READING AND STUDY SKILLS

FORM B

READING AND STUDY SKILLS is also available in an alternate edition known as Form A. Form A has essentially the same text as Form B but different reading selections and activities. An instructor can therefore use alternate versions of the text from one semester to the next.

READING AND STUDY SKILLS

FIFTH EDITION · FORM B

JOHN LANGAN
Atlantic Community College

McGRAW-HILL, INC.

*New York   St. Louis   San Francisco   Auckland   Bogotá   Caracas
Lisbon   London   Madrid   Mexico City   Milan   Montreal
New Delhi   San Juan   Singapore   Sydney   Tokyo   Toronto*

READING AND STUDY SKILLS, FORM B

Acknowledgments appear starting on page 555, and on this page by reference.

 This book is printed on recycled, acid-free paper containing a minimum of 50% total recycled fiber with 10% postconsumer de-inked fiber.

1 2 3 4 5 6 7 8 9 0   DOC   DOC   9 0 9 8 7 6 5 4

ISBN 0-07-036413-3

This book was set in Times Roman by Monotype Composition Company.
The editors were Alison Husting Zetterquist, Lesley Denton, Laurie PiSierra,
and Susan Gamer; the designer was Rafael Hernandez;
the production supervisor was Annette Mayeski.
R. R. Donnelley & Sons Company was printer and binder.

Library of Congress Cataloging-in-Publication Data

Langan, John, (date).
    Reading and study skills / John Langan.—5th ed., form B.
      p.   cm.
    Includes bibliographical references and index.
    ISBN 0-07-036413-3
    1. Study skills.   2. Reading (Higher education—United States.
I. Title.
LB2395.L346   1994
378.1'70281—dc20   93-36861

ABOUT
THE
AUTHOR

John Langan has taught reading and writing at Atlantic Community College near Atlantic City, New Jersey, for over twenty years. The author of a popular series of college textbooks on both subjects, he enjoys the challenge of developing materials that teach skills in an especially clear and lively way. Before teaching, he earned advanced degrees in writing at Rutgers University and in reading at Glassboro State College. He also spent a year writing fiction that, he says, "is now at the back of a drawer waiting to be discovered and acclaimed posthumously." While in school, he supported himself by working as a truck driver, machinist, battery assembler, hospital attendant, and apple packer. He presently lives with his wife, Judith Nadell, near Philadelphia. Among his everyday pleasures are running, working on his Macintosh computer, and watching Philadelphia sports teams or *60 Minutes* on TV. He also loves to read: newspapers at breakfast, magazines at lunch, and a chapter or two of a recent book ("preferably an autobiography") at night.

CONTENTS

PART SEVEN
MASTERY TESTS   **455**

PART EIGHT
ADDITIONAL LEARNING SKILLS   **517**

TO
THE
INSTRUCTOR

Reading and Study Skills will help students learn and apply the essential reading and study skills needed for success in college work. The book also provides a brief review of important word skills that students must have. And it will help students examine their attitudes about college and about studying, set goals for themselves, and take responsibility for their own learning.

The book covers a good number of skills because, quite simply, students often need to learn or review that many. In the best of academic worlds, students would have an unlimited amount of time to spend on study skills, word skills, motivation for achievement, and so on. In such an ideal scheme of things, they could use a series of books over several semesters to strengthen their learning ability. But in reality, students usually have only one or two semesters for improving their reading and study skills, and all too often they are asked to handle regular academic subjects at the same time as their developmental course. They should, then, have a book that presents all the central skills they need to become more effective learners. The book should also be organized in self-contained units, so that students can turn quickly and easily to the skills needed in a given situation.

With *Reading and Study Skills,* an instructor can cover a wide range of skills and activities that might otherwise require several books or one limited book and a bundle of handouts and supplementary exercises. In addition to its comprehensiveness, *Reading and Study Skills* has a number of other important features:

■   The book is highly *versatile.* Its eight parts, and many sections within these parts, are self-contained units that deal with distinct skills areas. An instructor can present in class those areas most suited to the general needs of students and then assign other sections for independent study. Also, because the book is so flexible, an instructor can more easily sustain students' attention by covering several skills in one session. For example, in a three-hour class period, work could be done on a study skill such as time control, a motivational skill such as setting goals, and a reading skill such as locating main ideas in short selections.

■   The book is *practical.* It contains a large number and wide range of activities so that students can practice skills enough to make them habits. There are, for instance, over sixty separate exercises in the section on study skills, over fifty activities in the section on reading comprehension skills, and twenty-five mastery tests that cover most of the skills in the book. No instructor is likely to cover all the exercises in the book, but the chances are good that an instructor will be able to select the combination of skills best suited to the needs of a reading class or individual students.

■   The book is *easy to use.* It has a simple, conversational style and explanations that are friendly without being patronizing. It presents skills as processes that can be mastered in a step-by-step sequence. Besides its many activities, the book often uses a question-answer format to help students learn the material. After a set of ideas is presented, one or more questions may follow so that students can check their understanding of those ideas. Such questions are signaled in the text with a bullet (■). Finally, the book features high-interest materials. For instance, selections on the meaning of love, everyday defense mechanisms, dependence on caffeine, and students' stress are used to practice reading skills.

■   The book is *realistic.* It uses material taken from a variety of college textbooks (in one instance, an entire textbook chapter) and gives practice in common study situations. Wherever possible, students are asked to transfer skills to actual study and classroom activities. A particular value of *Reading and Study Skills* for instructors should be its emphasis on activities that help students practice and apply study skills; the lack of such activities is a drawback in many currently available texts. In the past, too much attention has been given to increasing students' skill in reading selections rapidly and answering questions about the selections. Such drill has some value, but it does not prepare students to cope with an essay, control their study time, memorize material effectively (on those still-too-frequent occasions when memory work is emphasized), take useful classroom notes, or carry out the study assignments in a textbook chapter. *Reading and Study Skills* treats all the study skills that students need to survive in their courses at the same time they are working in other parts of the book to improve their reading skills.

■ The book is accompanied by *learning aids.* There is a set of forty *ditto masters,* free to instructors adopting the book, which provide extra activities and tests for many skills. A "user-friendly" *software disk* will help students review and practice many of the skills in the text. And an *Instructor's Manual and Test Bank* includes suggestions for using the book, a model syllabus, a full answer key, a guide to the computer disk, and additional activities and tests. These learning aids are available from the local McGraw-Hill representative or by writing to the College English Editor, McGraw-Hill, Inc., 1221 Avenue of the Americas, New York, New York 10020.

CHANGES IN THE FIFTH EDITION

There are some substantial changes in the fifth edition.

■ A *new opening chapter,* "Introduction," helps students determine right away what motivational skills, reading skills, and study skills they need to learn or strengthen.

■ The discussion of *textbook study* (which appeared as three chapters in previous editions) is now presented in one chapter—"Textbook Study I: The PRWR Study Method"—enabling students to see at once the whole process of studying a textbook.

　　As part of this change, a study method known as *PRWR (preview-read-write-recite)* has replaced the familiar SQ3R. I have not made this change lightly. But any instructor who has taught SQ3R knows as well as I do that there is a flaw in the formula: it does not specifically ask students to make writing a part of the study process. Students should be told explicitly to take written notes, because without note-taking a student cannot expect to master a chapter. Writing notes is as central to the learning process as reading the chapter and reciting the notes to oneself. And while the command "question" in SQ3R is helpful, it should be presented equally with other important advice: to look for definitions, examples, and basic enumerations. All three of these guidelines appear as substeps of PRWR.

For those instructors who still are more comfortable with SQ3R, I suggest telling students that "recite" in the SQ3R formula should be *written* recitation. With that step taken, it is easy enough to ask students to apply the SQ3R formula to all the practice materials in this new edition of *Reading and Study Skills.*

■ Following "Textbook Study I"—the overview of the textbook study process—are two chapters of *practice materials for studying textbooks.* "Textbook Study II" offers practice in a variety of textbook passages of intermediate and longer length. "Textbook Study III" gives students guided, hands-on experience in taking notes on an entire textbook chapter. (The chapter is from a popular introductory sociology text published in a fourth edition in 1991.) Students are shown specifically how to take a thirty-page chapter full of material and pull out the most important ideas, reducing the chapter to only five pages of written notes.

■ One part of the book, "A Brief Guide to Important Word Skills," has been moved. It now follows "Study Skills" and precedes "Reading Skills." Thus "Study Skills" comes immediately after "Motivational Skills," encouraging students to begin work right away on study skills they will need if they are taking content courses at the same time as their reading course.

■ The chapter on the *library* has been revised and updated; it now explains the computerized search facilities that are increasingly a part of today's libraries.

■ Part Eight, "Additional Learning Skills," is a reorganized and significantly expanded version of the former appendixes. In addition to its coverage of reading graphs and tables, studying mathematics and science, and understanding important connections between reading and writing, it now has three new chapters—"Reading Literature and Making Inferences," "Reading for Pleasure: A List of Interesting Books," and "Writing a Research Paper."

■ Throughout the book, much of the material has been expanded or freshened. For example, students are given more how-to advice in "Setting Goals for Yourself" in Part One. Some of the hints in "Taking Classroom Notes" in Part Two have been expanded. New tests have been developed for "Signal Words" in Part Four. Two new selections, both from textbooks, have been added to "Skim Reading" in Part Five, and a new reading has been added to "Rapid Reading" in Part Six.

■ A newly designed *Instructor's Manual* includes separate answer sheets for each skill; instructors can easily copy the sheets and pass them out to students for self-teaching.

■ A revised and expanded set of *ditto masters,* free to instructors adopting the book, provides many more tests and activities than were available previously.

ACKNOWLEDGMENTS

I owe thanks to the following reviewers and to the class testers of the book, who provided helpful suggestions and comments: Rebecca R. Ament, Muskingum Area Technical College; Michael L. Bettino, Cerritos College; Carl Zhonggang Gao, Mt. San Jacinto College; Pat Gent, Rogers State College; and Ken Haley, Prairie View A&M University.

I appreciate as well the help of my editors at McGraw-Hill: Lesley Denton, and Alison Husting Zetterquist, who secured detailed reviews and saw to it that I had dozens of representative college textbooks to examine; and Sue Gamer, who shepherded a challenging project through the many steps needed to bring it to publication. Finally, I remain grateful for the inspiration of my many students over the years who have had the desire to learn and sought only to find an effective means.

John Langan

READING AND STUDY SKILLS

FORM B

INTRODUCTION

While working my way through school, I had all kinds of summer and part-time jobs. One of my first summer jobs was as a drill-press operator in a machine shop. When I reported to work, the supervisor said to me, "Langan, I want you to spend the first couple of nights going around and observing the operators and picking up everything you can. Then I'll put you on a machine." So for three nights, I walked around and watched people, was bored stiff, and learned very little. I didn't learn the skill of operating a drill press until I was actually put on a machine with a person who could teach me how to run it and I began practicing the skill. I have found that my experience in the machine shop holds true for skill mastery in general. One picks up a skill and becomes good at it when a clear explanation of the skill is followed by plenty of practice. This book, then, tries to present clearly the reading and study skills that you will need to succeed in school or in your career. And it provides abundant activities so that you can practice the skills enough to make them habits.

The skills in this book should help make you an independent learner—a person who is able to take on and master almost any learning challenge. However, the book cannot help you at all unless you have a personal determination to learn the skills. In the machine shop, I quickly learned how to run the drill press because I had plenty of motivation to learn. The job was piecework, and the more skilled I became, the more money I could make. In your case, the more reading and study skills you master, the more likely you are not only to survive in college but also to do well in your courses.

OVERVIEW OF THE BOOK

Here are the eight parts into which this book is divided.

- *Part One: Motivational Skills.*   This part describes important steps you must take to get off to a strong start in college.
- *Part Two: Study Skills.*   Part Two explains and gives practice in all the key study skills you need to do well in your courses.
- *Part Three: A Brief Guide to Important Word Skills.*   The information here will help you quickly brush up on important word skills.
- *Part Four: Reading Comprehension Skills.*   Part Four explains and offers practice in comprehension skills that will help you read and take notes on your textbooks and other college materials.
- *Part Five: Skim Reading and Comprehension.*   Here you will learn how to do skimming, or selective reading.
- *Part Six: Rapid Reading and Comprehension.*   This part of the book will suggest a method for increasing your reading speed.
- *Part Seven: Mastery Tests.*   Part Seven consists of a series of mastery tests for many of the skills in the book.
- *Part Eight: Additional Learning Skills.*   This last part of the book presents other learning skills that can help you with your college work.

WHAT SKILLS DO YOU NEED TO MASTER?

Which learning skills do you need most? To help yourself answer this question, respond to the groups of statements that follow. The statements will tell you important things about yourself as a student.

The statements will make you aware, first, of your attitude toward study. By recognizing negative feelings you may have about yourself or about student life, you can begin to deal with those feelings. The statements will also make you aware of important reading and study skills you have—or do not have—right now. You can then use the book to master the skills you need.

Read and consider each statement carefully. Check the space for *True* if a statement applies to you most of the time. Check the space for *False* if a statement does not apply to you most of the time. Remember that your answers will be of value only if they are honest and accurate.

True	False	*Attitude about Studying*
____	____	1. I feel there are personal problems that I have to straighten out before I can be a good student.
____	____	2. I seem to be so busy all the time that I don't have the chance to do my schoolwork regularly.
____	____	3. If a subject is boring to me, I don't make the full effort needed to pass the course.
____	____	4. I often get discouraged about how much I have to learn and how long it's going to take me.
____	____	5. I will let myself be distracted by almost anything rather than concentrate on studying.
____	____	6. I want to be a successful student, but I hate studying so much that I often don't bother.
____	____	7. I often become moody or depressed, and when I do, I find that I am not able to study.
____	____	8. I keep trying to do well in school, but I don't seem to be making any real progress.
____	____	9. I am still trying to develop the willpower that I know I need in order to study consistently.
____	____	10. I am not completely sure that I want to be in school at this time.

Evaluating Your Responses: If you answered *true* more than twice in questions 1 to 10, you should read and work through all of Part One in this book. Part One will encourage you to think about the commitment you must make to become an independent learner. It will also help you set goals for yourself and will show you five important survival strategies.

It may also be important for you to discuss your situation with a counselor, a friend, an instructor, or some other person whose opinion you respect. All too often, people try to keep problems closed up inside themselves. As a result, they may limit their potential unnecessarily and waste valuable time in their lives. Talking with another person can help you get a perspective on your own situation and so help you deal better with that situation. If you care about making yourself strong and successful, you should take the risk of sharing your feelings and concerns with someone else.

True *False* *Taking and Studying Classroom Notes*

When I must take classroom notes,

____ ____ 11. I have trouble deciding what to write down.

____ ____ 12. I sometimes miss a point the instructor is making while I am writing down an earlier point.

____ ____ 13. I often get sleepy or begin to daydream when the instructor talks for long periods.

____ ____ 14. I don't know how to organize my notes, and so they are often hard to understand later.

____ ____ 15. I write down what the instructor puts on the board but usually don't take notes on anything else.

____ ____ 16. I seldom go over my notes after a class to make them easy to understand or to fill in missing points.

____ ____ 17. I don't have an effective way of studying my notes for a test.

Evaluating Your Responses: If you answered *true* more than twice in questions 11 to 17, you should read and work through the first chapter on study skills, ''Taking Classroom Notes'' (pages 39–67). The chapter will show you how to take effective notes in class and how to study those notes. If you are taking any content course such as business, psychology, sociology, or a science at the same time as your course in reading and study skills, you should *read this chapter first.*

True *False* *Time Control and Concentration*

____ ____ 18. I never seem to have enough time to study.

____ ____ 19. I don't have a schedule of regular study hours.

____ ____ 20. I never make up a list of what I need to study in a given day or week.

____ ____ 21. I don't write down test dates and paper deadlines in a place where I will see them every day.

____ ____ 22. When I sit down to study, I have trouble concentrating.

____ ____ 23. I often end up having to cram for a test.

Evaluating Your Responses: If you answered *true* more than twice in questions 18 to 23, you should read and work through ''Time Control and Concentration'' (pages 68–87) early in the semester. You'll learn how to use your time effectively—a key to success in college as well as in a career—and to develop consistent study habits.

True   *False*   ## Textbook Study

____ ____ 24. I'm not sure how to preview a textbook chapter.

____ ____ 25. It takes me a very long time to read and understand a textbook chapter.

____ ____ 26. When I have a lot of reading to do, my mind wanders or I get sleepy.

____ ____ 27. I'm never sure what is important when I read a textbook.

____ ____ 28. I don't have a method for marking important passages while reading a text-book chapter.

____ ____ 29. I don't have a really good way of taking notes on a textbook chapter.

____ ____ 30. I don't have a really good way of studying my notes on a textbook chapter.

Evaluating Your Responses: If you answered *true* more than twice in questions 24 to 30, you should read and work through the entire chapter ''Textbook Study I'' on pages 88–107. This chapter will provide immediate help to you as you begin getting textbook assignments in other courses. Then go on to ''Textbook Study II'' and ''Textbook Study III.''

As time permits, you will then want to work through Part Four of the book, which explains and offers practice in seven key reading comprehension skills. Students often ask, ''What can I do to understand and remember more of what I read?'' The first five skills (pages 319–365) will help you locate and understand important points in articles and textbook chapters. The sixth and seventh skills (pages 366–396) will enable you to take down and remember those key points in the form of clear and concise study notes.

True   *False*   ## Memory Training

____ ____ 31. I have trouble concentrating and often ''read words'' when I try to study.

____ ____ 32. I don't know any ''memory techniques'' to help me remember material.

____ ____ 33. I often forget something almost as soon as I have studied it.

____ ____ 34. I usually don't organize material in any special way before I try to study it.

____ ____ 35. I don't know how to study and remember a large amount of material for a test.

Evaluating Your Responses: If you answered *true* more than twice in questions 31 to 35, you should read and work through ''Building a Powerful Memory'' on pages 191–206. That chapter presents techniques to help you remember both classroom and textbook notes.

True	False	*Taking Tests*
___	___	36. When I take a test, I often panic and forget what I have learned.
___	___	37. Before a test, I never make a careful and organized review.
___	___	38. When I prepare for a test, I am never sure what is important enough to study.
___	___	39. I don't know how to go about preparing for an essay test.
___	___	40. When I write an essay answer, I have trouble organizing my thoughts.
___	___	41. I sometimes misread test questions and give an answer other than the one called for.
___	___	42. I don't know any hints to keep in mind when taking a true-false or multiple-choice test.
___	___	43. I sometimes spend too much time with some questions on a test and don't have enough time for others.

Evaluating Your Responses: If you answered *true* more than twice in questions 36 to 43, you should read and work through "Taking Objective Exams" (207–222) and "Taking Essay Exams" (223–231). These chapters show you how to prepare for both kinds of exams and explain test-taking techniques. Use them whenever exams are approaching.

True	False	*Using the Library*
___	___	44. I'm not sure how to look up or find a book in my library.
___	___	45. I don't know how to use the *Readers' Guide,* the *Magazine Index,* or other files for looking up magazine, newspaper, and journal articles.
___	___	46. I don't know how to look up information about books or articles by using the computer terminals in my library.
___	___	47. I don't know how to get a copy in the library of a magazine or journal article I want to read.
___	___	48. I don't know how to use subject headings to get ideas for a report or a research paper.

Evaluating Your Responses: If you answered *true* more than once in questions 44 to 48, you should read and work through "Using the Library" on pages 232–248. You'll learn all the basics you need to know in order to use the library for researching a topic and preparing a research paper.

True	False	Word Skills
____	____	49. I'm not sure how to use prefixes, suffixes, and roots to improve my pronunciation and spelling of words.
____	____	50. I have trouble pronouncing unfamiliar words.
____	____	51. I'm not sure how to use the dictionary for pronouncing words.
____	____	52. I feel that I should be a better speller.
____	____	53. If I see an unfamiliar word, I'm not able to guess its meaning by looking at the rest of the sentence.
____	____	54. I feel that a limited vocabulary keeps me from understanding my textbooks.
____	____	55. Very seldom, if ever, do I read a book for pleasure.

Evaluating Your Responses: If you answered *true* more than twice in questions 49 to 55, you should read and work through all of Part Three of the book. Part Three will help you improve your spelling and show you how to pronounce unfamiliar words, including specialized terms in your various subjects. You'll also learn ways to develop your vocabulary—a vital matter, because a small word base will limit your understanding of what you read. The concise information about word skills in Part Three can be supplemented with practice materials that are probably available in your college learning center.

True	False	Other Reading Skills
____	____	56. I have trouble locating definitions when I read.
____	____	57. I have trouble locating examples of ideas when I read.
____	____	58. I have trouble locating enumerations (lists of items) when I read.
____	____	59. I don't know how to use headings or subheadings when I read.
____	____	60. I don't know what kinds of words are used to signal important facts or ideas.
____	____	61. I have trouble locating main ideas in what I read.
____	____	62. I would benefit from practice in outlining and summarizing.
____	____	63. I don't know how to skim-read a textbook chapter effectively.
____	____	64. I think it would help me to learn how to speed-read.
____	____	65. I feel my lips moving as I read silently.
____	____	66. My eyes go back a lot to reread earlier lines on a page.

Evaluating Your Responses: If you answered *true* more than twice in questions 56 to 66, you should read and work through Parts Four, Five, and Six of the book. The chapters on textbook study in Part Two offer a quick course in becoming a better reader and note-taker; the chapters in Part Four provide a more detailed step-by-step process to strengthen your textbook reading and note-taking skills.

Part Five gives you practice in skim reading—going through a selection quickly and selectively to find important ideas. Skimming is a valuable technique when it is not necessary to read every word of a passage.

Part Six introduces you to rapid reading—processing words at a faster rate than is your normal habit. You will learn that rapid reading is not a cure-all for reading problems but simply one technique used by effective readers.

The overall purpose of Parts Four, Five, and Six is to make *you* an effective, flexible reader—able to apply "study reading," skim reading, or speed reading (or all three), depending on your purpose for reading and on the nature of the material. You will improve your comprehension, slowly but surely, if you isolate and work on important reading skills in a systematic way.

True	False	*Other Reading and Study Skills*
____	____	67. I have trouble making sense of charts and graphs.
____	____	68. I find it especially hard to deal with a math or science textbook.
____	____	69. I would like tips on reading short stories, poems, and other literary works.
____	____	70. I need to know just how to go about doing a research paper.
____	____	71. The connections between reading and writing are not clear to me.
____	____	72. I'd like to start reading some good books but have no idea what to read.

Evaluating Your Responses: If you answered *true* to any of questions 67 to 72, read and work through the appropriate chapter in Part Eight of the book.

ACHIEVING YOUR GOAL

You should now have a good sense of just what skills you most need to work on. Many students, I find, say that they want to improve in almost *all* the areas listed above. Whatever your specific needs, the material in this book should help.

Your goal as you begin your work is to become an independent learner—a person who can take on the challenge of any college course. Achieving the goal depends on your personal determination to do the work it takes to become a successful student. If you decide that you want to make your college time productive and worthwhile—something that only you can decide—this book will help you reach that goal. I wish you a successful journey.

PART ONE

MOTIVATIONAL SKILLS

PREVIEW

Part One is about important steps you must take to get off to a strong start in college. The point stressed throughout the first chapter, "Your Attitude: The Heart of the Matter," is that you must make a personal decision and commitment to do the diligent work that learning requires. The chapter describes several students who made or failed to make this commitment, and also asks a series of questions that will help you measure your own willingness to make it. The second chapter, "Setting Goals for Yourself," will encourage you to think actively about your eventual career goal and the practical steps you should take to start working toward that goal. In the third chapter, "Learning Survival Strategies," a successful student talks about the importance of planning for a realistic career, of getting organized, of learning how to persist, of being positive, and of remaining open to growth.

YOUR ATTITUDE: THE HEART OF THE MATTER

This book is chiefly about the reading and study skills you need to do well in your college work. But your *attitude* toward college work is even more crucial than any reading or study skill. Without the proper frame of mind, you might as well throw this book into the trash—and you may be wasting your time in school.

DOING THE WORK

Your attitude must say, "I will do the work." I have found that among the two hundred or so students I meet each year, there is almost no way of telling at first which students have this attitude and which ones do not. Some time must pass for people to reveal their attitude by what they do or do not do. What happens is that as the semester unfolds and classes must be attended and work must be done, some people take on the work and persist even if they hit all kinds of snags and problems; others don't take on the work or don't persist when things get rough. It then becomes clear which students have determined inside themselves, "I will do the work," and which have not.

The crucial matter is seldom the *speed* at which a person learns; the crucial matter is his or her determination—"I *will* learn." I have seen people who had this quality of determination or persistence do poorly in a course, come back and repeat it, and eventually succeed. And two years or so later, at commencement in June, I have heard their names being called out and have seen them walking up to the stage to get their degrees.

For example, I have seen the woman who wrote the following piece as her first assignment in a reading and writing class go up to receive her associate of arts degree:

Well its 10:48 and the kids are all in bed. I don't know yet what Im going to write about but I hope I think of something befor this ten minutes are up. boy I don't even like to write that much. I never send my letters or cards because I dislike writing, may be because I never took the time to sit down and really write, I've always wishes I could, put thing on paper that were in my mind. but my spelling isn't at all good, so when I had to take the time to look up a word or ask one of my children how to spell it, I said to heck with it, but, I can't do that with this any way I don't believ I can write for ten mintes straght, but Im trying I refus to stop until Ive made It. Ive always given my self credit for not being a quiter, so I guess I have to keep fighting at this and every thing else in the future, If I wish to reach my gols wich is to pass my GED and go in to nursing. I know it will take me a little longer then some one who hasen't been out of school as long as I have but no matter how long it takes I'm shure I will be well worth It and I'll be glad that I keep fighting. And Im shur my children will be very prowd of ther mother some day.

Through knowing determined people like this woman, I have come to feel that the single most important factor for survival and success in college is *an inner commitment to doing the work.* When the crunch comes—and the crunch is the plain hard work that college requires—the person with the commitment meets it head-on; the person without the commitment avoids it in a hundred different ways.

Doing the Work Despite Difficulties

A person who is committed to the work needed to succeed in college is not necessarily a person without confusions and difficulties in his or her life. One joke that is sometimes made about orientation—the day or so preceding the start of the first semester, when the entering student is introduced to college life—is that for some people orientation takes a year or more. The joke is all too often true. I can remember my own confusing first year at La Salle College in Philadelphia. I entered as a chemistry major but soon discovered that I could not deal with the mathematics course required. As hard as I tried, I couldn't pass even one of the weekly quizzes. I felt that the instructor was poor and the text unclear, but since other people were passing the tests, I felt that the problem was in me, too. It was a terribly confusing time. Because I doubted my ability to do the work, I began questioning my own worth.

At the same time that I began to doubt whether I *could* do the work in mathematics, I began to realize that I did not *want* to do the work. Even if I eventually passed the course and the other mathematics courses I would have to take, I could see that I did not want to spend my life working with numbers. Very quickly, my career plans disintegrated. I was not going to be a chemist, and I was left in the confused and anxious vacuum of wondering what I *was* going to be.

My career identity was not my only problem. My social identity was precarious as well. The one male friend that I had from high school had gone into the Army and was in Germany. And because I was shy, I found no one immediately at college to share experiences with. My one female friend—or supposed friend—from high school had gone off to a school in Chicago, and we did not bother to write to each other. I realized dismally that we didn't write because we didn't really know each other anyway. We had gone together in high school for the sake of form and convenience—so we would each have a partner for social events. There had never been real communication and sharing between two people. I had no one to help me shape my fragile social and sexual identities, and I felt very much alone. To make matters worse, in the midst of all this, my blood was burning. I yearned desperately for someone to burst into flame with—and felt lost that I had no one. In sum, my first year at college was a very worried, confused, and anxious time.

I responded to my general unhappiness partly by trying to escape. One way I did this was by resorting to games. In some respects my real major that first year at La Salle was the game room in the student center. Before and after classes I went there to play endless games of chess and Ping-Pong. I played, I now realize, not only to find relief from my worries but also as an indirect way of trying to meet other people. For a while I had a roommate who was in college only because his parents wanted him to be; he too was desperately unhappy. We seldom talked because we had very little in common, but we would spend entire evenings playing chess together. One day soon after midsemester grades were sent out, I came back to the dorm to find that my roommate, his clothes, his chessboard—everything—had disappeared.

The games were not enough escape for me, and so I decided to get a job. I did not absolutely need a job, but I told myself I did. Not only did I need an excuse to get away from my dismal days at the college; I also wanted to shore up my unsure self-image. If I could not be a successful student or friend or lover, I could at least be a successful wage earner. Fortunately, I did not get a full-time job but instead began working as a graphotype operator two nights a week in downtown Philadelphia. The job made me feel a little older and closer to being independent, so it helped lift my spirits.

Had I gotten a full-time job, it might have provided enough of an excuse for me to drop out of school, and I might have done so. As it was, I stayed, and—despite general unhappiness and partial escape through games and my part-time job—I did the work. Mathematics was hopeless, especially because there was no tutoring program or mathematics lab at the college, so I dropped the course. But I knew I would need the chemistry course that I was taking as a basic science requirement for graduation. The course meant a massive amount of work for me, and I studied and studied and went into a test hoping to get a grade that would reflect all the studying I had done. Instead, I always came out with D's. The grades were the more discouraging because I felt so generally displeased with myself anyway. They seemed to be saying to me, ''You are a 'D' person.'' However, I kept studying. I read and underlined the text, took lots of notes, and studied the material as best I could. I was determined to get the course behind me, and, with a final grade of low C, I did.

I have known students who experienced far rougher personal times at college than I did in my first year. But those people *who were determined to do the work,* despite all their difficulties, were the ones who succeeded. To overcome the worries, fears, and demands that may seem overwhelming during a semester, you must make a firm decision to do the work. Running from the work, you may lose precious time and opportunities in your life.

It is true that in a given situation you may decide it is better to drop a course or drop out for a semester than to try to do the work. You may be right, *but* it is important that you first talk to someone about your decision. One of the things that helped me stay in school during the hard first year was talking to an instructor I liked and felt I could trust. At your school you will find there are people—counselors, instructors, and others—who will care about listening to you and understanding your special situation. Talking with someone about your concerns will enable you to do something you cannot possibly do alone—get a perspective on yourself. From time to time we all need the insights into ourselves that can come from such perspectives. So if you are having trouble making yourself do the work that college requires, it is in your best interest to talk to someone about it.

Discovering the Commitment to Do the Work

I have often seen people come to college almost accidentally. Perhaps they are in doubt about what to do after high school, or are discontented with their limited job opportunities, or are looking for other interests to fill the time they once spent with their children. So they come to college uncommitted, vaguely looking for a change of pace in their lives. Without a commitment, they often drift along for a couple of weeks or months or semesters and then fade away—silent, shadowy figures in both their coming and their going.

But in some instances a spark ignites. These people discover possibilities within themselves or realize the potential meaning that college can have in their lives. As a result, they make the commitment to do the work that is absolutely essential to success in college. Here is one student's account of such a discovery:

My present feeling about college is that it will improve my life. My first attitude about college was that I didn't need it. I had been bored by high school, where it seemed we spent grades 9 to 12 just reviewing everything we had learned up through grade 8. I had a job as a bottle inspector at Wheaton's and was taking home over $105 a week. Then I was laid off and spent whole days hanging around with nothing to do. My roommate was going to Atlantic Community College and talked me into going, and now I hope I'll be thanking her one day for saving my life.

When I entered college in January I thought it was fun but that's all. I met a lot of people and walked around with college textbooks in my hand playing the game of being a college student. Some weeks I went to class and other weeks I didn't go at all and went off on trips instead. I didn't do much studying. I really wasn't into it but was just going along with the ball game.

Then two things happened. My sociology class was taught by a really cool person who asked us questions constantly, and they began getting to me. I started asking *myself* questions and looking at myself and thinking, "What am I about anyway? What do I want and what am I doing?" Also I discovered I could write. I wrote my own version of the Red Riding Hood story and it was read in class and everyone, including the teacher, roared. Now I'm really putting time into my writing and my other courses as well.

In my first version of this paper, the teacher asked me, "What is the point at which you changed? When was the switch thrown to 'On' in your head?" I don't know the exact moment but it was just there, and now it seems so real I can almost touch it. I know this is my life and I want to be somebody and college is going to help me do it. I'm here to improve myself and I'm going to give it my best shot.

Earlier in the semester things seemed so bad to me. I was busted for drugs, I got an eviction notice, and I was having man-trouble too. I was going to quit school and get a job and try to get a new start. But then I realized this is my start and this is where I will begin. I can tell you with a strong mind that nothing will discourage me, and that I will make it.

Running from the Commitment to Do the Work

I said earlier that as a semester unfolds and the crunch of work comes, people are put up against the wall. Like it or not, they must define their role in college. There are only two roads to take. One road is to do the work: to leave the game table, click off the stereo or television, turn down the invitation to go out, get off the telephone, stop everything and anything else, and go off by oneself to do the essentially lonely work that study is. The other road is to avoid the work, and there are countless ways of doing this.

Here is one student's moving account of the avoidance pattern in his life and his discovery of it:

Somewhere, a little piece of me is lost and crying. Someplace, deep in the shadows of my subconscious, a piece of my soul has sat down and anchored itself in defeat and is trying to pull me down into the darkness with it. This might sound strange to someone who is not familiar with the inner conflicts of a person that can tear and pull at his soul until he begins to stop and sink in his own deep-hollow depths. But sinking doesn't take much. It takes only one little flaw which left unattended will grow and grow . . . until like cancer it consumes the soul.

My flaw, the part of me that has given up, is best seen when it is winning. Then I am lost like a rudderless ship after the storm has abated, motor gone, drifting . . . pushed about by the eddying currents in little circles of lassitude and self-doubt, just waiting . . . just waiting . . . peering at the ominous dark clouds in the sky, waiting for help to arrive.

I know now, and I have always known, that help comes first from within. I know that if one doesn't somehow come to one's own rescue, then all is lost. I know it is time for me to look at myself, which I would rather avoid. But in order to break free of my own chains, I must look at myself.

I could relate the incidents of my youth. I could tell of the many past failures and what I think caused them. But I won't, for one example will show where I'm at. At the beginning of this summer I set my goals. These goals consisted of the college courses I wanted to complete and where I wanted to be physically and mentally when the summer was over. Listed among the goals to be accomplished were courses I needed in writing and accounting. To help me become at ease with my writing, I took English Composition 101, and to clear up my accounting deficiency, I took the course a second time. But now here, at the end of July, I am so far behind in both courses it looks as if I will fail them both. I ask myself, "Why?" I know that if I work enough I can handle the courses. So, why have I been so lazy? Why is it that the things I seem to want most, I either give up or in some way do not strive for? These are the questions I must try to answer.

I remember when I was about five or six—a little, dreamy boy living in the country—the much-older neighbor's boy told me one rainy afternoon, just when the rain had stopped and the sun peered with glistening rays of gold through gray and white fluffy clouds, that "there is a pot of gold at the end of the rainbow." And right then a pulsating, glowing rainbow of violets, blues, and golds raced from the clouds and down past the hill. It sent me scampering across the wet, weedy field and up the hill and down the other side, where fields with rows of wet corn stood. There my rainbow had moved a little farther on. I should have known then, but I kept walking through the puddles in the muddy fields watching my rainbow fade farther and farther away with each step. I started home when the rainbow faded, but in the puddles of water I saw little rainbows and dreamed that the next time I would get the pot of gold under the big rainbow.

I think it's time for me to stop chasing rainbows in the sky. It's time to stop looking into the sky waiting for help to arrive. It's time for me to start bailing the rot out of my mind, to stop dreaming and not acting, before I have nothing left to hope for. I can see now that I've never given it the total effort, that I've always been afraid I would fail or not measure up. So I've quit early. Instead of acting on my dreams I've laid back and just floated along. I've lived too much time in this world unfulfilled. I've got to make my dreams work. I've suffered enough in this world. I must do this now and all it takes is the doing. Somehow I must learn to succeed at success rather than at failure, and the time to start is now.

AVOIDANCE TACTICS

Described below are some of the tactics that people may use to avoid doing the hard work that college requires. If you see yourself in any of these situations, you should do some serious thinking about whether now is the right time for you to be in college. If you are unsure of your commitment, don't coast along, trying to ignore the situation. Instead, make an appointment with a counselor, your academic adviser, or some other interested person. That way you will confront your problem and begin to deal with it.

"I Can't Do It"

The only way people can really know that they are not able to do something is by first trying—giving it their best shot. The temptation is to use a defeatist attitude as an excuse for not making a real effort. Remember that many colleges can give you help if you decide to try. There may be a tutoring program and writing, reading, and mathematics labs. And you can often go to your instructor as well. If you think you "can't do it," the reason may be that you are not trying.

"I'm Too Busy"

Some people *make* themselves too busy, taking on a job that is not absolutely necessary or working more hours on a job than they need to. Others get overly involved in social activities on and off campus. Others allow personal or family problems to become so tangled and pressing that they cannot concentrate on their work. In some cases, of course, people really are so busy or so troubled that they cannot do their work. But in many cases, people unconsciously create conflicts in order to have an excuse for not doing what they know they should do.

"I'm Too Tired"

People who use fatigue as an excuse usually become tired as soon as it's time to write a paper or study a book or go to class. Their weariness clears up when the work period ends. The "sleepiness syndrome" also expresses itself as an imagined need for naps during the day and then ten hours or more of sleep at night. Students who sleep too much are, often literally, closing their eyes to the hard work that college demands.

"I'll Do It Later"

Everyone tends at times to procrastinate—to put things off. Some students, however, constantly postpone doing assignments and setting aside regular study hours. Time and time again they put off what needs to be done so they can watch TV, talk to a friend, go to the movies, play cards, or do any one of a hundred other things. These students typically wind up cramming for tests and writing last-minute papers, yet they often seem surprised and angry at their low grades.

"I'm Bored with the Subject"

Students sometimes explain that they are doing poorly in a course because the instructor or the subject matter is boring. These students want education to be entertainment—an unrealistic expectation. On the whole, college courses and instructors balance out: some are boring; some are exciting; many are in between. If a course is not interesting, students should be all the more motivated to do the work so that they can leave the course behind once and for all.

"I'm Here, and That's What Counts"

Some people spend their first weeks of college lost in a dangerous kind of fantasy. They feel, "All will be well, for I am now here in college. I have a student identification card in my pocket, a parking sticker on the bumper of my car, and textbooks under my arm. All this proves that I am a college student. I have it made." Such students have succumbed to a fantasy we all at times succumb to: the belief that we will get something for nothing. But everyone knows from experience that such a hope is false. Life seldom gives us something for nothing— and college won't either. College, like life, is demanding. And because this is so, to get somewhere and to become someone we must be prepared and able to make a solid effort. We must accept the fact that little can be won or achieved without hard work. The decision that each of us must make is the commitment to do the hard work required for success in college—and ultimately in life. By making such a decision, and acting on it, we assume control of our lives.

■ Questions to Consider

Your instructor may divide the class into small groups of three or four and ask you to take turns reading aloud to each other the discussion about attitude on pages 11–18. The instructor may then ask you to discuss with each other the questions that follow. Every person in the group should try to contribute to the sharing of experiences. The more honest and real you can be in exchanging individual experiences, the more meaningful and valuable the discussion can be.

1. Tell the group about some skill you have learned and how you went about learning it. Do you think the basic principles involved in learning that skill could hold true for reading and study skills as well?

2. "A person who does not go to class faithfully is showing that he or she is not committed to doing the work that college requires." Give your reasons for agreeing or disagreeing with this statement.

3. Have you or has anyone you've known had a "time of decision" like the one described by the person who wrote the paper on page 15?

4. Have you or has anyone you've known ever run from the commitment to do the work like the person who wrote the paper on pages 16–17?

5. Have you or has anyone you've known experienced the "sleepiness syndrome" described on page 18?

6. Have you or has anyone you've known ever experienced the "dangerous kind of fantasy" described on page 18?

7. Everyone uses avoidance tactics from time to time. Share with the group the tactics that you sometimes use. (You've already discussed two; four more are described on pages 17–18—and there may be other kinds of escape you can think of.) Also discuss whether you think avoidance tactics have ever been harmful to you in meeting goals in life.

8. What is your purpose, or what are your purposes, in taking college courses? Take a few minutes to write down on a separate sheet of paper your specific goals for four months from now, one year from now, and two years from now. Then share those goals with the other members of the group.

9. Do you think your chance of reaching your goals is 100 percent? 70 percent? 30 percent? Specifically, what odds would you give on yourself—and why? Share these odds with the group, and then give your reasons for setting the odds as you do. (Describe what you see as your strengths and weaknesses.)

Your instructor may ask you to write a paper that responds *in detail* to one of the preceding questions. He or she may stress that honesty—the expression of your real thoughts and feelings and experiences—will be more important than sentence skills in this paper.

SETTING GOALS FOR YOURSELF

If you asked a cross section of students why they are in college, you would probably get a wide range of responses. Following are some reasons people give for going to college. Check the reasons that you feel apply to you. Be honest; think a bit about each reason before you go on to the next one.

Reasons Students Go to College	*Apply in My Case*
■ To have some fun before getting a job	_____
■ To prepare for a specific career	_____
■ To please their families	_____
■ To educate and enrich themselves	_____
■ To be with friends who are going to college	_____
■ To fill in time until they figure out what they want to do	_____
■ To take advantage of an opportunity they didn't have before in their lives	_____
■ To find a husband or wife	_____
■ To see if college has anything to offer them	_____
■ To do more with their lives than they've done so far	_____
■ To take advantage of VA benefits or other special funding	_____
■ To earn the status that they feel comes with a college degree	_____
■ To get a new start in life	_____

Get together with one or more other students to compare and discuss your responses to this list. Talk about what you feel are the "bottom-line" reasons you are in college. Make a genuine effort to be as honest about yourself as possible.

Now write below the basic reason or reasons you have for being in college.

_____

_____

_____

_____

If you do not have one or more solid reasons for being in college, you may have trouble motivating yourself to do the hard work that will be required. When difficult moments occur, your concentration and effort will lag unless you can remember that you have good reasons for persisting.

LONG-TERM GOALS

For many students, one main reason for being in college is to prepare themselves for a career—the specific kind of work they intend to do in life. If you have not been thinking actively about this long-range goal, you should begin doing so during your first year of college. Here are four specific steps you can take to start formulating a career goal.

1   If you are not sure about your major, visit the college counseling center. The center probably administers an *interest inventory* and a *vocational preference test.* The first identifies what you like and can do well; the second points to careers that match your interests and abilities. With this information, the counseling staff at the center can help you decide on a possible major. You should begin taking courses in this prospective major as soon as you can in order to learn for sure that it is right for you.

2   Sometime early in your first year at college, make an appointment to talk with a faculty member in the department of your intended major. Most department advisers set aside a certain period of time to meet with students and discuss their courses of study. Ask such advisers the following questions:

What courses are required in the major?

What courses are recommended?

What courses, if any, offer practical work experience?

3   Also, plan to go to the placement office sometime during your first year to get specific information on careers. Many students have the mistaken notion that placement offices provide career information only to students who are about to graduate. That is not the case. *It is very important for beginning students to speak to the placement staff to obtain updated information about the future of specific fields.* For example, it would make little sense for you to plan to become a history teacher if that particular job market is expected to have few openings when you graduate.

4   See if your counseling center has the latest copy of the *Occupational Outlook Handbook,* which is a valuable source of information about the many kinds of jobs currently available and the best job prospects in the future. In fact, it makes sense to order the book for your personal reference soon after you enter college. Write to New Orders, Superintendent of Documents, P.O. Box 371954, Pittsburgh, PA 15250-7950, and ask for the latest paperback edition of the *Occupational Outlook Handbook,* or call 1-312-533-1886. The book will cost you about $23.

Activity

Answer the following questions.

1.   What is a vocational preference test? _____

_____

2.   Does your counseling center or library have a current copy of the *Occupational Outlook Handbook?* _____ What are three promising career fields identified in the *Handbook?*

a.   _____

b.   _____

c.   _____

3.   Have you asked a counselor for his or her professional opinion on the best job opportunities in your area of the country? _____

4.   Describe your long-range career goal (or what you think will be your goal):

_____

_____

5.   Mark with a check the expected job prospects in your major at the time when you will graduate. (You can answer this only after you have visited the placement center or spoken to a person knowledgeable in the field.)

_____ Excellent   _____ Good   _____ Fair   _____ Poor

SHORT-TERM GOALS

There is a familiar saying that the longest journey begins with a single step. To achieve your long-term career goal, you must set and work toward a continuing series of short-term goals. These can be as simple as a list of specific objectives that you have for your present semester in college. Activity 1 below gives an example—the short-term goals that one student, Barbara, set for herself.

Personal and Study Goals

Activity 1

Specific goals can consist of both *personal* goals and *study* goals. In the spaces beside the items on Barbara's list, indicate whether the goal listed is a personal or a study goal.

Barbara's Short-Term Goals

_____   1. To get to know at least two people in each of my classes

_____   2. To earn a B in my Basic Math class

_____   3. To earn a B or better in my reading class

_____   4. To earn a B in my Introduction to Business class

_____   5. To start exercising regularly

_____   6. To miss not more than three classes in any subject

_____   7. To limit my television watching to no more than five hours a week

_____   8. To spend at least ten study hours on my courses every week

You can help yourself succeed in your present semester of college by setting a series of personal and study goals. The goals must be honest oncs that you choose yourself—goals that you truly intend to work on and that you have the time to achieve during the semester. If necessary, you can change or add to your goals as needed. What matters is that you have a series of definite targets that will give you direction and motivation during the semester. A list of specific goals will help you do the *consistent* work that is needed for success.

Activity 2

Use the form below to set a series of short-term goals for yourself. Indicate in parentheses whether each goal is a personal or a study goal. Set real targets for yourself. At the same time, be realistic about how much you can achieve in one semester.

Goals for the _____ *Semester, 19*_____

1. _____
2. _____
3. _____
4. _____
5. _____
6. _____
7. _____
8. _____
9. _____
10. _____

_____

_____

_____

_____

_____

_____

Use the extra spaces provided if you decide to change or add to your goals. Refer frequently to your goals as the semester progresses. When a goal is completed, cross it out and write the date and your initials beside it.

Steps for Achieving Short-Term Goals

At the same time that you set short-term goals, you should decide on the *specific steps* you must take to achieve those goals. By looking closely at what you must do to reach your goals, you can determine whether they are realistic and practical. You can also get a good sense of just how you will reach them.

Look at some of the specific steps that Barbara decided she would have to take to reach her goals:

<u>Goal</u>: To take and earn Bs in three courses this semester.

<u>Specific steps for achieving this goal</u>:
I must get my mother to agree to watch my seven-year-old son three evenings a week.

I must get my ex-husband to agree to take my son one day every weekend.

My boss must agree to limit my work hours to no more than twenty a week.

I am going to have to do my food shopping and all my cleaning on Friday evenings, so that I can have more of the weekend free to study.

I need the phone numbers of at least two people in each class, so if I ever have to miss a class, I can find out right away what happened.

I must limit my television watching to no more than five shows a week.

Activity 3

Now choose three of your most important goals and list the specific steps you must take to achieve each of them.

Goal 1: _____

Specific steps for achieving goal 1:

_____

_____

_____

_____

_____

_____

_____

_____

Goal 2: _____

Specific steps for achieving goal 2:

_____

_____

_____

_____

_____

_____

Goal 3: _____

Specific steps for achieving goal 3:

_____

_____

_____

_____

_____

_____

Activity 4

Your instructor may now put you in a group with one or two other students so that you can compare your goals and discuss the steps you plan to take to achieve them. You should try to give each other feedback on what seems realistic about your goals—and what does not. Alternatively, your instructor may sit down with you individually to review your goals.

Activity 5

Answer the following questions as honestly as you can.

■ How important do you think it is to set specific goals for yourself and consciously work toward those goals?

Very important _____

Fairly important _____

Somewhat important _____

Unimportant _____

- How important do you think it is to work out the specific steps that you must take to achieve your goals?

  Very important _____

  Fairly important _____

  Somewhat important _____

  Unimportant _____

- Are you already a disciplined person? Or will you have to make a special effort to work consistently toward your goals during the semester?

  _____

- On the basis of your present situation in life and what you know about yourself, what do you think will be your greatest obstacles in reaching your short-term goals?

  _____

  _____

  _____

- How would you rate your chances for success in achieving your short-term goals?

  Excellent _____

  Good _____

  Fair _____

  Uncertain _____

LEARNING
SURVIVAL
STRATEGIES

Note: *Over the years I have spoken with a number of successful students who started college with a course in reading and study skills and then went on to earn their college degrees. Essentially, what I asked them was, ''What would you want to say to students who are just starting out in college? What advice would you give? What experiences would it be helpful to share?'' The comments of one student, Jean Coleman, were especially helpful. In several conversations I had with Jean, she identified some strategies for surviving in college that other students often spoke of as well. Jean's comments are presented, mostly in her own words, on the pages that follow.*

THE ADVICE AND EXPERIENCE
OF A SUCCESSFUL STUDENT

''Be Realistic''

The first advice that I'd give to beginning students is: ''Be realistic about how college will help you get a job.'' Some students believe that once they have college degrees, the world will be waiting on their doorsteps, ready to give them wonderful jobs. But the chances are that unless they've planned, there will be *nobody* on their doorsteps.

I remember the way you dramatized this point in our first class, John. You played a student who had just been handed a college degree. You opened up an imaginary door, stepped through, and peered around in both directions outside. There was nobody to be seen. I understood the point you were making immediately. A college degree in itself isn't enough. We've got to prepare while we're in college to make sure our degree is a marketable one.

At that time I began to think seriously about (1) what I wanted to do in life and (2) whether there were jobs out there for what I wanted to do. I went to the counseling center and said, "I want to learn where the best job opportunities will be in the next ten years." The counselor referred me to a copy of the *Occupational Outlook Handbook* published by the federal government. The *Handbook* has good information on what kinds of jobs are available now and which career fields will need workers in the future. In the front of the book is a helpful section on job hunting. The counselor also gave me a vocational interest test to see where my skills and interests lay.

The result of my personal career planning was that I graduated from Atlantic Community College with a degree in accounting. I then got a job almost immediately, for I had chosen an excellent employment area. The firm that I worked for paid my tuition as I went on to get my bachelor's degree. They're now paying for my work toward certification as a CPA, and my salary increases regularly.

By way of contrast, I know a woman named Sheila who majored in French. She earned a bachelor's degree with honors in French. After graduation, she spent several unsuccessful months trying to find a job using her French degree. Sheila eventually wound up going to a specialized school where she trained for six months as a paralegal assistant. She then got a job on the strength of that training—but her years of studying French were of no practical value in her career at all.

I'm not saying that college should serve only as a training ground for a job. People should take some courses just for the sake of learning and to expand their minds in different directions. At the same time, unless they have an infinite amount of money (and few of us are so lucky), they must be ready at some point to take career-oriented courses so that they can survive in the harsh world outside of college.

In my own case, I started college at the age of twenty-seven. I was divorced, had a six-year-old son to care for, and was working full time as a hotel night clerk. If I had had my preference, I would have taken a straight liberal arts curriculum. As it was, I did take some general-interest courses—in art, for example. But mainly I was getting ready for the solid job I desperately needed. What I am saying, then, is that students must be realistic. If they will need a job soon after graduation, they should be sure to study in an area where jobs are available.

"Get Organized"

One of the problems that can start a student off in the wrong direction is failing to get organized right at the beginning of the semester. It's funny, but even a disorganized first day—just one day—can set a negative tone for the semester that seems to snowball. For instance, I have seen students come to the first day of class as if the first class were some kind of unimportant rehearsal. They don't bother to bring pens or notebooks, and they let the important information they're receiving just float by. You get the feeling that they believe they'll catch up later, but they usually don't catch up.

I think students who are disorganized like this have never learned to take responsibility for their own behavior. They have had parents, teachers, and bosses telling them what to do, so they can't cope when they're placed in an atmosphere that says, "Nobody here is going to protect you from the consequences if you don't take care of things yourself." Students like this miss classes, fail to get the notes they missed, or don't know the most basic information, such as where their instructors' offices are. Then they act surprised when their grades take a nosedive—they feel as if they've been cheated because no one "rescued" them with warnings, reminders, or prodding.

I would tell all students to get organized right at the start of school. To help them do this, I would pass out the following checklist of important items:

_____ ▪ Remember that the first meeting of any class is crucial. Bring two pens and a notebook with you. Many instructors not only distribute basic information about assigned textbooks and requirements—they also start lecturing the first day.

_____ ▪ Don't put off getting your books, even if you have to wait in a long, boring line at the bookstore. You will need your books right away if you don't want to fall behind, so make the sacrifice.

_____ ▪ Find out, early in the semester, the names and phone numbers of some students in the class. Students who feel "funny" about this or are too shy to do it are really hurting themselves. If you miss one class, it's your responsibility to go *prepared* to the next class. At the college level, you can't get away with saying to an instructor, "I don't have the assignment because I was absent" or "Could you tell me what I missed?" If you have some of your classmates' telephone numbers, you can find out what happened in class and get the notes or assignments you missed. Of course, if you start missing too many classes or showing up late for your classes, just getting the notes won't help you keep up.

_____ ■ Have a specific place at home for all your school materials. In other words, have some kind of headquarters. You just can't study when you sit down to work and discover that your biology book is in the trunk of your brother's car, your lab notes are in a locker at school, and you can't find the handout the instructor gave you. All school-related materials should be kept somewhere convenient for you—a desk, a worktable, a closet, or a corner. This kind of very basic organization makes a big difference.

_____ ■ Decide, right from the start, how much work you can handle. If you are taking five courses, working at a full-time job, and caring for two children, for example, you're asking for a nervous breakdown—no matter how organized you are. I heard a good rule of thumb for this, and it seems accurate. For every ten hours per week you work, deduct one course from a full-time college course load. For example, if you don't work, you can do a good job on five courses; if you work ten hours, you should attempt only four courses; if you work twenty hours, take a maximum of three courses, and so on. You might have to bend this rule, however, depending on your family responsibilities and the level of difficulty of the courses you are taking.

I think what all this comes down to is that there seem to be two kinds of students—the ones who have a mature, professional attitude toward being a student and the ones who act like children who have to be taken care of. It's important to realize that college instructors aren't baby-sitters or disciplinarians. They want to teach, but they want to teach adults who meet them halfway and take responsibility for themselves. When I have seen students who have the attitude ''I'm sitting in class, so I've done my job—now you make me learn something,'' I have wanted to ask them, ''What are you doing here?'' They just never accept, or choose to ignore, the fact that _they_—not the instructors—are the ones who determine whether they will succeed or fail.

"Persist"

The older I get, the more I see that life visits some hard experiences on us. There are times for each of us when simple survival becomes a deadly serious matter. We must then learn to persist—to struggle through each day and wait for better times to come—as they invariably do.

I think of one of my closest friends, Neil. After graduating from high school with me, Neil spent two years as a stock boy at a local department store to save money for tuition. He then went to the guidance office at the small college in our town. Incredibly, the counselor there told him, ''Your IQ is not high enough for college work.'' Neil decided to go anyway and earned his degree in five years—with a year off to care for his father, who had had a stroke one day at work.

Neil then got a job as a manager of a regional beauty supply firm. He met a woman who owned a salon; they got married and soon had two children. Three years later he found out that his wife was having an affair. I'll never forget the day Neil came over and sat at my kitchen table and told me what he had learned. He always seemed so much in control, but that morning he lowered his head into his hands and cried. ''What's the point?'' he kept saying in a low voice over and over to himself.

But Neil has endured. He divorced his wife, won custody of his children, and learned how to be a single parent. Recently, Neil and I got letters informing us of the tenth reunion of our high school graduating class. Included was a short questionnaire for us to fill out that ended with this item, ''What has been your outstanding accomplishment since graduation?'' Neil wrote, ''My outstanding accomplishment is that I have survived.'' I have a feeling that most of our high school classmates, ten years out in the world, would have no trouble understanding the sad truth of his statement.

I can think of people who started college with me who had not yet learned, like Neil, the basic skill of endurance. Life hit some of them with unexpected low punches and knocked them to the floor. Stunned and dismayed, they didn't fight back and eventually dropped out of school. I remember Yvonne, still a teenager, whose parents involved her in their ugly divorce battle. Yvonne started missing classes and gave up at midsemester. There was Alan, whose girlfriend broke off their relationship. Alan stopped coming to class, and by the end of the semester he was failing most of his courses. I also recall Nelson, whose old car kept breaking down. After Nelson put his last $200 into it, the brakes failed and needed to be replaced. Overwhelmed by his continuing car troubles, Nelson dropped out of school. And there was Rita, discouraged by her luck of the draw with instructors and courses. In sociology, she had an instructor who wasn't able to express ideas clearly. She also had a mathematics instructor who talked too fast and seemed not to care at all about whether his students learned. To top it off, Rita's adviser had enrolled her in an economics course that put her to sleep. Rita told me she had expected college to be an exciting place, but instead she was getting busywork assignments and trying to cope with hostile or boring instructors. Rita decided to drop her mathematics course, and that must have set something in motion in her head, for she soon dropped her other courses as well.

In my experience, younger students seem more prone to dropping out than older students. I think some younger students are still in the process of learning that life slams people around without warning. I'm sure they feel that being knocked about is especially unfair because the work of college is hard enough without having to cope with some of life's special hardships.

In some situations, withdrawing from college may be the best response. But there are going to be times in college when students—young or old—must simply determine, ''I am going to persist.'' They should remember that no matter how hard their lives may be, there are many other people out there who are quietly having great difficulties also. I think of Dennis, a student in my introductory psychology class who lived mostly on peanut butter and discount store loaves of white bread for almost a semester in his first year. And I remember Estelle, who came to school because she was going to need a job to support her sons when her husband, who was dying of leukemia, would no longer be present. These are especially dramatic examples of the faith and hope that are sometimes necessary for us to persist

''Be Positive''

A lot of people are their own worst enemies. They regard themselves as unlikely to succeed in college and often feel that there have been no accomplishments in their lives. In my first year of college, especially, I saw people get down on themselves all too quickly. There were two students in my developmental mathematics class who failed the first quiz and seemed to give up immediately. From that day on, they walked into the classroom carrying defeat on their shoulders the way other students carried textbooks under their arms. I'd look at them slouching in their seats, not even taking notes, and think, ''What terrible things have gone on in their lives that they have quit already? They have so little faith in their ability to learn that they're not even trying.'' Both students hung on until about midsemester. When they disappeared for good, no one took much notice, for they had already disappeared in spirit after that first test.

They are not the only people in whom I have seen the poison of self-doubt do its ugly work. I have seen others with resignation in their eyes and have wanted to shake them by the shoulders and say, ''You are not dead. Be proud and pleased that you have brought yourself here to college. Many people would not have gotten so far. Be someone. Breathe. Hope. Act.'' Such people should refuse to use self-doubts as an excuse for not trying. They should roll up their sleeves and get to work. They should start taking notes in class and trying to learn. They should get a tutor, go to the learning center, see a counselor. If they honestly and fully try and still can't handle a course, only then should they drop it. Above all, they should not lapse into being ''zombie students''—students who have given up in their heads but persist in hanging on for months, going through hollow motions of trying.

Nothing but a little time is lost through being positive and giving school your best shot. On the other hand, people who let self-doubts limit their efforts may lose the opportunity to test their abilities to the fullest.

"Grow"

I don't think that people really have much choice about whether or not to grow in their lives. Not to be open to growth is to die a little each day. Grow or die—it's as simple as that.

I have a friend, Jackie, who, when she's not working, can almost always be found at home or at her mother's home. Jackie eats too much and watches TV too much. I sometimes think that when she swings open her apartment door in response to my knock, I'll be greeted by her familiar chubby body with an eight-inch-screen television set occupying the place where her head used to be.

Jackie seems quietly desperate. There is no growth or plan for growth in her life. I've said to her, "Go to school and study for a job you'll be excited about." She says, "It'll take me forever." Once Jackie said to me, "The favorite time of my life was when I was a teenager. I would lie on my bed listening to music and I would dream. I felt I had enormous power, and there seemed no way that life would stop me from realizing my biggest dreams. Now that power doesn't seem possible to me anymore."

I feel that Jackie must open some new windows in her life. If she does not, her spirit is going to die. There are many ways to open new windows, and college is one of them. For this reason, I think people who are already in school should stay long enough to give it a chance. No one should turn down lightly such an opportunity for growth.

In Conclusion

Maybe I can put all I've said into perspective by describing briefly what my life is like now. I have inner resources that I did not have when I was newly divorced. I have a secure future with the accounting firm where I work. My son is doing OK in school. I have friends. I am successful and proud and happy. I have my fears and my loneliness and my problems and my pains, to say the least, but essentially I know that I have made it. I have survived and done more than survive. I am tough, not fragile, and I can rebound if hard blows land. I feel passionately that all of us can control our own destinies. I urge every beginning student to use well the chances that college affords. Students should plan for a realistic career, get themselves organized, learn to persist, be positive, and open themselves to growth. In such ways, they can help themselves find happiness and success in this perilous but wonderful world of ours.

■ Questions to Consider

In groups of three or four, discuss the questions that follow. Every person in the group should try to contribute. The more honest you can be in sharing experiences, the more meaningful and valuable the discussion will be.

1. Do you know yet what kind of work you want to do after college?
   a. If your answer is *no,* have you visited the counseling center to take a vocational interest test?
   b. Are you thinking actively about possible careers and getting information on those careers?
   c. If your answer is *yes,* have you checked with the counseling center or teachers in the field or through your own reading about whether there will be good job opportunities available at the time you graduate?

2. Do you know any people with a recent two- or four-year college degree? How successful have they been in getting jobs? On the basis of their experiences, what areas seem to offer good job opportunities?

3. People often limit themselves by taking only career-oriented courses in college. Are there any courses you plan to take just for the sake of learning?

4. Were you aware of all the tips Jean Coleman discusses in her section on getting organized? Which of her suggestions do you practice, and which ones have you ignored? Describe how well or poorly your actions compare with the habits that Coleman recommends.

5. Have there been difficult times in life when you or one of your friends has simply had to persist, like Jean Coleman's friend Neil on pages 31–32?

6. Are any people you know like the four Jean Coleman describes on page 32 who dropped out of school when their lives became very hard? What do you think might have helped them decide to stay in school?

7. Are there any students you know who continued in school despite tough luck? What kinds of struggles did they have?

8. Do you know any students whose feelings of inferiority are keeping them from making an honest effort to learn in college? What do you think students with self-doubts could do to become more positive?

9. Do you know any ''zombie students'' like the ones Jean Coleman describes on page 33—students who are going through the motions of being college students but are not really committed to study? What are some of the ways in which they are deluding themselves?

10. Describe one person you know well who is open to growth in life and one person who is not open to such growth. How do they show willingness or reluctance to grow in their everyday lives?

Your instructor may ask you to write a paper that responds *in detail* to one of the preceding questions.

PART TWO

STUDY SKILLS

PREVIEW

Part Two presents study skills that you will need if you are to do well in your courses. Each skill is explained and illustrated, and a number of activities are given to help you practice and master it. "Taking Classroom Notes" lists a number of hints for note-taking, explains how to study your class notes, and discusses handwriting and listening efficiency. In "Time Control and Concentration," you will learn several ways to make better use of your time and to develop the persistence in your work that is vital to success in school. "Textbook Study I" describes a four-step method you can use to read and study chapters in your textbooks. "Textbook Study II" gives you practice in that method with short and medium-length textbook passages. "Textbook Study III" shows you how to apply the method to an entire textbook chapter. In "Building a Powerful Memory," you will learn seven steps you can take to improve your memory. "Taking Objective Exams" and "Taking Essay Exams" show you how to prepare for both kinds of exams and explain test-taking techniques. Finally, "Using the Library" prepares you for projects that require library research by explaining just how you can use the library to look up information about a subject.

TAKING CLASSROOM NOTES

This chapter will show you how to:

- Take effective classroom notes
- Study and remember your notes
- Improve your handwriting and listening efficiency

Introductory Projects

1. Consider this common study situation:

> Howard has trouble taking notes in all his classes. He is seldom sure about what is important enough to write down. Also, he has trouble organizing material when he does write it down. Often the only points he records are the ones the instructor puts on the board. The connections between these points are usually clear to him in class, for he spends most of his time listening carefully to the instructor rather than taking notes. However, several weeks later, when he is studying for a test, he has trouble remembering many of the relationships among points. His notes do not provide a complete, unified understanding of the subject but seem instead to consist of many isolated bits of information.
>
> One course that gives Howard special problems is sociology. In class the instructor asks students questions and uses their comments as takeoff points for discussing course ideas. Sometimes she is five minutes into an important idea before Howard realizes it is important—and he hasn't taken a single note on that point. He often winds up with such a frustrating shortage of notes that he decides not to go to class at all. In another course, biology, the instructor talks so fast that Howard cannot keep up. Also, he misspells so many words that it is often impossible for him to understand his notes when he tries to read them over weeks later, before an exam.

This chapter will provide answers to Howard's study problem. But take a few minutes first to examine your own ideas. What do you think are three specific steps that Howard could take to become a better note-taker?

2. Within a small group, read aloud to each other the thirteen hints for taking effective classroom notes described on the following pages. Someone should read the first hint to the group, someone else the second, and so on. Pay careful attention to each hint as it is being read. Think to yourself, "Do I practice this hint? If not, should I?"

   Then, as a group, decide which five hints seem most important. Argue about the five choices among yourselves; the final decision of the group should be based on your agreement about which five hints seem to be most necessary and useful. Write your final decisions in the spaces that follow.

3. If you are working on this section individually, read through the hints carefully. Then decide on the five most important ideas and list them here:

   a. _____

   b. _____

   c. _____

   d. _____

   e. _____

THE IMPORTANCE OF ATTENDING CLASS

If you really want to do well in a course, you must promise yourself that you will go to class faithfully and take good notes. This chapter will offer a series of tips on how to take effective classroom notes. However, the hints will be of no value if you do not attend class. The importance of *regular class attendance* cannot be emphasized enough. Students who cut classes rarely do well in college.

The alternatives to class attendance—reading the text or using someone else's notes—can seldom substitute for the experience of being in class and hearing the instructor talk about key ideas in the course. These ideas are often the ones you will be expected to know on exams.

If you do not attend classes regularly, you may be making an unconscious decision that you do not want to attend college at this time. If you think this may be how you feel, talk to a counselor, an instructor, or a friend. Another person can often help you clarify your own thoughts and feelings so that you can gain a perspective on your situation.

■ Have you made a personal decision (be honest!) to attend all your classes regularly? _____

■ If not, are you willing to think about why you are reluctant to make the commitment to college work? _____

THIRTEEN HINTS FOR TAKING EFFECTIVE CLASSROOM NOTES

Hint 1: Keep a Written Record

Get down a written record for each class. It's important that you write down the material covered, because forgetting begins almost immediately. Studies have shown that within two weeks you will probably forget 80 percent or more of what you have heard. And in four weeks you are lucky if 5 percent remains! The significance of these facts is so crucial that the point bears repeating: To guard against the relentlessness of forgetting, you must write down much of the information presented in class. Later, you will study your notes so that you understand and remember the ideas presented in class. And the more complete your notes are when you review them, the more likely you are to master the material.

How many notes should you take? If you pay attention in class, you will soon develop an instinct for what is meaningful and what is not. If you are unsure whether certain terms, facts, and ideas are significant, here is a good rule to follow: *When in doubt, write it down.* This doesn't mean that you should (or could) get down every word, but you should be prepared to do a good deal of writing in class. Also, do not worry if you don't understand everything you record in your notes. Sometimes an instructor will phrase an idea several different ways, and the third version of the idea may turn out to be the one you clearly understand. It is easy to cross out later the material that you don't need but impossible to recover material you never recorded in the first place. Keep in mind that writing too much, rather than too little, may mean the difference between passing and failing a course or between a higher grade and a lower one.

■   Explain briefly why you should get down a written record of each class.

_____

Hint 2: Sit Where You'll Be Seen

Sit where the instructor will always see you, and where you can see the blackboard clearly and easily. Your position near or at the front will help you stay tuned in to what the instructor does in class. If you sit behind someone, are hidden in a corner, or are otherwise out of the instructor's line of vision, it may be a reflection of your attitude — either you are worried that you may be noticed and called on (a common anxiety) or you don't really want to be in the classroom at all (something worth thinking about).

Analyze your attitude. If you're hiding, be aware that you're hiding and try to understand why. It is all right not to want to be in a class; instructors can be boring and subjects can be uninteresting. However, the danger in such cases is that you may slide into a passive state where you won't listen or take notes. Don't fool yourself. If a course is deadly, there is all the more reason to make yourself take good notes—that way you will pass the course and get out of it once and for all.

■   Explain briefly two reasons why you should sit near the front.

_____

_____

Hint 3: Do Some Advance Reading

Ideally, read in advance about the topic to be discussed in class. All too often, students don't read assigned textbook material on a topic until after class is over. Lacking the necessary background, they have trouble understanding the new ideas discussed in class. However, if they have made an initial breakthrough on a topic by doing some advance reading, they will be able to listen and take notes more easily and with greater understanding. And they should be able to write more organized and effective notes because they will have a general sense of the topic.

If you don't know what the topic is going to be, check with your instructor at the end of the preceding class. Simply ask, ''Is there a chapter in the textbook that I can read in advance of your next class? I'd like to get a head start on what you're going to cover.'' At the least, you are going to make a good impression on the instructor, who will appreciate your seriousness and interest.

In particular, try to read the textbook in advance when the subject is very difficult. Reading in advance is also a good idea if you have spelling problems that hinder note-taking. As you read through the text, write down key terms and recurring words that may come up in the lecture and that you might have trouble spelling.

■   Explain briefly why you should read your textbook in advance of a lecture.

_____

_____

_____

Hint 4: Record Notes Systematically

1   Use full-sized 8½- by 11-inch paper. Do *not* use a small note tablet. As explained below, you will need the margin space provided by full-sized paper. Also, on a single page of full-sized paper you can often see groups of related ideas that might not be apparent spread over several small pages.

2   Use a ballpoint pen. You will often need to write quickly—something that you cannot do as well with a pencil or a felt-tip pen. (Don't worry about making mistakes with a pen that makes marks you can't erase. Just cross out the mistakes!)

3   Keep all the notes from each course together in a separate section of a notebook. Use a loose-leaf binder with sections indicated by dividers and index tabs, or use a large spiral notebook that has several sections. A spiral notebook is simpler. But a loose-leaf binder has the advantage of letting you insert handout sheets and supplementary notes at appropriate points. If you use a binder, you may want to leave previous notes safe at home and just bring to each class the last day or so of notes and some blank paper.

4   Date each day's notes.

5   Take notes on one side of the page only and leave space at the top of the page and at the left-hand margin. (You might use notebook paper that has a light red line down the left side.) Using only one side of the paper eliminates the bother, when studying, of having to flip pages over and then flip them back to follow the development of an idea.

   Leaving wide margins gives you space to add to your notes if desired. You may, for example, write in ideas taken from your textbook or other sources. Also, the margins can be used to prepare study notes (see pages 50–51) that will help you learn the material.

6   Write legibly. When you prepare for a test, you want to spend your time studying—not deciphering your handwriting.

7   To save time, abbreviate recurring terms. Put a key to abbreviated words in the top margin of your notes. For example, in a biology class *ch* could stand for *chromosome;* in a psychology class *o c* could stand for *operant conditioning.* (When a lecture is over, you may want to go back and fill in the words you have abbreviated.) Also abbreviate the following common words, using the symbols shown:

+ = and	*def* = definition
w/ = with	∴ = therefore
eg = for example	*info* = information
ex = example	*1, 2, 3* = one, two, three, etc.

Note, too, that you can often omit words like *a, and,* and *the.*

8   Note prominently exams or quizzes that are announced as well as assignments that the instructor gives. It's a good idea to circle exam dates and mark assignments by putting a large *A* for *assignment* in the margin. (Be sure you have a definite system for keeping track of assignments. Some students record them on a separate small note pad; others record them at the back of the notebook devoted to a given course.)

■   What do you consider the three most helpful suggestions for recording notes?

_____

_____

_____

Hint 5: Use an Outline for Notes

Try to write down your notes in the following outline form. Start main points at the margin. Indent secondary ideas and supporting details. Further indent material that is subordinate to secondary points.

  Main points are listed at the margin.
    Secondary points and supporting details are indented.
      Material subordinate to secondary points is indented further.

Definitions, for instance, should always start at the margin. When a list of terms is presented, the heading should also start at the margin, but each item in the series should be set in slightly from the margin. Examples, too, should be indented under the point they illustrate.

  Here is another organizational aid: When the instructor moves from one idea or aspect of a topic to another, show this shift by skipping a line or two, leaving a clearly visible white space.

  In the rapid pace of a lecture, you won't always be able to tell what is a main point and what is secondary material. Be ready, though, to use the outline techniques of indentation and extra space whenever you can. They are the first steps toward organizing class material.

■   Explain briefly what is meant by *indentation.*

_____

_____

Hint 6: Be Alert for Signals

Watch for signals of importance:

1   Write down whatever your instructor puts on the board. Ideally, *print* such material in capital letters. If you don't have time to print, write as you usually do and put the letters *OB* in the margin to indicate that the material was written on the board. Later, when you review your notes, you will know which ideas the instructor emphasized. The chances are good that they will come up on exams.

2   Always write down definitions and enumerations. Most people instinctively write down definitions—explanations of key terms in the subject they are learning. But they often ignore enumerations, which are often equally important. An *enumeration* is simply a list of items (marked 1, 2, 3, etc., or with other symbols) that fit under a particular heading. (See also page 326.)

   Instructors use enumerations, or lists, to show relationships among ideas. Being aware of enumerations will help you organize material as you take notes. Enumerations are signaled in such ways as: "The four steps in the process are . . ."; "There were three reasons for . . ."; "Five characteristics of . . ."; "The two effects were . . ."; and so on. When you write a list, always mark the items with 1, 2, 3, or other appropriate symbols. Also, always be sure to include a clear heading that explains what a list is about. For example, if you list and number six kinds of defense mechanisms, make sure you write at the top of the list the heading "Kinds of Defense Mechanisms."

3   Your instructor may say, "This is an important reason . . ."; or "A point that will keep coming up later . . ."; or "The chief cause was . . ."; or "The basic idea here is . . ."; or "Don't forget that . . ."; or "Pay special attention to . . ."; and so on. Be sure to write down the important statements announced by these and other emphasis words, and write in the margin *imp* or some other mark (such as * or ≥ or →) to show their importance.

4   If your instructor repeats a point, you can usually assume that it is important. You might write *R* for *repeated* in the margin to remind yourself later that your instructor stressed the idea.

5   An instructor's voice may slow down, become louder, or otherwise signal that you are expected to write down exactly what is being said, word for word. Needless to say, do so!

■   Which two signals of importance do you think will be most helpful for you to remember? _____

_____

Hint 7: Write Down Examples

Write down any examples the instructor provides and mark them *ex.* Examples help you understand complex and abstract points. But if you don't mark them *ex,* you are likely to forget their purpose when you review them later for study. You may not need to write down every example that illustrates an idea, but you should record at least one example that makes a point clear.

Hint 8: Write Down Details That Connect or Explain

Be sure to write down the details that connect or explain main points. Too many students copy only the major points the instructor puts on the board. They do not realize that as time passes, they may forget the specifics that serve as connections between key ideas. Be sure, then, to record the connecting details the instructor provides. That way you are more apt to remember the relationships among the major points in your notes.

In science and mathematics classes especially, students often fail to record the explanations that make formulas or numerical problems meaningful. Their notes may consist only of the letters and numbers the instructor chalked on the board. But to understand how the letters and numbers are related, they should also write down accompanying explanations and details.

Always take advantage of the connections instructors often make at the beginning or end of a class. They may review material already covered and preview what is to come. Write down such overviews when they are presented and label them *review* or *preview,* as the case may be. An instructor's summaries or projections will help the course come together for you.

■   How often do you forget to write down connections between ideas?

_____ Frequently   _____ Sometimes   _____ Almost never

Hint 9: Leave Some Blank Spaces

Leave blank spaces for items or ideas you miss. Right after class, ask another student to help you fill in the gaps. Ideally, you should find a person in each course who will agree to be your note-taking partner — someone with whom you can compare and fill in notes after a class. If another person is not available, you might want to tape each class and play back the tape right away to get any missing material. (Don't ever, though, fall into the trap of relying on a tape recorder to take most of your notes. In no time at all, you'll have hours and hours of tape to go through — time you probably cannot afford to take. Use a tape only to help you fill in occasional missing spots.)

When you do fall behind in note-taking during class, don't give up and just stop writing. Try to get down what seem to be the main ideas rather than supporting facts and details. You may be able to fill in the supporting material later.

Hint 10: Ask Questions

If certain points are confusing to you, don't hesitate to ask the instructor about them. Probably, other students have the same questions but are reluctant to ask to have the material clarified. Remember that instructors look favorably on students who show interest and curiosity.

- How often do you ask questions in class?

    _____ Frequently

    _____ Sometimes

    _____ Almost never

Hint 11: Take Notes during Discussions

Do not stop taking notes during discussion periods. Many valuable ideas may come up during informal discussions, ideas that your instructor may not present formally later on. If your instructor puts notes on the board during a class discussion, it's a good sign that the material is important. If he or she pursues or draws out a discussion in a given direction, it's a clue that you should be taking notes. And don't forget the advice in hint 1 on page 41: When in doubt, write it down.

Hint 12: Take Notes Right Up to the End of Class

Do not stop taking notes toward the end of a class. Because of time spent on discussions, instructors may have to cram important points they want to cover into the last minutes of a class. Be ready to write as rapidly as you can to get down this final rush of ideas.

Be prepared, also, to resist the fatigue that may settle in during class. As a lecture proceeds, the possibility of losing attention increases. You do not want to snap out of a daydream only to realize that an instructor is halfway into an important idea and you haven't even begun writing.

- Are you one of the many students whose note-taking slows down at the end of a class? _____

Hint 13: Review Your Notes Soon

Go over your notes soon after class. While the material is still clear in your mind, make your notes as clear as possible. A day later may be too late because forgetting sets in almost at once.

As far as possible, make sure that your punctuation is clear, that unfinished ideas are completed, and that all words are readable and correctly spelled. You may also want to write out completely words that you abbreviated during the lecture. Wherever appropriate, add connecting statements and other comments to clarify the material. Make sure that important items—material on the board, definitions, enumerations, and so on—are clearly marked. Improve the organization, if necessary, so that you can see at a glance the differences between main points and supporting material as well as any relationships among the main points.

This review does more than make your notes clear: it is also a vital step in the process of mastering the material. During class, you have almost certainly been too busy taking notes to absorb all the ideas. Now, as you review the notes, you can roll up your sleeves, wrestle with the ideas presented, and think about the relationships among them. You can, in short, do the work needed to reach the point where you can smile and say, ''Yes, I understand—and everything I understand is written down clearly in my notes.''

- Explain briefly why you should go over your notes soon after class.

HOW TO STUDY CLASS NOTES

The best time to start studying your notes is within a day after taking them. Because of the mind's tendency to forget material rapidly, a few minutes of study soon after a class will give you more learning for less time and effort than almost any other technique you can practice.

One Effective Method for Studying Class Notes

Here is one effective way to study your notes:

1 Use the margin space at the side (or top) of each page. Jot down in the margin a series of key words or phrases from your notes. These key words or phrases, known as *recall words,* will help you pull together and remember the important ideas on the page.

On page 50 are notes from a business course. Take the time now to look them over carefully. You will notice in the side margin the recall words that the student, Janet, used for studying this page of notes.

2   To test yourself on the material, turn the recall words in the margin into questions. For instance, Janet asked herself, ''What is the origin of economics?'' After she could recite the answer without looking at it, she asked herself, ''What is the definition of economics?'' Janet then went back and retested herself on the first question. When she could recite the answers to both the first and second questions, she went on to the third one.

Shown below are most of the questions that Janet asked herself. Fill in the missing questions.

What is the origin of economics?
What is the definition of economics?

_____

What is the definition of economic resources?

_____

What are the two kinds of property resources and their definitions?
What are the three kinds of human resources and their definitions?

Janet tested herself on each of these seven questions and retested herself on those from earlier lectures until she could recite all of them from memory. (For more information on repeated self-testing, see page 195.)

This approach, if it is pursued regularly, will help you remember the material covered in your classes. With such a study method, you will not be left with a great deal of material to organize and learn right before an exam. Instead, you will be able to devote preexam time to a final intensive review of the subject.

Another Good Method for Studying Class Notes

Some students prefer to write out on separate sheets of paper the material they want to learn. They prepare study sheets, often using a question-and-answer format. The very act of writing out study notes is itself a step toward remembering the material. Shown on page 51 is a study sheet that Janet could have prepared.

At the left are the recall words Janet placed in the margin.

Janet's Classroom Notes

	Business 101 11-7-93 ec = economic(s) res = resource
Origin of ec	Economics—from Greek words meaning "HOUSE" and
	"TO MANAGE." Meaning gradually extended to cover not
	only management of household but of business and governments.
Def of ec	Ec (definition)—STUDY OF HOW SCARCE RESOURCES
	ARE ALLOCATED IN A SOCIETY OF UNLIMITED WANTS.
	Every society provides goods + services; these are available
	in limited quantities + so have value.
Imp	One of the most imp. assumptions of ec: Though res of
assumption	world are limited, wants of people are not. This means an ec
	system can never produce enough to satisfy everyone completely.
Def of ec res	Ec res—all factors that go into production of goods + services.
2 types of	Two types:
ec res	1. PROPERTY RES—2 kinds
2 kinds of	a. LAND—all natural res (land, timber, water, oil, minerals)
property	b. CAPITAL—all the machinery, tools, equipment, + building
res + defs	needed to produce goods + distribute them to consumers.
3 kinds of	2. HUMAN RES—3 kinds
human	a. LABOR—all physical and mental talents needed
res + defs	to produce goods + services
	b. MANAGEMENT ABILITY—talent needed to bring together
	land, capital, + labor to produce goods + services.
	c. TECHNOLOGY—accumulated fund of knowledge
	which helps in production of goods + services.

Sample Study Sheet

What is the origin of economics?

From Greek words "house" + "manage." Word gradually extended to include business + government.

What is economics?

Study of how scarce resources are allocated in a society of unlimited wants.

What is an important assumption of economics?

Resources are limited but people's wants are not.

What are economic resources?

All the factors that go into production of goods + services.

What are the two types of economic resources?

Property + human resources.

What are the two kinds of property resources?

a. Land—all natural resources (land, timber, water, oil, minerals).

b. Capital—all the machinery, tools, equipment, and building needed to produce goods + distribute them to consumers.

What are the three kinds of human resources?

a. Labor—all physical and mental talents needed to produce goods + services.

b. Management ability—talent needed to bring together land, capital, + labor to produce goods + services.

c. Technology—accumulated fund of knowledge which helps in production of goods + services.

TWO SPECIAL SKILLS THAT HELP NOTE-TAKING

Two special skills that will help you take effective classroom notes are handwriting efficiency and listening efficiency. The following pages explain and offer practice in these skills.

Increasing Handwriting Efficiency

Activity 1

To check your handwriting efficiency, write as fast as you can for ten minutes. Don't stop for anything. Don't worry about spelling, punctuation, erasing mistakes, or finding exact words. If you get stuck for words, write ''I am looking for something to say'' or repeat words until something comes. You have two objectives in this rapid-writing activity: to write as many words as you can in the ten minutes (you will be asked to count the words later) and to write words legibly enough so that you can still understand them several weeks from now.

Count the number of words you have written in the ten minutes and record the number here: _____.

Handwriting Speed and Legibility: In Activity 1, you should have been able to write at least 250 legible words in ten minutes—and ideally a hundred or so more than that. Handwriting speed is important because it is basic to effective note-taking in fast-moving lectures. If you cannot write quickly enough, you are likely to miss the valuable ideas presented in such classes. Also, you may have trouble writing out full answers on essay exams. And in either situation, if your handwriting is not legible, there is hardly any point in writing at all.

Improving Speed: There are several steps you can take to improve your handwriting speed.

One step is to practice *rapid writing*—writing nonstop for ten or fifteen minutes at a time about whatever comes into your head. Try to increase the number of pages you fill with words in the limited time period. With several practice sessions, you should be able to increase your handwriting speed significantly.

Another way to increase speed is to use abbreviations. Abbreviate words that occur repeatedly in a lecture class, and put a key for such words in the top margin of your notes. For example, if the name *Linnaeus* keeps recurring in a botany class, at the top of the page write *L = Linnaeus,* and from then on in your notes that day simply use *L.*

■ What keys could you make for a psychology class on Skinner and behaviorism?

_____   _____

Following is a list of other symbols that can be made part of a general ''shorthand'' for your writing. (Note that you can often omit *a, and, the,* and other connecting words.)

$$+ = \text{and}$$
$$\text{w/} = \text{with}$$
$$\text{eg} = \text{for example}$$
$$\text{ex} = \text{example}$$
$$\text{def} = \text{definition}$$
$$\text{imp} = \text{important}$$
$$\text{ind} = \text{individual}$$
$$\text{info} = \text{information}$$
$$\text{sc} = \text{science}$$
$$\text{soc} = \text{sociology}$$
$$\text{psy} = \text{psychology}$$
$$1, 2, 3, = \text{one, two, three, etc.}$$

Finally, you can write faster if you streamline your handwriting by eliminating unnecessary high and low loops in letters. For example,

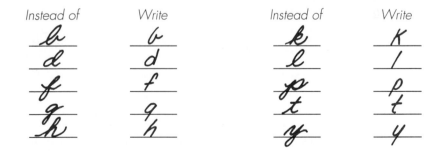

You will find that this streamlined, print-style writing can be learned easily and will help you write faster.

■ Go back and put the numbers 1, 2, and 3 in front of the three methods described for increasing handwriting speed.

Improving Legibility: To improve and maintain legibility, check a sample of your writing for the four common types of faulty handwriting illustrated here. Or give your writing sample to someone else to analyze for handwriting faults.

1 Overlapping letters from one line to the next. For example:

[handwriting sample] One of the main types of faulty handwriting is the overlapping of letters from one line to the next.

Note the improvement in legibility when this fault is eliminated:

[handwriting sample] One of the main types of faulty handwriting is the overlapping of letters from one line to the next.

2 Slanting letters in more than one direction. For example:

[handwriting sample] Another kind of faulty handwriting is to slant letters in all directions instead of just one.

Note how legibility improves when slants are consistent:

[handwriting sample] Another type of faulty handwriting is to slant letters in all directions instead of just one.

3 Making decorative capitals and loops. For example:

[handwriting sample] The use of decorative capitals and loops may result in a script that

You can greatly improve legibility by *printing* capital letters and restraining your loop letters.

4 Miswriting the letters *a, e, r, n,* and *t.* Common errors include writing the letter *e* like *i* (closing the loop) and putting a loop in nonloop letters like *i* and *t.* Check your handwriting to be sure you form these letters clearly. Also, look for other letters that you may miswrite consistently.

To improve legibility, follow two other tips as well. First, always use a ballpoint pen rather than a pencil. A dull-edged pencil will slow down your writing speed and hinder legibility. You can get a Bic pen for 45 cents. Second, be sure to hold your pen between the thumb and index finger, resting it against the middle finger. Don't grip the pen tightly; hold it just firmly enough to keep it from slipping. And don't hold it, as some people do, too close to the tip—you won't be able to see what you're writing. Hold it about ¾ inch from the point.

If you follow these suggestions, you should become a more efficient handwriter. Clear and rapid handwriting is a mechanical technique; once you decide to learn it and begin to practice, mastery is almost bound to follow. People should not allow failure to write skillfully to limit their note-taking performance, whether in school or on the job.

Activity 2

Write again for ten minutes without stopping. Try to write more words than you did in Activity 1. At the same time, be sure to keep your words legible.

Number of words in Activity 1: _____   In Activity 2: _____

Increasing Listening Efficiency

Activity 1

To take effective classroom notes, you must be able to listen attentively. This activity will test your ability to listen carefully and to follow spoken directions. The instructor will give you a series of thirteen directions. Listen closely to each one and then do exactly what it calls for. Each direction will be spoken only once.

If you are working on this book independently, get a friend to read the directions to you, or read each direction aloud once to yourself and then try to follow it. Do the same for other activities in this section as well.

Direction 1: Do not say a word at any point during this exercise. Do not raise your hand or look at your neighbor. There will be thirteen directions in the exercise. Follow every one of them except for the last direction, which you should disregard.

Direction 2: Get out a sheet of paper and write your full name in the upper-left-hand corner of the paper.

Direction 3: Write the numbers 1 to 8 down the left-hand side of the page.

Direction 4: Write beside space 2 the word *quiet,* which is spelled *q-u-i-e-t.*

Direction 5: Write beside space 3 the name of the street where you live. Do not write down the street number.

Direction 6: Think of the name of the high school that you went to. Do not write it down beside space 1.

Direction 7: Think of the name of the toothpaste that you use. Write it down on the back of your sheet of paper.

Direction 8: Listen to the following set of numbers and then put them down beside space 4. The numbers are 8, 12, 20, 31, 45.

Direction 9: Think of the name of a television show that you like, turn your paper upside down, and write the name of the show beside space 5.

Direction 10: Turn your paper back to the original position. Then count the number of people in the room, including yourself. Write out the number beside space 6.

Direction 11: Print in capital letters your first name or nickname beside space 7.

Direction 12: Write the word *banana*—spelled *b-a-n-a-n-a*—beside space 8. Then draw a picture of a pear on one side of the word *banana* and a picture of an apple under the word *banana*.

Direction 13: This is the last direction. Crumple your paper into a ball and throw it to the front of the room.

If you followed all directions correctly, you have done an effective job of attending closely. It is a skill that will help you be a good listener and note-taker.

Skills in Good Listening: Effective listening and note-taking require not only the ability to attend but other skills as well. At the same time that you are writing down what an instructor has said, you must be able to listen to what the instructor is now saying and to decide whether it is important enough to write down as well. Also, in a rapid lecture you must be able at times to store one or more ideas in your memory so that you will be able to write them down as soon as you finish writing down a previous idea. If you can ''listen ahead'' and process and remember what you hear at the same time as you are writing rapidly, you will be listening efficiently. Your brain will be able to work along with and ahead of your pen.

Activity 2

This activity will give you practice in developing your listening efficiency.

Group A: Your instructor will read each sentence in group A once, at a normal speaking speed. Listen carefully and, after the instructor has read the sentence, see if you can write down what has been said. The instructor will give you time to finish writing before starting the next sentence. Do not worry about getting down every little word; do try to get down the basic idea. (If there are words you cannot spell, try to spell them the way they sound. In actual note-taking situations, you can later look up correct spellings in your textbook or dictionary.) There are three practice sentences in group A.

1. Almost one in every seven Americans is affected by hypertension—that is, by high blood pressure.
2. A half hour of TV nightly news, if printed, would not fill one page of *The New York Times.*
3. In 1900 about one in thirteen marriages ended in divorce; today one in three ends in divorce.

Group B: The three examples in group B are almost twice as long as those in group A. They require, then, increased listening efficiency. Your instructor will read the two sentences in each example at a normal speaking rate. You can begin writing as soon as the instructor starts the first sentence. You will have to listen to and remember the second sentence in each example at the same time as you are writing the first sentence.

1.   The popular idea that you can tell the age of a rattlesnake by the number of rattles on its tail is false. A healthy snake can grow several new rattles in a single year.
2.   The usual age of retirement in the United States is sixty-five. Many experts are now questioning the fairness of a system that removes people from their jobs no matter how qualified they are.
3.   People have a great advantage over computers, for we can understand visual images drawn from our environment. Computers can process only facts that are put into numerical form.

Group C: The three examples in group C are about three times as long as those in group A. They create, then, an even more realistic note-taking situation, and they require a further increase in listening efficiency. Again, your instructor will read the sentences in each example at a normal rate of speed. You will have to "listen ahead" and remember what you hear at the same time as you are writing rapidly.

1.   When trapped in quicksand, do not struggle, or you will be sucked in deeper. The body floats on quicksand, so you should fall on your back, stretching out your arms at right angles, as if floating on water. Then, after working your legs free from the sand, begin rolling your entire body toward safe ground.
2.   Ralph Nader has suggested that voting be required in this country, as it is in several other countries. In Australia, students learn that if they don't vote at age eighteen, they may have to pay a fine equal to about $15 in American money. The result is that about 90 percent of qualified voters go to the polls.
3.   Babies seldom cry for no reason at all. They cry because of some discomfort that they feel. In the first year of life in particular, it is important that parents respond to a baby's cries rather than ignore them. A prompt response helps build a sense of security and trust in the baby.

You will receive additional practice in listening when you take notes on the short lectures that appear on pages 61–67.

PRACTICE IN TAKING CLASSROOM NOTES

Activity 1

Taking Notes: Evaluate your present note-taking skills by putting a check mark beside each of the thirteen note-taking hints that you already practice. Then put a check mark beside those steps that you plan to practice. Leave a space blank if you do not plan to follow a particular strategy.

Now Plan
Do to Do

_____ _____ 1. Take notes on classroom work.

_____ _____ 2. Sit near the front of the class.

_____ _____ 3. Read in advance textbook material about the topic to be presented in class.

4. Record notes as follows:

_____ _____   a. Use full-sized 8½- by 11-inch paper.

_____ _____   b. Use a ballpoint pen.

_____ _____   c. Use a notebook divided into parts.

_____ _____   d. Date each day's notes.

_____ _____   e. Take notes on one side of the page only.

_____ _____   f. Write legibly.

_____ _____   g. Abbreviate common words and recurring terms.

_____ _____   h. Indicate assignments and exams.

5. Write notes in outline form as follows:

_____ _____   a. Start main points at the margin; indent secondary points.

_____ _____   b. Use white space to show shift in thought.

6. Watch for signals of importance:

_____ _____   a. Write down whatever the instructor puts on the board.

_____ _____   b. Write down definitions and enumerations.

_____ _____   c. Write down points marked by emphasis words.

_____ _____   d. Record repeated points.

_____ _____   e. Note the hints given by the teacher's tone of voice.

_____ _____ 7. Write down examples.

_____ _____ 8. Write down connecting details and explanations.

9. Do as follows when material is missed:

_____ _____   a. Leave space for notes missed.

_____ _____   b. Try to get the broad sweep of ideas when you fall behind.

_____ _____ 10. Question the instructor when an idea isn't clear.

_____ _____ 11. Do not stop taking notes during discussion periods.

_____ _____ 12. Do not stop taking notes toward the end of a class.

_____ _____ 13. Go over your notes soon after class.

Studying Notes: Now, evaluate your skills in studying class notes.

Now   Plan
Do   to Do

_____ _____   ■ Jot in the margin key words to recall ideas.

_____ _____   ■ Turn recall words into questions.

_____ _____   ■ Use repeated self-testing to learn the material.

_____ _____   ■ Apply this study method regularly.

Activity 2

Write a one-page (or longer) essay in which you respond in detail to the study situation described on page 39. Apply what you have learned in this chapter to explain all the steps that Howard should take to become an effective note-taker.

Alternatively, your instructor may ask you to prepare an oral answer to this question. In this case, you should jot down brief notes (below) that you can refer to when presenting your answer to other people in your class.

Notes for Oral Answer

_____

_____

_____

_____

_____

_____

_____

_____

_____

_____

_____

_____

_____

_____

_____

_____

_____

Sociology 101   11-27-93

In the million years or so of life on earth, human beings have sought truth in many places. FIVE SOURCES OF TRUTH in particular are important to note: (1) intuition, (2) authority, (3) tradition, (4) common sense, and (5) science.

1. INTUITION—any flash of insight (true or mistaken) whose source the receiver cannot fully identify or explain.

    Ex.—Galen in second century made chart of human body showing exactly where it might be pierced without fatal injury. Knew which zones were fatal through intuition.

2. AUTHORITY—persons who are experts in a specific field.

Two kinds of authority:

a. SACRED—rests upon faith that a certain tradition or document—eg., the Bible—is of supernatural origin.

b. SECULAR—arises from human perception + is of two kinds:

    (1) secular scientific—rests upon empirical observation.

    (2) secular humanistic—rests upon belief that certain "great people" have had special insight.

Activity 3

On the opposite page is an excerpt from notes taken during an introductory lecture in a sociology class. In the margin of the notes, jot down key words or phrases that could be used to pull together and so recall the main ideas on the page.

Activity 4

Turn in to your instructor a copy of one day's notes that you have taken in one of your classes. These notes should fill at least one side of a sheet of paper. If you have never taken a full page of notes in class, add a second or third day's notes until you complete at least one sheet. In the top or left-hand margin of your notes, write down key words or phrases you could use to master the material in the notes.

Activity 5

The activity that follows will give you practice in taking lecture notes. The activity is based on a short lecture on listening given in a speech class. Take notes on the lecture as your instructor or a friend reads it aloud. Items that the original lecturer put on the board are shown at the top of the lecture. As you take your notes, apply the hints you have learned in this chapter. Then answer the questions that follow the selection by referring to your notes but *not* to the selection itself. Write your answers on separate sheets of paper.

LECTURE ABOUT LISTENING

On Board

Listening from the start	Appreciation
Three types of listening	Information
	Understanding

I'm going to be talking with you about listening—an aspect of communication you may never have thought much about.

In any kind of listening situation that you're in, there is one obvious but important point to remember. The point is that *you should be listening from the very start.* If you're not in it from the beginning, if you're not there to start on time, you're always going to be a little bit behind. You're never going to be able to catch up. And if you ask the person next to you about what you might have missed, you will make that person fall behind also.

With listening, an even more important point to consider is that we don't listen the same way all the time. In fact, it can be said that, in general, there are three major types of listening.

One type of listening would be called *listening for appreciation*. A second type of listening would be called *listening for information*. And a third type of listening would be called *listening for understanding*. This third type is also sometimes called *critical listening*. I'm going to give you informal definitions of all three types and examples of the types.

Listening for appreciation can be defined simply as listening for enjoyment or pleasure. Let's say you've had a rough day or a very exciting day and you just want to relax and unwind. You might get some records that you particularly like and go someplace where you can be by yourself, maybe to your room or to a listening room in the library. You turn on music and listen to the sound. You let your body feel the sound. You're not concerned with lines or chords or the way things go from one key into another (even if you've studied music appreciation or theory). You're just there, you relax, and you listen to the sound. And the sound just makes you feel good; you appreciate it.

Listening for information occurs most frequently when you get into a situation such as starting a new job or taking a new subject for the first time. Someone's giving you instructions, and—to get out to you a certain amount of information before you can begin—he or she gives you details. Listening for information can be defined simply as listening for details. People who are giving you details don't expect you to understand everything at once. There is a certain amount of information you have to have before you go on a job and before you can really begin to ask intelligent kinds of questions. In the situation you're in right now, taking notes, you're listening primarily for information.

A third kind of listening will frequently occur after this. You've taken in a certain amount of data; you've taken in a certain amount of information. And now you try to piece it together; you try to make sense out of it. You try to figure out what it all means, to understand it. This *listening for understanding* (or *critical listening*) can be defined simply as listening to gain a full and informed knowledge of a subject. It can occur when an instructor asks you to read and study the notes you've gotten in a class, and you then go to class the next day and discuss those notes and ideas. You look at them from all angles and ask questions. You relate them to your experience, voice agreements and disagreements, and in general deepen your comprehension of them. So a class discussion of a lecture can be seen as an example of listening for understanding.

That covers the three major types of listening. We have a good base now for going on and learning about how to become better listeners.

Questions on the Lecture about Listening

1. Why is it important to be involved in a listening situation from the start?
2. List the three types of listening.
3. Define the first type of listening and give an example.
4. Define the second type of listening and give an example.
5. Define the third type of listening and give an example.

Activity 6

Follow the directions given for Activity 5.

LECTURE ABOUT LOVE

On Board

Three states of mind	Martyring
Romanticizing	Manipulating
Two myths	Symbiotic relationships

In order to survive, human beings need food, water, and shelter. But we also need something else, something that seems to be the subject of just about any show you watch, song you hear, or book you read: love. Human beings need love. Some people find love and enjoy the happiness that goes with it. Other people spend a lot of their time looking for it. Human beings who are raised without love suffer severe emotional damage, for being loved gives us our sense of self-worth. Obviously, it's important to know what love is. One way to help do this is to first take the opposite approach and examine what love isn't. That's what we're going to look at now: what love is not. People are better off if they understand clearly the three states of mind that are often mistaken for love.

First of all, romanticizing is not love. *Romanticizing* can be defined as imagining or inventing many qualities of the person we want to love. In other words, we don't look at a person as he or she really is; instead, we create a false image of the loved one. For example, a person may build up an unreal image of the loved one as a person who never gets angry, or who is never afraid, or who always stays slim and attractive. Rick marries Kate, for instance, believing that she is always outgoing and fun-loving. Later, however, Rick cannot accept the fact that Kate—like everyone else—is occasionally depressed and moody. Rick feels that Kate has somehow betrayed his image of her.

Romanticizing usually involves one of two myths. One of these is that there is only one right partner in the world for each person and that a person knows it instantly when he or she meets this ideal. We have come to believe that the clichés we see in Hollywood movies exist in real life: Eyes meet across a crowded room, and it's love at first sight. Another myth that goes along with romanticizing is that true love conquers all. Partners disregard their lack of common interests, or their major problems, and trust that love will make everything work out for the best. This kind of romantic love is common among teenagers and often leads to early marriages that eventually fail. For instance, eighteen-year-olds Tina and Joe decide to marry even though they both hold minimum-wage jobs and Tina wants a family while Joe doesn't. Tina and Joe say that their love will somehow make everything turn out OK. Unfortunately, however, their relationship will probably not survive the stresses and strains it will have to undergo.

Why does romanticizing lead to a bad end? Romanticizing a relationship inevitably leads to disappointment when a partner fails to measure up to the ideal. Moreover, romanticizers, instead of accepting a partner's flaws, will usually conclude that they have made a mistake. They will say, "You've changed," or "You're not the person I thought you were," and then go off on another search for the "right" person.

Another thing that love isn't is martyring. *Martyring* can be defined as maintaining relationships by giving others more than one receives in return. Martyring involves a lopsided relationship. One person gives much more than the other. Martyrs may show several kinds of behavior. First, they do things for partners that often the partners would rather do for themselves. They'll run to the store or take over cooking a meal, for instance, even though the partner is perfectly content to do the job. Second, they hesitate to suggest what they would like; for example, they'll always leave a decision about a movie or a restaurant up to the partner. Third, martyrs help their partners develop talents and interests, but they neglect their own. They may help a spouse return to school or begin an exercise program, but they feel that they don't deserve to indulge in such activities themselves.

The martyr may sound unselfish, but a martyr is not showing real love. Martyrs don't express their own needs, and this prevents the openness and intimacy a relationship demands. If you're in a relationship and you often seem to be keeping your true feelings to yourself, you're not helping that relationship grow. In addition, martyrs often conceal growing feelings of anger and resentment at the one-sided relationship. These feelings can eventually explode.

Finally, manipulating is not love. *Manipulating* means seeking to control the feelings, attitudes, and behavior of one's partner. Manipulators believe that if they can get a partner to do something, then that partner truly loves them. For example, a manipulator may ask a partner to give up anything from a television show to a growing career to prove his or her love. In a way, manipulators are the opposites of martyrs. Manipulators expect partners to do things for them. Manipulators want the final say on all decisions. They also want to develop their own talents and interests while ignoring their partners' needs. In a sense, manipulators are constantly testing their partners. They do this because they secretly feel that they are unlovable; they often tell their partners, "You don't really love me." Manipulators also experience a great deal of guilt over the fact that they are taking advantage of others.

Manipulators and martyrs often seek each other out, since they have complementary needs. They form what are called *symbiotic relationships*. In a symbiotic relationship, each partner depends on the other for a sense of self-worth. This kind of relationship is often very strong and stable unless, of course, one of the partners tries to change. Then the delicate balance crumbles.

In conclusion, we have looked at three things love isn't: romanticizing, martyring, and manipulating. The major reason why these relationships are not love can be explained in a very simple way: All these relationships involve a refusal to accept oneself or one's partner realistically. If you do not accept yourself or your partner in a realistic way, you are probably not in a true loving relationship.

Questions on the Lecture about Love

1. What are three states of mind often mistaken for love?
2. What is romanticizing?
3. What are two myths involved in romanticizing?
4. What is martyring?
5. What is a symbiotic relationship?

Activity 7

Follow the directions given for Activity 5.

LECTURE ABOUT MEMORY

On Board

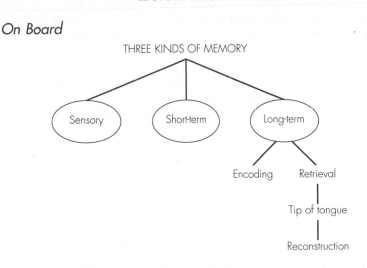

Today, I'd like to discuss the three kinds of memory that human beings have. First of all, we humans have something called *sensory memory*. We might define sensory memory as a brief shadow or fleeting impression of sensory experience, persisting for only a moment. For example, if you clap your hands once, you'll note how the distinctness of the sound fades gradually. Or, if you touch a sharp toothpick to the back of your hand, you'll retain that sensation momentarily, even after you remove the point. Because our senses are constantly bombarded by huge amounts of information, we take in, or register, the information and then forget it in less than a second. The reason for this is simple: we have to make room for new sensory information.

However, when we want to retain information for more than a second, we use the second type of memory we have—*short-term memory,* or *STM.* Suppose, for instance, that you're talking to a friend and your mind wanders to other matters, like an upcoming exam. Somehow you sense that your friend asked a question and is waiting for an answer. You're about to ask, "What did you say?" when, suddenly, you realize that you *do* know the exact question your friend asked. Somehow, almost without trying, you were able to dredge up the last fifteen to twenty seconds of conversation verbatim, that is, word for word. This is a commonplace experience. It seems to prove that humans can store meaningful information for several seconds with very little effort. And this ability is what we call short-term memory. Short-term memory contains whatever thoughts, information, and experiences are in a person's mind at any specific point in time.

Short-term memory has two functions: first, brief temporary storage (as in the example of recalling a bit of conversation); and second, overall management. *Overall management* means that STM somehow selects which materials are to be maintained momentarily and which are to be transferred permanently into long-term memory.

And this brings us to the third type of memory: *long-term memory,* or *LTM.* This system gives people the ability to recall large amounts of information for substantial periods—hours, days, weeks, years, and in some cases forever. Some examples of items stored in your own long-term memory are your name, the taste of popcorn, nursery rhymes, and the English alphabet. Psychologists feel that this system is virtually unlimited in its storage capacity. The next matter to look at is how, exactly, we manage to store this information in LTM. The entire process of readying information for storage is called *encoding.* Let me repeat that: encoding is the entire process of readying information for storage. We appear to store some visual material as pictures. We have mental images of places, people, and three-dimensional objects like our car or computer; we can call up these images quickly and accurately. Of course, we store information other than the three-dimensional, visual kind; for instance, we have to remember and recall verbal information. As you read a newspaper, you probably condense the words into a few ideas that you retain. For example, an entire story about energy-proofing your home might be condensed into the ideas of putting more insulation in your attic and adding storm doors. Very seldom do we remember the exact wording of what we've read. However, we can store precise wording if we need to, as when we must memorize a speech or a role in a play.

I've just discussed how we encode, or store, items in long-term memory. Now, I'd like to mention briefly how we *retrieve,* or call up, items in LTM. This retrieval seems to be a continuous process, with some retrievals being easier than others. For instance, you can call up your own address or your mother's name almost effortlessly. Occasionally, retrieval is more difficult. We've all experienced the rather frustrating *tip-of-the-tongue phenomenon,* when we're sure we know a bit of information and feel on the verge of remembering it. Usually, when we have trouble retrieving information from LTM, we resort to a problem-solving strategy. Psychologists call this strategy *reconstruction.* For example, if I asked you, "What were you doing one year ago on Monday afternoon in the second week of September?" you might think, "How should I know?" But if you really tried to recall the information through a series of steps, you might remember. You might say, "Well, it was my first semester in college then. I remember I had a speech class on Mondays. In fact, I think our class was doing short oral presentations then." Thus, through a series of logical steps, by breaking large questions into small ones, you might retrieve that long-term memory.

Let me sum up: I've discussed three kinds of memory—sensory, short-term, and long-term—and I've also touched on how we encode information and then retrieve it from our long-term memory.

Questions on the Lecture about Memory

1. What are the three types of memory?
2. Define sensory memory.
3. Name one of the two functions of short-term memory.
4. What is long-term memory?
5. Give an example of an item stored in the long-term memory.
6. What is encoding?
7. What is reconstruction, and how do we use it?

TIME CONTROL AND CONCENTRATION

This chapter will show you how to manage your time through the use of:

- A large monthly calendar
- A weekly study schedule
- A "to do" list
- A series of hints on concentration

Introductory Project

Consider this common study situation:

Cheryl has trouble managing her study time. She claims that the only time she can make herself study is right before a test. "If I'm not in a crisis situation with a test just around the corner," she says, "I usually won't study. When I'm in the right mood, I do try to study a bit to keep things from piling up. But most of the time I'm just not in the mood. Some mornings I get up and say to myself, 'Tonight you will do at least two hours of schoolwork.' Then, 95 percent of the time, I let something distract me." Cheryl recently had to face the shortcomings of her cramming method. She found herself with only one night to prepare for two exams and a report; the result was three disastrous grades.

This chapter will provide answers to Cheryl's study problem. But take a few minutes first to examine your own ideas. What do you think are three specific steps that Cheryl could take to prevent such a situation from happening again?

All of us need free time, hours without demands or obligations, so that we can just relax and do what we please. But it is easy to lose track of time and discover suddenly that there aren't enough hours to do what needs to be done. No skill is more basic to survival in college than time control. If you do not use your time well, your college career—and the life goals that depend on how well you do in college—will slip like sand through your fingers. This chapter describes three methods to help you gain control of your time: You will learn how to use a large monthly calendar, a weekly study schedule, and a daily or weekly "to do" list. There is also a series of hints on concentration—how to use your study time more effectively.

A LARGE MONTHLY CALENDAR

You should buy or make a large monthly calendar. Such a calendar is your first method of time control because it allows you, in one quick glance, to get a clear picture of what you need to do in the weeks to come. Be sure your monthly calendar has a good-sized block of white space for each date. Then, as soon as you learn about exam dates and paper deadlines, enter them clearly in the appropriate spots on the calendar. Hang the calendar in a place where you will see it every day, perhaps on your kitchen or bedroom wall. A monthly calendar made up by one student is shown below.

October

Sun.	Mon.	Tues.	Wed.	Thurs.	Fri.	Sat.
				1	2	3
4	5 Soc test	6	7	8	9 English essay due	10
11	12	13 Bio field trip	14	15 Psych quiz	16	17
18	19 Speech	20	21	22	23 English essay due	24
25	26 Bio test	27	28	29 Business report due	30	31

Activity

In the following spaces, write the names of the courses you are taking. Also, record the dates on which papers or other assignments are due and the dates on which exams are scheduled. Due dates are often listed in a course syllabus as well as announced by a course instructor.

Courses	Paper Due Dates	Exam Dates
_____	_____	_____
_____	_____	_____
_____	_____	_____
_____	_____	_____
_____	_____	_____

Transfer all this information to a monthly calendar.

■   Write here what you think would be the best place for you to post a monthly calendar:

_____

■   *Complete the following statement:*
   A monthly calendar will keep you constantly aware of exam and paper

   target days, so that you can _____
   well in advance.

A WEEKLY STUDY SCHEDULE

Evaluating Your Use of Time

A weekly study schedule will make you aware of how much time you actually have each week and will help you use that time effectively. Before you prepare a weekly study schedule, however, you need to get a sense of how you spend your time *each day*. The activities that follow will help you do that.

Activity 1

The daily schedule of one student, Jill, follows. Jill has three classes. Assuming that every hour of class time should receive at least one hour of study time, how could Jill revise her schedule so that she would have at least three full study hours in addition to time for "rest and relaxation"? Make your suggested changes by crossing out items and adding study time to her schedule. Your instructor may then have you compare your answers with those of others in the class.

Jill's Daily Schedule	
Time	Activity
7:30–8:30	Get up, wash, eat
8:30–9	Travel to school
9–10	Class (College Math)
10–11	Class (English)
11–12	Student center (read, talk to friends)
12–1	Cafeteria for lunch
1–2	Class (Intro. to Sociology)
2–3	Gym (use exercise equipment)
3–3:30	Drive to work
3:30–7	Work at Roy Rogers
7–8	Eat dinner at Roy Rogers, drive home
8–9:30	Read paper, check mail, do homework
9:30–11:30	Watch TV
11:30	Bed

Activity 2

Use the chart on the next page to record a *typical* school day in your life. Be honest: You want to see clearly what you are doing so that you will be able to plan ways to use your time more effectively.

| Your Daily Schedule | |
Time	Activity

Now, honestly evaluate your use of time. Write down the number of hours you *actually* used for study in your typical day: _____ hours. Next, go back to your chart and block off time in the day that you *could* have used for study. (Remember to still allow for ''rest and relaxation'' time, which is also needed.)

Write down the number of hours you could have used for study in the day: _____ hours.

Note: People sometimes learn from their schedules that they are victims of a time overload, for they have taken too much work on themselves with too little time to do it. If you think this is your case, you should talk with your instructor or a counselor about possibly dropping one or more courses.

Important Points about a Weekly Study Schedule

You are now ready to look over the master weekly schedule that Jill prepared to gain control of her time: it is shown on the next page. You should then read carefully the points that follow; all are important in planning an effective weekly schedule. Note that you will be asked to refer to Jill's schedule to answer questions that accompany some of the points.

Point 1: Plan, at first, at least one hour of study time for each hour of class time. Depending on the course, the grade you want, and your own efficiency in studying, you may have to schedule more time later. A difficult course, for example, may require three hours or more of study time for each course hour. Remember that learning is what counts, not the time it takes you to learn. Be prepared to schedule as much time as you need to gain control of a course.

- How many class hours, excluding lab and physical education, does Jill have? _____

- How many study hours has she scheduled? _____

Point 2: Schedule regular study time. To succeed in your college work, you need to establish definite study hours. If you do not set aside and stick to such hours on a daily or almost daily basis, you are probably going to fail at time control. Jot down in the following spaces the free hours each day that you would use as regular study time. The first column shows Jill's free hours on Monday.

For Jill	Your Possible Study Hours						
Mon.	Mon.	Tues.	Wed.	Thurs.	Fri.	Sat.	Sun.
11–12							
2–3							
8–12							

- How many separate blocks of study time has Jill built into her weekly schedule? _____

Jill's Weekly Schedule

	Mon.	Tues.	Wed.	Thurs.	Fri.	Sat.	Sun.	
6:00 A.M.								6:00 A.M.
7:00	B	B	B	B	B			7:00
8:00								8:00
9:00	Math	Psy	Math	Phys Ed	Math	B	B	9:00
10:00	Eng	↓	Eng	↓	Eng			10:00
11:00								11:00
12:00	L	L	L	L	L			12:00
1:00 P.M.	Soc		Soc		Soc	L	L	1:00 P.M.
2:00				Psy				2:00
3:00	Job	Job		↓	Job			3:00
4:00								4:00
5:00						Job		5:00
6:00	↓	↓	S	S	↓		S	6:00
7:00	S	S		Econ	S			7:00
8:00								8:00
9:00				↓	↓			9:00
10:00						S		10:00
11:00								11:00
12:00	Bed	Bed	Bed	Bed			Bed	12:00
1:00 A.M.								1:00 A.M.
2:00	③	④	④	③	①	⓪	⑤	2:00

B = Breakfast   ▨ = Study blocks   Econ = Economics   Eng = English
L = Lunch   ◯ = Study hours per day   Soc = Sociology   Phys Ed = Physical Education
S = Supper   Blanks = Free time   Psy = Psychology

There are many benefits to setting aside regular study hours. First of all, they help make studying a habit. Study times will be as automatically programmed into your daily schedule as, say, watching a favorite television program. You will not have to remind yourself to study, nor will you waste large amounts of time and energy trying to avoid studying; you will simply do it. Another value of regular study time is that you will be better able to stay up to date on work in your courses. You are not likely to find yourself several days before a test with three textbook chapters to read or five weeks of classroom notes to organize and study. Finally, regular study takes advantage of the proven fact that a series of study sessions is more effective than a single long ''cram'' session.

■ How many benefits of regular study hours are described above? (*Hint:* Word

  signals such as ''First of all'' are clues.) _____

Point 3: Plan at least one-hour blocks of study time.   If you schedule less than one hour, your study period may be over just when you are fully warmed up and working hard.

■ What is the largest single block of study time that Jill has during the week?

  (Write down the day and the number of hours.) _____

■ What is the largest single block of study time available to you each week?

  _____

Point 4: Reward yourself for using study time effectively.   Research shows that people work better if they get an immediate reward. So if your schedule permits, try to set up a reward system. Allow yourself to telephone a friend or watch television or eat a snack after a period of efficient study. On Jill's schedule, for example, nine to ten o'clock on Wednesday night is free for television as a reward for working well in the two-hour study slot before. When you are studying over a several-hour period, you can also give yourself ''mini-rewards'' of five to ten minutes of free time for every hour or so of study time.

Your reward system won't work if you ''cheat,'' so deprive yourself of such pleasures as television shows when you have not studied honestly.

■ Locate the other spots where Jill has built reward time into her schedule after

  study periods and indicate the hours here: _____

  _____

■ Do you think it is a good idea for Jill to reward herself with one day in the

  week (Saturday) free from study? Why or why not? _____

  _____

Point 5: Try to schedule study periods before and after classes. Ideally, you should read a textbook chapter before an instructor covers it; what you hear in class will then be a "second exposure," so the ideas are likely to be a good deal more meaningful to you. You should also look over your notes from the preceding class in case the instructor discusses the material further. Similarly, if you take a few minutes to review your notes as soon after class as possible, you will be able to organize and clarify the material while it is still fresh in your mind.

■ If a new textbook chapter were to be covered in Jill's psychology class on Thursday, where in her schedule should she plan to read it? _____

_____

Point 6: Work on your most difficult subjects when you are most alert. Save routine work for times when you are most likely to be tired. You might, for example, study a new and difficult mathematics chapter at 8 P.M. if you are naturally alert then and review vocabulary words for a Spanish class at 11 P.M., when you may be a little tired.

■ Assuming that Jill is most naturally alert early in the day and that math is her most difficult subject, in what time slots should she schedule her work on that subject? _____

■ At what time of day do you consider yourself most alert? _____

_____

Point 7: Balance your activities. Allow free time in your schedule for family, friends, sports, television, and so on. Note that there is a good deal of free time (empty space) in Jill's schedule, even with her classes, work, and study hours.

■ Where is the biggest block of free time in Jill's schedule? _____

_____

■ Where do *you* plan to have a substantial block of free time? _____

_____

Point 8: Keep your schedule flexible.   When unexpected events occur, trade times on your weekly timetable. Do not simply do away with study hours. If you find that your schedule requires constant adjustment, revise it. (Your in-structor may be able to give you extra copies of the schedule on the next page.) After two or three revisions, you will have a realistic, practical weekly schedule that you can follow honestly.

■   If Jill went to a family reunion on Sunday at 1 P.M. and didn't get back until eight o'clock that evening, where in her schedule could she make up the

missed hour of study time? _____

_____

Activity

Keeping the preceding points in mind, use the form on page 78 to make up your own realistic weekly study schedule. Write in your class and lab periods first; next add in your hours for job and meals; and then fill in the study hours that you need to do well in your courses. At the bottom of your schedule, make up a key that explains the symbols you have used in it. Also add up and circle the total number of study hours you realistically plan to set aside each day.

A DAILY OR WEEKLY "TO DO" LIST

How to Make a "To Do" List

A "to do" list is simply a list of things a person wants to accomplish within a limited period. Many successful people make the "to do" list a habit, considering it an essential step in using their time most efficiently each day. A "to do" list, made up daily or weekly, may be one of the most important single study habits you will ever acquire.

Prepare your "to do" list on four- by six-inch note pads or in a small notebook. (Such a notebook can also be used to record the daily assignments you receive in your different courses.) A weekly list is usually prepared on a Sunday for the week ahead; a daily list is prepared the evening before a new day or the first thing on the morning of that day. The list should include all the things you want to work on during that week or day.

Jill's "to do" list for one day appears at the top of page 79. (At the bottom of that page is a form for your own list, which you'll be asked to complete shortly.)

Your Weekly Schedule

	Mon.	Tues.	Wed.	Thurs.	Fri.	Sat.	Sun.	
6:00 A.M.								6:00 A.M.
7:00								7:00
8:00								8:00
9:00								9:00
10:00								10:00
11:00								11:00
12:00								12:00
1:00 P.M.								1:00 P.M.
2:00								2:00
3:00								3:00
4:00								4:00
5:00								5:00
6:00								6:00
7:00								7:00
8:00								8:00
9:00								9:00
10:00								10:00
11:00								11:00
12:00								12:00
1:00 A.M.								1:00 A.M.
2:00								2:00

Jill's "To Do" List

To Do   Monday

1. Think of topic for English essay
2. Read Chap. 6 of sociology text
3. Study class notes for psychology quiz on Tuesday
4. Find book in library for economics report
5. Have new tire put on car
6. Call Carol
7. Buy blouse on sale at Deb Shop
8. Borrow and copy notes from math class missed last week
9. Call my sister at her college
10. Watch comedy special on TV
11. Hem new jeans
12. Borrow George Michael album from Jim
13. Review math problems 1/2 hour before bed

Your "To Do" List

To Do

Important Notes about the "To Do" List

Point 1: Carry the list with you throughout the day. A small notebook can be kept in a purse, and a four- by six-inch slip of paper can be kept in a pocket or wallet.

Point 2: Decide on priorities. Making the best use of your time means focusing on high-priority items rather than spending hours completing low-priority activities. When in doubt about what to do at any given time in the day, ask yourself, "How can I best use my time at this point?" and choose a high-priority item on your list.

■ Look at Jill's list and label each item *A, B,* or *C* according to what you think is a reasonable priority level for that item.

Point 3: Cross out items as you finish them. Don't worry unnecessarily about completing your list; what is not done can usually be moved to the next day's list. What is important is that you make the best possible use of your time each day. Focus on high-priority activities!

Activity

Use the space at the bottom of page 79 to make up your own "to do" list for tomorrow. If you cannot think of at least seven items, then put down as well things that you want to do over the rest of the week. After completing the list, label the different items as priority *A, B,* or *C.*

CONCENTRATION

A monthly calendar, a weekly study schedule, and a "to do" list are essential methods of organizing your study time. Unfortunately, however, all your effort in creating them will be useless if you waste the study time you have set aside. Unless you master the art of *concentrating* on your work, you will learn very little.

Is concentrating difficult? The answer is both *yes* and *no.* The skill of concentration somewhat resembles a beating heart: when it works, we take it for granted and are hardly aware of it; any malfunction, however, is painfully obvious. For example, you probably find it very easy to concentrate on something you are extremely interested in—a television show, a certain magazine, an elaborate meal you are preparing for friends. But concentration may seem impossible when you are studying a biology chapter or mathematics problems.

■ Name an activity on which you can easily concentrate: _____
■ Name an activity on which you can concentrate only with great difficulty:

_____

Why People Can't Concentrate

Why is it often so difficult to concentrate on studying? There are several reasons; one or more of them may apply to you.

You equate studying with punishment. If you have a history of doing poorly in school, or if you have often received poor grades even though you tried to study, you will naturally have a negative reaction every time you sit down with your books. After all, you may think, the work is hard and probably not worthwhile. You are conditioned to see studying as torture. All your negative experiences have created a mental block that hinders your ability to concentrate.

- Do you think you have a block about studying because of past school experiences? _____
- If so, are you ready to break through your block by applying the study skills in this book? _____

You put everything off until the last minute. The Procrastinators Club holds its Christmas party in February. However, putting off your studies until the last minute is not as harmless and amusing as the Procrastinators' social schedule. Trying to study ten hours for an exam tomorrow or starting at nine o'clock in the morning to write a paper that is due by three o'clock in the afternoon is like trying to work with a gun at your head: concentration is difficult at best.

- Are you a procrastinator? _____
- If so, what do you do to avoid studying? _____
- Does procrastination make you feel anxious and guilty, as it does for most people? _____

You don't feel comfortable or settled. You're dying of thirst. The chair you're sitting in is sending shooting pains up your spine. Your head is pounding or your eyes are drooping. Your body feels so exhausted that it seems impossible to remain upright any longer. At the same time, dozens of other thoughts may crowd into your mind: next weekend's trip, the argument you had with your mother, the dirty laundry piling up in your closet. Such physical and mental distractions will soon overwhelm any amount of concentration you may have been able to achieve.

- Of the three reasons for not concentrating just listed, which one applies most in your case? _____

Ways to Concentrate

When you can't concentrate, you can take either of two routes. You can give in to defeat by rationalizing your failures. You can tell yourself, for example, that "nobody could understand this textbook" or "I hate this course anyway and I don't care if I fail" or "I don't know why I'm in school" or "I'll really concentrate next time." The better route to take is to decide that you will do everything you can to improve your concentration. Here are practical hints that will help you fix your attention on the studying you have to do.

Hint 1: Work on having a positive attitude.   It is a rare student who has a deep interest in every one of his or her college courses. Most students find that at least some of the studying they have to do involves uninteresting material. In such cases, it is essential to examine your priorities and goals. Don't let some less-than-stimulating courses block your route to the college degree you want. Decide that you will do the studying because someday the course will be forgotten, but your college education and degree will be benefiting your life.

■   What are the most unpleasant study tasks you will have this semester?

   _____

■   Is your college degree important enough for you to do these unpleasant
    tasks? _____

Hint 2: Prepare to work by setting specific study goals.   Don't stare at a foot-high pile of thick textbooks and wonder how you'll ever make it through the semester. Instead, go over your assignments and jot down a list of practical goals for the period of study time you have available. These will be the study items on your day's "to do" list. This technique helps you get organized; it also breaks your large study task into manageable units that you can accomplish one at a time. Here are typical study items from a student's daily "to do" list:

> *Answer review questions in Chapter 3 of business text.*
> *Do twenty minutes of freewriting for English class.*
> *Read Chapter 4 in psychology text.*
> *Complete ten mathematics problems.*

You may want to work first on the assignments that seem easiest, or least painful, to you. It's a good feeling to cross something off your list; knowing you've finished at least *one* thing can often give you the confidence you need to continue.

■ Jot down four specific assignments you must complete in the next school week.

_____

_____

_____

_____

Hint 3: Keep track of your lapses of concentration. When you start studying, jot down the time (for example, ''7:15'') at the bottom of your ''to do'' list of study items. When you find yourself losing interest or thinking about something else, write the time (for example, ''7:35'') on that same piece of paper. Catching yourself like this can help train your mind to concentrate for longer and longer periods. You should soon find that you can study for a longer span of time before the first notation appears. The notations, too, should become fewer and fewer.

■ Record the time here whenever you have a lapse in concentration while reading the rest of this chapter.

_____

Hint 4: Create a good study environment. Choose a room that is, first of all, quiet and well lighted. To avoid glare, make sure that light comes from above or over your shoulder, not from in front of you. Also, you should have more than one light source in the room. For example, you might use a ceiling light in addition to a pole lamp behind your chair.

■ Do you think that the place where you study is well lighted? _____

■ If not, what might you do to improve the lighting? _____

_____

Second, you should have a comfortable place to sit. Do not try to study in a completely relaxed position. A light muscular tension promotes the concentration needed for study. So sit on an upright chair or sit in a cross-legged position on your bed with a pillow behind you. Keep in mind, also, that you do not have to sit down to study. Many students stay alert and focused by walking back and forth across the room as they test themselves on material they must learn.

■ What is your usual position when you study? _____

_____

■ Are your muscles slightly tense in this position, or are they completely relaxed? _____

Make sure you have all the materials you will need: ballpoint pens, highlighter pens, pencils, loose-leaf or typing paper, and a small memo pad. Ideally (though not essentially), you should have a typewriter and a calculator as well.

Finally, to avoid interruptions in your study place, ask your family and friends to keep away during study hours. Tell them that you will return telephone calls after you finish studying. Preparing a good environment in advance ensures that when you do achieve concentration, nothing will interrupt you.

If you do not have a room where you can study, use a secluded spot in the library or student center, or find some other quiet spot. If you have one particular place where you usually do most of your studying, you will almost automatically shift into gear and begin studying when you go to that place.

Hint 5: Stay in good physical condition.   You do not want to tire easily or have frequent illnesses. Eat nourishing meals, starting with breakfast—your most important meal of the day. For some students, breakfast is simply coffee and doughnuts or a soda and cookies from a vending machine. But a solid breakfast is not merely a combination of caffeine and sugar. It is, instead, protein, as in milk, yogurt, or a whole-grain cereal. Protein will supply the steady flow of blood sugar needed to keep you mentally alert through the entire day.

Try to get an average of eight hours of sleep a night unless your system can manage with less. Also, try to exercise on a regular basis. A short workout in the morning (if only five minutes of running in place) will help sustain your energy flow during the day. Finally, do not hesitate to take a fifteen- to thirty-minute nap at some point during the day. Research findings show that such a nap can provide a helpful energy boost.

■   What is your typical breakfast? How could you realistically improve it?

_____

■   What other steps do you take—or should you take—to stay in good physical

condition? _____

Hint 6: Vary your study activities.   A study session need not be a four-hour marathon devoted to one subject. When you cannot concentrate anymore, don't waste time staring unproductively at, say, a mathematics problem. Switch over to your English paper or biology report. The change in subject matter and type of assignment can ease mental strain by stimulating a different part of your brain (verbal ability, for instance) while the other part (mathematical ability) rests. By varying your activities, you will stay fresh and alert longer than you would if you hammered away at one subject for hours.

Hint 7: Practice the study skills in this book. Many students can't concentrate on their studies because they don't know *how* to study. They look at the brief notes they took during a class lecture and wonder what to do with them. They start reading a textbook as casually as if they were reading the sports page of the newspaper, and then they wonder why they get so little out of it. They have perhaps been told that taking good notes and then reciting those notes are keys to effective study, but they are not sure how to apply these skills. Learning and practicing study skills will help you become deeply involved in your assignments. Before you know it, you are concentrating.

■ Of all the study skills in this book, which are the three most important for you to practice? _____ _____ _____

Hint 8: Use outside help when needed. Some people find that studying with a friend or friends helps concentration. Others, however, find it more of a distraction than an aid because they spend more time chatting than studying cooperatively. Use the technique of team study only if you think it will be of real value to you. Also, find out if your school has a tutoring service. If it does, do not hesitate to use the service to get help in a particular subject or subjects. Having a good tutor could make a significant difference in your grade for a course. And determine if your school, like many, has a learning center where you may work on developing writing, reading, study, and mathematics skills. Finally, learn the office hours of your instructors and find out whether you can see them if you need additional help.

■ Does your school have a tutoring service? _____

■ Does your school have a learning center? _____

■ If so, where is each located? _____

SOME FINAL THOUGHTS

You now have three practical means of gaining control of your time: a monthly calendar, a master study schedule, and a ''to do'' list. In addition, you have learned useful hints for aiding concentration. Use whatever combination of the techniques is best for you. These tools, combined with your own determination to apply them, can reduce the disorder of everyday life, where time slips quickly and silently away. Through time planning, you can achieve the consistency in your work that is absolutely vital for success in school. And through time control and steady concentration, you can take command of your life and accomplish more work than you have ever done before.

PRACTICE IN TIME CONTROL AND CONCENTRATION

Activity 1

Several skills for controlling time and several habits for studying and concentration are listed below. Evaluate yourself by putting a check mark beside each of the skills or habits that you already practice. Then put a check mark beside those steps that you plan to practice. Leave a space blank if you do not plan to follow a particular strategy.

Now   Plan
Do   to Do

_____ _____ ■ Use a large monthly calendar.

_____ _____ ■ Use a weekly study schedule.

_____ _____ ■ Use a daily or weekly "to do" list.

_____ _____ ■ Have regular study hours.

_____ _____ ■ Schedule as many hours as needed for a particular course.

_____ _____ ■ Give yourself rewards for using study time effectively.

_____ _____ ■ Work on difficult subjects at times when you are most alert.

_____ _____ ■ Balance activities.

_____ _____ ■ Try to have a positive attitude about all your courses.

_____ _____ ■ Set goals before starting work.

_____ _____ ■ Create a good study environment (comfortable but nondistracting).

_____ _____ ■ Stay in good physical condition.

_____ _____ ■ Vary your study activities.

_____ _____ ■ Use outside help when needed.

Activity 2

Several weeks into the semester, your instructor will ask you to hand in copies of the following:

■ One month from your monthly calendar

■ Your weekly study schedule

■ Your most recent daily or weekly "to do" list

Do not simply submit copies of the materials you have prepared while doing this chapter; instead, hand in recent and updated materials. And be honest: If you are not using one or more of these methods of time control, don't pretend that you are. Instead, write a short essay explaining why you have decided not to use one or more of the time-control methods in this chapter.

Activity 3

Write a short paper about some aspect of concentration skills. Here are some suggestions.

- Write a paragraph describing the reasons why you may not have concentrated effectively in the past. For example, you might have had a poor attitude; you might have procrastinated a great deal; you might have lacked certain study skills; you might have had a poor study environment. Use specific details to give a clear picture of your previous study habits.

- Write a narrative paragraph about your last study session. Be specific about how well *or* how poorly you concentrated and why.

- Write a paragraph detailing three specific changes you are planning to make in the place where you study.

- Write a paragraph on the mistakes the students you see around you make when they study. Note, for example, where you see students studying; the conditions under which they are trying to study; how they are going about studying; and so on.

Textbook Study I:

THE PRWR STUDY METHOD

This chapter will show you how to study a textbook chapter by:

- Previewing the chapter
- Reading the chapter
- Taking notes on the chapter
- Studying your notes

Introductory Project

Consider this common study situation:

> For tomorrow's test in his Introduction to Business course, Gary has to know three chapters from the textbook. At 1:30 P.M. yesterday, he sat down with a yellow marking pen and started reading the first chapter. At 3 P.M. he wasn't even halfway through the first chapter, and he felt bored and worn out. The sentences were long and heavy and loaded with details. Gary's head became so packed with information that as soon as he read a new fact, it seemed to automatically push out the one before it. When he looked back at what he had covered, he realized he had set off most of the text in yellow. Gary decided then to stop marking and just read. But the more he read, the sleepier he got, and the more his mind kept wandering. He kept thinking about all the things he wanted to do once the test was over. At 5:15 P.M. he had finished reading the first chapter, but he felt completely defeated. He still had to study the chapter, and he had no idea exactly what to study. On top of that, he had to plow through two more chapters and study them as well. He felt desperate and stupid—because he had waited so long to start with the text and because he was having such a hard time reading it.

This and the following two chapters will provide solutions for Gary's study problem. But take a few minutes first to examine your own ideas. What do you think are three specific steps Gary could take to read and study his textbook effectively?

USING YOUR TEXTBOOK: A CAUTION

To begin this chapter on textbook study, let me share an experience with you. When I first began teaching, I was still studying for my advanced degree in reading at a nearby state college. I remember especially a class in statistics I had every Monday night. I would travel to the college after a long day of teaching. I'd be exhausted, and I'd have to sit through a class that was hardly my favorite subject. There was a textbook, but I didn't understand much of it. I remember looking through it when I bought it and thinking, ''Good grief! How in the world am I going to survive this?''

As it turned out, the instructor didn't require us to do anything with the textbook. I wasn't too surprised, because in many of my undergraduate courses, although we had to buy a textbook, most of the learning actually took place in the classroom. The instructor's attitude seemed to be, ''Here is the textbook as a resource. But I'm going to give you the most important ideas in class.''

My statistics instructor did a lot of presenting in class. I remember sitting next to another student whose name also was John. We were a study in contrasts: he was very active in class, constantly asking questions and volunteering answers. In fact, he was so active that he didn't take many notes except to write down what the instructor put on the board. I said very little because I was so tired and neither my heart nor head was in the subject. I did little but sit there and take lots of notes. I wrote down not just everything the instructor put on the board but also the connections between those ideas. As the instructor explained things, I didn't just listen; I wrote it all down. My attitude was, ''I can't understand any of this stuff now, but later—when I don't feel turned off and brain dead—I'll be able to go through it and try to make sense of it.''

When I began to prepare for my midsemester exam, I was surprised to see that I had written some ideas down three or even four times. The instructor had repeated them, and I, getting everything down on paper, had repeated them as well. I had so many notes that I was able to make sense of the material. The instructor had done his job: he had used class time to help us understand a difficult subject. His explanations were very clear, and I had gotten them all down on paper. All I needed to study for that exam was right there in my notes. I didn't even open the textbook.

Do you want to guess who got the higher score in the midsemester exam— the other John or me? I got an 86; the other John got a 74. He saw my paper and felt, I think, a little chagrined. If he had asked me my secret, I would have said, ''Take lots of notes.''

The point of my story is this: *Don't underestimate the importance of taking class notes in doing well in a course.* If the truth be told, in a number of courses, good class notes will be enough to earn you a decent grade. In many courses, the textbook is only a secondary source of information for the ideas you need to know on exams.

Some students fail to take many notes in class because they think, "I'll get whatever else I need by reading the textbook." Whatever you do, don't make that mistake. An idea you can get down in five minutes in class might take you two hours to get out of a textbook—if it's there at all! Learn how to use the textbook, but don't *ever* make the mistake of trying to use it as a substitute for classroom note-taking.

■ In a chapter on textbook study, why is so much space devoted to a story about classroom note-taking? _____

_____

PRWR: A TEXTBOOK STUDY METHOD

To become a better reader—of textbooks or any other material—you should systematically develop a whole series of important reading skills, as presented in Part Four. This chapter will give you a plan of attack for dealing with a textbook assignment. It explains four steps needed for studying a chapter. The two chapters that follow give you practice in applying these four steps.

The four-step study method is known as PRWR and variations of it (the most familiar is known as SQ3R) are taught by many reading instructors. The letters stand for the four steps in the process: (1) *preview,* (2) *read,* (3) *write,* and (4) *recite.*

Step 1: Preview

A *preview* is a rapid survey that gives you a bird's-eye view of what you are reading. It involves taking several minutes to look through an entire chapter before you begin reading it closely.

Here is how to preview a selection:

■ Study the *title.* The title gives you in a few words the shortest possible summary of the whole chapter. Without reading a line of text, you can learn in a general way what the material is about. For example, if the assigned chapter in a psychology text is titled "Stress and Coping with Stress," you know that everything in the chapter is going to concern stress and how to deal with it.

■ Quickly read over the *first and last several paragraphs.* These paragraphs may introduce and summarize some of the main ideas covered in the chapter.

■ Then page through the chapter and look at the different levels of *headings.* Are there two levels of headings? Three levels? More? Are any relationships obvious among these headings? (For more detail on this, see "Recognizing Headings and Subheadings" in Part Four of this book.)

- Look briefly at words set in **boldface**, *italics*, and color; such words may be set off because they are important terms. (For more on this, see ''Recognizing Definitions and Examples'' in Part Four.)
- Glance at *pictures, charts, and boxed material* in the chapter.

Many students have never been taught to preview. They plunge right into a chapter rather than taking a minute or two to do a survey. But remember that it can help to get the ''lay of the land'' before beginning to read.

Activity 1

Answer the following questions.

1. Were you taught to preview as part of your reading instruction in school? _____
2. Do you think that previewing seems like a good idea? _____
3. What part of the preview do you think might be most helpful for you?

Activity 2

Take about two minutes to preview the following textbook selection; then answer the questions that follow it.

REFLEXES IN INFANTS

A second significant collection of behaviors we see in the newborn is *reflexes*. A reflex is a response that is automatic and is triggered involuntarily by some specific stimulus. As adults we have quite a collection of such reflexes, including the expansion and contraction of the pupil to dark and light, blinking when a puff of air hits the eye, the knee jerk, and so on. In the newborn there are dozens of reflexes, but psychologists are interested in only a few. Of these, the most important have to do with eating.

Feeding Reflexes

First, the infant comes equipped with a *rooting reflex*. If you touch infants on the cheek, anywhere near the mouth, they will turn their heads and root around to put the mouth on the object that touched them. This reflex is extremely sensible, if you think of the position in which a baby is held to be fed, particularly for breast-feeding. Next in the sequence is the *sucking reflex*. The baby will automatically make sucking movements if touched on the lips or if something is inserted in the mouth. Finally, there is the *swallowing reflex*. At this early stage babies haven't learned to stop breathing in order to swallow, to avoid taking in a lot of air, so they don't alternate these well. They swallow air and then have to burp it up again. But swallowing does occur reflexively from the very earliest days of life.

Primitive Reflexes

A second group of reflexes, although not as essential to the infant's survival as the various feeding reflexes, seems to be controlled by the midbrain, which is the part of the brain that develops earliest. As the more advanced parts of the brain such as the cortex develop and come to dominate during the first year or so of life, these primitive reflexes drop out.

The *Moro reflex* is one of these primitive reflexes. If a loud sound is made near the baby, if the baby's position is changed suddenly, or if there is some similar major change, the baby will throw both arms outward and bring them back. This response disappears at about three months of age, except in babies who have certain kinds of brain damage. Another of the primitive reflexes is the *Babinski reflex*. If you stroke babies on the bottom of the foot, they'll first spread out the toes and then curl them in. In an adult or an older baby, only the curling occurs. This response is all the more interesting because when it occurs in an adult, it's a sign of abnormality in the neurological system.

A further and perhaps more interesting primitive reaction is the *grasp reflex*. If you touch babies across the palm of the hand, their fingers will close tightly around the object touching them. Their grip is so strong, in fact, that a baby grasping a rod with both hands can often be lifted completely off the ground. Some psychologists have suggested that this reflex is a remnant of our evolutionary past, when we needed to be able to hang on to tree branches or on to part of the mother while she was moving. The reflex disappears by about six months of age, when the more mature parts of the brain have developed more fully.

Questions about the Preview

1. What is the selection about? (This question can be answered by studying the title.) _____

2. What are the two kinds of reflexes in infants? (This question can be answered by looking at the relationship between the title and the main headings.)

    a. _____

    b. _____

3. What are the three kinds of feeding reflexes? (This question can be answered by looking at the italicized words that follow the heading.)

    a. _____

    b. _____

    c. _____

4. What are the three kinds of primitive reflexes? (This question can also be answered by looking at the italicized words that follow the heading.)

    a. _____

    b. _____

    c. _____

The purpose of this activity is probably clear to you: Often a preview alone can help you key in on important ideas in a selection.

Step 2: Read

Read the chapter straight through. In this first reading, don't worry about understanding everything. There will be so much new information that it will be impossible to really comprehend it all right away. You just want to get a good initial sense of the chapter. If you hit snags — parts that you don't understand at all — just keep reading. After you have gotten an overall impression of the chapter by reading everything once, you can go back to reread parts that you did not at first understand.

Read the chapter with a pen in hand. Look for and mark off what seem to be important ideas and details. In particular, mark off the following:

- *Definitions* of terms — underline definitions
- *Examples* of those definitions — put an *Ex* in the margin
- Items in major *lists* (also called *enumerations*) — number the items *1, 2, 3,* and so on.
- What seem to be other *important ideas* — use a star or *Imp* in the margin.

(For more detail, see the chapters in Part Four on recognizing definitions and examples, enumerations, and main ideas.)

Notes about Marking: The purpose of marking is to set off points so that you can easily return to them later when you take study notes. Material can be marked with a pen or pencil, or it can be highlighted with a felt-tip pen.

Marking should be a *selective* process. Some students make the mistake of marking almost everything. You have probably seen textbooks, for example, in which almost every line has been highlighted. But setting off too much material is no better than setting off too little.

Here is a list of useful marking symbols:

Symbol	Explanation
―――――	Set off a definition by underlining it.
Ex	Set off helpful examples by writing *Ex* in the margin. Do not underline examples.
1, 2, 3	Use numbers to mark enumerations (items in a list).
☆ *Imp*	Use a star or *Imp* to set off important ideas.
|	Put a vertical line in the margin to set off important material that is several lines in length. Do not underline these longer sections because the page will end up being so cluttered that you'll find it difficult to make any sense of the markings.
✓	Use a check to mark off any item that *may* be important.
?	Use a question mark to show material you do not understand and may need to reread later.

Activity 1

Answer the following questions.

1. Why should you mark off definitions, examples, and enumerations when reading? _____

   _____

2. Why do you think you should *not* underline examples? _____

   _____

Activity 2

Go back and read and mark the textbook selection (''Reflexes in Infants'') you previewed in Activity 2 on pages 91–92. Remember to be selective. Mark only the most important points: definitions, key examples, enumerations, and what seem to be other important ideas.

Step 3: Write

I can still remember the time when I really learned how to study. I was taking an introductory history course. For our first test, we were responsible for three chapters in the textbook plus an abundance of classroom notes. I began by spending about two hours reading the first chapter — about thirty pages — and then I started to "study." My "studying" consisted of rereading a page and then looking away and reciting it to myself. After a half hour or so, I was still on the first page! "This is not going to work," I muttered. "I need a faster way to do this."

Here's what I did. I went through the first chapter, rereading and thinking about the material and making decisions about what were the most important points. I then wrote those points down on separate sheets of paper. In a nutshell, I went through a large amount of information and reduced it to the most important points. The very act of deciding what was most important and writing that material down was a valuable step in understanding the material. It took me a couple of hours to prepare my study sheets. Then I was able to close the book and just concentrate on studying those sheets.

I used that study technique successfully through college and graduate school. And when I began my own professional work in reading and study skills, I discovered that almost all successful students use some variation of the same basic strategy.

The third step, then, is to *write.* Following are specific directions for taking good notes. There are six points about *what* notes to write, followed by five points about *how* to write notes.

What to Write

1   Write the *title* of the chapter at the top of your first sheet of paper. Then write down each *heading* in the chapter. Under each heading, take notes on what seem to be the important points.

2   Rewrite headings as *basic questions* to help you locate important points. For example, if a heading is "One-Parent Families," you might convert it to the question, "How many one-parent families are there?" Then write down the answer to that question if it appears in the text. If a heading is "Choosing a Mate," you could ask "How do we choose a mate?" and write down the answer to that question.

3   Look for *definitions of key terms,* usually set off in color, **boldface,** or *italics.* Write down each term and its definition.

4   Look for *examples* of definitions. The examples will help make those definitions clear and understandable. Write down one good, clear example for
each definition.

5   Look for *major items in a list* (enumerations). Write them down and number
them *1, 2, 3,* and so on. For example, suppose the heading "Agents of
Socialization" in a textbook is followed by four subheads, "The Family,"
"Peers," "School," and "The Mass Media." Write down the heading. Then
write the four subheads under it and number them *1, 2, 3,* and *4.*

6   Remember that your goal is to take a large amount of information in a chapter
and reduce it to the most important points. Try not to take too many notes.
Instead, use headings, definitions, examples, and enumerations in the chapter
to help you focus on what is most important.

How to Write

1   Write your notes on letter-sized sheets of paper (8½ by 11 inches). By using
such paper (rather than smaller note cards), you will be able to see *relationships* among ideas more easily, because more ideas will fit on a single page.

2   Make sure your handwriting is clear and easy to read. Later, when you study
your notes, you don't want to have to spend time trying to decipher them.

3   Leave space in the left-hand and top margins of your study sheet so that you
can write down key words to help you study the material. Key words will
be described on page 99 of this chapter.

4   Don't overuse outlining symbols when you take notes. To show enumerations,
use a simple sequence of numbers (1, 2, 3, and so on) or letters (a, b, c, and
so on). Often, indenting a line or skipping a space is enough to help show
relationships among parts of the material. Notice, for example, that very few
outlining symbols are used in the sample study sheet on page 98, yet the
organization is very clear.

5   Summarize material whenever possible. In other words, reduce it to the fewest
words possible while still keeping the ideas complete and clear. For instance,
in the sample study sheet on page 98, the definition of the rooting reflex has
been summarized so that it reads simply, "If touched on cheek, will move
mouth in that direction."

Activity 1

Answer the following questions.

1. When you are taking notes on a chapter, how many of the headings in the chapter should you write down? _____

    _____

    _____

2. What are enumerations? _____

    _____

    _____

3. In "What to Write" on pages 95–96, what do you consider the three most helpful guidelines?

    a. _____

    _____

    _____

    b. _____

    _____

    _____

    c. _____

    _____

    _____

4. In "How to Write" on page 96, what do you consider the three most helpful tips?

    a. _____

    _____

    _____

    b. _____

    _____

    _____

    c. _____

    _____

    _____

Activity 2

A sample study sheet for the selection ''Reflexes in Infants'' follows. Refer to the selection (on pages 91–92) to fill in the notes that are missing.

	Developing Person, Chapter 4: "The Newborn Infant"
	Reflexes in Infants
	Reflex—A response that is triggered involuntarily
	by some specific stimulus.
	Ex—Blinking when puff of air hits eye
	Kinds of reflexes in infants:
	1. Feeding
	a. Rooting—If touched on cheek, will move mouth
	in that direction.
	b.
	c. Swallowing—Hasn't yet learned to stop breathing
	in order to swallow.
	2. Primitive (source is midbrain; the part that
	develops earliest)
	a.
	b. Babinski—Will spread out and then curl in toes if
	stroked on bottom of foot.
	c.

Step 4: Recite

Let's review what you need to do to study a textbook chapter. First, you *preview* the chapter. Second, you *read* it through once, marking off what appear to be important ideas. Third, you reread it, decide on the important ideas, and *write* study notes. Fourth, you need to learn your notes. How can you do this?

To learn your notes, you *recite* the material to yourself. Using key words and phrases—also known as *recall words*—will help you do this. Write the recall words in the margins of your notes. For example, look at the recall words in the margin of the following notes:

Recall words	Notes
Def & ex of reflex	Reflex—A response that is automatic and is triggered involuntarily by some specific stimulus.
	Ex—Blinking when puff of air hits eye
2 kinds of reflexes	Kinds of reflexes in infants:
3 kinds of feeding reflexes	1. Feeding
	a. Rooting—If touched on cheek, will move mouth in that direction.

After you have written the recall words, use them to study your notes. To do so, turn each recall word into a question and go over the material until you can answer the question without looking at the page. For example, look at the recall words *Def & ex of reflex* and see if you can recite that definition and example to yourself without looking at the material. Go back and reread the items if necessary. Then look away again and try once more to recite the material. Next, look at *2 kinds of reflexes* and see if you can say them to yourself without looking at the page.

After you finish a section, go back and review the previous sections. For instance, after you can recite the two kinds of reflexes, go back and make sure you can also recite the definition of *reflexes* and an example. Continue like this—studying, reciting, and reviewing—as you move through all the material.

You will discover that recitation helps you pay attention. There is simply no way you can sleepwalk your way through it. Either you do it or you don't. Recitation is, in fact, a surefire way of mastering the material you need to learn. More information about recitation is given in the chapter "Building a Powerful Memory" (page 191).

Activity

Answer the following questions.

1. In the past, have you studied material mainly by reading and rereading it or mainly by reading and reciting? _____

    _____

2. A number of experiments have found that students who spend 25 percent of their time reading and 75 percent reciting remember much more than students who spend all their time reading. Will this fact make you spend more of your study time reciting? _____

3. Suppose you learn a group of four definitions until you can say them without looking at them. Then you go on and learn a group of several more definitions. What should you do after learning the second group of definitions?

    _____

    _____

4. What are recall words? _____

    _____

5. Where should you write recall words? _____

    _____

LEARNING TO USE PRWR

The following activities will give you practice in the four steps of PRWR: previewing, reading, writing notes, and reciting.

Activity 1: A Short Passage from a Sociology Text

Preview: Take about thirty seconds to preview the following short textbook passage. The title tells you that the passage is about _____.
How many words are set off in **boldface** within the passage? _____

INNOVATION

The process of introducing an idea or object that is new to a culture is known as **innovation.** There are two forms of innovation: discovery and invention. A **discovery** involves making known or sharing the existence of an aspect of reality. The finding of the DNA molecule and the identification of a new moon of Saturn are both acts of discovery. A significant factor in the process of discovery is the sharing of newfound knowledge with others. By contrast, an **invention** results when existing cultural items are combined into a form that did not exist before. The bow and arrow, the automobile, and the television are all examples of inventions, as are Protestantism and democracy.

Source: *Sociology,* Fourth Edition, by Richard T. Schaefer and Robert P. Lamm. McGraw-Hill, 1992.

Read (and Mark):   Read the passage straight through. As you do, underline the three definitions you will find. Also, number the two kinds of innovation as 1 and 2. Finally, write *Ex* in the margin beside each example of a definition.

Write: Complete the following notes about the passage:

Innovation — _____
Kinds of innovation:

1.   _____ — _____

   _____

   Ex. — _____

   _____

2.   _____ — _____

   _____

   Ex. — _____

Note that the keys to the main ideas here are an enumeration and definitions.

Recite: What key words could you write in the margin to help you study this passage?

_____

   After you can recite to yourself the definition of *innovation*, you should then study until you can say to yourself the definitions and examples of the two kinds of innovation. What should you then do? _____

Activity 2: A Short Passage from a Health Text

Preview: Take about thirty seconds to preview the following short textbook passage. The title tells you that the passage is about _____. How many words are set off in **boldface** within the passage? _____

ANXIETY DISORDERS

Anxiety can become incapacitating for some people. Unlike the usual type of anxiety people experience, true **anxiety disorders** involve a severe and persistent level of fear or worry that can be almost as damaging to an individual's everyday functioning as a serious mental illness is. Two important types of anxiety disorder are phobias and panic disorders.

Phobias are characterized by a persistent and irrational fear of a specific stimulus—an object, activity, or situation—that leads to a compelling desire to avoid it. Many people experience unreasonable fear when confronted by a harmless stimulus such as a tiny spider. The fear is considered a phobia only if it becomes a significant source of distress or interferes with normal functioning. It is estimated that one in nine adult Americans suffers from some kind of phobia.

Panic disorders are often characterized by recurrent panic attacks that may occur unpredictably or as a result of a specific situation such as driving a car or being in a crowded place. They are a common type of disorder, often starting in adolescence. The panic attacks may be confined to a period of several weeks or months or may become chronic. The individual is often nervous between attacks, sometimes to the point of being unwilling to be alone or in public places away from home.

Source: *Life and Health,* by Marvin R. Levey, Mark Dignan, and Janet H. Shirreffs. McGraw-Hill, 1992.

Read (and Mark):   Read the passage straight through. As you do, underline the three definitions you will find. Also, number the two kinds of anxiety disorders as 1 and 2. Finally, write *Ex* in the margin beside each example of a definition.

Write: Complete the following notes about the passage:

Anxiety disorders—_____
Kinds of anxiety disorders:

1. Phobias—_____

     Ex.—_____

2. Panic disorders—_____

     Ex.—_____

Recite: What key words could you write in the margin to help you study this passage? _____
After you can recite to yourself the definition of *anxiety disorder*, you should then study until you can define to yourself the two kinds of anxiety disorders.
What should you then do? _____

Activity 3: A Short Passage from a Business Text

Preview: Take about thirty seconds to preview the following short textbook passage. The title tells you that the passage is about _____.
How many subtitles appear? How many words are set off in **boldface** within the passage? _____ How many words are set off in *italics?*
_____

THE NATURE OF ECONOMIC SYSTEMS

What exactly is an **economic system?** Simply put, it's a basic set of rules used to allocate a society's resources to satisfy its citizens' needs. Although every nation has a unique way of distributing resources, economic systems all have certain features in common and may be measured in similar ways.

Factors of Production

A society's resources are referred to by economists as the **factors of production.** One factor of production, *natural resources,* includes things that are useful in their natural state, such as land, forests, minerals, and water. The second, *labor,* consists of the human resources used to produce goods and services. The third factor of production is *capital,* which includes human-made inputs such as machines, tools, and buildings, as well as the money that buys other resources.

A fourth factor of production is *entrepreneurship,* which refers to the development of new ways to use the other economic resources more efficiently. Entrepreneurs acquire materials, employ workers, invest in capital goods, and engage in marketing activities. In some societies, entrepreneurs risk losing only their reputations or their positions if they fail. In the United States, entrepreneurs also risk losing their own personal resources. On the other hand, American entrepreneurs reap the benefits if they succeed and this motivates them to take the risk of trying something new.

_____

Source: *Business Today,* Seventh Edition, by David J. Rachman et al. McGraw-Hill, 1993.

Read (and Mark): Read the passage straight through. As you do, underline the six definitions you will find. Also, number the factors of economic production as 1, 2, 3, and 4.

Write: Complete the following notes about the passage:

Economic system—_____

_____

Factors of production:

1. Natural resources—_____

_____

2. Labor—_____

_____

3. Capital—_____

_____

4. Entrepreneurs—_____

_____

Recite: To help yourself study this passage, you could write *economic system* in the margin as one key term and _____ as the other key term.

Activity 4: A Short Passage from a Biology Text

Preview: Take about thirty seconds to preview the following short textbook passage. The title tells you that the passage is about _____

_____.

What words are set off in **boldface** within the passage? _____

_____.

FUNDAMENTAL PRINCIPLES:
CAUSALITY AND UNIFORMITY

A lightning bolt flashes in a cloud-darkened sky. A man eating in a restaurant becomes enraged and abusive when the waitress tells him that they are out of apple pie. Modern scientists assume that events like these are due to natural causes, a principle they call **causality.** The ancient Greeks, on the other hand, believed that thunderbolts arose when the god Zeus hurled them at the earth and that a mentally disturbed person was possessed. Today's scientists may not yet fully understand the natural causes of a phenomenon like mental illness, but they firmly believe that by applying the scientific process, they someday will.

A second fundamental principle of science is the **uniformity** of phenomena in time and space. Scientists contend that the same natural laws operating today functioned in the same way at the dawn of time, during the emergence of life, and all during its evolution on the planet. A biologist can feel confident that the laws of nature operate the same way today in Columbus, Ohio, as they did in Olduvai Gorge, in East Africa, one million years ago or in the cloud of dust or gases that existed before our solar system formed billions of years ago. The principle of uniformity is important to biologists because events that led to life's origin and diversity occurred long before people were alive to observe them.

Source: *The Nature of Life,* Second Edition, by John H. Postlethwait and Janet L. Hopson. McGraw-Hill, 1992.

Read (and Mark):   Read the passage straight through. As you do, underline the two definitions you will find.

Write: Complete the following notes about the passage by filling in the definitions.

1. Causality—_____

2. Uniformity— _____

Recite: After you can say one definition without looking at it, make sure that you can say the second _____ without looking at it.

Activity 5: A Short Passage from a Psychology Text

Preview: Take about thirty seconds to preview the following short textbook passage. The title tells you that the passage is about _____.
How many terms are set off in *italics* within the passage? _____

BEHAVIOR MODIFICATION

Behavior modification refers to a technique that uses principles of conditioning to reach a desirable goal. A desired behavior is identified, and then each progressive step toward the desired behavior is rewarded. Careful records are kept to show progress. Behavior may be used either to help others or for self-help.

One researcher reported an interesting use of behavior modification by a hardware company. The business was having problems with employees who were late and absent from work. To reward the employees who came to work on time every day, the company had a monthly drawing for home appliances. Employees who had been late or absent during the month were not eligible. At the end of six months, the company held a special drawing for a color television set. Only those employees who had been to work on time every day for six months could participate. The company found that employees with colds or mild problems were coming to work rather than staying at home as they had done in the past. After the program was in effect for one year, absenteeism and lateness had been reduced by 75 percent.

Recently behavior modification has been used in pain-control clinics. Here the concern has been with patients who become so totally preoccupied with their pain that they cannot take an interest in anything else. In most cases these patients have not been able to receive help in any other way. Staff members are instructed to walk away from any patient who begins to talk or complain about pain. The only time a patient is permitted to discuss pain is during an appointment with a physician who asks about the location and extent of the pain. Staff members give special attention to patients who talk about subjects other than pain or who become involved in other activities. Usually more than half the patients who receive this kind of behavior modification will be helped.

Source: *Applying Psychology,* Second Edition, by Virginia Nichols Quinn. McGraw-Hill, 1990.

Read (and Mark):   Read the passage through, underlining the one definition you will find. Also, write *Ex* in the margin beside the two examples of the definition.

Write: Complete these notes about behavior modification by filling in the definition and then *summarizing* one example in your own words. Summarizing the example will help you understand it and reduce it in size.

Behavior modification—_____

_____

Ex.—_____

_____

_____

_____

Recite: After you can say the definition without looking at it, make sure that you can say the _____ without looking at it.

USING PRWR

This chapter will help improve your textbook study by

- Explaining two helpful memory techniques
- Providing note-taking practice on a series of textbook passages
- Presenting hints and comments on good note-taking

This chapter will provide further practice in the PRWR study system explained in "Textbook Study I." You'll use PRWR with ten readings that are longer than the readings in "Textbook Study I" and have more varied activities. Readings 1 to 5 will give you guided practice: each of these passages appears on a left-hand page, with activities and comments on the opposite right-hand page. Readings 6 to 10 will give you more independent practice: these are still longer passages with introductory hints, for which you'll do note-taking on your own.

Before you start on the readings, you should master two valuable memory techniques that will help you recite and learn your notes after you have read and taken notes on a passage. *Catchwords* and *catchphrases* will therefore be explained briefly here. (They are also described in detail on pages 197–199.)

TWO MEMORY AIDS FOR PRWR

Catchwords

In "Textbook Study I," you took notes on four factors in production (page 103): (1) natural resources, (2) labor, (3) capital, and (4) entrepreneurship. Chances are that you might forget at least one of the four factors. To help ensure that you remember all *four* factors, you could create a catchword. A *catchword* is a word made up of the first letters of the words you want to remember. The first letters of the four factors are R (for *natural resources*), L (*labor*), C (*capital*), and E (*entrepreneurship*). If necessary, rearrange the letters to form an easily recalled catchword. It can be a real word or a made-up word. For example, you might remember the letters RLCE with the made-up word CLER.

After you create a catchword, test yourself until you are sure that each letter stands for a key word in your mind. Make sure, for example, that C stands for *capital,* that L stands for *labor,* that E stands for *entrepreneurship,* and that R stands for *natural resources.* In each case, the first letter serves as a "hook" to help you pull an entire idea into your memory.

This memory device is a proven method of remembering a group of items. Learn to use and apply it!

■ Suppose that you have just taken notes on four kinds of crowds: casual crowds, conventional crowds, expressive crowds, and acting crowds. The first letter of these four kinds are C (*casual*), C (*conventional*), E (*expressive*), and A (*acting*). Make up a catchword that would help you remember the four kinds

   of crowds. *Catchword:* _____

Catchphrases

Sometimes you can't easily make up a catchword. In such cases, create a catchphrase instead. A *catchphrase* is a series of words in which each word begins with the first letter of a word you want to remember.

Suppose you have just taken notes on three kinds of noise: external noise, internal noise, and semantic noise. The first letters of the three kinds are E (*external*), I (*internal*), and S (*semantic*). You might not be able to make a good catchword out of E, I, and S, but you could make a catchphrase.

For example, I have a friend named Ed, and I quickly came up with the catchphrase, ''I shot Ed.'' This is an outrageous sentence, since I do not expect to shoot Ed or anyone else, or even hold a gun in my hand. But the point is that because I created the sentence, I would automatically remember it. That's what you want to do: create a sentence that you'll be sure to remember. The catchphrase does not have to be a model of grammar or make perfect sense. It can be so outrageous that you would not want anyone else to know what it is. All that matters is that you create a line that will stick in your memory.

The purpose of the catchphrase is to give you the first letters of the words you want to remember. After you create a phrase, test yourself until you are sure each letter stands for a word in your mind. If you were studying noise and used the catchphrase ''I shot Ed,'' you'd make sure that *I* helped you recall *internal,* *S* helped you recall *semantic,* and *E* helped you recall *external.*

If you were asked on a test to list and describe the three kinds of noise, you would think immediately, ''I shot Ed.'' You would have the first letters *I, S,* and *E.* The letter *I* would be a memory hook to help you remember that one kind of noise is *internal, S* would help you remember that another kind is *semantic,* and *E* would help you remember that the third kind is *external.*

■ Suppose that you have just taken notes on four kinds of extrasensory perception. The first letters of these four factors are T (*telepathy*), C (*clairvoyance*), P (*precognition*), and P (*psychokinesis*). Make up a catchphrase that would help you remember the letters T-C-P-P. (Note that you can put the letters in any order when creating your sentence.)

   Catchphrase: _____

GUIDED PRACTICE IN PRWR

Reading 1: A Passage from a Sociology Text

NORMS

All societies have ways of encouraging and enforcing what they view as appropriate behavior while discouraging and punishing what they consider to be improper conduct. "Put on some clean clothes for dinner" and "Thou shalt not kill" are examples of norms found in American culture, just as respect for older people is a norm in Japanese culture. **Norms** are established standards of behavior maintained by a society.

In order for a norm to become significant, it must be widely shared and understood. For example, when Americans go to the movies, we typically expect that people will be quiet while the film is showing. Because of this norm, an usher can tell a member of the audience to stop talking so loudly. Of course, the application of this norm can vary, depending on the particular film and type of audience. People attending a serious artistic or political film will be more likely to insist on the norm of silence than those attending a slapstick comedy or horror movie.

Types of Norms   Sociologists distinguish between norms in two ways. First, norms are classified as either formal or informal. **Formal norms** have generally been written down and involve strict rules for punishment of violators. In American society, we often formalize norms into laws, which must be very precise in defining proper and improper behavior. In a political sense, **law** is the "body of rules, made by government for society, interpreted by the courts, and backed by the power of the state." Laws are an example of formal norms, although not the only

type. The requirements for a college major and the rules of a card game are also considered formal norms.

By contrast, **informal norms** are generally understood but are not precisely recorded. Standards of proper dress are a common example of informal norms. Our society has no specific punishment or sanction for a person who comes to school or to college dressed quite differently from everyone else. Making fun of nonconforming students for their unusual choice of clothing is the most likely response.

Norms are also classified by their relative importance to society. When classified in this way, they are known as *mores* and *folkways*.

Mores (pronounced "MOR-ays") are norms deemed highly necessary to the welfare of a society, often because they embody the most cherished principles of a people. Each society demands obedience to its mores; violation can lead to severe penalties. Thus, American society has strong mores against murder, treason, and child abuse that have been institutionalized into formal norms. **Folkways** are norms governing everyday behavior whose violation raises comparatively little concern. For example, walking up a "down" escalator in a department store challenges our standards of appropriate behavior, but it will not result in a fine or a jail sentence. Society is more likely to formalize mores than it is folkways. Nevertheless, folkways play an important role in shaping the daily behavior of members of a culture.

Source: *Sociology,* Fourth Edition, by Richard T. Schaefer and Robert P. Lamm. McGraw-Hill, 1992.

Activity for Reading 1

Preview: Take about thirty seconds to preview the textbook passage on the opposite page. The title tells you that the passage is about _____.
How many other headings are in the passage? _____ How many words are set off in **boldface** in the passage? _____

Read and Mark: Read the passage straight through. As you do, underline the definitions you find. Write *Ex* in the margin beside an example that makes each definition clear for you. Also, number the items in the two enumerations that you'll find.

Write: On separate paper, take notes on "Norms."

1. Write down the definition of *norms* and an example of a norm.
2. Write down and number the two ways in which sociologists distinguish between types of norms. Include definitions and examples.

Recite: To remember the four norms, create a *catchphrase:* a short sentence made up of the first letters of the four norms: *f* for *formal, i* for *informal, m* for *mores,* and *f* for *folkways:*

Your sentence: *F* _____ *I* _____ *M* _____ *F* _____

Comments on Reading 1: After you can say the definition and an example of *norm* to yourself without looking at them, go on and see if you can say the four norms to yourself. Doing this should be easy because you will have created a catchphrase that will automatically give you the first letters (*F, I, M, F*) of those four norms. You can then use the first letters as "hooks" to help you pull the words themselves into memory. Test yourself, then, to make sure that the first *F* stands in your head for *formal, I* stands for *informal, M* stands for *mores,* and the second *F* stands for *folkways.*

DEFENSE MECHANISMS

Even for those of us who have developed a reasonably healthy self-concept, there will always be aspects of our psychological experience (e.g., ugly dreams, unacceptable sexual desires) that violate the standards we have set for ourselves. How do we manage to prevent these intruders from blackening our picture of ourselves? In formulating his theory of the personality, Sigmund Freud concluded that human beings unconsciously resort to various distortions of reality in order to protect themselves from the anxiety that comes from recognizing one's baser motives. These distortions he called *ego defense mechanisms*. Let us look at a few of them.

Repression

Repression is the most common of all the defense mechanisms, and it is the basis on which the others operate. In *repression* a person experiencing an unacceptable impulse unknowingly forces that impulse out of his or her awareness and into the unconscious mind. For example, a young boy who feels intense jealousy of his baby sister and wishes she would be run over by a car may simply banish this intolerable thought from his consciousness. This does not mean that the hostility actually disappears. It may surface in his dreams, and it may affect his behavior in subtle ways. But his self-esteem remains unaffected, at least superficially.

Intellectualization

In *intellectualization,* a rather subtle defense mechanism, the person hides unacceptable feelings behind a smokescreen of intellectual analysis and thereby avoids the pain of confronting these feelings head-on. For example, a person may spin out impressive-sounding generalizations about how difficult it is for two generations to understand one another, how parents and children invariably disappoint one another, and how we are all alone as we face the existential void, whereas what he or she really means is: "My mother never loved me, and I hate her for it."

Projection

In *projection* the individual, experiencing an impulse that is threatening to his or her self-esteem, unconsciously transfers the unwanted impulse to another person and then poses as the innocent victim.

For example, a man terrified by what he imagines are his own homosexual inclinations may complain that homosexuals are always making disgusting passes at him.

Displacement

Displacement, like projection, involves a transfer of emotion. In displacement, however, what is switched is the object, rather than the originator, of the emotion. Let us take as an example a woman whose self-concept does not allow her to feel hostility toward her child. She has read a lot of books on how to raise emotionally healthy children and considers herself the ideal loving mother. It would be very threatening for her to deviate from this self-image, since it constitutes the basis of her self-esteem. Thus, at the end of a day on which her son has tortured the cat and flushed his underwear down the toilet, she still remains calm and affectionate with the child. But when her husband comes home from work, she finds some pretext to lash out at him and thereby release her repressed anger.

Rationalization

Rationalization is the substitution of "respectable" motives for "unrespectable," instinctual motives in explaining one's behavior. For example, a man may ransack his children's trick-or-treat bags after the children have gone to sleep and then explain to his wife that he is protecting the children from tooth decay, whereas the real reason is that he simply wanted to eat the candy. Rationalization is an extremely common defense mechanism.

How do defense mechanisms affect the self-concept? Are these common self-deceptions damaging to the self? Yes and no. On the one hand, defense mechanisms are useful adaptive techniques. We all resort to them, and, according to Freud, we have to resort to them in order to adjust to the demands made on us by reality and by our own consciences. On the other hand, defense mechanisms can also prevent us from looking at ourselves realistically. If the individual's self-image must continuously be protected from his or her true feelings, then this is a good indication that the self-concept is rigid and unrealistic and that the person is making it more so by blocking out large chunks of experience.

Source: *Psychology of Adjustment,* Third Edition, by James F. Calhoun and Joan Ross Acocella. McGraw-Hill, 1990.

Activity for Reading 2

Preview: Take about thirty seconds to preview the textbook passage on the opposite page. The title tells you that the passage is about _____. How many other headings are in the passage? _____ How many words are set off in *italics*? _____

Read and Mark: Read the passage straight through. As you do, underline the definitions you find. Write *Ex* in the margin beside an example that makes each definition clear for you. Also, number the items in an enumeration that you'll find. And note what seem to be important details.

Write: On separate paper, take notes on "Defense Mechanisms."

1. Write down the definition of *defense mechanisms.*
2. Write down the definitions and examples of the five types of defense mechanisms.

Recite: To remember the five kinds of defense mechanisms, you might want to create a catchword. Use the first letters of the five words:

Repression—*R*
Projection—*P*
Displacement—*D*
Intellectualization—*I*
Rationalization—*R*

From these five letters—*R, P, D, I, R*—create a nonsense word that will help you remember them: _____. Then test yourself repeatedly until you are sure that each letter stands for a word in your head.

Comments on Reading 2: A basic enumeration, definitions, and examples help you focus on the important ideas in the passage. The use of a catchword will ensure that you do not forget any of the five kinds of defense mechanisms.

Reading 3: A Passage from a Business Text

THE JOB OF BUILDING A BUSINESS

Suppose you decide to join the ranks of business owners. What are your chances of success? According to one recent study, roughly 80 percent of new businesses make it through the third year. It's worth noting, however, that those results were obtained during the late 1980s, when the economy was strong.

Finding an Opportunity

If you decide to take the risk, there are three ways to get into business for yourself: start from scratch, buy an existing operation, or obtain a franchise. Starting from scratch is the most common route, and probably the most difficult as well. Most of the people who succeed do so because they have enough experience to minimize the risks. They start with something they know how to do and capitalize on an existing network of professional or industry contacts. Tom Scholl, the CEO of an Inc. 500 ad agency, is a typical example. He spent thirteen years working in the advertising industry before setting up his own agency and seeking out clients he thought his former employer (Young & Rubicam) was overlooking.

Buying an existing business tends to reduce the risks—provided, of course, that you check the company out carefully. When you buy a business, you instantly acquire a known product or service and a system for producing it. You don't have to go through the painful period of building a reputation, establishing a clientele, and hiring and training employees. And financing the venture is generally much easier; lenders are reassured by the history and assets of the going concern. With these major details already settled, you can concentrate on making improvements.

Obtaining a franchise is another alternative. The franchiser's name, product, and system are already established, and you can build on that base. However, owning a franchise is no guarantee that your business will succeed. According to one study, your chances are no better with a franchise operation than with a start-up.

Deciding on a Form of Ownership

Once you have identified a promising opportunity, you need to decide on the form of business you will use. You can choose a sole proprietorship, a partnership, or a corporation, depending on your needs and the advantages and disadvantages of each. For each type of organization, certain legal formalities must be met.

Developing a Business Plan

One of the first steps you should take toward starting a new business is to develop a written business plan that explains what you're going to do. Preparing such a plan will help you decide how to turn your idea into reality, and if you need outside financing, the plan will also help you persuade lenders and investors to back your business. Your business plan may be relatively informal if you're starting out on a small scale and using your own money, but at a minimum, it should describe the basic concept of the business and outline specific goals, objectives, and resource requirements.

Obtaining Financing

With your business plan in hand, you can begin the search for financing. The most common sources of funds for new businesses fall into two basic categories: debt and equity. **Debt** must be repaid; **equity** does not have to be repaid, but it entitles the investor to a piece of your company and a share of future profits. Most businesses are financed with a mix of debt and equity.

Once the business is launched, it will have a continuing need for money. You can't expect to obtain all the financing you need in one fell swoop. Although a few businesses do grow entirely through internally generated funds, most businesses need repeated transfusions from outside lenders or investors.

Source: *Business Today,* Seventh Edition, by David J. Rachman, et al. McGraw-Hill, 1993.

Activity for Reading 3

Preview: Take about thirty seconds to preview the textbook passage on the opposite page. The title tells you that the passage is about _____. How many subtitles are there in the passage? _____

Read and Mark: Read the passage straight through. As you do, number the enumerations that you find.

Write: On separate paper, take notes on ''The Job of Building a Business.''

1. Write down the four steps involved in building a business.
2. Write down the enumerations that occur within those steps (three ways to find a business opportunity, three kinds of ownership, two categories of financing).
3. Write down the definitions of the two terms that are defined: *debt* and *equity.*

Recite: To remember the four steps involved in building a business, you may want to create a catchphrase. Do so by first circling a key word in each step:

Finding an opportunity
Deciding on a form of ownership
Developing a business plan
Obtaining financing

Now take the first letters in the key words and create a short sentence with those four words:

Your sentence: *O* _____ *F* _____ *P* _____ *F* _____

Comments on Reading 3:   Remembering the four steps in building a business should be easy because you will have a catchphrase that will automatically give you in sequence the first letters (*O, F, P, F*) of the four steps. You can then use those first letters as ''hooks'' to help you pull the words themselves into memory. Test yourself, then, to make sure that *O* stands in your head for *opportunity,* that *F* stands for *form of ownership,* that *P* stands for *business plan,* and that *F* stands for *financing.*

Use catchphrases or catchwords to remember the other enumerations in the passage as well.

CAFFEINE

History

Coffee drinking in the United States is an extension of the European custom brought to this country centuries ago. In Europe, coffeehouses were the common meeting places for conversation, political argument, and camaraderie. The drinking of coffee continues to be a custom that gives people an excuse to sit down to have a conversation or take "time out." The coffee break became a national institution partly because of the need for a rest from work, but also because of the stimulation this beverage offers.

Classification

Caffeine is the stimulant found in coffee, tea, and soft drinks labeled *cola* or *pepper*. It is a chemical that belongs to the xanthine group of drugs. Xanthines are powerful amphetaminelike stimulants that can increase metabolism and create a highly awake and active state. They also trigger release of the stress hormones that, among other factors, are capable of increasing heart rate, blood pressure, and oxygen demands on the heart.

How Taken into the Body

Coffee (from the *Coffea arabica* tree) is the most frequently consumed source of caffeine in the United States, with those over the age of seventeen drinking six or more cups of coffee or tea a day. Other caffeine sources are chocolate, cola, other soft drinks containing the name *pepper*, and anti-sleep preparations such as No-Doz. Caffeine may also be found in other over-the-counter drugs such as appetite suppressants and analgesics.

Characteristics of Dependence

People who drink more than one or two cups of coffee every day develop some tolerance, physical dependence, and most likely some psychological dependence on their coffee habit. Individuals who drink more than one or two cups of coffee a day often feel that they cannot get started in the morning without their coffee and continually drink it throughout the day just to keep going. Withdrawal from caffeine occurs when the drug is abruptly discontinued by those who have become tolerant to it.

Symptoms of withdrawal include headache, irritability, lethargy, mood changes, sleep disturbance, and mild physiological arousal.

Pharmacology

It appears that caffeine interferes with adenosine, a naturally occurring chemical that acts as a natural tranquilizer in the brain. It attaches to sites on neurons and makes them less sensitive to other neurotransmitters that would normally excite them. Caffeine also attaches to brain cells and blocks adenosine from acting on them, making the receptor cells more sensitive to chemical stimulation.

Effects on the Body

Caffeine consumption of more than 250 milligrams per day is considered by many to be excessive because it can have adverse effects on the body. (The average brewed six-ounce cup of coffee contains about 110 milligrams of caffeine, as well as other xanthines, theobromine, and theophylline.) In addition, it has been reported that a significantly higher number of psychological complaints exist among persons drinking seven or more cups a day than among those whose intake is more moderate. A lethal dose of caffeine could be consumed in the form of twenty cups of coffee, if drunk all at once. Frequent side effects of excessive coffee intake are anxiety, irritability, diarrhea, arrhythmia (irregular heartbeat), and the inability to concentrate. Coffee may also stimulate the secretion of the digestive enzyme pepsin within the stomach. In an empty stomach, this enzyme, combined with the natural oils in coffee, can irritate the stomach lining, a reason why those who already have ulcers should cut out caffeine products.

Special Danger

Caffeinism is a recent clinical term that characterizes the acute or chronic overuse of caffeine, with subsequent caffeine toxicity. The symptoms of the syndrome include anxiety, mood changes, sleep disturbances, and other psychological complaints. Symptoms are usually dose-related extensions of caffeine's usual effects.

Source: *Drugs: A Factual Account,* Fifth Edition, by Dorothy E. Dusek and Daniel A. Giardano. McGraw-Hill, 1993.

Activity for Reading 4

Preview: Take about thirty seconds to preview the textbook passage on the opposite page. The title tells you that the passage is about _____.

How many other headings are in the passage? _____

Read and Mark: Read the passage straight through. To help yourself decide what is important, turn each heading into a basic question and read to find details that answer that question. For example, turn the heading "History" into the question, "What is the history of caffeine?" Turn the heading "Classification" into the heading, "What is the classification of caffeine?" Turn the heading "How Taken into the Body" into the question, "How is caffeine taken into the body?" and so on.

The technique of turning headings into basic questions starting with words like *What, How, When,* and *In what ways* is a good way to locate and focus on important details within a section.

Write: On separate paper, take notes on "Caffeine." In this case, your notes will be in the form of short summaries that answer the basic questions you have asked about the headings. For example, the first question, "What is the history of caffeine?" can be answered with a summary like the following: "Coffee drinking in the United States derived from the European custom of people meeting to talk with each other and take time out." Write summaries that answer each of the following questions:

1. What is the classification of caffeine?
2. How is caffeine taken into the body?
3. What are characteristics of dependence on caffeine?
4. What is the pharmacology of caffeine?
5. What are the effects of caffeine on the body?
6. What is a special danger of caffeine?

Recite: To study the material, look at each of the basic questions and see if you can recite the answer to yourself without looking at your notes. After you learn each answer, go back and review all the previous answers until you have studied all the material.

Comments on Reading 4: In a passage like this one, you must turn headings into questions to help yourself focus on the major points presented in each section. Asking basic questions that are based on headings can be an excellent way to get inside a block of material. The questions help you both to understand the material and to identify the most important ideas and details.

Reading 5: A Passage from a Political Science Text

BUREAUCRACY

Bureaucracy is essentially a method of organizing people and work. As a form of organization, bureaucracy is the most efficient means of getting people to work together on tasks of great magnitude and complexity.

Bureaucracy is a system of organization and control that is based on three principles: hierarchical authority, job specialization, and formalized rules. **Hierarchical authority** refers to a chain of command, whereby the officials and units at the top of a bureaucracy have control over those in the middle, who in turn control those at the bottom. In **job specialization,** the responsibilities of each job position are explicitly defined, and there is a precise division of labor within the organization. **Formalized rules** are the standardized procedures and established regulations by which a bureaucracy conducts its operations.

These features are the reason that bureaucracy, as a form of organization, is unrivaled in the efficiency and control it provides. Hierarchy speeds action by reducing conflict over the power to make decisions: the higher an individual's position in the organization, the more decision-making power he or she has. Hierarchy is also the basis by which superiors control subordinates and maintain a commitment to organizational goals. Specialization yields efficiency because each individual is required to concentrate on a particular job: specialization enables workers to develop advanced skills and expert knowledge. Formalized rules enable workers to act quickly and precisely because decisions are made on the basis of predetermined guidelines. Formalized rules also enhance control: workers make decisions according to established organizational standards rather than their personal inclinations.

The Persian Gulf war demonstrated the power of bureaucracy as a means of accomplishing tasks.

Within five months of Iraq's invasion of Kuwait on August 2, 1990, 540,000 American combat troops and their equipment had been moved into the Gulf region. The orders were sent from the top by President Bush and channeled to each unit and its commander. All personnel had deployment assignments and, once in the Gulf area, an exact mission to perform. This operation could not have been carried out with the same speed and efficiency by any form of organization other than the bureaucratic one.

The characteristics of bureaucratic organizations were first described by the noted German sociologist Max Weber (1864–1920), who concluded that bureaucratic efficiency is achieved at a high price. Bureaucracy transforms people from social beings to rational actors: they perform not as whole persons but as parts of an organizational entity. Their behavior is dictated by position, specialty, and rule. A bureaucracy grinds on, heedless of the personal feelings of its members. In the process, they lose a sense of the place of their narrow role and specialty within the larger context and become bound to rules without regard for the insensitivity of those rules to human circumstance. "Specialists without spirit" was Weber's unflattering description of bureaucrats.

Yet Weber also saw that all large-scale, task-oriented organizations have no realistic alternative to the bureaucratic form. It alone facilitates the coordination of a massive work force. The superiority of the bureaucratic form of organization as a means of accomplishing tasks is apparent from its prevalence. Although Americans tend to associate the word *bureaucracy* with government, bureaucracy is found wherever there is a need to manage large numbers of people and tasks. All major American corporations are bureaucratic organizations. So are most foundations, churches, lobbying groups, and colleges.

Source: *The American Democracy,* by Thomas E. Patterson. McGraw-Hill, 1993.

Activity for Reading 5

Preview: Take about thirty seconds to preview the textbook passage on the opposite page. The title tells you that the passage is about _____.
How many words are set off in **boldface** in the passage? _____

Read and Mark: Read the passage straight through. As you do, underline the definitions you find. Also, number the items in the enumeration. Finally, jot down what seem to be important details within the passage.

Write: On separate paper, take notes on "Bureaucracy."

1. Write down the definition of *bureaucracy.* Also write down one or two examples, which appear later in the passage.
2. Write down the three principles of bureaucracy and their definitions.
3. Write down what seem to be important ideas in the passage. Think carefully about the other ideas and details that the passage develops. As you read, you will realize that the passage talks about the advantages of a bureaucracy and that it also describes one drawback of a bureaucracy. Summarize those points.

Recite: After you can recite the definition of a bureaucracy, test yourself to make sure that you can explain the three principles of bureaucracy. Then see if you can state the advantages of a bureaucracy and the drawback the author describes. Finally, review the first material you studied. Remember that constant review is a key to effective study.

Comments on Reading 5:   Definitions and a basic enumeration help you focus on some of the important content of this passage. And by reading carefully, you can determine the other important ideas—the benefits and one drawback of a bureaucracy. The author could have provided you with further help by using subheadings: "Benefits of a Bureaucracy" and "One Drawback of a Bureaucracy." Since he does not do this, he leaves more work for you to do. The moral here is simply this: You must be quick to take advantage of the clues that an author does provide. But you must also be ready to do your own digging into the material when an author does not give you clear signals that something is important.

INDEPENDENT PRACTICE IN PRWR

Following are several longer textbook passages. Apply the PRWR—*preview, read, write, recite*—method to study the material in each passage. Use your own paper to take study notes. Hints for note-taking are provided at the start of each selection.

Reading 6: A Passage from a Communications Text

Hints: Definitions, examples, and enumerations are the keys to important ideas in this selection.

Remember that a good way of taking notes is to write down all the headings and to write your notes under those headings. Textbook authors often organize their information carefully through a series of headings and subheadings—that is, major and minor headings. By writing those headings down, you help organize your own notes.

THE ELEMENTS OF COMMUNICATION

The communication process is made up of various elements. These elements are: senders and receivers, messages, channels, feedback, noise, and setting.

Sender-Receivers

People get involved in communication because they have information, ideas, and feelings they want to share. This sharing, however, is not a one-way process where one person sends ideas and the other receives them, and then the process is reversed. In most communication situations, people are **sender-receivers**—both sending and receiving at the same time.

> *Bobby and Rebecca are discussing baseball. Bobby is sending a message by talking and Rebecca is receiving it by listening. Bobby is enthusiastic, animated, and a little loud as he tells her of his heroics in last night's game. As Rebecca listens, she also sends a message to Bobby. She has one hand on her hip, one eyebrow slightly raised, and an expression which says, "I don't believe a word of this." Both Bobby and Rebecca are sender-receivers.*

Message

The **message** is made up of the ideas and feelings that a sender-receiver wants to share. In the case of Bobby and Rebecca, Bobby's message was what he was doing and feeling while Rebecca's message was a reaction to what Bobby was telling her.

Ideas and feelings can be communicated only if they are represented by symbols. A **symbol** is something that stands for something else. All our communication messages are made up of two kinds of symbols: verbal and nonverbal.

Every word in our language is a **verbal symbol** that stands for a particular thing or idea. Verbal symbols are limited and complicated. For example, when we use the word *chair,* we agree that we are talking about something we sit on. Thus, *chair* is a **concrete symbol,** a symbol which represents an object. However, when we hear the word *chair,* we all might have a different impression: a chair could be a recliner, an easy chair, a beanbag, a lawn chair—the variety is very great.

Even more complicated are **abstract symbols,** which stand for ideas. Consider, for example, the vast differences in our understanding of words such as *home, hungry,* and *hurt.* How we understand these words will be determined by our experience. Since people's experiences differ to some degree, they will assign different meanings to these abstract words.

Nonverbal symbols are anything we communicate without using words, such as facial expressions, gestures, posture, vocal tones, and appearance. As with verbal symbols, we all attach certain meanings to nonverbal symbols. A yawn means we are bored or tired; a furled brow indicates confusion; not looking someone in the eye may mean we have something to hide. Like verbal symbols, nonverbal symbols can be misleading. We cannot control all our nonverbal behavior, and we often send out information of which we are not even aware.

> *Rosa has tried several times to talk to Xavier, who sits next to her in biology class. Each time she speaks to him, his answer has been short and he has turned away quickly. Rosa concludes that Xavier is stuck-up, and so she decides not to pay any more attention to him. The truth is that Xavier thinks Rosa is the most beautiful woman he has ever seen, but every time she talks to him, he becomes hopelessly tongue-tied. By being so, he has inadvertently communicated the wrong message and possibly halted any chance for a relationship.*

Whether or not we are aware of them, nonverbal symbols are extremely important to messages. Some communication scholars believe that over 90 percent of the messages we send and receive are made up of nonverbal symbols.

Channels

The **channel** is the route traveled by a message, the means it uses to reach the sender-receivers. In face-to-face communication, the primary channels are sound and sight: we listen to and look at each other. We are familiar with the channels of radio, television, records, newspapers, and magazines in the mass media. Other channels communicate nonverbal messages. For example, when Denise goes to apply for a job, she uses several nonverbal signals to send out a positive message: a firm handshake (touch), a light perfume (smell), nice clothes (sight), and a respectful voice (sound). In her case, the senses she is appealing to are the channels.

Feedback

Feedback is the response of the receiver-senders to each other. You tell me a joke and I smile. That's feedback. You make a comment about the weather and I make another one. More feedback.

Feedback is vital to communication because it lets the participants in the communication see whether ideas and feelings have been shared in the way they were intended. If Sally tells John, for example, that she will pick him up at 8 P.M. and he is ready and waiting at that time, he shows by his behavior that the message has been understood. However, let's suppose at another time they agree to meet at the intersection of Brown and Keller Streets at 8 P.M. They both arrive on time but wait at different corners. When they finally discover each other, at nine, they have a big fight and each accuses the other of being in the wrong place. In this case they thought they had understood the message but come to realize that not enough feedback had occurred. One of them should have asked, "*Which* corner of Keller and Brown?"

Sender-receivers who meet in a face-to-face setting have the greatest opportunity for feedback. In this kind of setting, they have a chance to see whether the other person understands and is following the message. A teacher working with a child, for example, can readily see by the child's face whether he or she is confused. She can also see when the child is getting bored, by the way he or she fidgets and begins to lose attention. A speaker in a large lecture hall, however, is not as aware of the feedback from the audience. Those listeners the lecturer can see might look attentive, but the ones in the back rows may be having a quiet snooze. In general, the fewer the people involved in the communication event, the greater the opportunity for feedback.

Noise

Noise is interference that keeps a message from being understood or accurately interpreted. Noise occurs between the sender-receivers, and it comes in three forms: external, internal, and semantic.

External noise comes from the environment and keeps the message from being heard or understood. Your heart-to-heart talk with your roommate can be interrupted by a group of people yelling in the hall, a helicopter passing overhead, or a power saw outside the window. External noise does not always come from sound. You could be standing and talking to someone in the hot sun and become so uncomfortable that you can't concentrate. Conversation might also falter at a picnic when you discover that you are sitting on an anthill and ants are crawling all over your blanket.

Internal noise occurs in the minds of sender-receivers when their thoughts or feelings are focused on something other than the communication at hand. A student doesn't hear the lecture because he or she is thinking about lunch; a wife can't pay attention to her husband because she is thinking about a problem at the office. Sometimes internal noise occurs when someone doesn't want to hear what is being said: a child might look attentive when being scolded by a parent, but he or she is working hard on not listening.

Semantic noise is caused by people's emotional reactions to words. Many people tune out a speaker who uses profanity because the words are so offensive to them. Others have negative reactions to people who make ethnic or sexist remarks. Semantic noise, like external and internal noise, can interfere with all or part of the message.

Setting

The **setting** is where the communication occurs. Settings can be a significant influence on communication. Some are formal and lend themselves to formal presentations. An auditorium, for example, is good for giving speeches and presentations but not very good for conversation. If people want to converse on a more intimate basis, they would be better off in a smaller, more comfortable room where they can sit and face each other.

Setting is made up of several components, which can range from the way a place is lighted to the colors used for decoration. Your local discount store is lighted with fluorescent lights. These lights communicate a message: you are there not to relax, but to do business and move on. On the other hand, if you are going to buy designer clothing in a department store, you are not going to find fluorescent lighting. The lighting will be subdued, and the showroom will probably look more like your living room than like a store.

The color of a room might determine how comfortable you feel. A room that is painted red might be very striking when you first see it, but after you are in it for a while, you will probably feel nervous and uncomfortable. Public buildings such as schools and offices are often painted "institutional green"—a cool color that means business, not relaxation, but has been found by researchers to reduce the restlessness of students.

The arrangement of furniture in a setting can also affect the communication that takes place. For example, at one college, the library was one of the noisiest places on campus. The problem was solved by rearranging the furniture. Instead of sofas and chairs arranged so that students could sit and talk, the library used study desks—thus creating a quiet place to concentrate.

■

All communication is made up of senders and receivers, messages, channels, feedback, noise, and setting. Every time people communicate, these elements are somewhat different. They are not the only factors that influence communication, however. Communication is also influenced by what we bring to it. That is the subject of our next section.

Source: *Communicating Effectively*, Third Edition, by Saundra Hybels and Richard L. Weaver II. McGraw-Hill, 1992.

Reading 7: A Passage from a Speech Text

Hints: A basic enumeration is the key to important ideas in this selection. Notice that each of the headings under ''Four Causes of Poor Listening'' is part of an enumeration. When you take notes, you should number these headings. You should also provide short summaries of the author's explanation of each cause of poor listening. You'll see that there is a minor enumeration to help organize the information presented about one cause of poor listening; be sure to include it in your notes.

FOUR CAUSES OF POOR LISTENING

Not Concentrating

The brain is incredibly efficient. Although we talk at from 125 to 150 words a minute, the brain can process from 400 to 800 words a minute. This would seem to make listening very easy, but actually it has the opposite effect. Because we can take in a speaker's words with ease and still have plenty of spare ''brain time,'' we are tempted to interrupt our listening by thinking about other things. And thinking about other things is just what we do. Here's what happens:

Joel Nevins is the youngest member of the public relations team for a giant oil company. He is pleased to be included in the biweekly staff meetings. After two dozen or so meetings, however, he is beginning to find them rather tedious.

This time the vice president is droning on about executive speech writing—an area in which Joel is not directly concerned. The vice president says, ''When the draft of a speech hits the president's desk . . .''

''Desk,'' thinks Joel. ''That's my big problem. It's humiliating to have a metal desk when everyone else has wood. There must be some way to convince my boss that I need a new wooden desk.'' In his imagination, Joel sees himself behind a handsome walnut desk. He is conducting an interview, and his visitor is so impressed. . . .

Sternly, Joel pulls his attention back to the meeting. The vice president has moved on to a public relations problem in Latin America. Joel listens carefully for a while, until he hears the words ''especially in the Caribbean.''

''Oh, if only I could get away for a winter vacation this year,'' he thinks. He is lost in a reverie featuring white beaches, tropical drinks, exotic dances, scuba diving, sailboats, himself tanned and windblown. . . .

''. . . will definitely affect salary increases this year'' brings him back to the meeting with a jolt. What did the vice president say about salary increases? Oh, well, he can ask someone else after the meeting. But now the vice president is talking about budgets. All those dreary figures and percentages. . . . And Joel is off again.

His date last night, Margie, really seems to like him and yet. . . . Was it something he did that made her say good night at the door and go inside alone?

Could she have been that tired? The last time she invited him in for coffee. Of course, she really did have a rough day. Anybody can understand that. But still. . . .

". . . an area that Joel has taken a special interest in. Maybe we should hear from him." Uh, oh! What area does the vice president mean? Everyone is looking at Joel as he tries frantically to recall the last words said at the meeting.

It's not that Joel *meant* to lose track of the discussion. But there comes a point at which it's so easy to give in to physical and mental distractions—to let your thoughts wander rather than to concentrate on what is being said. After all, concentrating is hard work. Louis Nizer, the famous trial lawyer, says, "So complete is this concentration that at the end of a court day in which I have only listened, I find myself wringing wet despite a calm and casual manner."

Later in this chapter, we will look at some things you can do to concentrate better on what you hear.

Listening Too Hard

Until now we have been talking about not paying close attention to what we hear. But sometimes we listen *too* hard. We turn into human sponges, soaking up a speaker's every word as if every word were equally important. We try to remember all the names, all the dates, all the places. In the process we often miss the speaker's point by submerging it in a morass of details. What is worse, we may end up confusing the facts as well.

The car with out-of-state plates and ski racks on the roof pulled up outside a Vermont farmhouse. The driver called out to the farmer, "Can you tell us how to get to Green Mountain Lodge?"

"Well," replied the farmer, "I guess you know it's not there anymore. Terrible thing. But if you want to know where it used to be, you go down the road two miles, take a left at the blinking light, make the next right at the cheese shop, and follow the mountain road for about eight miles until you get to the top. Really a sad thing it's all gone."

"Let me make sure I heard you right," said the driver. "Two miles down the road, and then a left at the light, a right at the cheese shop, and then up the mountain road for eight miles to the top?"

"That's it," answered the farmer. "But you won't find much when you get there."

"Thanks a lot," called the driver as the car drove away.

When the car had pulled out of sight, the farmer turned to his son. "Do you suppose," he said, "they don't know the lodge burned down last summer?"

This is a typical example of losing the main message by concentrating on details. The driver of the car had set his mind to remember directions—period. In so doing, he blocked out everything else—including the information that his destination no longer existed.

The same thing can happen when you listen to a speech: you pick up the details but miss the point. It just isn't possible to remember everything a speaker says. Efficient listeners usually concentrate on main ideas and evidence. We'll discuss these things more thoroughly later in the chapter.

Jumping to Conclusions

Janice and David are married. One day they both come home from work exhausted. While Janice struggles to get dinner onto the table, David pours a glass of wine for each of them and then falls down in front of the television set to watch the evening news. Over dinner, this conversation takes place:

JANICE: *There's going to be a big change around here.*

DAVID: *I know, I know. I haven't been pulling my share of the cooking and cleaning, but I'm really going to try to be better about it.*

JANICE: *Well, that's certainly true, but it's not the only thing . . .*

DAVID: *Look, I know I didn't take out the garbage last night and you had to do it. I promise I won't forget the next time.*

JANICE: *No, you're not listening. I'm talking about a much more basic change, and . . .*

DAVID: *I hope you don't want to write up a formal schedule saying who does what on which days. Because I think that's ridiculous. We can work this out sensibly.*

JANICE: *No, I don't mean that at all. You're not paying attention. I mean something a lot more basic, and . . .*

DAVID: *Janice, we're both reasonable, intelligent people. We can work this out if we just approach it rationally.*

JANICE: *Of course we can. If you would only listen for a minute. I'm trying to tell you I had a call from my sister today. She's lost her job and she doesn't have any money. I told her she could stay with us for a few months until she finds another one.*

Why is there so much confusion here? Clearly, Janice is unhappy about the amount of household work David does and has mentioned it several times. Equally clearly, David feels guilty about it. So when Janice starts to talk about a "change," David jumps to a conclusion and assumes Janice is going to bring up household work again. This results in a breakdown of communication. The whole problem could have been avoided if, when Janice said "There's going to be a big change . . . ," David had asked "What change?"—and then *listened.*

This is one form of jumping to conclusions—putting words into a speaker's mouth. It is one reason why we sometimes communicate so poorly with the people we are closest to. Because we are so sure we know what they mean, we don't listen to what they actually say. Sometimes we don't even hear them out.

Another way of jumping to conclusions is prematurely rejecting a speaker's ideas as boring or misguided. We may decide early on that a speaker has nothing valuable to say. Suppose you are passionately committed to animal rights and a speaker's announced topic is "The Importance of Animals to Scientific Research." You may decide in advance not to listen to anything the speaker has to say. This would be a mistake. You might pick up useful information that could either strengthen or modify your thinking. In another situation, you might jump to the conclusion that a speech will be boring. Let's say the announced topic is "Looking toward Jupiter: Science and the Cosmos." It sounds dull. So you tune out—and miss a fascinating discussion of possible extraterrestrial life-forms.

Nearly every speech has something to offer you—whether it be information, point of view, or technique. You are cheating yourself if you prejudge and choose not to listen.

Focusing on Delivery and Personal Appearance

George Matthews had just received his engineering degree from a major university—magna cum laude and Phi Beta Kappa. Several good firms were interested in hiring him. At his first interview the company's personnel manager took him to meet the hiring executive, with whom George spent nearly an hour. At the end of the interview George felt he had made an excellent impression.

Later, the personnel manager called the executive and asked, "What did you think of Matthews?" The executive replied, "He won't do. He's a lightweight. Everything he said made me think he's not serious about a career in engineering."

"Funny," said the personnel manager, "he didn't seem like a lightweight to me. What exactly did he say?"

The executive hemmed and hawed. He couldn't remember the precise words, but the guy was definitely a lightweight. He would not be able to handle the work load or make a contribution to the firm. Still the personnel manager persisted. What was the problem? Finally, the executive was pinned down.

"The man wouldn't fit in," he said. "He had on a double-knit suit, and we're a Brooks Brothers type of company. To tell you the truth, I didn't hear a word he said, because the minute he walked in, I knew he wouldn't do. For crying out loud, he was wearing yellow socks!"

This story illustrates a very common problem. We tend to judge people by the way they look or speak and therefore don't listen to what they *say*. Some people are so put off by personal appearance, regional accents, speech defects, or unusual vocal mannerisms that they can't be bothered to listen. This kind of emotional censorship is less severe in the United States now than it was a decade or two ago, but we need always to guard against it. Nothing is more deadly to communication.

Source: *The Art of Public Speaking,* Fourth Edition, by Stephen E. Lucas. McGraw-Hill, 1992.

Reading 8: A Passage from a Sociology Text

Hints: Definitions, examples, enumerations, and headings are all keys to important ideas in this selection.

Remember that a good way of taking notes is to write down all the headings in the selection and to write your notes under those headings. Textbook authors often organize their information carefully through a series of headings. By writing those headings down, you help organize your own notes.

FORMS OF COLLECTIVE BEHAVIOR

Drawing upon the emergent-norm, value-added, and assembling perspectives—and upon other aspects of sociological examination—sociologists have examined many forms of collective behavior. Among these are crowds, disaster behavior, fads and fashions, panics and crazes, and rumors.

Crowds

Crowds are temporary groupings of people in close proximity who share a common focus or interest. Spectators at a baseball game, participants at a pep rally, and rioters are all examples of crowds. Sociologists have been interested in what characteristics are common to crowds. Of course, it can be difficult to generalize, since the nature of crowds varies dramatically. For example, in terms of the emotions shared by crowds, hostages on a hijacked airplane experience intense fear, whereas participants in a religious revival feel a deep sense of joy.

Like other forms of collective behavior, crowds are not totally lacking in structure. Even during riots, participants are governed by identifiable social norms and exhibit definite patterns of behavior. Sociologists Richard Berk and Howard Aldrich examined patterns of vandalism in fifteen American cities during the riots of the 1960s. They found that stores of merchants perceived as exploitive were likely to be attacked, while private homes and public agencies with positive reputations were more likely to be spared. Apparently, looters had reached a collective agreement as to what constituted a "proper" or "improper" target for destruction.

If we apply the emergent-norm perspective to urban rioting, we can suggest that a new social norm is accepted (at least temporarily) which basically condones looting. The norms of respect for private property—as well as norms involving obedience to the law—are replaced by a concept of all goods as community property. All desirable items, including those behind locked doors, can be used for the "general welfare." In effect, the emergent norm allows looters to take what they regard as properly theirs.

Disaster Behavior

Newspapers, television reports, and even rumors bring us word of many disasters around the world. The term **disaster** refers to a sudden or disruptive event or set of events that overtaxes a community's resources so that outside aid is necessary.

Traditionally, disasters have been catastrophes related to nature, such as earthquakes, floods, and fires. Yet, in an industrial age, natural disasters have now been joined by such "technological disasters" as airplane crashes, industrial explosions, nuclear meltdowns, and massive chemical poisonings.

Sociologists have made enormous strides in disaster research despite the problems inherent in this type of investigation. The work of the Disaster Research Center—established at Ohio State University in 1963 and later relocated to the University of Delaware in 1985—has been especially important. The center has teams of trained researchers prepared to leave for the site of any disaster on four hours' notice. Their field kits include material identifying them as center staff members, recording equipment, and general interview guidelines for use in various types of disasters. En route to the scene, these researchers attempt to obtain news information in order to learn about the conditions they may encounter. Upon arrival, the team establishes a communication post to coordinate fieldwork and maintain contact with the center's headquarters.

Since its founding, the Disaster Research Center has conducted more than 520 field studies of natural and technological disasters in the United States, as well as twenty-four in other nations. Its research has been used to develop effective planning and programming for dealing with disasters in such areas as delivery of emergency health care, establishment and operation of rumor-control centers, coordination of mental health services after disasters, and implementation of disaster-preparedness and emergency-response programs. In addition, the center has provided extensive training and field research for over one hundred graduate students. These students maintain a professional commitment to disaster research and often go on to work for such disaster service organizations as the Red Cross and civil defense agencies.

Remarkably, in the wake of many natural and technological disasters, there is increased structure and organization rather than chaos. In the United States, disasters are often followed by the creation of an emergency "operations group" which coordinates public services and even certain services normally carried out by the private sector (such as food distribution). Decision making becomes more centralized than in normal times.

Fads and Fashions

An almost endless list of objects and behavior patterns seems temporarily to catch the fancy of Americans. Examples include silly putty, Davy Crockett coonskin caps, hula hoops, *Star Wars* toys, the Rubik cube, break dancing, Cabbage Patch Kids, *The Simpsons* T-shirts, and Nintendo games. Fads and fashions are sudden movements toward the acceptance of some life-style or particular taste in clothing, music, or recreation.

Fads are temporary patterns of behavior involving large numbers of people; they spring up independently of preceding trends and do not give rise to successors. By contrast, *fashions* are pleasurable mass involvements that feature a certain amount of acceptance by society and have a line of historical continuity. Thus, punk haircuts would be considered a fashion, part of the constantly changing standards of hair length and style, whereas adult roller skating would be considered a fad of the early 1980s.

Typically, when people think of *fashions,* they think of clothing, particularly women's clothing. In reality, fads and fashions enter every aspect of life where choices are not dictated by sheer necessity—vehicles, sports, music, drama, beverages, art, and even selection of pets. Any area of our lives that is subject to continuing change is open to fads and fashions. There is a clear commercial motive behind these forms of collective behavior. For example, in about seven months of 1955, over $100 million of Davy Crockett items was sold, including coonskin caps, toy rifles, knives, camping gear, cameras, and jigsaw puzzles.

Fads and fashions let people identify with something different from the dominant institutions and symbols of a culture. Members of a subculture may break with tradition while remaining "in" with (accepted by) a significant reference group of peers. Fads are generally short-lived and tend to be viewed with amusement or lack of interest by nonparticipants. Fashions, by contrast, often have wider implications because they can reflect (or give a false impression of) wealth and status.

Panics and Crazes

Panics and crazes both represent responses to some generalized belief. A **craze** is an exciting mass involvement which lasts for a relatively long period of time. For example, in late 1973, a press release from a Wisconsin congressman described how the federal bureaucracy had failed to contract for enough toilet paper for government buildings. Then, on December 19, as part of his nightly monologue on the *Tonight Show,* Johnny Carson suggested that it would not be strange if the entire nation experienced a shortage of toilet paper. Millions of Americans took his humorous comment seriously and immediately began stockpiling this item out of fear that it would soon be unavailable. Shortly thereafter, as a consequence of this craze, a shortage of toilet paper actually resulted. Its effects were felt into 1974.

By contrast, a **panic** is a fearful arousal or collective flight based on a generalized belief which may or may not be accurate. In a panic, people commonly perceive that there is insufficient time or inadequate means to avoid injury. Panics often occur on battlefields, in overcrowded burning buildings, or during stock market crashes. The key distinction between panics and crazes is that panics are flights *from* something whereas crazes are movements *to* something.

One of the most famous panics in the United States was touched off by a media event: the 1938 Halloween radio dramatization of H. G. Wells's science fiction novel *The War of the Worlds.* This CBS broadcast realistically told of an invasion from Mars, with Martians landing in New Jersey and taking over New York City fifteen minutes later. The announcer indicated at the beginning of the broadcast that the account was fictional, but about 80 percent of the listeners tuned in late.

Clearly, a significant number of listeners became frightened by what they assumed to be a news report. However, some accounts have exaggerated people's reactions to *The War of the Worlds.* One report concluded that "people all over the United States were praying, crying, fleeing frantically to escape death from the Martians." In contrast, a CBS national survey of 460 listeners found that only 91 (or about 20 percent) were genuinely scared by the broadcast. Although perhaps a million Americans *reacted* to this program, many reacted by switching to other stations to see if the "news" was being carried elsewhere. When viewed properly, this "invasion from outer space" set off a limited panic rather than mass hysteria.

It is often believed that people engaged in panics or crazes are unaware of their actions, but this is certainly not the case. As the emergent-norm perspective suggests, people take cues from one another as to how to act during such forms of collective behavior. Even in the midst of an escape from a life-threatening situation, such as a fire in a crowded theater, people do not tend to run in a headlong stampede. Rather, they adjust their behavior on the basis of the perceived circumstances and the conduct of others who are assembling in a given location. To outside observers studying the events, people's decisions may seem foolish (pushing against a locked door) or suicidal (jumping from a balcony). Yet, for that individual at that moment, the action may genuinely seem appropriate—or the only desperate choice available.

Rumors

A man responding to an advertisement came to the designated address and asked if the ad was correct. "Yes," said the woman at the door, "this almost-new Porsche will be yours for only $50." Hardly believing his good fortune, the man gave the car a test run and presented the woman with a $50 bill. The man finally asked her if she realized that the Porsche she had sold would be a bargain at $5,000. Her reply was simple: "My husband ran off with his secretary and left a note instructing me to sell the car and send him the money."

This story has reappeared in newspapers for years, often with such vague introductions as "a doctor at Dallas General said." In 1980, columnist Ann Landers reported the account as fact. However, there is no proof that the incident actually took place. Concerted efforts to investigate its authenticity by the *Chicago Tribune* led to the conclusion that it was a rumor that had spread across the nation. The $50 sports car thus joins such legendary rumors as the alligators in city sewers ("Years ago a boy flushed two pet alligators down the toilet. They were long forgotten until a sewer worker came upon hundreds of giant alligators . . ."). Stories such as these illustrate how people believe, hope, or fear that unlikely events have taken place.

Not all rumors that we hear are so astonishing, but none of us is immune from hearing or starting rumors. A **rumor** is a piece of information gathered informally which is used to interpret an ambiguous situation. As the American novelist James Fenimore Cooper noted, it is very tempting to accept a story when one is unable to confirm or deny it—especially if the rumor is entertaining and vaguely plausible.

Rumors about celebrities—whether politicians, movie stars, or members of royal families—have long been a popular pastime around the world. In 1986, for example, Isabelle Adjani, one of the leading actresses in France, had to appear on French television to dispel widespread rumors that (1) she had AIDS and (2) she had died. Similarly, a number of American film stars have responded to rumors that they have AIDS by making public appearances and denials.

Like celebrities, business firms find that rumors can be damaging. One type of rumor that is particularly worrisome for manufacturers involves ill-founded charges of contamination. In the late 1970s, it was rumored that General Foods' Pop Rocks and Cosmic Candy would explode in children's mouths, with tragic results, yet no such explosions took place. Another popular theme of rumors in the marketplace focuses on the charge that a company is using its profits for evil purposes.

Source: *Sociology,* Fourth Edition, by Richard T. Schaefer and Robert P. Lamm. McGraw-Hill, 1992.

Reading 9: A Passage from a Psychology Text

Hints: Definitions, examples, enumerations, and headings and subheadings are all keys to important ideas in this selection.

Remember that a good way of taking notes is to write down all the headings in the selection and to write your notes under those headings. Textbook authors often organize their information carefully through a series of headings and subheadings. By writing those headings down, you help organize your own notes.

OPERANT CONDITIONING

The type of learning that occurs because of rewards and punishments is labeled either *operant conditioning* or *instrumental conditioning.* Both terms refer to the same technique, a method of conditioning based on rewards, or positive reinforcers, and punishments or other negative reinforcers. In classical conditioning, association is the significant feature. In operant conditioning, reinforcers and punishments are the key. Reinforcers and punishments provide feedback.

Positive Reinforcement

Suppose someone asked you to sit on top of a flagpole for twelve hours and promised you a reward. The reward was a stick of gum. Would you be likely to repeat the flagpole-sitting behavior? Chances are you would not unless there was a severe gum shortage and you craved gum. Although the gum was a reward, it would not serve as a *positive reinforcement.* The purpose of a positive reinforcement is to increase the same behavior. What would it take to make you climb up and sit on top of the flagpole again? Perhaps a good positive reinforcer for you would be a new car, or a headline in the newspaper, or a screen test from a movie studio. If these did not serve as reinforcers, maybe you would sit there for an invitation to the White House or a tour of the Greek islands. Perhaps just smiles of approval from your friends would work. For a positive reinforcement to be effective and increase behavior, it must be appropriate. Finding the right reinforcer can be difficult. Some people can be rewarded with money; others seek only attention and approval.

Behavioral psychologists believe that your entire personality is shaped by reinforcers. If you are talkative, your parents and friends have probably found appropriate ways to reinforce your conversation. Simply paying attention and listening is a way of showing approval and is a positive reinforcement. You may have learned some successful flirting techniques or ways of hedging an answer when you are uncertain. Again, approval was the likely reinforcer.

For a reinforcement to be effective, it should occur immediately or as soon as possible after the desired behavior. If a man is training his dog to beg and delays the dog-biscuit reward for an hour after the begging behavior, the pet will not recognize the biscuit as a reward for begging. Instead, the dog may connect the biscuit with more recent behaviors that may have included barking, chewing the furniture, or chasing a cat.

Negative Reinforcement

Like positive reinforcements, *negative reinforcements* are used to increase behavior. However, while positive reinforcements present pleasant stimuli when you behave as desired, negative reinforcements remove unpleasant stimuli when you behave as desired. For example, suppose your roommate constantly nags you to pick up your messy clothes and clean the room. If you keep your area tidy, the nagging stops. Nagging, the negative reinforcer, is increasing the likelihood of your cleanup behavior. You want to escape from the nagging, so you pick up your clothes and maintain a neat room. In many instances, negative reinforcement is indeed effective in increasing specific behaviors that will permit an escape.

Punishment

The purpose of *punishment* is to weaken a behavior or lessen its likelihood. Punishment can be effective. A study by Sherman and Berk found that men who were arrested for wife beating were less likely to beat their wives during the next six months than men who were not arrested. The experiment was carefully controlled and the men were arrested for only twenty-four hours.

However, many other studies have found disadvantages and problems with punishment. Generally punishment will suppress a response for only a short time. In most cases the undesired response will reappear later. If your kid brother annoys you by tapping his foot all through dinner, you might decide that an appropriate reaction would be a swift kick under the table. Your "punishment" might eliminate the behavior for the present, but chances are his undesired foot-tapping behavior will reappear. Similarly, a mother who washes her daughter's mouth with soap to clean up her language may find that the cleaning will not last very long, particularly if the mother is not around. Unfortunately, people often punish others when they are angry and upset. As a result, the punishment seems unreasonable and little is learned.

Guidelines for Punishment

Effective punishment can help eliminate an undesirable behavior. However, if the punishment is not chosen carefully, there can be unexpected side effects.

Sometimes a punishment can have elements of positive reinforcement. A teacher may believe that he or she is punishing a six-year-old boy by shouting, "Mike, don't tell me you are out of your seat again. You never sit still!" In reality, Mike is gaining the attention he is seeking. Classmates turn and notice him, and the teacher becomes totally preoccupied with his problem. What she thought was a punishment turns out to be a positive reinforcement. The next time Mike feels a need for attention, he will know that getting out of his seat and walking around the classroom will win the notice he wants. Similarly, a hockey player put in the penalty box for a clash and fight often gets cheers from the crowd. The player's rowdy behavior may well increase because of the attention of the crowd.

Psychologists have developed several guidelines for punishment. Four important rules are:

- Avoid combining rewards with punishments.
- Punish immediately or reinstate the situation that caused the need for punishment.
- Avoid inadequate punishment.
- The punishment should suit the crime.

Types of Punishment

Several categories or types of punishment have been identified. Coopersmith described three types.

Corporal Punishment   *Corporal* refers to the body, and corporal punishment involves inflicting bodily harm when a person behaves in an undesirable way. A spanking, a whipping with a switch, a slap across the face, and a punch in the nose would all qualify as corporal punishments.

Withdrawal of Love and Approval   Parents sometimes reprimand their children for misbehavior by threatening to remove their love. Statements like "If you go outside the yard again, I won't love you anymore" and "I hate you because you just spilled your juice" are examples. If this technique is used persistently, the child will feel that the parents' love is weak and undependable. The child is given the impression that love and affection have to be earned. As a result the child may become anxious and show such symptoms as nail biting, bed-wetting, or thumb sucking.

Management   *Management* permits the person to escape the punishment and gain a reward. A parent who states, "If you don't eat your spinach, you may not have dessert" is permitting the reward of dessert for a desired behavior (eating spinach) and a punishment of no dessert for the undesired behavior (not eating spinach). Of the three techniques, Coopersmith found this to be the most effective.

Reinforcements versus Punishments

You are probably familiar with the conflicting adages "Spare the rod and spoil the child" and "You can catch more flies with honey than with vinegar." Which should you believe? Will you spoil a child by not using punishments, or is it better to stick with rewards? Most psychological research concludes that a child disciplined with rewards will show better emotional adjustment than one disciplined with punishments. If a child is punished harshly by parents and teachers, an aversion or dislike for them is likely to develop. In addition, the child will tend to avoid activities associated with the parents and teachers. Family activities and school studies could become unpopular.

Further, since punishment is generally either painful or frustrating, it can lead to aggression. A study by Bandura found that boys who were severely punished for aggression at home tended to be overly aggressive in school. Punishment is most effective and least damaging when a rewarding alternative is offered. If a father scolds his daughter for not completing her homework, he should also praise her when she does complete her assignments. Unfortunately, repeated corporal punishments can result in child abuse. Parents who use punishments rather than rewards may cause serious problems for preschool children.

As mentioned in the previous section, a punishment that draws attention to a person can serve more as a positive than as a negative reinforcement. One way the teacher could avoid this dilemma is to put more emphasis on Mike's positive behavior. Remarks such as "Look at how nicely Mike is sitting in his seat. I wish everyone would sit and work like that" would give Mike a rewarding alternative. Punishment would be still more effective if the teacher offered an alternative directly: "If you stay in your seat, you can play a special game. If you walk around, you will not play the game."

Punishment situations arise far beyond the classroom and home. Prisons are a prime example of attempts at punishments that sometimes work and sometimes do not. Statistics on repeat offenders are alarming. Again it seems that punishment is more effective when it is combined with a positive experience or alternative.

Source: *Applying Psychology,* Second Edition, by Virginia Nichols Quinn. McGraw-Hill, 1990.

Reading 10: A Passage from a Health Text

Hints: Definitions, enumerations, and headings are all keys to important ideas in this densely packed passage from a health text.

Remember that a good way of taking notes is to write down all the headings in the selection and then to write your notes under those headings. Textbook authors often organize their information carefully through a series of headings and subheadings. By writing those headings down, you will help organize your own notes.

DEFENSE AGAINST INFECTIOUS DISEASE

Suppose a pathogenic agent invades the body. What can the body do to fight off the pathogen and prevent it from causing disease? The body has three basic lines of defense: the skin and mucous membranes, the inflammatory response, and immunity.

First-Line Defenses

The skin and mucous membranes are the body's first line of defense. An invading microorganism must find its way through the skin or the mucosae, the mucus-coated membranes that line the respiratory, digestive, and urogenital tracts and form an "inner skin." Secretions such as tears, perspiration, skin oils, and saliva, which contain chemicals that can kill bacteria, are part of this defense system. In addition, the respiratory passages are lined with fine, short moving hairs called *cilia* that spread a carpet of sticky mucus. The mucus works like flypaper to trap inhaled microorganisms and foreign matter and carry them to the back of the throat, where they are removed by sneezing, coughing, or nose blowing or are swallowed and disposed of by digestive fluids.

Besides the cilia, other body hairs (the eyelashes, for example) may fend off invading microorganisms. Reflexes such as coughing, blinking, and vomiting are also part of the body's first line of defense, as are high acid levels in the stomach and vagina, which help destroy invaders.

inflammation—
*a general
defense
mechanism
in the blood
and tissues
to ward off
an irritant
or foreign
body. Also
called the*
inflammatory
response.

The Inflammatory Response

Sometimes microorganisms get beyond the body's outer defenses—through a cut in the skin, for example. They then face a second line of defense in the blood and the tissues—**inflammation,** or the **inflammatory response.** The inflammatory response is a general one; it helps ward off any irritant or foreign matter, whether it is a relatively large physical object (such as a splinter), a chemical substance, or a microorganism.

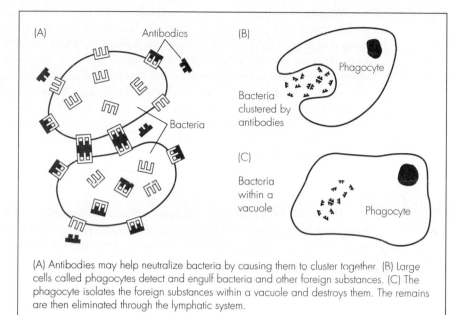

(A) Antibodies may help neutralize bacteria by causing them to cluster together. (B) Large cells called phagocytes detect and engulf bacteria and other foreign substances. (C) The phagocyte isolates the foreign substances within a vacuole and destroys them. The remains are then eliminated through the lymphatic system.

phagocytes— white blood cells that protect the body from infection by engulfing and digesting invading microorganisms, toxins, and other foreign substances.

The white blood cells in the bloodstream form a vital part of the body's defense system. Some are of a type known as **phagocytes,** a term that literally means "cells that eat." A phagocyte is made up of a semiliquid jellylike substance with a cell wall holding it together; it can actually flow around a foreign substance, take it apart chemically, and digest it (see the illustration).

During the inflammatory response, the supply of blood to the endangered area increases while the flow of blood through the area slows down. As a result, some *blood plasma* (the fluid that transports red and white blood cells) leaks through the walls of the blood vessels into the spaces between the cells in the endangered area, bringing with it special proteins that help destroy pathogens. Meanwhile, phagocytes rush to the area to engulf bacteria and foreign particles.

If the infection is localized in one part of the body, the patient usually shows the signs of inflammation only in that area; these signs include redness, local warmth, swelling, and pain. Such signs indicate that the invaders are being counterattacked. However, if the battle is being waged throughout the body, the patient usually will have a generalized fever, which is caused at least in part by toxins produced by the invaders or released by them while they are being destroyed. These toxins interfere with the regulatory mechanisms that control the temperature of the body. While the resulting elevated temperatures may be harmful to normal body functions, fever can be helpful as well: it stimulates the body to produce more white blood cells and may even kill the invading organism, since most pathogens cannot survive in above-normal body temperatures.

Whether the inflammatory response is sufficient to knock out the infection depends on how many invading organisms there are, how strong they are, and how well the body is able to defend itself. Sometimes the battle comes to a standstill at the local level. As more and more local tissue is destroyed, the body may form a cavity, or **abscess,** filled with sticky yellow-white pus that consists of fluid, battling cells, and white blood cells that have died in the battle. The struggle is resolved when enough invading organisms have been killed or inactivated to halt the infection. In more severe cases, this line of defense fails and the invading organisms begin to spread through the tissues and even into the bloodstream. The infection then becomes generalized and highly dangerous.

Immunity

The body's third line of defense against disease is **immunity,** a group of mechanisms that help protect the body against specific diseases. Immunity is the body's most efficient disease-preventing weapon; it can help fight either a viral infection or a bacterial one.

The Role of Lymphocytes   In the immune mechanism, as in the inflammatory response, white blood cells become involved in fighting infection. Here the protective white blood cells are of a type known as **lymphocytes,** including two key subtypes: B and T lymphocytes.

B lymphocytes, or B cells, are believed to originate in the bone marrow (hence the letter B). When foreign or invading pathogens are present in the body, these cells help produce substances called immunoglobulins, or **antibodies.** Antibodies react specifically to the parts of a pathogen that link up to human cells and cause damage. These parts, which are called **antigens,** are thus neutralized. If the invaders are viruses, the antibodies lock on to their antigens and prevent them from entering the target cells. If the invaders are bacteria, the antibodies lock on to them and cause them to clump together, making it easier for phagocytes to engulf and digest them. These bacterial-antibody clumps also activate certain *bactericidal* (bacteria-killing) substances in the blood. Antibodies can also lock on to bacterial toxins to make them less harmful to the body.

T lymphocytes, or T cells, named for their origin in the thymus gland, fight infection in three major ways. First, some T lymphocytes spur the phagocytes to eat foreign substances faster. Second, some help stimulate the production of antibodies by B lymphocytes. Third, some can attack foreign cells (such as cells in tissues that have been transplanted), cells that have been killed by viruses, and possibly cancer cells.

Natural Immunity   When a virus attacks the body, it helps bring about its own destruction by triggering the production of interferon. Natural immunity works in somewhat the same way. When an invading antigen enters the body, it stimulates the body to produce certain antibodies that can inactivate it. When antigens lock on to specific receptor sites on a body cell's plasma membrane, the immune response is set in motion and antibodies are produced. As was mentioned above, antibodies work only on the specific antigens that trigger them: measles antibodies work only on the measles virus, mumps antibodies on the mumps virus, and so on. There are over a million different specific antibodies, each capable of fighting one antigen. That means that over a million different foreign antigens can stimulate the immune system to take action.

Acquired Immunity   In the past, having a disease was the only way to develop immunity to it (natural immunity through the development of antibodies to fight the current infection and subsequent ones). Today, however, immunity may be induced artificially by means of **vaccines,** which consist of killed or weakened viruses, taken orally or by injection. Several days or weeks after an individual receives a vaccination, the body starts to produce specific antibodies, which circulate in the bloodstream, ready to attack the initiating antigen.

People who contract a disease or receive a vaccine for it usually develop **active immunity.** But what happens if a person is exposed to a serious disease and it is too dangerous to wait for the person's body to produce its own antibodies? In this instance a physician may confer **passive immunity** by giving the person antibodies from another person or an animal. These antibodies are found in certain proteins in the donor's blood that are collectively called **gamma globulin.** Gamma globulin is used to confer passive immunization against infectious hepatitis and other diseases for which an effective vaccine has not been devised.

In general, active immunity is long-term and in some cases lifelong, whereas passive immunity generally lasts only a few weeks or months. Babies have passive immunity at birth because antibodies that pass through the placental membrane become part of the fetus's immune system. Within six weeks after birth, however, passive immunity begins to weaken, and the baby will need to receive vaccinations to start the development of active immunity against certain diseases.

Source: *Life and Health,* by Marvin R. Levey, Mark Dignan, and Janet H. Shirreffs. McGraw-Hill, 1992.

CHECKING YOUR MASTERY OF PRWR: QUIZZES

After you study each of the readings in this chapter, you can use the following quizzes to test your understanding of the material. It may take you too much time to study each passage as fully as you would if you were taking a test in a course. However, the very act of reading the material, making decisions on what is important, taking notes, and applying some memory techniques should give you a good basic sense of the material. That is what will be tested in the quizzes.

■ Quiz on Reading 1

1. A law is an example of
   a. a formal norm.
   b. an informal norm.
   c. a folkway.
   d. none of the above.

2. *True or false?* _____ Someone who violates a folkway will probably be given less severe punishment than someone who violates a more.

3. A norm
   a. is a standard that is shared by a large number of people.
   b. encourages what is believed to be appropriate behavior.
   c. punishes what is believed to be improper behavior.
   d. does all of the above.

4. Sociologists distinguish between norms in how many ways?
   a. two
   b. three
   c. five

■ Quiz on Reading 2

1. The most common of all defense mechanisms is
   a. repression.
   b. intellectualization.
   c. projection.
   d. rationalization.

2. Which two defense mechanisms involve the transfer of the threatening emotion to something or someone that is innocent?
   a. repression and rationalization
   b. intellectualization and projection
   c. rationalization and displacement
   d. projection and displacement

3. Which defense mechanism involves using a barrier of impressive-sounding generalizations in order to avoid confronting feelings head-on?
   a. repression
   b. intellectualization
   c. projection
   d. displacement

4. *True or false?* _____ A man who eats the last piece of pie and states that he is doing this so that his children will not spoil their appetite for dinner is using rationalization.

■ Quiz on Reading 3

1. How many ways are there to get into business for yourself?
   a. two
   b. three
   c. four
   d. five

2. After deciding on the form of ownership of your business, you should
   a. develop a business plan.
   b. obtain financing.
   c. work on developing contacts in the field.
   d. decide how you will repay the initial debt.

3. Which of the following statements is true?
   a. Starting a business from scratch is the most common route and probably the easiest.
   b. Lenders are usually more willing to finance an existing operation than to finance a new business.
   c. Those who open a franchise operation generally have much better chances at success than those with a start-up.
   d. It is always better to enter into a partnership than to start a sole proprietorship.

4. *True or false?* _____ Debt differs from equity in that debt does not need to be repaid.

■ Quiz on Reading 4

1. Caffeine interferes with what naturally occurring chemical that acts as a natural tranquilizer in the brain?
   a. *Coffea arabica*
   b. adenosine
   c. xanthines
   d. neurons

2. Caffeine is found in
   a. chocolate.
   b. some antisleep preparations.
   c. tea.
   d. all of the above.

3. Caffeine consumption of more than 250 milligrams a day is considered by many to be excessive and harmful to the human body. About how many six-ounce cups of coffee is this?
   a. half a cup
   b. one cup
   c. 1½ cups
   d. slightly over two cups

4. *True or false?* _____ People who drink more than one or two cups of coffee a day develop some dependence on it.

■ Quiz on Reading 5

1. Which of the following statements about bureaucracy is true?
   a. It is the most efficient means of getting people to work together on large, complex tasks.
   b. It was viewed by Max Weber as a cold system in which individuals are lost within the larger organization.
   c. Max Weber acknowledged that because of its high efficiency, there is no realistic alternative to bureaucracy.
   d. All of the above are true.

2. Bureaucracy is based on how many principles?
   a. two
   b. three
   c. four
   d. five

3. In a hierarchy, the person with the most power
   a. is located at the top of the system of organization.
   b. is located at the bottom of the system of organization.
   c. is located at the top of each level within the system.
   d. None of the above is true; everyone has equal power within a hierarchy.

4. *True or false?* _____ During the Persian Gulf war, soldiers were able to act quickly and efficiently because their tasks were highly specialized.

■ Quiz on Reading 6

1. How many elements are there in the communication process?
   a. four
   b. six
   c. eight
   d. ten

2. A yawn is an example of what kind of symbol?
   a. verbal
   b. concrete
   c. abstract
   d. nonverbal

3. The greatest opportunity for feedback occurs
   a. when sender-receivers meet face to face.
   b. when a speaker addresses a number of students in a quiet lecture hall.
   c. over the radio.
   d. when sender-receivers write editorials to their local newspapers.

4. When a person tunes out a speaker's words because of a racist remark the speaker has made, that interference is known as
   a. external noise.
   b. internal noise.
   c. semantic noise.
   d. feedback interruption.

■ Quiz on Reading 7

1. *True or false?* _____ Listening might actually be easier if our brains were not so incredibly efficient.

2. When we listen too hard, we
   a. forget to concentrate on detail.
   b. are unable to pick out the main ideas.
   c. Both of the above are true.
   d. Neither of the above is true.

3. In the example about George Matthews, a recent graduate with an engineering degree,
   a. the executive jumped to a conclusion about Matthews on the basis of Matthews's dress.
   b. the executive was turned off by Matthews's use of slang.
   c. Matthews probably was not qualified for the job.
   d. Matthews's superior academic record meant more than how he conducted himself at the interview.

4. Our communication with the people we are closest to
    a. is usually clear and meaningful.
    b. may often be poor because we jump to conclusions about what we assume the other person is going to say.
    c. is usually insignificant.
    d. can usually be handled with passive listening.

■ Quiz on Reading 8

1. Crowds
    a. are made up of people who share a common focus or interest.
    b. may develop their own social norms on a temporary basis.
    c. do not lack structure.
    d. All of the above are true.

2. *True or false?* _____ The Disaster Research Center has found that there is increased structure and organization after many disasters.

3. Which of the following is *not* true of a panic?
    a. It is based on a generalized belief which may or may not be accurate.
    b. It often occurs in situations where there is a great possibility of physical harm.
    c. It involves fear.
    d. It is a movement *to* something.

4. A piece of information that is gathered informally and is used to interpret an ambiguous situation is a
    a. craze.
    b. rumor.
    c. fad.
    d. panic.

■ Quiz on Reading 9

1. Negative reinforcement
    a. presents pleasant stimuli when you behave as desired.
    b. removes unpleasant stimuli when you behave as desired.
    c. is used only by experienced psychiatrists.
    d. None of the above is true.

2. A positive reinforcer
    a. is used to increase the same behavior.
    b. may involve extra attention or approval.
    c. must be appropriate to the action.
    d. All of the above are true.

3. Which of the following is *not* a proper guideline for punishment?
    a. Combine rewards with punishments.
    b. Punish immediately after the offense.
    c. Avoid inadequate punishment.
    d. Make sure the punishment suits the crime.

4. *True or false?* _____ Research has shown that a child disciplined with punishments will show better emotional adjustment than one disciplined with rewards.

■ Quiz on Reading 10

1. How many basic lines of defense does the body have?
    a. two
    b. three
    c. four
    d. five

2. Which of the following is *not* a part of the defense system that involves the skin and mucous membranes?
    a. tears
    b. perspiration
    c. phagocytes
    d. cilia

3. The cells that can flow around a foreign substance, take it apart chemically, and digest it are known as
    a. cilia.
    b. phagocytes.
    c. antigens.
    d. vaccines.

4. What is the body's most efficient disease-preventing weapon?
    a. immunity
    b. an abscess
    c. the mucous membranes
    d. phagocytes

APPLYING PRWR TO A TEXTBOOK CHAPTER

This chapter will help improve your textbook study by:

- Reviewing the PRWR study method
- Providing note-taking practice on an entire textbook chapter
- Presenting hints and comments on good note-taking

To make your practice in textbook study as realistic as possible, you are now going to apply the PRWR method to an entire chapter from a college textbook. The book, *Sociology: An Introduction,* by Michael S. Bassis, Richard J. Gelles, and Ann Levine, was published in a fourth edition in 1991. This McGraw-Hill book is widely used in colleges throughout the country.

You will read and take notes on the entire chapter by completing the "activities and comments" pages placed at four different spots within the chapter. The work you do will help show you just how the enormous amount of information presented within a chapter can be reduced to a limited number of notes. You will also become aware of the techniques that authors use to help communicate their ideas in an organized way.

Ideally, before studying this chapter, you should work through all the reading skills in Part Four of this book. If you have practiced such individual skills as locating definitions, enumerations, and main ideas, you will be better able to take on an entire textbook chapter. On the other hand, if you need practical guidance right away in how to read and study a textbook, you may want to proceed now with the sample chapter.

A REVIEW OF PRWR

To read and study this or any textbook chapter, apply the four steps in the PRWR study method. Following is a summary of those steps.

Step 1: Previewing the Chapter

Note the title and reflect for a moment on the fact that this entire chapter is going to be about "Social Stratification." Then skim the chapter (which goes to page 186) to answer the following questions:

- How many major heads are in the chapter? (You'll note that major heads are set off in boldface capital letters.) _____
- Look at the major head on page 150: "Social Stratification." How many subheads (which are set off in **boldface** capital and lowercase letters) appear under this main head? _____
- What is the first term that is set off in **boldface** print in the text? _____
- What is the first idea that is set off in *italicized* print in the text? _____
- How many tables, figures, and photographs are in the chapter? _____
- How many boxes with related added material are in the chapter? _____
- Does the chapter have an introduction? _____
- Does the chapter have a summary? _____
- Is there a list of key terms that are central to understanding the chapter? _____

Step 2: The First Reading

Read the chapter all the way through once. As you do so, mark off as a minimum the following: *definitions* (underline them), *examples* (write *Ex* in the margin), *major enumerations* (number them 1, 2, 3, and so on), and what seem to be *important ideas* (make a check in the margin).

Remember that while you mark, you should not worry about understanding everything completely. Understanding is a process that will come gradually while you continue to work with the text. Bit by bit, as you reread the text, as you take notes on it, and as you study your notes, you will increase your understanding of the material.

Step 3: Writing Notes on the Chapter

As you proceed, write down all the headings and subheadings—that is, major and minor headings—in the chapter. The authors have used these headings to organize their material, and you can use the same headings to help organize your notes. Under the headings, write down definitions, examples, enumerations, and main ideas. (You will be shown just how to take such notes.)

Use common sense when taking textbook notes for your actual courses. Write down only what adds to ideas you have learned in class. Have your class notes in front of you while taking textbook notes. If a good definition of a term has been given to you by the instructor, there may be no need to write down a definition that appears in the textbook.

Step 4: Reciting Your Notes

Use the key words you have written in the margin of your notes to go over the material repeatedly until you have mastered it.

STUDYING THE SAMPLE CHAPTER

How to Proceed

Preview, read, and take notes on the textbook chapter that follows. While previewing, you will see that four sets of "activities and comments" appear within the chapter. All the notes you need for the chapter will go on those "activities and comments" pages. Doing the activities will give you a solid, realistic grounding in the skills needed to read and study textbook material.

C H A P T E R

8

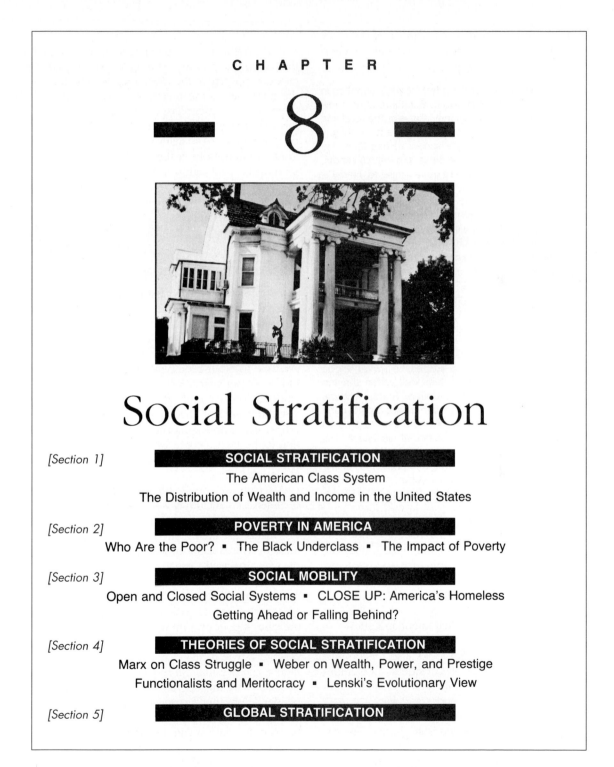

Social Stratification

Despite the myth of equal opportunity in America, the deck is stacked.

> Jimmy is a second grader. He pays attention in school, and he enjoys it. School records show that he is reading slightly above grade level and has a slightly better than average IQ. Bobby is a second grader in a school across town. He also pays attention in class and enjoys school, and his test scores are quite similar to Jimmy's. Bobby is a safe bet to enter college (more than four times as likely as Jimmy) and a good bet to complete it—at least twelve times as likely as Jimmy. Bobby will probably have at least four years more schooling than Jimmy. He is twenty-seven times as likely as Jimmy to land a job which by his late forties will pay him an income in the top tenth of all incomes. Jimmy has about one chance in eight of earning a median income.
>
> These odds are the arithmetic of inequality in America. They can be calculated with the help of a few more facts about Bobby and Jimmy. Bobby is the son of a successful lawyer whose annual salary...puts him well within the top ten percent of the United States income distribution.... Jimmy's father, who did not complete high school, works from time to time as a messenger or a custodial assistant. His earnings...put him in the bottom ten percent. Bobby lives with his mother and father and sister. Jimmy lives with his father, mother, three brothers, and two sisters. (de Lone, 1979, pp. 3–4)

The distribution of social rewards—not only high-income jobs and "all the things money can buy," but also political influence, social esteem, and simple respect—is far from equal. Opportunities are determined as much by race, ethnic origin, gender, and social class as they are determined by individual talent and effort.

This is the first of three chapters on social inequality. This chapter looks at socioeconomic inequality. Chapter 9 considers inequalities based on race and ethnicity, and Chapter 10 inequalities based on gender and age.

This chapter begins with a look at social stratification. Does the United States have a class system? How wide is the gap between the rich and the poor in this country? The second section focuses on poverty in the United States. Who are the poor? Are some members of our society trapped in an "underclass"? If so, why? Section three discusses social mobility. Is this "the land of opportunity," as so many people believe? The fourth section looks at theories of social stratification. Is stratification an inevitable part of social life? The last section steps back from the United States and views social stratification from a global perspective.

[Section 1 begins.]

SOCIAL STRATIFICATION

The term **social stratification** refers to the division of a society into layers (or strata) whose occupants have unequal access to social opportunities and rewards. People in the top strata (such as Bobby) enjoy privileges that are not available to other members of society; people in the bottom strata (like Jimmy) endure penalties that other members of society escape. In a stratified society, inequality is part of the social structure and is passed from one generation to the next. People who occupy the same layer of the socioeconomic hierarchy are known as a **social class.**

A society can be stratified along a number of dimensions, including wealth, occupation, education, power, prestige, celebrity, or anything else that is distributed unequally. In most cases these measures of social standing overlap. People who are wealthy usually went to college and work in prestigious occupations; people who are poor are likely to be high school dropouts who work at menial jobs. But this is not always the case. A poet or a minister may enjoy great prestige but have little personal wealth. Conversely, a drug dealer may be wealthy but has little social prestige. Moreover, some markers of social standing operate more or less independently of other factors. Children have very little power, regardless of whether they are rich or poor. In some situations the fact that a per-

A very small number of families make up the "exclusive club" of the upper class in America. Passing family wealth from one generation to the next helps maintain social stratification—the unequal access to social rewards and opportunities.

son is a member of a minority group or a female overrides other indicators of social standing.

The United States may be one of the richest nations in the world today, but (as everyone knows) some Americans are far better off than others. What form does social stratification take in the United States? What is the extent of inequality?

The American Class System

The United States, unlike European countries, has never had an officially defined class system with a titled aristocracy. But we are far from being a "classless society." Sociologists have used three different methods to analyze the American class structure. The first is to examine objective criteria—such things as amount of education, amount and source of income, and type and place of residence. A second method is to study subjective factors, such as occupational prestige. A third method is to conduct reputational studies, asking people how they classify themselves and others.

The number of classes a sociologist identifies in American society depends in part on which approach he or she takes. A researcher who asks people to identify their social class will probably find that the majority of Americans think of themselves as middle-class. A researcher who looks at the educations, incomes, and occupations of these self-declared middle-class Americans will find that some are far better off and some are well below the mean for this group.

The latter approach might yield six social classes (Gilbert and Kahl, 1987; Rossides, 1976) (see Table 8-1). The *upper class* (about 1 percent of the population) is a small, exclusive "club" of families who have accumulated wealth and privilege over a number of generations. Their wealth is based on inherited assets, which they, in turn, pass on to their children. Although they do not have to work, they often serve on the boards of major corporations (and so make decisions that affect millions of workers and stockholders, not to mention consumers), own newspapers and television stations, and run for public office (or make substantial campaign contributions), and so have a great deal of power and influence.

The *upper middle class* (10 to 15 percent of the population) is composed of top-level exec-

TABLE 8-1   Model of the American Class Structure

PROPORTION OF HOUSEHOLDS	CLASS	EDUCATION	OCCUPATION	FAMILY INCOME
1%	Capitalist	Prestige university	Investors, heirs, executives	Over $500,000 mostly from assets
10–15%	Upper middle	College, often with postgraduate study	Upper managers and professionals; medium business people	$75,000 or more
30–35%	Middle	At least high school; often some college or apprenticeship	Lower managers; semiprofessionals; sales, nonretail; elite craftspeople; supervisors	About $50,000
40–45%	Working	High school	Operatives; low-paid craftspeople; clerical workers; retail sales workers	About $30,000
20–25%	Poor	Some high school	Service workers; laborers; low-paid operatives and clericals	Below $20,000
1%	Underclass	Primary school	Unemployed or part-time; welfare recipients	Below $15,000

Source: Adapted from D. Gilbert and J. A. Kahl, *The American Class Structure: A New Synthesis,* 3rd Ed. (Pacific Grove, CA: Dorsey Press, 1987), table 11-1, p. 332.

utives and highly paid professionals who have "made it" by most people's standards. Virtually all have college degrees, and most have postgraduate education as well. With household incomes in excess of $75,000, they can afford comfortable suburban homes, country clubs, travel, expensive cars, and other symbols of success. Career-oriented, they expect their children to do as well as they have. They are often active in local political and cultural affairs.

The *middle class* (30 to 35 percent of the population) is composed of *small* business owners, *semi*professionals (police, clergy, social workers), and *middle* managers. Many have had some college education. They hold respectable white-collar jobs, but their authority and oppor-

tunities for advancement at work are limited. Their household income is about $50,000; their jobs are relatively secure; and they are able to lead comfortable if not extravagant lives.

The *working class* (40 to 45 percent of the population) is made up of factory workers, farmhands, clerical workers, salespeople, and the like. Their jobs tend to be routine, mechanized, and closely supervised, and they are more likely to be laid off than are middle-class workers. They rarely have more than a high school education, or earn more than $30–35,000 a year. They try to maintain a simple but decent lifestyle. Since 1973, working-class wages (adjusted for inflation) have held steady. But the cost of the American dream—owning a home of one's

Social stratification is reduced somewhat in modern industrialized societies. These auto workers probably earn as much as a pharmacist or computer programmer and more than a college professor. But their jobs depend on decisions over which they have no control.

own, sending a child to college—has skyrocketed. As a result many working-class families cannot enjoy the lifestyle their parents enjoyed (see Figure 8-1).

The *poor* (20 to 25 percent of the population) are unskilled laborers and low-paid factory workers who may be above the official poverty line, but are barely able to make ends meet. Some have graduated from high school, but many have not. Many are single mothers. Most experience frequent spells of unemployment. With household incomes below $20,000, they are rarely able to save or plan ahead, living in a state of constant financial insecurity. Given this precarious position, having an extended family and friendship network whose members can be called on during hard times takes on added importance.

The *underclass* (about 1 percent of the population) is composed of individuals who live in a chronic state of poverty, often magnified by discrimination, physical or mental illness, and other problems (discussed later in this chapter under "Poverty in America").

Note that occupation plays an important role in class identification in the United States, particularly in the middle classes. How a person ranks in our society depends in large part on what he or she does for a living. Surveys conducted over a forty-year period (National Opinion Research Center, 1988) reveal a high degree of consensus about occupational prestige: Americans agree on who "counts." Moreover, these rankings are relatively stable over time. (See Table 8-2.)

The Distribution of Wealth and Income in the United States

The great majority of Americans see themselves, and are seen by others, as middle or working class. At the opposite extremes of the social spectrum are the very rich and the poor. Investigation shows that the rich in this country are richer, and the poor are poorer and more numerous than most Americans imagine.

In measuring economic inequality, social scientists distinguish between wealth and income.

The Biolsi Family

Astoria, Queens
Harry Biolsi, truck driver
Arlene Biolsi
Four children

Base pay	$26,000
Salary with regular overtime	30,000
Monthly take-home pay	1,800
Monthly expenses	
Food	600
Rent	325
Telephone	108
Savings for gifts, vacation	130
Car insurance	56
Loan	152
Cable television	24
Life insurance	34
Interest on credit	17
Credit cards	87
Tuition	142
Computer fee	10
TOTAL	**$1,685**

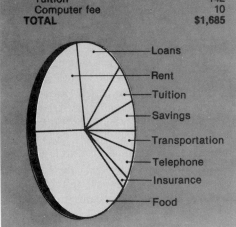

Figure 8-1 Making It on Working-Class Wages. "I am very lucky," says Harry Biolsi, a New York City truck driver who earns $30,000 a year. He and his family are able to scrape by because they live with his mother in a home she bought in 1944. *(From "The Biolsi Family," The New York Times, October 3, 1989. Copyright © 1989 by The New York Times Company. Reprinted by permission.)*

Wealth refers to the things people own, to such assets as stocks, bonds, and real estate. *Income* refers to the money people earn in the form of

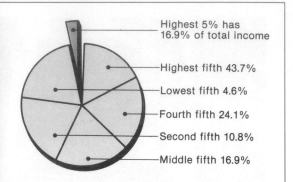

Figure 8-2 The Distribution of Income in the United States, 1987. This figure shows how income is distributed among each fifth of the earning population. *(From U.S. Bureau of the Census, 1988.* Current Population Reports, *"Money Income and Poverty Status of Families and Persons in the United States: 1987," table 4, p. 17, series P-60, no. 157.)*

wages or salaries, interest or dividends from investments, rent on property, and the like. A person may receive a high salary but spend everything he or she earns and so have little wealth. Conversely, an individual may own valuable property (say, a collection of Picasso's paintings) but earn little or no income from these assets.

One way to analyze the distribution of wealth and income is to divide the population into fifths and compare each segment's "share of the pie." As shown in Figure 8-2, the wealthiest fifth of the population earns more each year than the poorest three-fifths combined. Moreover, the level of economic inequality in our society is increasing. Since 1980, the incomes of the wealthiest fifth of Americans have increased, while the incomes of all other levels have declined (*Current Population Reports*, 1980, 1989).

But income does not tell the full story. In the United States the richest fifth of the population owns three-quarters of the nation's wealth, while the poorest fifth owns a mere five-hundredth of the nation's assets. The majority of Americans have very little wealth: About half the population does not own stocks or bonds, real estate, or even a car, and has savings of less than $5,000

TABLE 8-2   Selected Occupational Prestige Ratings*

Physicians	82	Secretaries	46
Teachers, college and university	78	Firemen	44
Judges and lawyers	76	Postal clerks	43
Dentists	74	Teachers, except college and university	43
Physicists	74	Farm owners and managers	41
Bank officers	72	Plumbers	41
Architects	71	Carpenters	40
Pilots	70	Automobile repairmen	37
Clergy	69	Airline stewardesses	36
Engineers	68	Bill collectors	36
Biologists	68	Brickmasons	36
Social scientists	66	Bulldozer operators	33
Laboratory technician	61	Butchers	32
Registered nurses	62	Truck drivers	32
Painters and sculptors	56	Salesclerks	29
Actors	52	Lumbermen	26
Embalmers	52	Miners	26
Social workers	52	Child-care workers	25
Athletes	51	Garage and gas station workers	22
Computer programmers	51	Taxicab drivers	22
Radio and TV announcers	51	Bartenders and waiters	20
Bank tellers	50	Farm laborers	18
Office managers	50	Garbage collectors	17
Bookkeepers	48	Janitors	16
Machinists	48	Barbers	14
Policemen and detectives	48	Bootblacks	9
Insurance agents	47		

*The average ratings, on a scale of 1 to 100, Americans give different occupations.
Source: National Opinion Research Council. General Social Surveys, 1972–1988. Reprinted by permission. Data provided by the Roper Center for Public Opinion Research, University of Connecticut.

(Page, 1983). According to studies conducted by the University of Michigan, the richest 1 percent of the population saw their share of the nation's wealth increase by nearly 40 percent over the last two decades, while the share held by the bottom 90 percent of the population dropped by 20 percent. The wealthiest 1 percent of the population is composed of the "super rich" (420,000 households with assets worth an average of $8.9 million) and the "very rich" (420,000 households with assets of $1.4 to $2.5 million). All told, the combined wealth of the 200 richest Americans exceeds the gross national product of any nation in sub-Saharan Africa (except South Africa). Inequality is just as pronounced in the business world: The top 1 percent of the nation's almost 2 million corporations control four-fifths of all corporate assets (Domhoff, 1983; Galbraith, 1978, chap. 7; *Statistical Abstracts*, 1989, p. 536).

At the opposite extreme are America's poor.

[Section 1 ends.

POVERTY IN AMERICA   *Section 2 begins.]*

In 1987, 32.5 million Americans—about 13.5 percent of the population—were officially counted as poor (*Statistical Abstracts*, 1989, p. 452). They fell below the official **poverty line**, which is based on the federal government's estimate of a minimal budget for a family of four. Both the count and the poverty line have been the subject of much debate. Some critics argue

Studying Section 1

Activities for Section 1

Notice that the title page of the chapter lists all the headings and subheadings (major and minor headings) within the chapter. You'll see that social stratification is examined in five different ways, starting with ''Social Stratification'' and ending with ''Global Stratification.''

Now read the first text page of the chapter (page 150) and answer the following question:

■   Which of the opening three paragraphs explains the purpose of the chapter and also previews what will be covered in each section of the chapter?

_____ First paragraph   _____ Second paragraph
_____ Third paragraph

By giving you a quick overview of the entire chapter, the authors help prepare you to read and understand it.

The notes below cover the first six pages of the sample chapter, beginning with the first heading. A main idea is presented under that heading, as well as an example of the idea. Complete the notes. You will have to add several definitions along with items in an enumeration.

SOCIAL STRATIFICATION

Social stratification—_____

_____

   Ex.—People in the top strata (such as Bobby, son of a lawyer) enjoy privileges not available to others; people in bottom strata (such as Jimmy, son of a part-time janitor and messenger), endure penalties escaped by others.

Social class—_____

_____

The American Class System:

Six social classes—

1. Upper class (about 1 percent of population) is a small, exclusive "club" of families that have accumulated wealth and privilege over a number of generations.

2. _____

   _____

3. _____

_____

4. _____

_____

5. _____

_____

6. _____

_____

Note that occupation plays an important role in class identification in the United States, particularly in the middle classes.

The Distribution of Wealth and Income in the United States:

Study shows that the rich in this country are richer, and the poor are poorer, than most Americans realize.

Wealth—_____

Income—_____

The richest 1 percent of the population saw their share of nation's wealth increase by 40 percent over last two decades, while the share held by the bottom 90 percent dropped by 20 percent.

Comments on Section 1

- As a general rule, take notes on a chapter by writing down all the headings and subheadings (major and minor headings). Then write down whatever seem to be the most important ideas that fit under those headings. This is an extremely important guideline to keep in mind when taking notes on a chapter. In a nutshell, write down headings, definitions, examples, enumerations, and what seem to be other important ideas.

  In particular, writing definitions while note-taking is typical with introductory textbooks, where you are often learning the special vocabulary of a subject.

- Add details that seem noteworthy. The notes above include the interesting detail that _____ plays an important role in class identification in the United States, particularly in the middle classes. Such noteworthy details are likely to be included in a multiple-choice exam.

- Don't use any more symbols than you need to when taking notes. When you do use symbols, make sure they really mean something. In the notes above, the symbols "1" to "6" refer to the six kinds of social classes. Many students overuse and misuse note-taking symbols. Keep your notes simple!

that the count of the nation's poor is too high because it fails to take into account such "in kind" (non-cash) aid as food stamps and Medicare. If this aid were treated as income, the poverty count might drop by 4 million or more. Others argue that the poverty line has been set too low, and that the "official poor" should include all those who earn less than half the median income. By this measure, more than 50 million Americans are living in poverty.

Between 1983 and 1987, inflation rose faster than incomes for the working poor. As a result, there is a $250 gap between a poor family's income and its budget. In 1987 they could afford $250 less in goods and services than they could in 1983 (even though their paychecks had increased). For families who are only scraping by, this means a substantial decline in standard of living—less meat on the table, fewer clothes for growing children, home remedies or over-the-counter medicine instead of trips to the doctor....

Gallup polls have found that 15 to 20 percent of Americans had experienced times in the preceding months when they did not have enough money to buy food; 35 percent say they worry "all the time" or "most of the time" that their household income will not be enough to meet family expenses and pay the bills (*The Gallup Report*, No. 234, March 1985, p. 22; 1987, No. 256–7, p. 17).

In considering economic inequality in the United States, it is important to distinguish between absolute and *relative poverty* (see Chapter 7). To a subsistence farmer in Central America or Africa, the poorest Americans might seem well-off in terms of cash flow (though not in terms of vulnerability to crime, drug abuse, and other contemporary problems). Many Americans whose incomes fall below the poverty line have shoes, indoor plumbing, electricity, a telephone, and a TV set. But this is little consolation to families who compare their situation to that of middle-income Americans. In terms of relative deprivation, the poor in the United States are poorer than low-income groups in

most other advanced industrial nations (see Figure 8-3).

Who Are the Poor?

The face of poverty has changed significantly in the last two to three decades. First, poverty in the United States today is increasingly an *urban* phenomenon. In the nation's fifty largest cities, the number of people living in poverty increased 20 percent between 1970 and 1980, even though the total population of those cities declined by 5 percent. The concentration of the urban poor in pockets of poverty, and the gap between rich and poor urban residents, have also increased. More and more, poverty has become a "big-city, central-city" problem (Wilson et al., 1988, p. 125).

Second, poverty in the United States has become increasingly *feminized*. More than half the poor families in the United States today are headed by single women. Never-married, deserted, or divorced mothers (and their children) are five times more likely to be poor as two-parent families. Many do not receive child support from their children's father; many work only part-time at low-paying jobs; many who work full-time spend a large proportion of their income on child care; and many are unable to keep above the poverty line. Some sociologists have argued that the popular phrase "the feminization of poverty" is misleading. (Gimenez, 1987; Preston, 1984). They maintain that the percentage of poor women has remained more or less stable since the 1960s. What has changed is the distribution of poverty among women: Fewer older women are poor, but more young women are poor. This, in turn, reflects the fact that unemployment rates for young men have risen. Young working-class and minority males have been hardest hit by changes in the economy. As a result, more mothers in these categories have become the main or sole support of their children.

Third, although the great majority of the poor (two-thirds) are white, *racial minorities* are

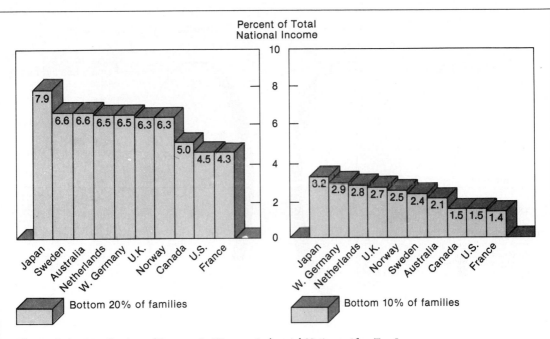

Figure 8-3   Distribution of Income in Western Industrial Nations: After-Tax Income Shares. *(Adapted from* Minding America's Business *by Ira C. Magaziner and Robert B. Reich. Reprinted with the permission of Prentice Hall Law & Business.)*

overrepresented in the ranks of poverty (see Figure 8-4). Blacks are more than three times as likely as whites to be poor, and Hispanics almost three times as likely. One reason is that minority members are less likely to complete high school and college than whites are. But even those minority members who hold degrees earn about 20 percent less than whites with equivalent educations (see Chapter 9).

Finally, many of the poor are *children*. Twenty percent of American children under age eighteen—and 39 percent of Hispanic children and 45 percent of black children—are being raised by families whose incomes fall below the poverty level (National Research Council, 1989).

Within the group defined as poor are a number of subgroups. The "working poor" are men and women whose part-time jobs or seasonal employment as day laborers, waitresses, and the like do not earn enough to lift them above the poverty level (Schiller, 1984). Migrant laborers

are particularly vulnerable to recurrent unemployment. But many other low-skilled adults work at marginal and sometimes illegal jobs, with little or no job security, and without such benefits as health insurance and sick leave. Indeed, a full-time job for the federal minimum wage ($3.35 an hour; $6,968 a year) is not enough to keep an individual (much less a family) above the poverty line. As Dr. Janet Norwood, the Commissioner of Labor Statistics, testified before a House panel, "there are many people who are working full time at very low incomes" (*The New York Times*, July 22, 1986, p. A20). Poverty for this large group cannot be explained by their failure to work or to seek jobs when they are out of work. Rather, their subemployment is built into the economic system.

The "new poor" are men and women who have fallen below the poverty line in recent years because of changes in the economy, es-

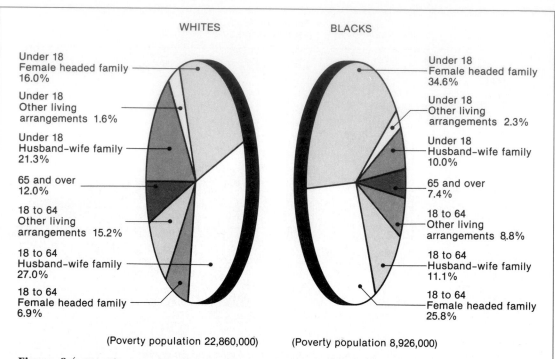

WHITES   BLACKS

Under 18
Female headed family
16.0%

Under 18
Other living
arrangements 1.6%

Under 18
Husband–wife family
21.3%

65 and over
12.0%

18 to 64
Other living
arrangements 15.2%

18 to 64
Husband–wife family
27.0%

18 to 64
Female headed family
6.9%

Under 18
Female headed family
34.6%

Under 18
Other living
arrangements 2.3%

Under 18
Husband–wife family
10.0%

65 and over
7.4%

18 to 64
Other living
arrangements 8.8%

18 to 64
Husband–wife family
11.1%

18 to 64
Female headed family
25.8%

(Poverty population 22,860,000)   (Poverty population 8,926,000)

Figure 8-4   Distribution of Poverty, by Race, Age, and Living Arrangements (1985). *(Source: Data from decennial census and 1985 Current Population Survey; From G. O. Jaynes and R. M. Williams, Jr., Eds.*, A Common Destiny: Blacks and American Society. *Copyright © 1989 by the National Academy of Sciences, National Academy Press, Washington, D.C.)*

pecially the decline of such old-line industries as automobile manufacturing. Farmers have also been hurt. The technical term for their situation is *structural unemployment*: Changes in the structure of the economy have made their skills obsolete. Many working-class families have experienced a decline in their standard of living (Harrington, 1984; O'Hare, 1985). Young male workers have been particularly hard hit. The average earnings of males ages twenty to twenty-four have declined 30 percent since 1973. Whereas the average incomes of men who turned thirty in 1973 kept pace with inflation, those who turned thirty in 1983 had already experienced a 35 percent decline in buying power (*Dollars & Sense*, 1987).

The good news is that for most Americans, poverty is only a temporary condition (Duncan,

1984). The same people are not poor year in, year out; rather they fall into or out of poverty because of personal fortune, economic cycles (and structural unemployment), and/or their stage in the life cycle. For example, a single mother may go on welfare for a time, but return to work when her children reach school age.

The bad news is that some Americans never find a place in the labor market. The term "underclass" refers to a heterogeneous population of individuals who are chronically unemployed, lack training and skills, have experienced extended periods of poverty and/or reliance on welfare, and may drop out of the labor force, turning to the underground economy (street vending, bartering services, and the like) or crime for survival (Wilson, 1987). The financial problems of the underclass are compounded by the fact that many live in neighborhoods where crime rates are high, drug abuse is rampant, schools are substandard, unwed teenage pregnancy is common, housing is rundown, and prices are high.* All of America's poor experience some of these problems, but they are most acute in black, inner-city neighborhoods.

The Black Underclass

The emergence of an urban black underclass is largely a modern phenomenon. Consider Chicago (Wacquant and Wilson, 1989). In the 1950s, Chicago's South Side was a racially segregated but economically integrated community, composed of a small number of middle-class professionals and white-collar workers, a large number of working-class machine operators and laborers, and a lower class of marginally employed workers. Chicago was at the height of its industrial might, with some 10,000 manufacturers employing half a million blue-collar workers. The rate of black employment was about the same as that for all Chicagoans, and the median black income was about two-thirds the city average. The South Side may not have been affluent, but it was a lively, vital community. Because of racial segregation, the diverse skills of people of all income and educational levels were concentrated in the black community. As a result, the South Side had its own doctors and lawyers, schools and churches, theaters and clubs, markets and retail stores. Maids and ditchdiggers lived on the same streets, attended the same churches, and shopped at the same stores as school teachers, clergy, and other professionals.

Today the South Side is unrecognizable (Duncan, 1987; Wacquant, 1989). The author Studs Terkel has compared Chicago's South Side to Soweto, the black township outside Johannesburg, South Africa (in Wacquant, 1989, p. 509). Two out of three adults are unemployed. Half have not completed high school. Six in ten are on welfare. Median income has dropped to one-third the city average; half of South Side families make do with household incomes of less than $7,500. During the mid-1980s, a period of economic recovery for most of the nation, residents of the South Side reported that their situation stayed the same—or deteriorated. Three quarters do not have even one of the following assets: a personal checking or savings account, a retirement account or pension plan, stocks or bonds, or a prepaid burial plan. Owning a home and a car—staples of the American dream—are well beyond reach. (See Table 8-3.) A stable family life is also elusive. Nearly half of ghetto residents say they do not have a current partner (someone they are dating, living with, or married to) (Wacquant and Wilson, 1989). As many as six out of ten babies are born to unmarried women, and two-thirds of households are headed by single mothers (Wilson, 1987).

As Troy Duster (1988) has pointed out, black Americans have endured hardships in the past by pinning their hopes on their children. But this hope may be turning to despair. Since 1960, the unemployment rate for young blacks sixteen to nineteen years old has quadrupled, reaching a staggering 48.3 percent. Of the original class of 1984 enrolled in inner-city Chicago schools, only two-thirds were still in school in ninth grade. Of these 25,500 ninth graders, only 16,000 graduated from high school, and only 2,000 of these graduates read at or above the national average (*The Bottom Line*, 1985). There are more young blacks in prison today than on college campuses (Duster, 1988).

The South Side story is not unique. In city after city, both the relative and absolute numbers of blacks living in poverty have increased.†

---

*Stores typically charge more for food, clothing, furniture, appliances, and the like in poor neighborhoods on the grounds that they have to make up for the costs of shoplifting, theft, and nonpayment of bills.

†"Relative" meaning the proportion of blacks compared to the proportion of whites, and "absolute" meaning actual numbers.

TABLE 8-3   **Economic Exclusion and Deprivation in Chicago's Ghetto, 1986–1987**

	ALL RESPONDENTS	FEMALES
Class position		
not employed	61%	69%
working class	33	21
middle class	6	10
did not finish high school	51	50
Public aid		
on aid when a child	41%	44%
currently on aid	58	69
receives food stamps	60	70
Assets		
household income < $7,500	51%	59%
finances not improved or worse	79	80
has checking account	12	10
has savings account	18	14
household owns home	21	8
household owns a car	34	26

Source: Urban Poverty and Family Life Survey, 1987; L. J. D. Wacquant, "The Ghetto, the State, and the New Capitalist Economy." *Dissent* (Fall 1989), table 1, p. 509. Reprinted by permission of the Foundation for the Study of Independent Social Ideas, Inc.

The concentration of poor blacks (and other minorities) in deteriorating neighborhoods increased by 230 percent, or 2.3 million individuals, between 1970 and 1980 (Ricketts & Mincy, 1989). Poverty has also become more persistent (Adams, Duncan, and Rodgers, 1988). For two-fifths of urban blacks, there is a strong likelihood that they will never find a decent job or stable marriage partner, and that their children will share their fate.

Popular explanations of the black underclass invoke a "welfare mentality" or "culture of poverty" characterized by low aspirations, sexual irresponsibility, impulsiveness, and general laziness. According to this view, members of the underclass do not attach the same value to education, work, and family as other members of our society do. Men abandon their families; women see nothing wrong with having babies out of wedlock and going on welfare; young people drop out of school in their early teens, "hang out" on the street, and often become involved with drugs and crime. These antisocial values, passed from generation to generation,

prevent members of the underclass from climbing out of poverty. From this perspective, government assistance is viewed as perpetuating the cycle.

Sociologists (for example, Wilson, 1987) counter that conditions in black ghettoes are the result of structural changes in society, not moral defects in individuals. The difference between the underclass and other members of society is not that the poor hold different values, but that they have many fewer opportunities to achieve such basic goals as earning a living wage and maintaining a stable family life. After a series of low-paying jobs and long, frequent spells of unemployment, members of the underclass may stop trying to find conventional jobs—not because they are "lazy," but because experience has shown that such jobs are beyond their reach. Realizing how few people around them achieve a conventional work and family life, they may defend themselves by pretending they never wanted these in the first place (Anderson, 1989; Liebow, 1967). Some may turn to "hustling"; others, to drink or drugs. These adjustments may be self defeating, but they are more a consequence than a cause of extreme poverty. What, then, is the cause?

Part of the explanation of the growing black underclass lies in the *deindustrialization* of the nation's major cities (especially northeastern and north central cities). In recent decades, these cities have been transformed from industrial to information-processing centers (Kasarda, 1989). Manufacturing plants have moved from the inner city to the suburbs, the Sun Belt, and foreign countries. Between 1950 and 1980, Chicago lost half its factories and mills, and 63 percent of its blue-collar jobs. These jobs had been the main support of the black community: In 1950, 42,000 residents of the South Side were employed as machine operators, transport workers, laborers, and the like. Today, only 6,200 blue-collar workers remain (Wacquant, 1989). For people with limited education (a large percentage of today's inner city black youth), blue-collar jobs also served as the main entry to the labor force. In the past, entry-level blue-collar jobs often were a ladder to better-paying jobs that could lift a family out of poverty. Now these jobs are gone. Wholesale and retail trade have followed a similar pattern, moving warehouses to rural areas and stores to suburban shopping malls. Also, government cutbacks have reduced the number of public sector jobs (such as postal workers), which provided a route out of poverty for previous generations.

The decline of manufacturing and trade in major cities has been offset in part by the growth of such information-intensive services as accounting, advertising, brokerage, and law. But most jobs in these areas require educational credentials that most inner-city blacks do not have (Wilson et al., 1988). The remaining service jobs—at gas stations, fast-food establishments, dry cleaners—do not pay a living wage. In short, "the poorly educated are trapped in dead-end jobs for a life time of poverty" (Moore, 1989, p. 267). As the formal wage market declines, people look for other means of support, including welfare, the underground economy, and crime (both petty and organized).

A second reason for the growth of the black underclass is the *social restructuring of the ghetto*. Black neighborhoods used to be economically integrated communities, as described above. One of the unintended consequences of the civil rights legislation that outlawed discrimination in housing was to drain inner-city neighborhoods of middle- and working-class black families. The exodus of nonpoor blacks from city centers has had numerous repercussions (Wilson, 1987, 1988). First, and most obviously, many of the black professionals who once served the ghetto (physicians, lawyers, social workers, teachers) now work outside the community. This means services within the ghetto have been cut back. It also means that ghetto residents who used to see a family doctor who lived nearby, knew their parents, and attended their church now travel to an impersonal clinic.

Second, the working and middle classes bring stability to a community. They patronize its churches, stores, banks, and recreational facilities; they send their children to its schools; they participate in PTAs, community organizations, local political clubs, block associations, and other associations. When the middle and working classes leave, some of these institutions (stores, banks, community organizations) close their doors; others (churches, schools) cut back on activities. Because of the concentration of the poor in ghetto neighborhoods, school buildings are run-down, many students are ill-prepared for the classroom, and teachers become discouraged: They expect failure and trouble, and often get what they expect. As institutions become weaker, illegal and deviant behavior become more open. A former resident of Chicago's ghetto reflects,

> The sixties gave us people in higher places, but the rank and file is worse off than they was then. They're on a destruction course. We have more killings, more murder. We have dropouts. Our schools is gone. Our churches is gone. And our

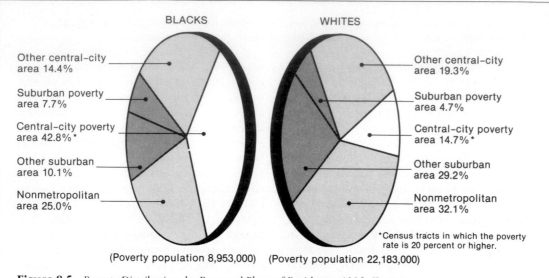

BLACKS WHITES

Other central-city area 14.4%

Suburban poverty area 7.7%

Central-city poverty area 42.8%*

Other suburban area 10.1%

Nonmetropolitan area 25.0%

Other central-city area 19.3%

Suburban poverty area 4.7%

Central-city poverty area 14.7%*

Other suburban area 29.2%

Nonmetropolitan area 32.1%

*Census tracts in which the poverty rate is 20 percent or higher.

(Poverty population 8,953,000) (Poverty population 22,183,000)

Figure 8-5 Poverty Distribution, by Race and Place of Residence, 1986. *(Source: Data from current population surveys; G. O. Jaynes and R. M. Williams, Jr., Eds.,* A Common Destiny: Blacks and American Society. *Copyright © 1989 by the National Academy of Sciences, National Academy Press, Washington, D.C.)*

business is gone. (Quoted in Blauner, 1989, p. 175)

Third, the middle and working classes act as role models for young people whose parents are not so well off. They provide concrete evidence that "education is meaningful, that steady employment is a viable alternative to welfare, and that family stability is the norm, not the exception" (Wilson, 1988, p. 13). The child whose father is chronically unemployed or whose mother is alcoholic knows personally other, intact families in which fathers and mothers are successfully playing the roles of breadwinner and homemaker. Every day the child sees adults with briefcases or toolboxes hurrying to get to work on time. When the middle and working classes depart, these role models disappear. Young people may come to think of hustling as a job, single-parent families as the norm, and welfare as something everyone needs from time to time.

Finally, the departure of the middle and working classes cuts off access to the networks that might enable ghetto residents to find work. Most people get jobs not through newspaper ads or employment agencies, but through their own networks. In today's black ghetto, connections to the world of work have been largely destroyed. In their place, one finds networks for drug dealing, fencing stolen goods, and the like (Wacquant, 1989). The decline of job networks affects children as well as adults. In working-class neighborhoods young people see education not just as valuable in itself, but as a necessary credential for many of the jobs available through their family and neighborhood connections (Sullivan, 1984). Youngsters in the black ghetto have less reason to believe that education will "pay off."

The combination of racial and economic segregation creates a high degree of social isolation (see Figure 8-5) (Wilson, 1988). Often the only contacts blacks in today's ghetto have with the working and middle classes emphasize their subordinate status as marginal students, low-level employees, and clients of public health and welfare agencies.

In contrast, a majority of poor whites live in economically integrated neighborhoods. Hispanics are almost as likely as blacks to be poor, but Hispanic inner-city neighborhoods have not changed so dramatically in recent decades (Moore, 1989). Working- and middle-class families did not leave the barrio suddenly and in large numbers, most institutions are still strong,* and networks are intact. Moreover low-wage industries (in textiles, apparel, and furniture manufacturing) and local, Hispanic-owned businesses provide the barrio with a wage-based (rather than welfare-based) economy. Likewise, ethnic identification, extended-kin networks, and family businesses have helped recent Asian immigrants avoid permanent poverty and social dislocation (Boyd, 1988).

The Impact of Poverty

Social stratification can be a matter of life and death. For example, in Vietnam enlisted men (the majority of whom were poor or working class and a disproportionate number of whom belonged to minority groups) were much more likely to be killed than were officers (Zeitlin, Lutterman, and Russell, 1977). According to one estimate, life expectancy for Americans in the lowest income groups is six years shorter than that for the highest income groups (Antonovsky, 1972).

The impact of poverty on *life chances* begins even before birth. Poor women are more likely than other women to suffer from protein, vitamin, and mineral deficiencies, untreated infections, and emotional stress during pregnancy. They are less likely to seek prenatal care. They are often younger when they have their first baby, and older when they have their last child, than are other mothers. As a result, their babies are more likely to be born prematurely, to have low birth weights, and even to die during infancy. Thanks to Medicare, poor children today

*The exception, according to Moore, is the school system. Rates of dropping out and underachievement are as high in the barrio as in the black ghetto.

visit a doctor nearly as often as middle-class children do. Even so, they have many more health problems growing up, ranging from dental cavities and poor eyesight to tuberculosis and dysentary (diseases often associated with Third World populations) (deLone, 1979).

As adults, America's poor are more likely to suffer from chronic and infectious diseases, to feel sick, and to worry about their health. They lose more days of work because of illness and injury. They are also more likely to suffer from occupational diseases, such as black lung disease among coal miners. Yet they are much less likely to see physicians, dentists, or other medical professionals. It is not simply that they cannot afford medical care—although this is a problem, especially for the "working poor" who don't qualify for Medicaid. Mild illnesses have a low priority in poor households. A slight fever is tolerated in the face of more pressing problems, such as putting food on the table. Moreover, to receive medical treatment, poor people may have to travel long distances to a clinic and wait there for hours. Treatment is impersonal and rarely is the same doctor seen twice. Many seek medical attention only as a last resort.

When they do receive treatment it may not be the same treatment given wealthier Americans. For example, psychologically disturbed members of the lower class are often confined to mental hospitals, where they receive drug therapies and custodial care. Middle- and upper-class individuals are more likely to be treated as outpatients, to see a private psychologist, and to receive some form of psychotherapy.

Numerous studies have shown that poor Americans are more likely than better off Americans to suffer from emotional disorders (Hollingshead and Redlich, 1958; Srole et al., 1975; Wheaton, 1978). But there is much debate about whether poverty is a cause or an effect of mental illness (Kessler, 1982; Link, 1989). Some sociologists have argued that the poor not only are exposed to more life stresses, but also have fewer resources for coping with problems. According to this view, poverty causes (or makes people vulnerable to) mental disturbance. Others have argued the reverse, that emotional problems cause people to "drift" into poverty. Still others have argued that the real issue is the quality of care people at different economic levels receive for psychological problems (Mollica and Milie, 1986).

Broad *social and economic trends* also affect different classes in different ways. In times of inflation or recession, the poor suffer more from rising prices and are more likely to lose their jobs (Caplovitz, 1979). Because they have no "disposable income" (money left over when necessities are paid for), the poor are hit hardest by rises in the cost of living. Suppose the cost of food for a family of four is $5,800 a year. This represents 33 percent of the budget of a family with an income of $17,500 a year (about half the median income and $5,000 above the poverty line). Food would amount to only 19 percent of the budget of a family with an income of $30,000 a year. If food prices rise by 25 percent, the additional cost ($1,450) represents a much larger share of the poorer family's income (8 percent) than of the moderate family's income (5 percent). The same principle applies to housing, utilities, and other necessities. Efforts to cut the federal budget also have a greater impact on the poor (as well as the working class and large segments of the middle class) than on the well-to-do (Waxman, 1983, chap. 7). This was particularly true of the budget cuts made in the early 1980s (Wilson and Aponte, 1985), which hit social welfare programs particularly hard.

The poor are more likely to be arrested and sent to prison for committing crimes, and also more likely to be the victims of crime (Chapter 6). They are more likely to be divorced or separated than are affluent Americans (Chapter 12). Schools in low-income neighborhoods are more likely to emphasize discipline and vocational training, whereas schools in affluent neighborhoods encourage academic performance and college preparatory programs (Chapter 13). The poor are less likely to vote or to participate in political and other organized social activities (Chapter 15). In short, few areas of a person's life are not affected by poverty. Being homeless adds insult to injury (see "Close Up," below).

Poverty in the United States is all the more puzzling because it challenges one of our cherished beliefs: the idea that anyone who works hard enough can get ahead.

*[Section 2 ends.
Section 3 begins.]*

SOCIAL MOBILITY

Nearly all Americans are descended from immigrants who saw this nation as the land of opportunity. Our literature and folklore contain hundreds of stories of people who rose "from rags to riches." Americans may resign themselves to a modest lifestyle, but they do not give up the hope that their children will get ahead. How realistic is that hope? How much social mobility is there in the United States?

The term **social mobility** refers to movement up or down the socioeconomic ladder. Social mobility can be measured by comparing an individual's position to that of his or her parents, or by assessing the degree of success or failure experienced in a lifetime. Individuals who gain property, power, and prestige, improving their living conditions, are said to display *upward mobility*. An example is a college professor whose father was an automobile worker. People who lose property, power, and prestige and do not live as well or stylishly as they or their parents once did are said to display *downward mobility*. A salesclerk whose mother was a judge is an example.

Open and Closed Social Systems

The degree of social mobility in different societies varies. In a **closed system** opportunities to better oneself are severely limited, if they exist at all. The traditional caste system in India is

Studying Section 2

Activities for Section 2

Continue your note-taking on the chapter by completing the partial notes below. These notes cover pages 158–166.

POVERTY IN AMERICA

Official poverty line—_____

_____

     In 1987, 32.5 million Americans (about 13.5 percent of the population) were officially counted as poor.

     It is important to distinguish between absolute and relative poverty. To a farmer in Central America, our poorest might seem well off in some ways. But this is little consolation to families who compare their situation with that of middle-income Americans.

Who Are the Poor?

Changes in face of poverty in last two to three decades:

1. Increasingly an urban phenomenon. More and more, poverty is a big-city, central city problem.

2. _____

   _____

   _____

3. _____

   _____

   _____

4. _____

   _____

   _____

Subgroups:

1. "Working poor"—people whose part-time jobs do not lift them above the poverty level.

2. "New poor"—_____

   _____

Technical term for situation of the new poor is structural unemployment—_____

_____

Underclass—_____

_____

The Black Underclass:

Emergence of the black underclass is a modern phenomenon. Compare Chicago's South Side in the 1950s with the South Side today.

Causes of the black underclass:

1. Deindustrialization of the nation's major cities. Cities have changed from industrial to information-processing centers. Entry-level blue-collar jobs of past are gone; they were often a ladder that could lift a family out of poverty.

2. _____

    _____

    _____

Effects of departure of nonpoor blacks from city centers:

1. Many black professionals who once served the ghetto now work outside the community, which means services have been cut back.

2. _____

    _____

3. _____

    _____

4. _____

    _____

    _____

    In contrast, a majority of poor whites live in economically integrated neighborhoods.

The Impact of Poverty:

1. Life expectancy in the lowest income groups is six years shorter than for those in the highest income groups.

2. Impact of poverty on life chances begins even before birth. Poor mothers have many health problems, and their children have many more health problems growing up.

3. _____

    _____

4. _____

_____

5. _____

_____

6. _____

_____

Comments on Section 2

- The notes above, which cover nine pages in the sample chapter, consist mostly of definitions and enumerations. Two of the enumerations are apparent because the authors set off the items in each enumeration by using signal words along

  with (*complete the missing word*) _____ type in the text.
- The final enumeration is made up of examples of the impact of poverty. While the items in the enumeration are not set off with signal words or with italic type in this section, it becomes apparent as you read that almost every paragraph develops a different example. A good way to organize these examples is simply to number them in your notes.

CLOSE UP
America's Homeless

The most important thing in a man's life is shelter. Once you have shelter, then you are able to get yourself together, then you are able to develop the idea of how to get yourself out of the trouble you are in.
—A homeless man in New York City (Quoted in Baxter and Hopper, 1981, p. 48)

No one knows exactly how many Americans are homeless. Estimates range from 250,000 to 3 million or more. What is clear is that the number and visibility of the homeless have increased dramatically in the last decade.

Who are the homeless? Fifteen years ago the typical streetperson was an alcoholic male, age fifty or older (Sloss, 1984). Today the homeless are a varied group. Using data from studies of homeless people receiving medical treatment, seeking shelter, and living on the streets, James Wright (1988) drew up a sample of 1,000 (see Fig-

ure 8-6). The largest group in this sample (625 of 1,000) are male, most of whom are alone and in their middle thirties. Only a small proportion of today's homeless (17 of 1,000) are men age sixty-five or older. One reason may be that Social Security benefits are tied to the cost of living, enabling older men to afford housing. But Wright suspects an equally important reason is that few homeless men live to age sixty-five. Their average life span is about twenty years shorter than the national average.

A relatively large proportion of homeless men (188 of 1,000) are veterans, many of the Vietnam war. Some of these veterans are suffering from war-related physical or psychiatric disabilities, and some from drug and alcohol abuse. Nearly all re-

Ultimately, the root causes of homelessness lie in changes in the structure of society, not the case histories of individuals.

port chronic unemployment. Interviews suggest that many of the men who fought in Vietnam were from lower socioeconomic groups and enlisted because they believed military service would lead to better educational and employment opportunities. For a variety of reasons (the unpopularity of the war, cutbacks in benefits, and general economic conditions), these hopes did not materialize.

About 122 of the remaining men in the sample are mentally disabled. Although not a threat to themselves or others, they are not fully capable of holding a job and caring for themselves. About 28 cannot work because of non-war-related physical disabilities. About an equal

Sociologist James Wright found that nearly 10 percent of the homeless persons in his study were children living on the street with one or both of their parents.

(Continued)

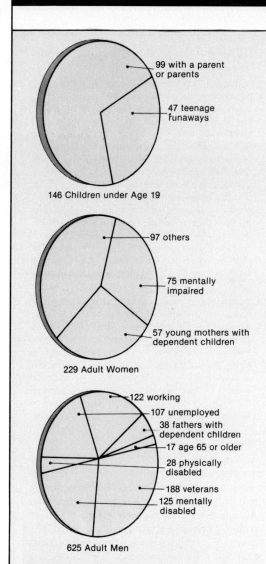

Figure 8-6 Who Are the Homeless? From a sample of 1,000. *(Data adapted from J. D. Wright, "The Worthy and Unworthy Homeless." Published by permission of Transaction Publishers, from* Transaction Society, *Vol. 25, No. 5 [July/August 1988], pp. 64–69. Copyright © 1988 by Transaction Publishers.)*

number (122 unattached men and 38 fathers) are working sporadically, but not earning enough to pay for housing. The remainder are unemployed.

Today's homeless population includes a smaller but growing number of women (229 of 1,000). About 75 homeless women in the sample are mentally disturbed (the stereotype of the "bag lady"). These women are more likely to be white and middle-aged than are other homeless. About 57 are young mothers. These women are less likely than other homeless people to be suffering from psychological problems or from drug or alcohol abuse. But many of the remaining homeless women have lost their homes and families in part because of drug and/or alcohol abuse.

Almost one-tenth of the homeless (99 in the sample) are children under the age of sixteen who are with either one or, less frequently, both parents. Because many children of homeless parents live with relatives or in foster care, the actual number of children affected by homelessness is actually much higher. An additional 47 children in the sample are teenagers who have either run away from, or been thrown out of, their homes. Often these teenagers suffered physical and/or sexual abuse in their homes; many survive on the streets by turning to crime (especially prostitution); and a high percentage are heavy users of drugs and/or alcohol.

The homeless are only a small fraction (less than 3 percent) of the nation's extremely poor, who subsist on incomes of about $2,000 a year (about $165 a month) (Rossi, 1988; Rossi and Wright, 1989). How do others get by? Some spend all their income on rent (usually space in a single room occupancy, or SRO, hotel), and depend on soup kitchens and charities for other necessities. Others live with family (usually parents or siblings) or friends, for little or no charge.

Three features distinguish the homeless from others who are extremely poor. The first is length of unemployment: The average homeless person has not held a steady job for four and a half years. The second is the level of disability. Three out of four homeless people report being in only "fair" or poor health; have been in a mental hospital or detoxification unit; receive scores on psychological tests that indicate a need for treatment for depression or psychotic thinking; or have been convicted of a crime. One of these problems might not push an extremely poor person into homelessness; but a majority of the homeless experience two or more such problems. The third feature of homelessness is social isolation. A majority of homeless people (57 percent) have never been married. One in three say they have no contact with their families whatsoever, and one in four report no contact with family or friends.

Comparisons of individuals are useful in identifying the special difficulties the homeless experience. But it is impossible to say whether these problems are causes or effects of homelessness. Ultimately, the root causes of homelessness lie in changes in the structure of society, not the case histories of individuals. Peter Rossi and James Wright (1989) identify the basic causes of homelessness as:

1 A decline in the demand for low-skilled workers (detailed in the discussion of the underclass earlier in this chapter).

2 Cutbacks in welfare programs for the poor. Subsidies to the poor through General Assistance (GA) and Aid to Families with Dependent Children (AFDC) declined by an average of 20 percent in the 1970s. This has both direct and indirect effects. Cutbacks in GA make it all but impossible for a single person to afford even the cheapest housing,* and cutbacks in AFDC make it more difficult for

*In Chicago, for example, to qualify for GA a single person must earn less than $1,848 a year. But GA payments of $154 a month will not pay for an SRO unit, at an average monthly rental of $194 (not to mention other necessities).

families to shelter an adult relative who has fallen on hard times.

3 Cutbacks in subsidies for the disabled—including a reduction in the number of people eligible for disability support, reductions in the amount of support, and deinstitutionalization. In the 1960s, the government set out to reduce the number of patients confined to mental hospitals. This policy, known as "deinstitutionalization," was based on good intentions. State mental institutions offered little more than custodial care to the mentally ill; new drugs promised that many could function outside the hospital; community centers would ease the transition, helping them to cope with the problems of everyday life. Between 1960 and 1980, the rate of hospitalization for mental illness dropped by about 75 percent. But plans for a network of community clinics and halfway houses did not materialize. After release, many patients were on their own.

4 Reductions in the supply of low-income housing. Cutbacks in federal spending for low-income housing, reductions in tax incentives for private investment in housing, the deterioration of housing projects built in the 1950s and 1960s, and gentrification of urban neighborhoods combined to decrease the amount of housing available to the poor while the number of poor was growing. The greatest decline has been in low-cost housing for single people. In 1980 to 1983 alone, Chicago lost nearly 25 percent of its SRO units.

Current policies toward the homeless focus on providing emergency services, not on correcting root causes. Shelters for the homeless provide beds on a nightly basis, reinforcing their sense of rootlessness. Life on the streets may create or worsen psychological and physical disabilities. Many of the homeless suffer from malnutrition, heart and respiratory diseases, and chronic leg ulcers. Alcohol may become a form of self-medication, an escape from depression, pain, and cold. Not knowing what tomorrow will bring can intensify mental disorientation. "The danger is that emergency measures may create "a permanently disenfranchised group for whom 'makeshift' has become a way of life" (Hopper, 1984, p. 13).

the classic example of this. According to ancient Hindu legends, the sacrifice of the man-god Purusha created the universe. Purusha, and all Indian society, was divided into four. His mouth became the Brahmin caste (the priests and scholars); his arms became the Kshatriya caste (nobles and warriors); his thighs, the Vaisya caste (merchants and traders); and his feet, the Sudra caste (peasants, laborers, and artisans). The Harijans, or "Untouchables" (street sweepers, scavengers, leather workers, and swineherds), who make up about 20 percent of the population of India today, have no status at all, according to this system. They are, literally, "outcastes." (These castes are, in turn, divided into thousands of subcastes.)

Individuals are born into one caste or another. Caste determines not only their social standing, but also their function in life (their occupation). An elaborate system of etiquette ensures caste purity. Marriage between members of different castes and such activities as eating or sitting together are strictly forbidden. The only route to "social mobility" between castes (wealth may vary considerably within castes) in the Hindu system is through reincarnation. Birth into a higher caste is believed to be a reward for correct behavior in one's previous life.

In closed systems, then, social status is ascribed: People are assigned a more or less arbitrary and permanent social status on the basis of traits over which they have no control (such as blood relationships, skin color, sex, or age). Individual ability and effort do not count (Kemper, 1974).

In contrast, an **open system** attempts to reduce the obstacles to social mobility by providing equal opportunity to all. In its ideals, the American class system is an example.

Most Americans subscribe to the belief that all individuals are equal in the sight of God. Our traditions emphasize individualism, hard work, competition, and freedom of choice. Theoretically, people are free to be whatever they want to be. Our institutions are designed to provide everyone with the same political and legal rights, the same educational and occupational opportunities. Class differences are attributed to differential achievement, particularly in economic pursuits. Ideally, this system is like a giant marathon race with a few first prizes, more second prizes, and many third prizes. (The prizes are wealth, power, and prestige.) In theory, all individuals start at the same point; where they finish depends on them.

In an open system, then, social status is achieved: status is awarded on the basis of individual ability and effort. Ideally, such factors as family of origin, skin color, sex, and age do not matter.

No society is entirely open or entirely closed. In India a member of a caste may improve his or her position on the local level by taking over a valued new occupation or by adopting upper-caste customs. Westernization, mass education, the media, and laws to protect "Untouchables" are breaking down caste barriers. In the United States, equal opportunity is still a dream. Social status is based on ascription as well as achievement (as shown in Chapters 9 and 10). How open or closed is the American social system?

Getting Ahead or Falling Behind?

Statistics indicate that many Americans are upwardly mobile. In 1940, only 25 percent of the adult population had high school diplomas; in 1987, 76 percent did (*Statistical Abstracts*, 1989, pp. 131, 147). The proportion of Americans employed in white-collar and service occupations (teaching, nursing, sales, and other jobs that do not involve the production of goods) rose from 45 percent in 1945 to 68 percent in 1982 (Rossides, 1976; *Statistical Abstracts, 1985*). Personal income has also increased, from $9,063 per capita in 1970 to $12,955 in 1987 (adjusting for inflation) (Census Bureau, 1989). Contrary to popular belief, however, the rate of social mobility is no higher in the United States than in other industrialized nations such as Switzer-

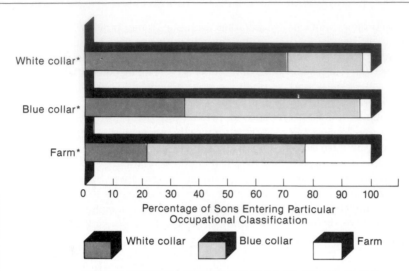

White collar

Blue collar

Farm

Percentage of Sons Entering Particular
Occupational Classification

*Father's occupational classification when son was sixteen years of age

Figure 8-7 Following in Father's Footsteps: The Correlation between the Occupations of Fathers and Sons. A study by Blau and Duncan revealed that the majority of sons tended to find employment within the same broad occupational classifications as their fathers. Thus, for example, 71 percent of the boys whose fathers had worked in white-collar jobs, also entered white-collar employment. *(Reprinted with permission of The Free Press, a Division of Macmillan, Inc. from The American Occupational Structure by Peter M. Blau and Otis Dudley Duncan. Copyright © 1967 by Peter M. Blau and Otis Dudley Duncan.)*

land, France, Japan, Sweden, and Germany. A leap from rags to riches is rare (see Figure 8-7). Most upward mobility involves a small step up: The child of a factory worker becomes a supervisor; the child of a pharmacist becomes a physician.

Much of the mobility in the United States is the result of structural change, not individual success stories (Levy, 1988). **Structural mobility** occurs when technological innovations, urbanization, economic booms or busts, wars, and other events alter the number and kinds of occupations available in a society. As a result, people are "pulled" onto a higher social level or "pushed" onto a lower one.

Structural mobility has been an important factor in the rising standard of living in the United States. Urbanization and mechanization increased the demand for professionals, man-

agers, and office workers. The upper classes (who tend to have small families) did not bear enough children to fill the increasing number of jobs. People from working-class backgrounds were "pulled" into the lower middle class. This "pulled" people who grew up on farms (and who were already being "pushed" off farms by the mechanization of agriculture) toward factory jobs in the cities.

The early post–World War II years were a period of exceptional growth and prosperity for this country. In the 1950s and 1960s, the number of Americans who were able to realize the middle-class dream—a home of their own, one or two cars, a washing machine and drier, a dishwasher, a color TV, college education for the children—grew steadily. Because of rising income tax revenues, government support for poor families also increased. Americans came to expect that their standard of living would improve over their working life, and that they would be better off at retirement than their parents had been.

The 1970s and 1980s, however, brought economic stagnation (Levy, 1988). The country did not fall into a deep depression, but the rate of economic growth slowed. Families who had already achieved the dream—who had job security, a home they had purchased with a low, fixed-rate mortgage, and a pension plan—were able to stay on track. But younger workers found that the dream was becoming more and more expensive. To attain the standard of living their parents enjoyed required more education, two wage earners, assuming a large amount of debt, and postponing parenthood and/or having fewer children. The average worker who was thirty-five in 1965 had seen her wages increase steadily; the average worker who was thirty-five in 1985 was treading water. The proportion of two-income families with annual incomes of $30,000 (adjusted for inflation) dropped from 51 percent in 1973 to 45 percent in 1984,* in spite of the fact that many more women were working.

Young workers just entering the job force were hardest hit (Cutler, 1989). Between 1973 and 1986, the median income of households headed by someone under age twenty-six dropped from $20,229 to $14,900. In part as a result of declining wages, many young people postponed marriage. The proportion of married men ages twenty to twenty-four living with their spouses fell from 39 to 19 percent. Home ownership among this age group went from 23 to 16 percent.

These trends do not mean a permanent reversal of America's fortunes, just that the country has been going through a difficult period

---

*If postwar growth rates had continued, 60 percent of two-income families would have had incomes in excess of $30,000 in 1985.

(Levy, 1988). In the years ahead, the pool of young workers will shrink. Businesses will have to not only compete for highly educated workers (by raising their wages), but also hire and train less educated workers (and raise their wages to keep them). The housing crunch of the 1970s, when the baby boom generation began settling down, may become a housing glut in the year 2000. In short, the tide may turn. But this depends on how the United States fares in the changing global economy (see Chapter 16). *[Section 3 ends. Section 4 begins.]*

THEORIES OF SOCIAL STRATIFICATION

In the musical *My Fair Lady*, Professor Henry Higgins sets out to prove that he can transform Eliza Doolittle, a poor, wretched girl from London's underclass, into a member of the upper class simply by teaching her to speak properly. Professor Higgins's experiment is a success. Eliza passes as a member of the aristocracy. Of course, in real life, speech is only one of the characteristics that assign people to different social classes. For Eliza to become an actual member of the upper class, she would require wealth, a "proper" education, connections with the "right" people, and other social assets. Indeed, in George Bernard Shaw's play *Pygmalion*, on which *My Fair Lady* is based, Liza ends up marrying her less desirable suitor Freddy—not the wealthy, aristocrat Professor Higgins—and running a flower shop. The musical reflects the American dream of upward mobility; the play is closer to reality.

Social stratification is a persistent social fact in this and other modern societies. Why should this be so? Why are social rewards, and even life chances, distributed unevenly? Theories of stratification attempt to answer these questions. Two of the first sociologists to analyze social stratification were Karl Marx and Max Weber. Their different conclusions are still debated among sociologists.

Studying Section 3

Activities for Section 3

Continue your note-taking on the sample chapter by completing the partial notes below. These notes cover pages 170–175.

SOCIAL MOBILITY

Social mobility —_____

_____

1. Upward mobility—_____

_____

2. Downward mobility—_____

_____

Open and Closed Social Systems:

Closed system—_____

_____

   Ex.—_____

_____

Open system—_____

_____

   Ex.—_____

Getting Ahead or Falling Behind:

Statistics show that many Americans are upwardly mobile, but the rate of mobility is no higher in the United States than in other industrialized nations, such as Japan or Germany.

Much of the mobility in the United States is the result of structural mobility—_____

_____

_____

Much structural mobility in the 1950s and 1960s, but economic stagnation in the 1970s and 1980s. Younger workers found that the dream of their parents (job security, own home, pension plan) was becoming more expensive and harder to realize.

America's Homeless:

According to one sample, the homeless fall into the following groups:

1. Largest is adult men, alone and in their middle thirties.
2. Large proportion of these men are veterans, many of the Vietnam war.
3. Many are mentally disabled.
4. _____
5. _____

Three features distinguish the homeless from the poor:

1. _____
2. _____
3. _____

Basic causes of homelessness:

1. _____
2. _____
3. _____
4. _____

Comments on Section 3

■ Once again, definitions and enumerations are the keys to important ideas in this section of the sample chapter.

■ Some notes are based on main ideas or key details within paragraphs. For example, in the section "Getting Ahead or Falling Behind," the first sentence of notes contains the main idea of the first paragraph. The final two sentences of notes (contrasting the 1950s and 1960s with the 1970s and 1980s) include a key detail presented in the section. As you practice taking notes, you will develop an instinct for writing down important material that does not appear in an obvious way within a definition or an enumeration.

■ Notes are also included here on the boxed "Close-Up" feature concerning the homeless. Note that there are several enumerations within this feature. Unless your instructor indicates otherwise, you should assume that such features may be included on tests.

Marx on Class Struggle

"The history of all hitherto existing society," wrote Marx and his collaborator, Friedrich Engels, in *The Communist Manifesto* (1848/1960) "is the history of class struggles." Marx believed that the emergence of a division of labor laid the foundation for the division of society into antagonistic classes. For Marx, a social class is a category of people who have a common relationship to the means of production (to the raw materials, technology, and so on). Those who control the means of production (the landed aristocracy in a feudal society, the factory owners and bankers in a capitalist society) exploit those who do not (the serfs or workers). Although the subordinate class provides all or most of the labor, the dominant class reaps all or most of the benefits. In feudal societies, barons exploited serfs by imposing high taxes and tithes (a proportion of the serf's produce); in capitalist societies, business owners pay workers less than the value of what they produce. Thus social stratification is determined by *the relations of production*—that is, the social relationships into which people must enter to obtain food, clothing, and other goods at a given stage of technological and economic development.

Marx argued that the class that controls the economic life of a society is in a position to control other aspects of social life as well. The law is designed to protect the interests of the dominant class; religion supports the status quo (for example, by teaching that those who accept hardship in this life will be rewarded in the next); and so on. "The ruling ideas of each age have ever been the ideas of its ruling class" (1864/1960). Marx argued, further, that the class into which a person is born largely determines that individual's modes of thinking and behaving. "It is not the consciousness of men that determines their existence, but on the contrary their social existence determines their consciousness" (1859). For Marx, economic relationships and material conditions were all-important.

Marx's theory of social stratification was grounded in his reading of history. He held that each stage in history is defined by a particular *mode of production*, which in turn gives rise to a distinctive form of social stratification. Capitalism, for example, depends not only on industrial technology (a mode of production), but also on private ownership of the means of production; this draws owners and nonowners into specific social-class relationships. Although he acknowledged periods of stagnation and historical "dead ends," Marx believed the overall trend was toward higher levels of production and higher standards of living. Feudalism represented an advance over tribalism, and capitalism, an advance over feudalism. In advanced capitalist societies there is greater choice of occupation, more room for personal development, more leisure time. Nature exerts less complete control over human activities.

In Marx's view, technological advances and social and political change are intertwined. As a society progresses, its own achievements make it obsolete, provoking revolution. For example, feudal societies laid the foundation for capitalist enterprises by producing surplus goods that could be traded and the raw materials for industrialization. But capitalism could not develop under existing relations of production. Feudal society was based on inherited social position and land; capitalism required opportunities for personal advancement based on technological innovations and investment of profits. The famous revolutions in England, France, and America in the sixteenth and seventeenth centuries, according to Marx, were revolutions on behalf of the rising capitalist class—what he called the *bourgeoisie*—against the constraints imposed by the old aristocracy. Similarly, Marx predicted that capitalism would eventually reach a point where its own advances could no longer be contained in a system where a relatively small number of people owned and controlled nearly all the means of production. Like the bourgeoisie before them, the workers—the *proletariat*—would unite to overthrow the system that held them back. For the first time in history, a class representing the majority of the population would control the means of production. Marx believed that ultimately the workers' socialist state would give rise to a communist society without class distinctions. Communism would mark the end of history based on class struggle, and the beginning of a new history determined by human potential.

Marx thought that proletarian revolutions were most likely to occur in advanced capitalist states—in his day, England, the Netherlands, and the United States. Because these societies were becoming more democratic, he thought the revolution might even be peaceful—though he doubted the bourgeoisie would give up power so easily. As it happened, most revolutions inspired by Marx occurred in less advanced countries during the transition from feudal, agricultural to industrial, capitalist production. Why have capitalist societies "avoided" revolution? In Marx's theory, revolution depends on increasing polarization, on a clear separation of class interests that provides the basis for organization, mobilization, and eventually revolutionary collective action (see Chapter 7). In other words, Marx believed that common exploitation would override other sources of group identity (religion, ethnicity, occupation, even nationality), uniting workers in a revolution against capitalism and its ruling elite. At least so far, this has not been the case.

Weber on Wealth, Power, and Prestige

Although he agreed with many of Marx's points, Max Weber found his analysis of social stratification oversimplified. Weber did not believe societies inevitably divide into two opposing camps of "haves" and "have nots," as Marx had argued. Where Marx saw sharply divided classes, Weber saw subtle, continuous gradations, with many intermediate groups. Moreover, he did not believe that politics, religion, and ideas are simply reflections of economic relationships. Although in some cases economics may determine the shape of religion, in others, religious beliefs shape economic pursuits (1904/1958). Whereas Marx was a strict materialist, Weber was more of an idealist, concerned with the meanings people attach to their actions in different social and historical contexts. (See Coser, 1977.)

Weber held that social stratification depends on the distribution of three resources: wealth (economic resources), power (political resources), and prestige (social resources). In many cases, the three go together. Thus, in our society wealthy business owners often gain power by contributing to political campaigns and earn prestige by making large donations to charity or to the arts. In other cases, however, the three are not linked. For example, in our society an individual who acquires wealth by criminal means acquires less prestige (in most circles) than someone who acquires comparable wealth by legitimate means. Artists, the clergy, and others may enjoy prestige but not wealth. On occasion people with few economic resources and little social prestige—bureaucrats, for instance—exercise considerable power. Each element in Weber's model deserves elaboration.

Ordinarily we think of wealth in terms of possessions: money, a house, a car. Both Marx and Weber used the term **wealth** to refer to rights over socially desirable objects as well as to ownership of the objects themselves. For example, oil companies can purchase the right to drill in the ocean (although not the ocean itself). Writers can copy*right* their ideas. A slave in Greece or the American South was "property" in the sense that the slave owner exercised rights over that person.

Marx and Weber differed on a central point, however. Marx emphasized production relations. He analyzed class position by asking, What does a person *do*? (Is he an owner-capitalist or a worker?) Weber emphasized market relations. For him the question was, How much does a person *get*? (Is she rich or poor?) And whereas Marx saw wealth as the decisive factor in social stratification, Weber believed that power and prestige were also significant.

Weber defined **power** as the ability of individuals or groups "to realize their own will in a communal action even against the resistance of others who are participating in that action" (1946, p. 180). Marx believed that in capitalist societies power is always rooted in economic relations. Weber agreed that this is often the case, but argued that power may come from other sources, too. For example, in some cases power automatically accompanies a social role. Thus in our society the President, police officers, professors, and parents exercise power over certain other people by virtue of their social positions. (Marx would say that, at least indirectly, these actors serve ruling-class interests.) In other cases power depends on the threat or use of physical force. Generals have power; so do street gangs. In still other cases, power derives from personal qualities such as intelligence, charm, and the ability to inspire and organize others—what Weber called "charisma." (See Chapter 15.)

Prestige refers to social standing, to the degree of respect or esteem a person receives from others. Marx believed that the way a person earns a living determines his or her *status*, or position in the social hierarchy. Weber held that the way a person *spends* his or her earnings is also significant. Cultural notions of proper consumption patterns and proper life style influence social standing. According to Weber, prestige also depends on how highly a culture values such characteristics as a person's ethnic and family background, religion, occu-

pation, and education. It depends on what people in a society define as beautiful, or courageous, intelligent, or holy. For example, in industrial societies occupation is a major source of prestige.

Weber held that because stratification is multidimensional, the formation of groups depends on which interests or identities people choose to emphasize. In capitalist societies, for example, ethnic and national identifications have proved more important than economic or class identification. Interests, in turn, shape strategies of group formation. For example, people who want to form groups based on prestige generally need to exclude outsiders. Exclusivity becomes a means of establishing elite domination. Subordinate groups who wish to challenge the elite need all the members they can get, however, and thus adopt an inclusive strategy (see Parkin, 1974). Thus, in Weber's view, Marx's division of society into two opposing classes ignored the complexities of social conflict in modern societies. The relationship between economics and power and prestige is variable. Modern societies are divided into different political parties and status groups as well as different economic classes. Sometimes the three aspects coincide, but other times they do not.

Functionalists and Meritocracy

A third theory of social stratification was introduced by Emile Durkheim and other European sociologists, but found its chief support among American sociologists. Functionalists argue that some form of social stratification is an inevitable and necessary part of social life. The classic statement of this view was made by the sociologists Kingsley Davis and Wilbert Moore (1945). Davis and Moore reasoned this way: Societies depend on individuals occupying a variety of interdependent social positions and performing the roles associated with those positions. If everyone had the ability and skills to fit any role, and if all roles were equally desirable and important, it wouldn't matter who occupied which position.

In fact, however, some roles are far more important and demanding than others. Moreover, everyone is not qualified to fill every role. Some roles require special talents and extensive training. To ensure that the right people take on important positions and are motivated to do their best, societies develop systems of unequal rewards. For example, in our society, physicians are rewarded with high income and prestige for the many years they spend in training and for the important but often unpleasant work they do. Digging ditches may also be socially necessary, but the job of ditch digger does not require a high degree of intelligence or a long period of training. For these reasons it is not highly rewarded. Functionalists maintain that this system of distributing unequal rewards ultimately benefits everyone.

Underlying the functionalist theory of stratification is the American ideal of a **meritocracy**—a system in which social rewards are distributed on the basis of achievement. What matters is what you yourself do. A meritocracy is based on equality of opportunity, not equality of outcome. Functionalists argue that some degree of inequality is necessary to motivate people to fill socially important roles.

Herbert Gans's analysis of the uses of poverty (1973) is a somewhat more sophisticated version of the functionalist position. Gans points out that poverty creates jobs—for public health and social workers, police officers and criminologists, pawnbrokers and journalists, not to mention racketeers and loan sharks. By working as migrant laborers, the poor reduce the costs of fruits and vegetables for other Americans. By working as domestics, they free middle- and upper-class people to pursue their careers and other interests full-time. The poor provide a market for inferior goods, such as day-old bread and secondhand clothes, and for inferior services, such as second-rate doctors and teach-

ers. They help to "keep the aristocracy busy" with charity drives. As the last example suggests, Gans is speaking tongue-in-cheek. But his point is a serious one: Many people derive some benefit from the existence of a poor underclass. In this sense, social stratification is "functional" for some segments of the population.

Lenski's Evolutionary View

Rather than examining the internal dynamics of one society, evolutionary theorists look at the pattern of change over the history of human societies (see Chapter 5). The most important statement of this point of view is found in Gerhard Lenski's *Power and Privilege* (1966). Examining different types of societies, Lenski concludes that through most of human history, advances in technology and productivity have led to increases in stratification. In other words, the more advanced a society becomes, the greater the gap between the top and bottom layers of society. Social inequalities are minimal

The extremes of inequality found in more complex societies do not exist in hunter-gatherer bands or horticultural villages, where each family produces what it needs to survive and no one works for a boss.

TABLE 8-4 Stratification and Social Systems

TYPE OF SOCIETY	ECONOMIC INEQUALITY	POLITICAL INEQUALITY	PRESTIGE
Hunters and gatherers	Nonexistent: resources communally owned; norms of sharing food and other goods	No formal leadership	Social honor achieved through individual talent and effort; ascribed on the basis of sex
Horticulturalists	Slight: rights to land controlled by clans, but redistribution of food and other goods institutionalized in feasts and potlach	"Big men" and warriors have no formal authority; chiefs may have authority over kin groups, but do not control resources or weapons	Social honor achieved through conspicuous display of generosity or bravery; ascribed status differences between the sexes more pronounced
Agrarian states	Pronounced and institutionalized: kings or emperors control resources in a territory by divine right; command economy .	A ruling elite monopolizes weaponry; exacts taxes, tribute, and forced labor; absolute rule; serfdom and slavery institutionalized	Institutionalization of rigid social strata; status inherited, not earned; little or no social mobility
Industrial nations	Gap between top and bottom strata narrows, and overall standard of living improves, but inequalities remain	Usually accompanied by adoption of democratic or socialist constitution promising equal rights to all citizens, but rights are variable in practice	Status increasingly based on achievement, especially education, occupation, and income; greater social mobility; but mobility limited by ascribed criteria based on race, ethnicity, religion, and sex

in hunter-gatherer societies, slight in horticultural societies, but pronounced in agrarian states. With the emergence of agrarian states, chiefs became kings and emperors, and ordinary people became serfs or even slaves. Extreme social inequalities were institutionalized; the individual's social status was ascribed at birth. Rights to land were hereditary, as was the right to rule. The *loss* of rights and obligation to labor and/or pay taxes were also hereditary. The result was marked differences in wealth, power, and prestige.

Looking to modern, industrial societies, Lenski concludes that this pattern (advances in technology and productivity equal increases in social inequality) has begun to reverse. Industrial societies are far from egalitarian. But neither are they as rigidly stratified as agrarian states. The overall effect of industrialization has been to reduce the gap between the top and bottom layers of society somewhat, and to raise the overall standard of living. Wealth, power, and prestige are more widely distributed. Individuals have greater opportunities to rise above the social level at which they were born, especially through education and occupation. There is more movement from one social class to another. But opportunities are limited by such factors as race, ethnicity, sex, and social origins.

These changes in the degree and form of social stratification over the course of human history are summarized in Table 8-4.

In Third World nations like El Salvador, a large proportion of the people are peasant farmers. Even so, most do not produce enough food to feed their populations.

In Lenski's view, one of the ironies of the industrial revolution is that while it reduced inequalities within industrial nations, it had the opposite effect on the world system, widening the gap between rich and poor nations (Lenski and Lenski, 1987).

*[Section 4 ends.
Section 5 begins.]*

GLOBAL STRATIFICATION

Immanuel Wallerstein (1974, 1980) was one of the first social scientists to point out that economic relations are no longer confined within national boundaries, but form an international "world system." Following Wallerstein, Daniel Chirot (1986) argues that the industrial prosperity that Europe and North America have achieved over the last century was due in large part to the development of a global system of social stratification. In 1900, Europeans and Americans controlled much of the world, directly (as colonies) or indirectly (through influence and power). This led to a global division of labor. The wealthy, economically diversified, industrial powers of the Northern Hemisphere operated as an international upper class. The undeveloped nations of the Southern Hemisphere—what we now call the Third World—functioned as an international lower class, supplying raw materials, agricultural products, and cheap labor. A few nations like Japan, which were neither colonized nor industrialized in 1900, took on characteristics of an international middle class. Europeans ran their colonies like plantations. The government of, or

TABLE 8-5   Gross National Product Per Capita and Life Expectancy for Selected Countries*

	GNP PER CAPITA	LIFE EXPECTANCY AT BIRTH
Ethiopia	$ 130†	47 years
Bangladesh	160	51
China	290	69
Bolivia	580	53
Egypt	680	61
Thailand	850	64
Turkey	1,210	64
Mexico	1,830	69
Brazil	2,020	65
Yugoslavia	2,480	71
Korea, Republic of	2,690	69
Greece	4,020	76
Spain	6,010	77
Saudi Arabia	6,200	63
Israel	6,800	75
Singapore	7,940	73
Australia	11,100	76
France	12,790	77
Canada	15,160	77
Japan	15,760	78
United States	18,530	75
Switzerland	21,330	77

*Note that while life expectancy is in general correlated with gross national product per capita, there are striking exceptions. China, for example, has a very high life expectancy for its income group, due largely to its advanced health care policies and the fairly even distribution of income. Saudi Arabia has a relatively low life expectancy for its income level because that income is very recent and based overwhelmingly on one product (oil) not yet matched by overall level of economic development.
†In 1987 dollars.
Source: Adapted from *World Development Report 1989* by the World Bank. Copyright © 1989 by the International Bank for Reconstruction and Development/The World Bank. Reprinted by permission of Oxford University Press, Inc.

companies from, the colonial power controlled mineral rights, transportation systems, the import-export business, and sometimes land. Their representatives acted as supervisors, making decisions about what would be produced in the colony and sometimes employing forced labor.

Although nearly all these former colonies have won political independence, the global system of stratification remains intact, for a number of reasons. First, while Western nations became increasingly diversified economically, colonies were encouraged to specialize in exporting agricultural crops and raw materials—coffee, peanuts, rubber, tin, and the like. Today, as nations, their economies are still centered on these exports. The price of coffee (or even oil) on the international market is not only lower than the price of manufactured goods, but fluctuates widely. Some conflict theorists (Paige, 1975) hold that stratification systems based on export agriculture are responsible for many of the revolutions in Third World nations. Others (Arrighi, 1972; Amin, 1981) hold that First World nations keep the price of manufactured goods artificially high to maintain their economic dominance over these nations.

Second, the populations of Third World nations have expanded rapidly. In many, a substantial majority of the people are dependents, too young or too old to work. Even though these nations are predominantly agricultural, they do not produce enough food to feed their populations, and depend on imports and aid from rich nations. Though necessary, such aid can be disruptive. For example, free or cheap food undercuts domestic food prices (Harrell-Bond, 1986).

Third, although Third World nations now control their own natural resources, industrial nations control most of the *technology* of mining, transportation, and trade (Goldthorpe, 1985). Third World nations must buy equipment, and sometimes hire technicians, from industrial nations. Capital for investments is scarce. When foreign investors build factories and plants, opportunities for internal development decline (Evans, 1979). (For example, Coca-Cola may replace local beverages produced by small entrepreneurs.) Multinational corporations that operate in Third World nations create low-level jobs, but often fill top managerial positions with personnel from industrial nations. Even when they do hire local managers, they tend to create a class of well-to-do people who are dependent on, and responsible to, foreign interests (Evans, 1979).

Some "middle-class" nations have improved their position in the global system—Japan being the most spectacular example. But movement out of a "lower-class" position is rare and largely dependent on the accidents of geography, such as possession of a valuable resource like oil. (See Table 8-5.) In some cases, rapid progress in industrialization has been made, only to be met by later crises. The OPEC countries are obvious examples. Mexico, Malaysia, and South Korea also met at least temporary problems in sustaining high economic growth rates. These newly industrial nations are particularly vulnerable to worldwide recessions and to fluctuations in prices on particular markets (such as oil).

By almost any measure, the United States today is in an upper-class position among nations. Nevertheless, competition with other industrial nations (such as Japan) and industrializing nations has weakened a number of industries (most notably the steel and automobile indus-

tries). Where this country will rank in the global stratification system in the year 2000 or 2050 remains to be seen.

[Section 5 ends.]

SUMMARY

A system of **social stratification** exists when social inequalities are institutionalized so that society is divided into layers or **social classes** whose occupants do not have equal access to social opportunities and rewards.

Most sociologists divide American society into six social classes. At one extreme is the upper class, which controls a major share of the nation's wealth. At the opposite extreme, more than 32 million Americans live below the federal **poverty line**, including many urbanites, women, children, and minority members. The black urban underclass is a recent phenomenon, brought about by the deindustrialization of cities and the combination of economic and racial segregation within cities. The consequences of poverty include shorter life spans and generally poor health, as well as greater vulnerability to economic swings.

The degree of **social mobility** varies from one society to another. In a **closed system**, like India's caste system, opportunities for upward mobility are almost nonexistent. In an **open system**, like the U.S. class system, equal opportunity for all is held as an ideal. In practice, however, social mobility is limited by such factors as race and sex. Upward mobility usually takes the form of small steps up the social ladder, not giant leaps "from rags to riches"—**structural mobility**, rather than individual success stories.

Why is social stratification so pervasive? Marx and Weber were pioneers in the analysis of social stratification. Marx emphasized the relations of production, and saw society as divided into opposing camps of haves and have-nots. Weber argued that there are many gradations in a society and that **power** and **prestige** (or social esteem) can be as important as **wealth** in determining social positions. Functionalists main-

tain that society needs a system of unequal rewards to ensure that qualified people will fill
important but demanding positions. Evolutionary theorists link stratification to technology. In
the past, technological advances led to increases
in social stratification, but this pattern has begun to reverse in modern industrial societies.

Recent history has produced a global system
of stratification, dividing the world into rich and
poor nations. Although an "upper-class nation,"
the United States is not immune to competition
from "lower-" and "middle-class" nations.

KEY TERMS

closed system
meritocracy
open system
poverty line
power
prestige
social class
social mobility
social stratification
structural mobility
wealth

Studying Sections 4 and 5

Activities for Sections 4 and 5

Continue taking notes. An enumeration will help you take notes and understand
this section of material, which covers pages 178–186.

THEORIES OF SOCIAL STRATIFICATION

1. Marx on Class Struggle:

   Key ideas in Marx's theory:

   a. Relations of production—_____

   _____

   b. Mode of production—_____

   _____

   c. Bourgeoisie—_____

   _____

   d. Proletariat—_____

   _____

2. Weber on Money, Power, and Prestige:

    Key ideas in Weber's theory:

    a. Wealth—_____

    _____

    b. Power—_____

    _____

    c. Prestige—_____

    _____

3. Functionalists and Meritocracy:

    Meritocracy—_____

    _____

4. Lenski's Evolutionary View:

    _____

    _____

    GLOBAL STRATIFICATION

    In 1900, Europeans and Americans controlled much of the world, directly (as colonies) or indirectly (through influence and power). This led to a global division of labor, with wealthy nations operating as an international upper class and undeveloped nations— the Third World—as an international lower class.

    Reasons why this global system remains intact:

    1. _____

    _____

    2. _____

    _____

    3. _____

    _____

Comments on Sections 4 and 5

- Notice here how headings, an enumeration, and definitions (signaled by terms set off in italic type) can help you take notes on the large amount of dense material included in "Theories of Social Stratification." First of all, each heading refers to a different theory, and so you should number the headings in your notes. Under each heading appear words that the authors have set off in italics while explaining each theory. As a minimum, make sure that you write down and understand those terms. In the case of Lenski's view, simply try to answer the question that you can form from the heading itself, "What is Lenski's evolutionary view?"

- The material under "Theories of Social Stratification" is extremely dense; it represents a summary of entire chapters on such theories in other books. With such material, it is possible that your instructor may expect you to remember only the high points about each theory that he or she may present within a class lecture. At the least, if you understand the terms set off in italics within the text, you should have a working sense of each theory.

- In general, it is your recognition and use of enumerations that can help you take organized notes on this closing section of the chapter.

Closing Comments

In the process of taking notes, you have reduced thirty pages of material to about four pages! These four pages provide an anchor for your understanding of the chapter. Keep in mind that if your instructor intends to test you on just this chapter, you may need to have a very detailed knowledge of the material, and you may want to do more rereading and add even more notes. On the other hand, if the instructor intends to test you on, say, this chapter and two other chapters, plus several weeks of classroom notes, it may well be that the four pages of notes will be more than enough. You will quickly develop skill at making a good judgment call about just how much you need to learn.

- Complete the following description of the final stage of textbook study:

  After taking as many notes as you need, your final step is to study the notes. To do so, put _____ words in the margin. For instance, the words "def of social strat." and "6 social classes" would help you learn the material on the first page of your notes. Your purpose would be to study until you could _____ to yourself the definition of *social stratification* and the six social classes without looking at them. You could then go on to study the other three pages of notes. After completing each page of notes, you should go back and _____ the previous pages. Through this process of repeated self-testing, you will effectively learn the material.

CHECKING YOUR MASTERY:
A QUIZ ON THE SAMPLE CHAPTER

After you have finished taking notes on the sample chapter, you or your instructor may decide that you should spend some time studying the notes. You can then use the following quiz to see how well you have learned the material.

■ Quiz on "Social Stratification"

1. *True or false?* _____ Occupation does not play an important role in class identification in the United States.
2. Wealth includes
   a. the real estate someone owns.
   b. a person's salary.
   c. rent collected on property.
   d. all of the above.
3. The departure of nonpoor blacks from city centers has had all of the following effects *except*
   a. a decrease in services (such as the work done by doctors, lawyers, and teachers) in the ghettos.
   b. lack of positive role models for black children who live in the ghettos.
   c. lack of networks that might enable ghetto residents to find work.
   d. increased stability among inner-city schools and businesses.

Items 4–6: Match each term with its definition.

4. Underclass _____   a. Men and women who have fallen below the poverty line in recent years because of changes in the economy.

5. Working poor _____   b. Men and women whose part-time jobs or seasonal employment do not pay enough to lift them above the poverty level.

6. Wealth _____   c. A hetergeneous population of individuals who are chronically unemployed, lack training and skills, and may drop out of the labor force, turning to the underground economy or crime for survival.
   d. The things people own, including stocks, bonds, and real estate.
   e. Social standing, the degree of respect or esteem a person receives from others.

7. In a closed social system, *all but which* of the following are true?
   a. Social status is determined by traits a person cannot control.
   b. Marriage between members of different castes is forbidden.
   c. Emphasis is placed on rewarding individual talent and hard work.
   d. An individual's caste will also determine his or her occupation.

8. *True or false?* _____ Structural mobility was an important factor in the rising standard of living in the United States in the 1950s and 1960s.

9. Meritocracy
   a. is a system in which social rewards are distributed on the basis of achievement.
   b. is based on equality of opportunity.
   c. emphasizes an individual's hard work and talents.
   d. All of the above are true.

10. All of the following are causes of increased homelessness *except*
    a. a decline in the demand for low-skilled workers.
    b. cutbacks in welfare programs for the poor.
    c. increased community clinics and halfway houses for the mentally ill.
    d. reductions in the supply of low-income housing.

BUILDING
A POWERFUL
MEMORY

This chapter will show you how to develop your memory by:

- Organizing the material to be learned
- Intending to remember
- Testing yourself repeatedly
- Using specific memory techniques
- Spacing memory work over several sessions
- Overlearning
- Studying before sleep

Introductory Projects

Project 1: Mastering class names.   Your instructor may present this activity on memory skills in one of the first classes of the semester, when you still do not know the names of the other people in the class. The instructor will ask you to learn each other's first names and (so as not to get in your way while you do this) will leave the room for ten or fifteen minutes. On returning, the instructor will call for volunteers to introduce him or her on a first-name basis to all the people in the room.

Afterward, the instructor will ask you to describe *how* you went about mastering the first names of all the people in the class. You will then have a chance to compare ideas with others on the memory processes that were used. You will probably find that in most cases the methods used to learn the names were similar. You may also realize for the first time that there *is* a definite process, or sequence of steps, involved in an act of memorization.

Project 2: A study problem.   Consider this common study situation:

> In two days, Steve will have a biology quiz in which he will have to write the definitions of ten terms that have been discussed in the course. As a study aid, the instructor has passed out a list of thirty terms that students should know thoroughly. Steve has gone through his class notes and textbook and copied down the definitions of the thirty terms. He tries to study the terms by reading them over and over, but he has trouble concentrating and merely keeps "reading words." He decides to write out each definition until he knows it. Hours later, he has written out ten definitions a number of times and is still not sure he will remember them. He begins to panic at spending such an enormous amount of time for such meager results. He decides to play Russian roulette with the terms—to study just some of them and hope they are the ones that will be on the test.

This chapter will provide answers to Steve's study problem. But take a few minutes first to examine your own ideas. What do you think are three specific steps that Steve could take to learn the thirty definitions?

Perhaps you think that memorizing material for a test is a waste of time; you may be convinced that you will forget what you memorize as soon as a test is over. Moreover, because some instructors believe that memorization and learning are incompatible, they may tell you that you shouldn't *memorize* material; rather, you should *understand* it.

Memorization, however, can be an important aid to understanding—and not just in situations where basic, uncomplicated material is involved. Effective memorizing requires that you organize and repeatedly test yourself on the material to be learned. As you do this, you are sure to enlarge your comprehension of the material and notice relationships you had not seen before. In short, memorization and understanding *reinforce* one another. Together, they help you learn—and learning is the goal of education. What you need, then, is a series of strategies, or steps, to help you memorize effectively. The following pages present seven such steps:

1 Organize the material to be learned.
2 Intend to remember.
3 Test yourself repeatedly on the material to be learned.
4 Use specific memory techniques.
5 Space memory work over several sessions.
6 Overlearn the material.
7 Use as a study period the time just before going to bed.

STEP 1: ORGANIZE THE MATERIAL TO BE LEARNED

The first key to effective remembering is *organizing the material to be learned* in some meaningful way. For example, in the memorization activity described on page 191, students often begin by introducing themselves in isolated pairs. This is not an effective method for learning all the names, however, and someone usually suggests that the introductions be done in an organized manner. What then happens is that, one by one, people take turns giving their names. Some students even jot down a rough seating chart (another organizational device) to aid them in learning all the names. The point is that some meaningful kind of *organization* is a vital first step in the memory process. The following two examples should also show how organizing material will aid memory.

Example A: Suppose that you had to memorize these numbers in any sequence:

> 1, 10, 7, 12, 22, 28, 20

You could eventually memorize the numbers by sheer mechanical repetition. However, you could learn them far more quickly, and remember them far longer, by grouping them in a meaningful and logical way:

$$10 + 12 = 22$$
$$1 + 7 + 20 = 28$$

Example B: Suppose that before leaving for school or work, you were asked to look at a shopping list on the kitchen blackboard and to pick up the items later at the store. To save the time of writing down the items, and to exercise your memory, you look over the list:

> Vaseline
> cheese
> Bufferin
> graham crackers
> Oreo cookies
> minute steaks
> Crest
> pressed ham
> M & M's

It would be difficult to memorize these items at random, and so you organize them into meaningful groupings, as shown on the following page.

Medicine-Chest Items	Snacks	Staples
Crest	graham crackers	cheese
Bufferin	Oreo cookies	minute steaks
Vaseline	M & M's	pressed ham

The three groups of related items are far easier to study and remember than the nine random items.

To be an effective student, you must learn how to organize the material in classroom lectures and reading assignments. It is easier to remember ideas and details that are related to one another than ones that are isolated, unorganized, and unrelated. In this book, ''Taking Classroom Notes'' will help you learn how to organize the material in classroom lectures, and the three chapters on textbook study (pages 88–190) will help you tie together ideas and details in reading assignments. You will then be ready to memorize any of the information that it is necessary for you to remember.

■ Material in your class notes and textbooks should be _____ in some meaningful way before you attempt to memorize it.

STEP 2: INTEND TO REMEMBER

A second important aid to memory is *deciding to remember*. This bit of advice appears to be so obvious that many people overlook its value. But if you have made the decision to remember something and you then work at mastering it, you *will* remember. Anyone can have a bear-trap memory by working at it; no one is born with a naturally poor memory.

In the introductory project on memorizing class names, students are often surprised at their ability to learn the names so quickly and completely. A main reason for their success is that they have *decided* to learn—for it might be embarrassing to be the only one not to have mastered the names when the instructor returned. The lesson here is that *your attitude is crucial in effective memorization:* You must begin by saying, ''I am going to master this.''

■ Do you ever have trouble, as many people do, in remembering the names of persons you are introduced to? _____ Yes _____ No

■ If you do, the reason is probably that you did not consciously decide to remember their names. Suppose you were introduced to a person who was going to borrow money from you. Is it safe to say you would make it a point to remember (and so *would* remember) that person's name? _____ Yes _____ No

STEP 3: TEST YOURSELF REPEATEDLY
ON THE MATERIAL TO BE LEARNED

After you have organized the material you intend to learn, memorize it through *repeated self-testing.* Look at the first item in your notes; then look away and try to repeat it to yourself. When you can repeat the first item, look at the next item; look away and try to repeat it. When you can repeat the second item, *go back* without looking at your notes and repeat the first *and* second items. After you can recall the first two items without referring to your notes, go on to the third item, and so on. In short, follow this procedure: *After you learn each new item, go back and test yourself on all the previous items. This constant review is at the heart of self-testing* and is the key to effective memorization.

■ If you were memorizing a list of ten definitions, what would you do after you mastered the second definition? The sixth? The tenth?

_____

STEP 4: USE SPECIFIC MEMORY TECHNIQUES

The following techniques will help you in the self-testing process:

1 Use several senses.
2 Use key words.
3 Use catchwords.
4 Use catchphrases.

The last two techniques are sometimes called *mnemonic* (*nǐ mǒn'ǐk*) devices. (The term is derived from the Greek word for *memory.*) Each technique is explained and illustrated on the pages ahead.

Use Several Senses

Use *several senses* in the self-testing process. Studies have shown that most people understand and retain information more effectively when several senses are involved in learning the material. Do not, then, merely recite the information silently to yourself. Also repeat it out loud so that you *hear* it, and write it down so that you both *see* and, as it were, *touch* it. These steps will help you learn more than you would if you only repeated the information silently to yourself.

■ What senses do you use in studying material? _____

_____

Use Key Words

Key words can be used as "hooks" to help you remember ideas. A *key word* stands for an idea and is so central to the idea that if you remember the word, you are almost sure to remember the entire concept that goes with the word.

Here is an illustration of how key words may function as hooks to help you recall ideas. Assume that your biology instructor has announced that the class will be tested on a textbook chapter dealing with the ecology of urban life. This is one important paragraph taken from that chapter.

> Urban planners who want to replace living plants with plastic ones seem to think that the city does not need to have living plants in it. Actually, plants do many useful things in a city even if they are not producing food for people. Plants improve the quality of the air by giving off oxygen and woodsy-smelling compounds, such as those emitted by pine trees. Smog contains some gases that, in low concentrations, can be used as nutrients by plants. Thus plants can absorb some air pollutants. Evaporation of water from plants cools the air; also, the leaves of plants catch falling dust particles. Trees and shrubs muffle the noise of what otherwise could be the deafening sound of street traffic and construction work. Finally, the roots of plants—even weeds on vacant lots—help to hold earth in place and reduce the number of soil particles blown into the air and washed into sewers.

Since you want to learn this information, you would first prepare study notes that might look something like this:

Uses of Plants in City

1. *Give off oxygen (and pleasant smell)*
2. *Absorb air pollutants (gases used as nutrients)*
3. *Cool the air (evaporation from leaves)*
4. *Catch dust particles*
5. *Muffle noises (traffic, construction)*
6. *Hold earth in place*

It is now necessary for you to memorize the study notes, and to do that you will need a technique.

One way to memorize these study notes is to use key words as hooks. What you do is circle a key word from each of the listed items. The word you select should help you pull into memory the entire idea that it represents. Write each of the words, one after the other, under the study notes.

Here is how your notes would look.

Uses of Plants in City

1. Give off（oxygen）(and pleasant smell)
2. Absorb air（pollutants）(gases used as nutrients)
3.（Cool）the air (evaporation from leaves)
4. Catch（dust）particles
5.（Muffle）noises (traffic, construction)
6. Hold（earth）in place

Key words: oxygen, pollutants, cool, dust, muffle, earth

After you pick out key words, the next step would be to test yourself repeatedly until you remember each of the six key words *and* the concepts they stand for.

■   Take five minutes to study your six key words for the uses of plants in the city. Test yourself until you can recite from memory all the words and the ideas they stand for. Your instructor may then ask you to write from memory the six words and concepts on a sheet of paper.

Use Catchwords

Sometimes people who use key words to pull central ideas into memory can't remember one of the key words, and so they forget the entire concept represented by that word. Using catchwords is one way to ensure that you remember an entire series of key words and the ideas they stand for. *Catchwords* are words made up of the first letters of other words. (See also page 108.)

Follow these guidelines when you prepare catchwords. First, circle the key words in your study notes. Then write down the first letter of each key word. Here are the first letters for the key words in the paragraph about city plants: O (oxygen), P (pollutants), C (cool), D (dust), M (muffle), and E (earth). Now, if necessary, rearrange the letters to form an easily recalled catchword. It can be a real word or a made-up word. For example, you might remember the letters O-P-C-D-M-E with the made-up word MEDCOP.

What matters is that you create a word that you can automatically remember and that the letters in the word help you recall the key words (and so the ideas the key words represent).

After you create a catchword, test yourself until you are sure each letter stands for a key word in your mind. Here is how you might use the catchword MEDCOP to pull into memory the textbook paragraph about city plants:

MEDCOP
M = muffle
E = earth
D = dust
C = cool
O = oxygen
P = pollutants

Cover the key words (*muffle, earth,* etc.) with a sheet of paper, leaving only the first letter exposed. Look at the letter M and see if you can recall the key word *muffle* and the idea that plants muffle noise. Next, look at the letter E and see if you remember the key word *earth* and the idea that plant roots hold the earth in place. Then do the same for the other four letters. In each case, the letter serves as a hook to pull into memory the key word and then the whole idea.

Here is an illustration of how first letters and key words help you remember ideas. As shown here, the first letter helps you remember the key word, which helps you pull the entire idea into memory.

First Letter	Key Word	Entire Idea
M ⟶	muffle ⟶	muffle noise of traffic and construction
E ⟶	earth ⟶	hold earth in place
D ⟶	dust ⟶	catch dust particles
C ⟶	cool ⟶	cool the air
O ⟶	oxygen ⟶	give off oxygen
P ⟶	pollutants ⟶	absorb air pollutants

■ An instructor in a psychology class described the following four techniques used in behavior therapy: (1) extinction, (2) imitation, (3) reinforcement, and (4) desensitization. Make up a catchword that will help you remember the four techniques and write the word here: _____

Use Catchphrases

Another way to remember key words is to form some easily recalled *catchphrase* (see page 109). Each word in a catchphrase begins with the first letter of a different key word. For example, suppose you had to remember the six uses of city plants in the exact order in which they are presented in the textbook paragraph (*oxygen, pollutants, cool, dust, muffle, earth*). You would write a six-word phrase with the first word beginning with *O*, the second with *P*, the third with *C*, and so on. Here is a catchphrase you might create to help remember the order of the six letters and the key words they stand for:

> *Our parents cook dinner most evenings.*

Your catchphrase does not have to be perfect grammatically; it does not even have to make perfect sense. It simply needs to be a phrase which will stick in your memory and which you will automatically remember.

Once you create a catchphrase, follow the testing process described above in the section on catchwords. Note that the first letter of each word in the catchphrase pulls into memory a key word, and the key word recalls an entire idea. For example, the O in *Our* recalls the key word *oxygen* and the idea that plants give off oxygen, the P in *parents* helps you remember the key word *pollutants* and the idea that plants absorb air pollutants, and so on.

■ Suppose an instructor wants you to learn the following five influences on a child's personality. The influences are listed in order of importance.

Influences on Children

One: Parents
Two: Siblings (brothers and sisters)
Three: Friends
Four: Close relatives
Five: Teachers

Make up a catchphrase that will help you remember in sequence the five influences on children and write the phrase here:

_____

STEP 5: SPACE MEMORY WORK
OVER SEVERAL SESSIONS

If you try to do a great deal of self-testing at any one time, you may have trouble absorbing the material. Always try to *spread out your memory work.* For instance, three two-hour sessions will be more effective than one six-hour session.

Spacing memory work over several time periods gives you a chance to review and lock in material you have studied in an earlier session but have begun to forget. Research shows that we forget a good deal of information right after studying it. However, review within a day reduces much of this memory loss. So try to review new material within twenty-four hours after you first study it. Then, if possible, several days later review it again to make a third impression or ''imprint'' of the material in your memory. If you work consistently to retain ideas and details, they are not likely to escape you when you need them during an exam.

■ Do you typically try to study the material for a test ''all at once,'' or do you spread out your study over several sessions?

_____

■ How might you spread out six hours of memory work that you need to do for a biology exam?

_____

_____

STEP 6: OVERLEARN THE MATERIAL

If you study a subject beyond the time needed for perfect recall, you will increase the length of time that you will remember it. You can apply the principle of *overlearning* by going over several times a lesson you have already learned perfectly. The method of repeated self-testing is so effective partly because it forces you to overlearn. After you study each new idea, the method requires that you go back and recite all the previous ideas you have studied.

Another way to apply the principle of overlearning is to devote some time in each session to review. Go back to restudy—and overlearn—important material that you have studied in the past. Doing so will help ensure that you will not push old ideas out of memory at the time you are learning new ones.

■ If you memorize a list of ten definitions using the process of repeated self-testing, how many times, at a minimum, will you have tested yourself on the

first definition? _____

STEP 7: STUDY BEFORE GOING TO BED

Study thoroughly the material to be learned. Then go right to sleep without watching a late movie or allowing other activities to interfere with your new learning. *Studying just before going to bed* will let your mind work through and absorb much of the material during the night. Set your clock a half hour earlier than usual so that you will have time to go over the material as soon as you get up. The morning review will complete the process of solidly fixing the material in your memory.

■ Have you ever used this technique and found it to be helpful? _____

_____

■ Do you think you should practice the technique daily or more as a study aid

in the review period before an exam? _____

PRACTICE IN BUILDING A POWERFUL MEMORY

Activity 1

1. A sociology instructor describes the following four elements of social class. Make up a catchword that will help you remember all four elements:

    Elements of Social Class
    Money
    Occupation
    Education
    Self-identification

2. A data-processing instructor writes on the board five types of electrical accounting machines. Make up a catchword that will help you remember the five kinds of machines.

    Electrical Accounting Machines
    Sorter
    Reproducer
    Collator
    Interpreter
    Accounting machine

3. The following six sources of nutrients are presented in a lecture on nutrition. Use a catchword or catchphrase to memorize the sources in any order.

   Sources of Nutrients
   Carbohydrates
   Fats
   Proteins
   Minerals
   Vitamins
   Water

4. You have memorized three groups of items individually. Now take ten to fifteen minutes to prepare for a quiz in which you will be asked to write from memory the four elements of social class, the five kinds of accounting machines, and the six sources of nutrients.

Activity 2

1. A psychology text explains the five stages of the dying process identified by Elisabeth Kübler-Ross. The sequential stages are listed below.

   Five Stages of the Dying Process
   Denial
   Anger
   Bargaining
   Depression
   Acceptance

   Use a catchphrase to memorize these five stages *in sequence*.

2. A business text describes five modes of transportation used for moving goods. These modes are arranged in order from the least expensive to the most expensive.

   Five Modes of Moving Goods
   Waterways
   Motor trucks
   Pipelines
   Railroads
   Airplanes

   Use a catchphrase to memorize these five modes *in sequence*.

3. You have memorized two groups of items individually. Now take about five minutes to prepare for a quiz in which you will be asked to write from memory, and in sequence, the five stages of the dying process and the five modes of transportation.

Activity 3

1. Read the following selection from a psychology text. Then look over the study notes on the selection.

INFLUENCING BEHAVIOR THROUGH APPROVAL

In order to make your approval truly reinforcing to the other person, you should follow a few rules. First, increase your rate of approval gradually. Don't wake up one morning and start complimenting everything about other people; they will begin to wonder what you want from them. Second, praise things that other people consider important—things that they have worked on and care about. If a woman doesn't give a hoot about her cooking but prides herself on being witty, praise her wit rather than her cooking. Third, be specific in your praise. Don't just say, "You were awfully witty tonight." Pick out specific details (for example, "I loved it when you told Suzanne . . ."). This will show the person that you're not just manufacturing compliments; you really did notice. The fourth and by far the most important rule is: be sincere. Most people despise insincere praise; they rightfully take it as an insult to their intelligence. Furthermore, most people can easily sniff out insincere praise. So the most crucial aspect of an approval-increasing program is the last step: finding things in the other person that you really *do* approve.

Study Notes

Rules for Reinforcing the Behavior of Others

First: Increase rate of approval gradually.

Second: Praise things the other person considers important.

Third: Be specific in your praise.

Fourth: Be sincere.

Pick out a key word for each of the four rules and then use a catchword or catchphrase to memorize the rules. *Hint:* Do not use the word *praise* as a key word, for praise is included or implied in all the rules.

2. Read the following selection from a sociology text. Then look over the study notes on the selection.

BUILT-IN PROBLEMS OF MARRIAGE

Even happily married people jokingly speak of the "ball and chain," admitting that in marriage, freedom is reduced. Whenever we are close to another person, whether in marriage or in friendship, we have to take the other person's needs into account. In our type of society, which values individual freedom, people may resent this. Many newlyweds find it hard to learn the art of give-and-take.

Making decisions is not always easy. Conflicts are sure to arise. In these situations, it is easy for the person who cares most about the marriage to become the loser, feeling that he or she must always "give in" to keep the peace. There are dangers that if the same person constantly gives in, resentments will build up.

When setting up a new household turns out to be more expensive than expected, arguments about money may arise. In fact, arguments over money are among the most common conflicts in marriage.

The romantic myth may also lead the partners to expect greater harmony than is usually possible between people. The unrealistic expectations that are part of the romantic myth may lead to disillusionments. The problem is that the intoxication of falling in love is at variance with the everyday routine of marriage.

In American society, the family is often an isolated unit, located far from relatives and without strong neighborhood ties. In less mobile societies, the extended family (relatives) provides strong support to marriage and family life. Anthropologists have noted the contrast between the two types of society and see isolation as a particularly severe problem for American families.

Study Notes

Problems of Marriage

One: Freedom is limited.

Two: Decision making is not always easy.

Three: Arguments about money may arise.

Four: Unrealistic and romantic expectations may lead to disillusionments.

Five: Family is often an isolated unit.

Pick out a key word for each of the five problems and then use a catchword or catchphrase to memorize the problems.

3. You have memorized two groups of items individually. Now take about ten minutes to prepare for a quiz in which you will be asked to write from memory the four rules for reinforcing behavior and the five problems of marriage.

Activity 4

Here is a study outline of the selection on pages 409–415 of this book that describes the process of job hunting. Use several catchwords to memorize the entire study outline.

Four Stages in Getting a Job

A. Make contact through:
    1. College placement bureau
    2. Want ads and employment agencies
    3. Telephone calls
    4. Personal connections
B. Prepare essential written materials
    1. Résumé
    2. Cover letter
C. Go out on interview
    1. Interview etiquette
    2. Prepare responses to some typical questions
        a. "Why are you interested in this job?"
        b. "What are your greatest strengths and weaknesses?"
        c. "Tell me about yourself."
        d. "Why should we hire you?"
    3. Come across as a competent person
D. Follow up on interview with thank-you note

Activity 5

This activity will help you apply memory techniques to different kinds of lecture and textbook notes. Use catchwords or catchphrases to do one or more of the following:

■ Learn the three states of mind that are not love (pages 63–64).
■ Learn the concentration hints (pages 82–85).
■ Learn the six elements in communication (pages 120–123).

Activity 6

From one of your course textbooks or the class notes from one of your courses, select a list of important items that you will need to remember. Then do three things:

1. Write the full list on a sheet of paper.
2. Circle key words that will help you remember each item on the list.
3. Make up a catchword or catchphrase to remember the first letters of the key words.

Turn in a copy of your work to your instructor.

Activity 7

Select four lists of important items to remember from the sample textbook chapter on pages 149–186. Then do the three things listed in Activity 6.

TAKING OBJECTIVE EXAMS

This chapter will show you how to:

- Prepare for and take tests in general
- Prepare for objective exams
- Take objective exams
- Cram when you have no other choice

Introductory Project

Consider this common study situation:

> Most of the exams Rita takes include both multiple-choice and true-false questions as well as at least one essay question. She has several problems with such tests. She often goes into the test in a state of panic. "As soon as I see a question I can't answer," she says, "big chunks of what I do know just fly out the window. I go into an exam expecting to choke and forget." Another problem is her timing. "Sometimes I spend too much time trying to figure out the answer to tricky multiple-choice or true-false questions. Then I end up with only fifteen minutes to answer two essay questions." Rita's greatest difficulty is writing essay answers. "Essays are where I always lose a lot of points. Sometimes I don't read a question the right way, and I wind up giving the wrong answer to the question. When I do understand a question, I have trouble organizing my answer. I'll be halfway through an answer and then realize that I've skipped some material I should have put at the start or that I've already written down something I should have saved for the end. I have a friend who says that essays are easier to study for because she can usually guess what the questions will be. I don't see how this is possible. Essay tests really scare me, since I never know what questions are coming."

This chapter and the following chapter will provide answers to Rita's study problem. But take a few minutes first to examine your own ideas. What do you think are three specific steps that Rita should take to begin dealing more effectively with tests?

AVOIDING EXAM PANIC

A familiar complaint of students is, "I'm always afraid I'll panic during an exam. I'll know a lot of the material, but when I sit down and start looking at the questions, I forget things that I know. I'll never get good grades as long as this happens. How can I avoid it?" The answer is that if you are *well prepared,* you are not likely to block or panic on exams.

"How, then," you might ask, "should a person go about preparing for exams?" The answer is plain: You must go to class consistently, read the textbook and any other assigned material, take class and textbook notes, and study and at times memorize your notes. In short, you must start preparing for exams in the first class of the semester. The pages that follow offer a series of practical suggestions to help you use your study time efficiently.

Note: Many suggestions in this chapter assume that you know how to take effective classroom and textbook notes and how to memorize such notes. If you have not developed these essential skills, refer to the appropriate chapters.

- *Complete the following sentence:* You are unlikely to forget material during

   exams if you are _____.

WHAT TO STUDY

You will not always know beforehand if a scheduled exam will be an objective or an essay test (or a combination of both). To be prepared for whichever kind is given, you should, throughout the course, pay attention to the following.

Key Terms: Look for key terms, their definitions, and examples that clarify their meaning (see also page 319). Look for this material in your class and textbook notes. If your textbook notes are not complete, go back to the original reading material to locate key terms. They are often set off in *italic* or **boldface** type.

- Which of the courses you are now taking involves a number of new terms

   that you will probably have to know for exams? _____

Enumerations: Look for enumerations (lists of items) in your class and textbook notes (see also page 326). Enumerations are often the basis of essay questions.

Items in a list will probably have a descriptive heading—for example, characteristics of living things, major schools of contemporary psychology, primary consequences of the Industrial Revolution—and the items may be numbered. Be sure to learn the heading that describes the list as well as the items in the list.

Points Emphasized: Look for points emphasized in class or in the text. Often phrases such as *the most significant, of special importance, the chief reason,* and so on (see page 348) are used to call attention to important points in a book or a lecture. When you take notes on such material, mark these significant points with the abbreviation *imp,* an asterisk (*), or some other mark.

Also, as you go through your class notes, concentrate on areas the instructor spent a good deal of time discussing. For example, if the instructor spent a week talking about present-day changes in the traditional family structure, you can reasonably expect to get a question on this emphasized area. Similarly, review your textbook. If many pages in a chapter deal with one area, you may be sure that subject is important, and so you should expect a question about it on an exam.

- Write below the name of one of your courses and an area that your instructor has spent a good deal of time discussing in the course.

  Course: _____

  Area: _____

Topics Identified by the Instructor: Pay attention to areas your instructors have advised you to study. Some instructors conduct in-class reviews during which they tell students what material to emphasize when they study. Always write down these pointers; your instructors have often made up the test or are making it up at the time of the review and are likely to give valuable hints about the exam. Other instructors indicate the probable emphasis in their exams when they distribute reviews or study guides. You should, of course, consider these aids very carefully.

- One study-skills instructor has said, "I sometimes sit in on classes, and time and again I have heard instructors tell students point-blank that something is to be on an exam. Some students quickly jot down this information; others sit there in a fog." Which group of students do you belong to?

  _____

- What are some specific study aids instructors have given to help you prepare for tests? _____

  _____

Questions on Earlier Tests: Pay attention to questions on past quizzes and reviews as well as tests at the end of textbook chapters.

If you follow these suggestions, you will have identified most, if not all, of the key concepts in the course.

GENERAL TIPS: BEFORE THE EXAM

The following hints will help you make the most of your time before a test.

Hint 1:   Spend the night before an exam making a final review of your notes. Then go right to bed without watching television or otherwise interfering with the material you have learned. Your mind will tend to work through and absorb the material during the night. To further lock in your learning, get up a half hour earlier than usual the next morning and review your notes.

■   Do you already review material on the morning of an exam? _____

    If so, have you found it to be very helpful? _____

Hint 2:   Make sure you take with you any materials (pen, paper, eraser, dictionary, and other aids allowed) you will need during the exam.

Hint 3:   Be on time for the exam. Arriving late sets you up to do poorly.

Hint 4:   Sit in a quiet spot. Some people are very talkative and noisy before an exam. Since you don't want anything to interfere with your learning, you are better off not talking with others during the few minutes before the exam starts. You might want to use those minutes to make one final review of your notes.

■   How do you typically spend the minutes in class right before an exam?

    _____

Hint 5:   Read over carefully *all* the directions on the exam before you begin. Many students don't take this important step and end up losing points because they fail to do what is required. Make sure you understand how you are expected to respond to each item, how many points each section is worth, and how many questions you must answer. Also listen carefully to any oral directions or hints the instructor may give. Many students wreck their chances at the start because they do not understand or follow directions. Don't let this happen to you.

■   Do you already have the habit of reading all the directions on an exam carefully

    before you begin? _____

Hint 6:   Budget your time. Take a few seconds to figure out roughly how much time you can spend on each section of the test. Write the number of minutes in the margin of your exam paper or on a scratch sheet. Then stick to that schedule. Be sure to have a watch or to sit where you can see a clock.

Exactly *how* you budget your time depends on what kinds of questions you are good at answering (and so can do more quickly) and the point value of different sections of the test. Keep in mind that the reason for budgeting your time is to prevent you from ending up with ten minutes left and a fifty-point essay still to write or thirty multiple-choice questions to answer.

Activity 1

This activity will check your skill at following written directions.

A Test in Following Directions: First read all ten directions carefully. Then follow them.

_____   _____

1. Print your full name in capital letters, last name first, on the line at the right-hand side above.
2. Write your first and last names, first name last, followed by your middle initial, on the line at the left-hand side above.
3. Count the number of vowels (*a, e, i, o,* or *u*) in your first name and enter the number in the margin to the right of this line.
4. Fold this sheet of paper in equal thirds, lengthwise, and then open it again.
5. Read the following question carefully and answer it in the space provided. "What was the last thing Thomas Jefferson said after he died?"

_____

6. Disregard the fourth instruction.
7. Write down the name of your brother or sister's father's wife, *or* write down the name of your grandfather's son's son or daughter.

_____

8. Draw a small equilateral triangle around the number of this question; then use a dotted line to draw a half-inch square around the number of the next question.
9. Cross out the three-letter words, circle the four-letter words, and underline the five-letter words in this sentence. Then indicate in the space that follows

   the number of words left unmarked. _____
10. If a zatron lorked two statergills of reprocene, how many hollybutts cranched the zatron?

_____

Activity 2

Here is an activity that will check your skill at budgeting time. Suppose that you had two hours for a test made up of the following sections:

Part 1:   10 true-false questions worth 10 points   (_____minutes)

Part 2:   40 multiple-choice questions worth 40 points   (_____minutes)

Part 3:   2 essay questions worth 50 points   (_____minutes)

In the spaces provided, write how much time you would spend on each part of this test.

One possible division of time is to spend an hour on the first two parts (about ten minutes on the true-false questions and fifty minutes on the multiple-choice questions) and a half hour on each essay question. Because the essay questions are worth half the points on the test, you want at least an hour to work on them.

PREPARING FOR AND TAKING OBJECTIVE EXAMS

Objective exams may include multiple-choice, true-false, fill-in, and matching questions. Perhaps you feel that objective tests do not require as much study time as essay exams do. A well-constructed objective test, however, can evaluate your understanding of major concepts just as well as an essay exam and can demand just as sophisticated a level of thinking. Therefore, do not cut your study time short just because you know you will be given an objective test.

To do well on objective tests, you must know how to read test items carefully. The pages that follow describe a number of strategies you can use to deal with the special problems posed by objective tests.

Getting Ready for Objective Exams

Hint 1:   Be prepared to memorize material when studying for an objective test. The test may include short-answer questions. For example, the instructor may give several technical terms and ask you to define them. Or the instructor may give headings such as ''Three Values of the Social Security Act'' and expect you to list the values underneath. He or she may include fill-in questions such as ''An important leader of the stimulus-response school of psychology has been

_____.''

Even objective tests made up only of multiple-choice and true-false questions can include such fine distinctions that memorization may be necessary. In addition, memorization helps keep your study honest: it forces you to truly *understand* the material you are learning.

There is one difference worth noting between the kind of memorizing needed for essay exams and the kind needed for objective tests. In an essay test, you are expected to actually *recall course material.* For example, an essay test might ask you to list and explain three kinds of defense mechanisms. In an objective test, you are expected to *recognize the correctness of statements about course material.* For instance, an objective test might give you a defense mechanism followed by a definition and ask you whether that definition is true or false. In either kind of test, however, memory is required.

■ Describe the specific kinds of objective exams that your instructors give:

_____

Hint 2: Ask your instructor what kind of items will be on the test. Not all instructors will provide this information. However, finding out beforehand that an exam will include, let's say, fifty multiple-choice and fill-in items relieves you of some anxiety. At least you know what to expect.

Hint 3: Try to find a test that is similar to the one you will be taking. Some instructors distribute past exams to help students review. Also, some departments keep on file exams given in earlier semesters. Looking at these exams closely can familiarize you with the requirements, format, and items you may reasonably expect on your exam.

Hint 4: Be sure to review carefully all the main points presented in the course. These were detailed in ''What to Study'' on pages 208–209. To sharpen your understanding of the course's key material, apply the techniques of repeated self-testing (page 195) to the recall words written in the margin of your class and textbook notes (pages 48 and 99).

Hint 5: Make up practice test items when you study. That way you will be getting into the rhythm of taking the test, and you may even be able to predict some of the questions the instructor will ask.

Taking Objective Exams

Hint 1: Answer all the easier questions first. Don't lose valuable time stalling over hard questions. You may end up running out of time and not even getting a chance to answer the questions you can do easily. Instead, put a light check mark ($\sqrt{}$) beside difficult questions and continue working through the entire test, answering all the items you can do right away. You will find that this strategy will help give you the momentum you need to go confidently through the rest of the exam.

Hint 2: Go back and spend the time remaining with the difficult questions you have marked. Often you will find that while you are answering the easier questions, your unconscious mind has been working on questions you at first found very difficult. Or later items may provide just the extra bit of information you need to answer earlier items you found difficult. Once you answer a question, add a mark to the check you have already made ($\sqrt{}$) to show that you have completed that item.

Hint 3: Answer *all* questions unless the instructor has said that points will be deducted for wrong answers. Guess if you must; by doing so, you are bound to pick up at least a few points.

Hint 4: Ask the instructor to explain any item that isn't clear. Not all instructors will provide explanations, but probably many will. Most experienced instructors realize that test questions may seem clear and unambiguous to them as they make up the exam but that students may interpret certain questions in other and equally valid ways. In short, you can't lose anything by asking to have an item clarified.

Hint 5: Put yourself in the instructor's shoes when you try to figure out the meaning of a confusing item. In light of what was covered in the course, which answer do you think the instructor would say is correct? If a test item is worded so ambiguously that no single response seems correct, you may—in special situations—use the margin of your test paper to explain to the instructor what you feel the answer should be. Obviously, use this technique only when absolutely necessary.

Hint 6: Circle or underline the key words in difficult questions. This strategy can help you untangle complicated questions and focus on the central point in the item.

Hint 7: Express difficult questions in your own words. Rephrasing the item in simpler terms and then writing it down or even saying it to yourself can help you cut through the confusion and get to the core of the question. Be sure, however, not to change the original meaning of the item.

Hint 8: Take advantage of the full time given and go over the exam carefully for possible mistakes. People used to say that it is not a good idea to change the first answer you put down. However, as long as you have a good reason, you *should* change your earlier answers if they seem incorrect. At the same time, be on guard against last-minute anxiety that prompts you to change, without good reason, *many* of your original answers. You should control any tendency you may have to make widespread revisions.

Activity

Write here what you consider the three most important of the preceding hints for taking objective exams.

1. _____

2. _____

3. _____

Specific Hints for Answering Multiple-Choice Questions

1 Remember that in multiple-choice exams the perfect answer to a question may not be offered. You must choose the best answer *available.*

2 Cross out answers you know are incorrect. Eliminating wrong answers is helpful because it focuses your attention on the most reasonable options. If you think all options are incorrect, the correct answer is "none of the above."

3 Be sure to read all the possible answers to a question, especially when the first answer is correct. Remember that the other options could also be correct. In this case, "all of the above" would be the correct response.

4 Minimize the risk of guessing the answer to difficult items by doing either of the following:

   a Read the question and then the first possible answer. Next, read the question again and the second possible answer and so on until you have read the question with each separate answer. Breaking down the items this way will often help you identify the option that most logically answers the question.

   b Try not to look at the answers when you return to difficult items. Instead, read the question, supply your own answer, and then look for the option on the test that is closest to your response.

5 Use the following clues, which may signal correct answers, *only* when you have no idea of the answer and must guess.

a   The longest answer is often correct.

- *Use this clue to answer the following question:* The key reason students who are well prepared still don't do well on exams is that they (a) are late to the test, (b) don't have all their materials, (c) forget to jot down catchphrases, (d) haven't studied enough, (e) don't read all the directions before they begin the test.

    The correct answer is *e,* the longest answer.

b   The most complete and inclusive answer is often correct.

- *Use this clue to answer the following question:* If you have to cram for a test, which of these items should receive most of your attention? (a) The instructor's tests from other years, (b) important ideas in the class and text notes, including such things as key terms, their definitions, and clarifying examples, (c) the textbook, (d) class notes, (e) textbook notes.

    The correct answer is *b,* the most complete and inclusive choice. Note that the most complete answer is often also the longest.

c   An answer in the middle, especially if it is longest, is often correct.

- *Use this clue to answer the following question:* Many students have trouble with objective tests because they (a) guess when they're not sure, (b) run out of time, (c) think objective exams are easier than essay tests and so do not study enough, (d) forget to double-check their answers, (e) leave difficult questions to the end.

    The correct answer is *c,* which is in the middle and is longest.

d   If two answers have opposite meanings, one of them is probably correct.

- *Use this clue to answer the following question:* Before an exam starts, you should (a) sit in a quiet spot, (b) join a group of friends and talk about the test, (c) review the textbook one last time, (d) read a book and relax, (e) study any notes you didn't have time for previously.

    The correct answer is *a.* Note that *a* and *b* are roughly opposite.

e   Answers with qualifiers, such as *generally, probably, most, often, some, sometimes,* and *usually,* are frequently correct.

■   *Use this clue to answer the following question:* In multiple-choice questions, the most complete and inclusive answer is (a) never correct, (b) often correct, (c) always correct.

The correct answer is *b,* the choice with the qualifying word *often.* Note also that answers with absolute words, such as *all, always, everyone, everybody, never, no one, nobody, none,* and *only,* are usually incorrect.

■   *Use this clue to answer the following question:* In multiple-choice questions, the answer in the middle with the most words is (a) always correct, (b) always incorrect, (c) frequently correct.

The correct answer is *c;* the other answers use absolute words and are incorrect.

Activity

Write here what you consider the three most helpful clues when guessing the answer to a multiple-choice question.

1.   _____

2.   _____

3.   _____

Specific Hints for Answering True-False Questions

1   Simplify questions with double negatives by crossing out both negatives and then determining the correct answer.

■   *Use this hint to answer the following question: True or false?* _____
You won't be unprepared for essay exams if you anticipate several questions and prepare your answers for those questions.

The statement is true. It can be reworded to read, ''You will be prepared for essay exams if you anticipate several questions and prepare your answers for those questions.''

2 Remember that answers with qualifiers such as *generally, probably, most, often, some, sometimes,* and *usually* are frequently true.

■ *Use this hint to answer the following question: True or false?* _____ Some instructors tell students what kinds of items to expect on an exam.

The statement, which contains the qualifier *Some,* is true.

3 Remember that answers with absolute words such as *all, always, everyone, never, no one, nobody, none,* and *only* are usually false.

■ *Use this hint to answer the following question: True or false?* _____ You should never review your notes on the morning of an essay exam.

The statement, which contains the absolute word *never,* is false.

Specific Hints for Answering Fill-In Questions

1 Read the questions to yourself so that you can actually hear what is being asked. If more than one response comes to mind, write each response lightly in the margin. Then, when you review your answers later, choose the answer that feels most right to you.

2 Make sure each answer you provide fits logically and grammatically into its

slot in the sentence. For example: An _____ lists ideas in a sequence. The correct answer is *enumeration.* Note that the word *an* signals that the correct answer begins with a vowel. (Note, however, that test developers may phrase items to avoid giving hints, using devices like "A/An.")

3 Remember that not every fill-in answer requires only one word. If you feel that several words are needed to complete an answer, write in all the words unless the instructor or the directions indicate that only single-word responses will be accepted.

Specific Hints for Answering Matching Questions

1 Don't start to answer matching items until you read both columns and get a sense of the choices. Often, there's an extra item or two in one column. This means that not all items can be paired. Some will be left over. For example:

1. Sentence-skills mistakes _____
2. Absolute words _____
3. Connecting words _____
4. Qualifying words _____
5. Direction words in instructions _____

a. compare, explain, analyze
b. often, usually, most
c. from, over, in, with
d. misspelled and omitted words
e. all, never, only
f. first, second, next, also

The correct answers are 1-*d,* 2-*e,* 3-*f,* 4-*b,* and 5-*a.* Item *c* is extra.

2   Start with the easiest items in a matching question. One by one, focus on each item in one column and look for its match in the other column. Cross out items as you use them.

A FINAL NOTE:
HOW TO CRAM WHEN YOU HAVE NO OTHER CHOICE

Students who always cram for tests are not likely to be successful; they often have to cram because they have not managed their time well. However, even organized students may sometimes need to cram because they run into problems that disrupt their regular study routine. If you're ever in this situation, the following steps may help you do some quick but effective studying.

1   Accept the fact that, in the limited time you have, you are not going to be able to study everything in your class notes and textbook. You may even have to exclude your textbook if you know that your instructor tends to base most of a test on class material.

2   Read through your class notes (if you have them, also read through your textbook notes) and mark off those ideas that are most important. Use as a guide any review or study sheets that your instructor has provided. Your purpose is to try to guess as many as possible of the ideas your instructor will put in the test.

   Important ideas often include definitions, enumerations (lists of items), points marked by emphasis words, and answers to basic questions made out of titles and headings. See also the discussion of ''What to Study'' on pages 208–209.

3   Write the ideas you have selected on sheets of paper, using one side of a page only. Perhaps you will wind up with three or four ''cram sheets'' full of important points to study.

4   Prepare catchwords or catchphrases to recall the material and then memorize the points using the method of repeated self-testing described earlier, on page 195.

5   Go back, if time remains, and review all your notes. If you do not have textbook notes, you might skim your textbook. Do not use this time to learn new concepts. Instead, try to broaden as much as possible your understanding of the points you have already studied.

PRACTICE IN TEST TAKING

Activity 1

Evaluate your present test-preparation and test-taking skills. Put a check mark beside each of the following steps that you already practice. Then put a check mark beside those steps that you plan to practice. Be honest; leave a blank space if you do not plan to follow a particular point.

Now Plan
Do   to Do   *What to Study*

____ ____ Key terms, definitions, and examples

____ ____ Enumerations (lists of items)

____ ____ Points emphasized in class

____ ____ Reviews and study guides

____ ____ Questions in past quizzes and textbook chapters

General Tips before an Exam

____ ____ 1. Study right before sleep.

____ ____ 2. Take materials needed to the exam.

____ ____ 3. Be on time for the exam.

____ ____ 4. Sit in a quiet spot.

____ ____ 5. Read all directions carefully.

____ ____ 6. Budget your time.

Getting Ready for Objective Exams

____ ____ 1. Memorize as necessary.

____ ____ 2. Ask instructor about makeup of test.

____ ____ 3. Look at similar tests.

____ ____ 4. Review carefully all main points of course.

____ ____ 5. Make up practice test items.

Taking Objective Exams

____ ____ 1. Answer all easier questions first.

____ ____ 2. Do difficult questions in time remaining.

____ ____ 3. Answer all questions.

____ ____ 4. Ask instructor to explain unclear items.

____ ____ 5. For difficult questions, think of the instructor's point of view.

____ ____ 6. Mark key words in difficult questions.

____ ____ 7. State difficult questions in your own words.

____ ____ 8. Use all the time given.

____ ____ 9. Use the specific hints given for multiple-choice, true-false, fill-in, and matching questions.

Activity 2

All the questions that follow have been taken from actual college tests. Answer the questions by using the specific hints below for multiple-choice and true-false questions. Also, in the space provided, give the letter of the hint or hints used to determine the correct answer.

Hints for Test Taking

a   The longest multiple-choice answer is often correct.

b   The most complete and inclusive multiple-choice answer is often correct.

c   A multiple-choice answer in the middle, especially the one with the most words, is often correct.

d   If two multiple-choice answers have the opposite meaning, one of them is probably correct.

e   Answers with qualifiers, such as *generally, usually, probably, most, often, some, may,* and *sometimes,* are usually correct.

f   Answers with absolute words, such as *all, always, everyone, everybody, never, no one, nobody, none,* and *only,* are usually incorrect.

Hint _____   1. *True or false?* _____ Denial and intellectualization always reduce anxiety.

Hint _____   2. Newton's third law of motion is
   a. $x = 2y$.
   b.   "force equals mass times acceleration."
   c.   "for every force there is an opposing force of equal value."
   d.   a measure of inertia.

Hint _____   3. With a policy of exclusive market coverage, a manufacturer
   a.   expands the availability of a product.
   b.   restricts the availability of a product.
   c.   seeks multiple retail outlets.
   d.   advertises in low-circulation magazines.

*Hint*_____   4. *True or false?* _____ Too much thyroxine can often result in tenseness and agitation.

*Hint*_____   5. Charismatic authority is based on
    a. law.
    b. established behavior.
    c. belief in the extraordinary personal qualities of the ruler.
    d. religious beliefs.

*Hint*_____   6. Schizophrenics labeled *paranoid*
    a. always display "waxy flexibility."
    b. usually fear that they are being persecuted.
    c. are invariably the children of schizophrenics.
    d. always display multiple personalities.

*Hint*_____   7. Prohibition
    a. was supported mainly by urban dwellers.
    b. caused a decrease in crime.
    c. was an unqualified success.
    d. failed because of widespread violations, an upsurge in crime, and inadequate enforcement.

*Hint*_____   8. *True or false?* _____ A charged cloud may cause an induced charge in the earth below it.

*Hint*_____   9. A covalent bond is
    a. a bond between two atoms made up of a shared pair of electrons.
    b. impossible in organic compounds.
    c. an extremely unstable chemical bond.
    d. the basis of all inorganic compounds.

*Hint*_____   10. *True or false?* _____ The only factors influencing the decision of the United States to enter World War I were economic ones.

TAKING
ESSAY EXAMS

This chapter will show you:

- Two key steps in preparing for an essay exam
- Three key steps in writing an exam essay

Essay exams are perhaps the most common type of writing you will do in school. They include one or more questions to which you must respond in detail, writing your answers in a clear, well-organized manner. Many students have trouble with essay exams because they do not realize there is a sequence to follow that will help them do well on such tests. Here are five steps you should master if you want to write effective exam essays:

1 Anticipate probable questions.
2 Prepare and memorize an informal outline answer for each question.
3 Look at the exam carefully and do several things.
4 Prepare a brief, informal outline before answering an essay question.
5 Write a clear, well-organized essay.

Each step will be explained and illustrated on the pages that follow.

STEP 1: ANTICIPATE PROBABLE QUESTIONS

Because exam time is limited, the instructor can give you only a few questions to answer. He or she will reasonably focus on questions dealing with the most important areas of the subject. You can probably guess most of them.

Go through your class notes with a colored pen and mark those areas where your instructor has spent a good deal of time. The more time spent on any one area, the better the chance you'll get an essay question on it. If the instructor spent a week talking about the importance of the carbon molecule, or about the advantages of capitalism, or about key early figures in the development of psychology as a science, you can reasonably expect that you will get a question on the emphasized area.

In both your class notes and your textbooks, pay special attention to definitions and examples and to enumerations—basic lists of items. Enumerations in particular are often the key to essay questions. For instance, if your instructor spoke at length about the causes of the Great Depression, or about the long-range effects of water pollution, or about the advantages of capitalism, you should probably expect a question such as ''What are the causes of the Great Depression?'' or ''What are the long-range effects of water pollution?'' or ''What are the advantages of capitalism?''

If your instructor has given you study guides, look for probable essay questions there. (Some instructors choose their essay questions from among those listed in a study guide.) Look for clues to essay questions on any short quizzes that you may have been given. Finally, consider very carefully any review that the instructor provides. Always write down such reviews—your instructor has often made up the test or is making it up at the time of the review and is likely to give you valuable hints about the test. Take advantage of them! Note also that if the instructor does not offer to provide a review, do not hesitate to *ask* for one in a friendly way. Essay questions are likely to come from areas the instructor may mention.

- *Complete the following sentence:* Very often you can predict essay questions,

  for they usually concern the most _____ areas of a subject.

STEP 2: PREPARE AND MEMORIZE AN
INFORMAL OUTLINE ANSWER FOR EACH QUESTION

Write out each question you have made up and, under it, list the main points to be discussed. Put important supporting information in parentheses after each main point. You now have an informal outline that you can go on to memorize.

If you have spelling problems, make up a list of words you might have to spell in writing your answers. For example, if you are taking a psychology test on the principles of learning, you might want to study such terms as *conditioning, reinforcement, Pavlov, reflex, stimulus,* and so on.

An Illustration of Step 2: One class was given a day to prepare for an essay exam on the study schedule hints on pages 41–48. The students were told that the question would be, "Describe five hints to remember when planning a weekly study schedule." One student in the class, Kurt, made up the following outline answer for the question:

Five hints to remember when planning a weekly study schedule:

1. *Schedule (regular) study time (makes studying a habit, stay up to date, more effective).*
2. *Plan (one) hour blocks of study time (less is only a warm-up).*
3. *(Reward) yourself (people work better with rewards).*
4. *Study periods (before) and after classes (prepare for classes, review recent material).*
5. *Keep schedule (flexible) (juggle schedule when unexpected occurs).*

RORBF (Red oars row boats fast.)

Activity

See whether you can complete the following explanation of what Kurt has done in preparing for the essay question.

First, Kurt wrote down the heading and then numbered the five hints under it. Also, in parentheses beside each point he added _____. Then he picked out and circled a key _____ in each hint, and he wrote down the first _____ of each key word underneath his outline. Kurt then used the first letter in each key word to make up a catchphrase that he could easily remember. Finally, he _____ himself over and over until he could recall all five of the words that the first letters stood for. He also made sure that each word he remembered truly stood for an _____ in his mind and that he recalled much of the supporting material that went with each idea.

STEP 3: LOOK AT THE EXAM CAREFULLY
AND DO SEVERAL THINGS

1 Get an overview of the exam by reading *all* the questions on the test.

2 Note the direction words (*compare, illustrate, list,* and so on) for each question. Be sure to write the kind of answer that each question requires. For example, if a question says "illustrate," do not "compare." The list on the opposite page will help clarify the distinctions among various direction words.

3 Budget your time. Write in the margin the number of minutes you should spend for each essay. For example, if you have three essays worth an equal number of points and a one-hour time limit, figure twenty minutes for each one. Make sure you are not left with only a couple of minutes to do a high-point essay.

4 Start with the easiest question. Getting a good answer down on paper will help build your confidence and momentum. Number your answers plainly so that your instructor will know which question you answered first.

An Illustration of Step 3:   When Kurt received the exam, he circled the direction word *describe,* which meant that he should explain in detail each of the five hints. He also jotted "30" in the margin when the instructor said that students would have a half hour to write the answer.

Activity

Complete the short matching quiz below. It will help you review the meanings of some direction words.

1. Enumerate _____   a. Give the development or history of a subject

2. Compare _____   b. Explain by giving examples

3. Illustrate _____   c. List points and number them 1, 2, 3, etc.

4. Interpret _____   d. Show similarities between things

5. Trace _____   e. Explain the meaning of something

Direction Words Used in Essay Questions

Compare	Show similarities between things.
Contrast	Show differences between things.
Criticize	Give the positive and negative points of a subject as well as evidence for these positions.
Define	Give the formal meaning of a term.
Describe	Tell in detail about something.
Diagram	Make a drawing and label it.
Discuss	Give details and, if relevant, the positive and negative points of a subject as well as evidence for these positions.
Enumerate	List points and number them 1, 2, 3, and so on.
Evaluate	Give the positive and negative points of a subject as well as your judgment about which outweighs the other and why.
Illustrate	Explain by giving examples.
Interpret	Explain the meaning of something.
Justify	Give reasons for something.
List	Give a series of points and number them 1, 2, 3, and so on.
Outline	Give the main points and important secondary points. Put main points at the margin and indent secondary points under the main points. Relationships may also be described with symbols, as follows:

1. _____

    a. _____

    b. _____

2. _____

Prove	Show to be true by giving facts or reasons.
Relate	Show connections among things.
State	Give the main points.
Summarize	Give a condensed account of the main points.
Trace	Describe the development or history of a subject.

STEP 4: PREPARE A BRIEF, INFORMAL OUTLINE BEFORE ANSWERING AN ESSAY QUESTION

Use the margin of the exam or a separate piece of scratch paper to jot down quickly, as they occur to you, the main points you want to discuss in each answer. Then decide in what order you want to present these points. Write 1 in front of the first item, 2 beside the second item, and so on. You now have an informal outline to guide you as you answer your essay question.

If there is a question on the exam that is similar to one of the questions you anticipated and outlined at home, quickly write down the catchphrase that calls back the content of the outline. Below the catchphrase, write the key words represented by each letter in the catchphrase. The key words, in turn, will remind you of the concepts they represent. If you have prepared properly, this step will take only a minute or so, and you will have before you the guide you need to write a focused, supported, organized answer.

An Illustration of Step 4: Kurt immediately wrote down his catchphrase "Red oars row boats fast." He next jotted down the first letters in his catchphrase and then the key words that went with each letter. He then filled in several key details and was ready to write his essay answer.

Here is what Kurt's brief outline looked like:

Red oars row boats fast.

R	*Regular study hours*
O	*One-hour blocks of study time*
R	*Reward yourself*
B	*Before—study before and after class*
F	*Flexible—keep schedule flexible*

STEP 5: WRITE A CLEAR, WELL-ORGANIZED ESSAY

If you have followed the suggestions to this point, you have done all the preliminary work needed to write an effective essay. Be sure not to wreck your chances of getting a good grade by writing carelessly. Instead, as you prepare your response, keep in mind the principles of good writing: unity, support, organization, and clear, error-free sentences.

First, start your essay with a sentence that clearly states what it will be about. Then make sure that everything in your essay relates to your opening statement.

Second, though you must obviously take time limitations into account, provide as much support as possible for each of your main points.

Third, use transitions to guide your reader through your answer. Words such as *first, next, then, however,* and *finally* make it easy for the reader to follow your train of thought.

Last, leave time to proofread your essay for sentence-skills mistakes you may have made while you concentrated on writing your answer. Look for illegible words; for words omitted, miswritten, or misspelled (if possible, bring a dictionary with you); for awkward phrasings or misplaced punctuation marks; and for whatever else may prevent the reader from understanding your thoughts. Cross out any mistakes and make your corrections neatly above the errors. If you want to change or add to some point, insert an asterisk at the appropriate spot, put another asterisk at the bottom of the page, and add the corrected or additional material there.

An Illustration of Step 5:   Read through Kurt's answer, and then do the activity.

	The five hints that follow are helpful to remember when
	planning a weekly study schedule. First, schedule regular
	study time. This helps make studying a habit and helps you
	stay up to date in your course work. Also, it has been shown
	that regular study is more effective than "cramming."
	Second, plan at least one-hour ^blocks^ of study time. Shorter study
	periods are over just when you are fully warmed up and
	working hard. Another hint is to reward yourself for
	studying. People work better ^when^ they are ~~rev~~ rewarded for their
	efforts; therefore, you ^should^ schedule some free time, a snack, or
	other "bonus" for hard work. A fourth hint is to schedule
	study periods before and after classes. Studying before a
	class can help you review ~~pri~~ previous material.* Studying
	after class helps you review and ~~orgin~~ organize material
	while it is still ^fresh^ in your mind. Finally, you should keep your
	schedule ~~flexa~~ flexible. When unexpected events occur, you
	should shift your study time, not do away with it. But if
	your schedule requires constant adjustments, you may have
	to reorganize it.
	*or preview a new chapter.

Activity

The following sentences comment on Kurt's essay. Fill in the missing word or words in each case.

1. Kurt begins with a sentence that clearly signals what his paper _____.
   Always begin with such a clear signal!

2. Notice the various _____ that Kurt made when writing and proofreading his paper. He crossed out awkward phrasings and miswritten words; he used his _____ after he had finished the essay to correct misspelled words; he used insertion signs ($^\wedge$) to add omitted words; and he used an asterisk to add an omitted detail.

3. The transition words that Kurt used to guide his reader, and himself, through the five points of his answer include:

   _____

   _____

   _____

   _____

   _____

PRACTICE IN PREPARING FOR AND TAKING ESSAY EXAMS

Activity 1

Evaluate your present skills in preparing for and taking essay tests. Put a check mark beside each of the following steps that you already practice. Then put a check mark beside those steps that you plan to practice. Leave a space blank if you do not plan to follow a particular point.

Now Do	Plan to Do	
____	____	1. List ten or so probable questions.
____	____	2. Prepare a good outline answer for each question and memorize the outline.
		3. Look at the exam carefully and do the following:
____	____	a. Read *all* the questions.
____	____	b. Note direction words.
____	____	c. Start with the easiest question.
____	____	4. Outline answer before writing it.

5. Write a well-organized answer by doing the following:
    a. Have a main-idea sentence.
    b. Use transitions throughout the answer.
    c. Write complete sentences.
    d. Proofread paper for omitted words, miswritten words, unclear phrasing, punctuation problems, and misspellings.

Activity 2

The student paragraph below was written in response to the essay question about a weekly study schedule on page 225. On separate paper, rewrite the paragraph, expanding and correcting it. Begin with a clear opening statement, use word signals throughout your answer, and make sure that each point and the supporting details for that point are clearly presented.

	First, study before and after class. This will help you know
	what's going to happen in a class. Also study for at least one
	hour. Regular study time is important, too; this is why a
	schedule is necessary. However, you can change the schedule
	if it's not working out. Reward yourself when you study.
	Last, work on your most difficult subject at the best time.
	This will depend on you.

Activity 3

Spend a half hour getting ready to write a one-paragraph essay on the question "Describe seven steps you can take to improve your memory." Prepare for the test by following the advice given in step 2 on page 224.

Activity 4

Prepare five questions that you might be expected to answer on an essay exam in one of your courses. Make up an outline answer for each of the five questions. Memorize one of the outlines, using the technique of repeated self-testing (see page 195). Finally, write a full essay answer, in complete sentences, to one of the questions. Your instructor may ask you to hand in your five outlines and the essay.

USING THE LIBRARY

This chapter will show you how to use the library and its:

- Main desk
- Book file
- Book stacks
- Magazine file
- Magazine holdings area

Introductory Project

Consider this study situation:

> Pete had been out of school for ten years before he enrolled in college. During his first semester, his sociology instructor asked him to "compile a list of ten books and articles about single-parent families." In addition, Pete's business instructor asked him to do a research paper on "benefits of the Japanese quality circle in American companies." Pete dreaded these projects because he had no idea where or how to begin them. Before class one night, he walked into his college library and wandered around for a while, aimlessly and shyly. He felt especially intimidated by the people who sat typing in front of computer screens and seemed to know exactly what they were doing. Pete felt completely out of his element—like a visitor in a foreign land. He didn't even know what questions to ask about how to use the library.

This chapter will explain exactly how Pete, or anyone, can use the library to get the information needed for course work. But take a few minutes first to examine your own ideas. What do you think are two specific things that Pete could do to get the information he needs?

This chapter provides the basic information you need to use your college library with confidence. It also describes basic steps to follow in researching a topic.

Most students seem to know that libraries provide study space, typing facilities, and copying machines. They also seem aware that a library has a reading area with recent magazines and newspapers. But the true heart of a library consists of the following: a *main desk*, a *book file*, *book stacks*, a *magazine file*, and a *magazine storage area*. Each of these will be discussed on the pages that follow.

PARTS OF THE LIBRARY

Main Desk

The main desk is usually located in a central spot. Check at the main desk to see if there is a brochure that describes the layout and services of the library. You might also ask if the library staff provides tours of the library. If not, explore your library to find each of the areas described below.

Activity

Make up a floor plan of your college library. Label the main desk, book file, book stacks, magazine file, and magazine storage area.

Book File

The book file will be your starting point for almost any research project. The book file is a list of all the books in the library. It may be an actual card catalog: a file of cards alphabetically arranged in drawers. Increasingly, however, the book file is computerized, and it appears on a number of computer terminals located at different spots in the library.

Finding a Book—Author, Title, and Subject: Whether you use an actual file of cards or a computer terminal, it is important for you to know that there are three ways to look up a book: you can look it up according to *author, title,* or *subject.* For example, suppose you want to see if the library has *The Population Explosion* by Paul R. Ehrlich and Anne H. Ehrlich. You could check for the book in any of three ways:

1 You could go to the *title* section of the book file and look it up there under ''P.'' Note that you always look up a book under the first word in the title, excluding the words *A, An,* and *The.*

2   You could go to the *author* section of the book file and look it up there under
"E." An author is always listed under his or her last name. Here is the author
entry in a card catalog for Ehrlich's book *The Population Explosion:*

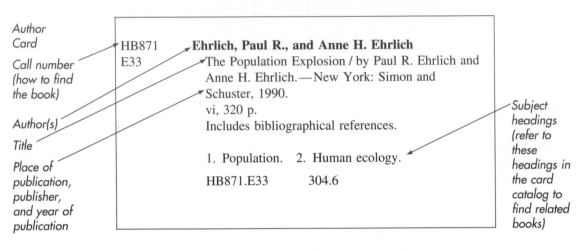

Author
Card

Call number
(how to find
the book)

Author(s)

Title

Place of
publication,
publisher,
and year of
publication

HB871
E33

Ehrlich, Paul R., and Anne H. Ehrlich
The Population Explosion / by Paul R. Ehrlich and
Anne H. Ehrlich.—New York: Simon and
Schuster, 1990.
vi, 320 p.
Includes bibliographical references.

1. Population.   2. Human ecology.

HB871.E33   304.6

Subject
headings
(refer to
these
headings in
the card
catalog to
find related
books)

3   Or, since you know the subject that the book deals with—in this case the
subject is obviously "population"—you could go to the *subject* section of
the book file and look it up under "P."

Generally, if you are looking for a particular book, it is easier to use the
author or *title* section of the book file.

On the other hand, if you hope to find other books about population, then
the *subject* section is where you should look. You will get a list of all the books
in the library that deal with population. You'll also be given related subject
headings under which you might find additional books about the subject.

Using a Computerized Book File: Recently, I visited a local library that had
just been computerized. The card catalog was gone, and in its place was a table
with ten computer terminals. I approached a terminal and looked, a bit uneasily,
at the instructions placed nearby. The instructions turned out to be very simple.
They told me that if I wanted to look up the author of a book, I should type
"A =" on the keyboard in front of the terminal and then the name of the author.
I typed "A = Ehrlich," and then (following the directions) I hit the Enter/Return
key on the keyboard.

In two seconds a new screen appeared showing me a numbered list of several
books by Paul R. Ehrlich, one of which was *The Population Explosion.* This title
was numbered "3" on the list, and at the bottom of the screen was a direction
to type the number of the title I wanted more information about. So I typed the
number "3" and hit the Enter/Return key. I then got the screen shown on the
next page.

AUTHOR:	Ehrlich, Paul
TITLE:	The Population Explosion
PUBLISHER:	Simon and Schuster, 1990.
SUBJECTS:	Population. Human ecology.

Call Number	Material	Location	Status
362.5097	Book	Cherry Hill	Available

I was very impressed. The terminal was easier and quicker to use than a card catalog. The screen gave me the basic information I needed to know about the book, including where to find it. In addition, the screen told me that the book was ''Available'' on the shelves. (A display card nearby explained that if the book was not on the shelves, the message under ''Status'' would be ''Out on loan.'') I noticed other options. If the book was not on the shelves at the Cherry Hill location of the library, I would be told if it was available at other libraries nearby, by means of interlibrary loan.

The computer gave me two other choices. I could type ''T = '' plus a name to look up the title of a book. Or I could type ''S = '' plus the subject to get the names of any books that the library had dealing with the subject of population.

Using Subject Headings to Research a Topic: Whether your library has a card catalog or a computer terminal, it is the subject section that will be extremely valuable to you when you are researching a topic. If you have a general topic, the subject section will help you find books on that general topic and also on more specialized topics within that subject.

For example, I typed ''S = Population'' to see how many books there were dealing with the subject of population. In seconds, a screen came up showing me thirty-three different titles! In addition, the screen informed me of related headings under which I could find dozens of other books about population. These related headings included ''human ecology,'' ''environmental health,'' ''contraception,'' ''conservation of nature,'' and ''bioengineering.'' With the help of all these headings and titles, a student could really begin to think about a limited research topic to develop within the general subject of population.

There are two points to remember here: (1) Start researching a topic by using the subject section of the book file. (2) Use the subtopics and related topics suggested by the book file to help you begin to narrow your topic. Chances are, you will use the library to do research on a paper of anywhere from five to twenty pages or so. You do not want to choose a topic so broad that it could be covered only by an entire book or more. Instead, you want to come up with a limited topic that can be covered adequately in a relatively short paper.

Activity

Part A: Answer the following questions about the card catalog.

1. Is your library's book file an actual file of cards in drawers, or is the book file on computer terminals? _____

2. What are the three ways of looking up a book in the library?

    a. _____

    b. _____

    c. _____

3. Which section of the book file will help you research and limit a topic?

    _____

Part B: Use your library book file to answer the following questions.

1. What is the title of one book by Arthur C. Clarke? _____

    _____

2. What is the title of one book by Toni Morrison? _____

    _____

3. Who is the author of *A Distant Mirror?* (Remember to look up the title under *Distant,* not *A.*) _____

4. Who is the author of *Darkness at Noon?* _____

5. List two books and their authors dealing with the subject of handicaps:

    a. _____

    _____

    b. _____

    _____

6. List two books and their authors dealing with the subject of Eleanor Roosevelt:

    a. _____

    _____

    b. _____

    _____

7. Look up a book titled *The Children of Sánchez* or *Profiles in Courage* or *The Fate of the Earth* and give the following information:

    a. Author _____

    b. Publisher _____

    c. Date of publication _____

    d. Call number _____

    e. Subject headings: _____

8. Look up a book written by Studs Terkel or Margaret Mead or B. F. Skinner and give the following information:

    a. Title _____

    b. Publisher _____

    c. Date of publication _____

    d. Call number _____

    e. Subject headings: _____

Book Stacks

The book stacks are the library shelves where books are arranged according to their call numbers. The call number, as distinctive as a social security number, always appears on a book file for any book. It is also printed on the spine of every book in the library.

If your library has *open stacks* (ones that you are permitted to enter), follow these steps to find a book. Suppose you are looking for *The Population Explosion,* which has the call number HB871.E33 in the Library of Congress system. (Libraries using the Dewey decimal system have call letters made up entirely of numbers rather than letters and numbers. However, you use the same basic method to locate a book.) You go to the section of the stacks that holds the H's. After you locate the H's, you look for the HB's. After that, you look for HB871. Finally, you look for HB871/E33, and you have the book.

If your library has *closed stacks* (ones you are not permitted to enter), you will have to write the title, author, and call number on a slip of paper. (Such slips of paper will be available near the card catalog or computer terminals.) You'll then give the slip to a library staff person, who will locate the book and bring it to you.

Activity

Use the book stacks to answer one of the following sets of questions. Choose the set of questions related to the classification system of your library.

Library of Congress System (Letters and Numbers)

1. Books in the BF21 to BF833 area deal with
   a. philosophy.
   b. sociology.
   c. psychology.
   d. history.

2. Books in the HV580 to HV5840 area deal with what type of social problem?
   a. drugs
   b. suicide
   c. white-collar crime
   d. domestic violence

3. Books in the PR4740 to PR4757 area deal with
   a. James Joyce.
   b. Jane Austen.
   c. George Eliot.
   d. Thomas Hardy.

4. What aspect of the environment is dealt with in the area between TD196 and TD763?
   a. air
   b. water
   c. soil
   d. vegetation

Dewey Decimal System (Numbers)

1. Books in the 320 area deal with
   a. self-help.
   b. divorce
   c. science.
   d. politics.

2. Books in the 546 to 547 area deal with
   a. biology.
   b. chemistry.
   c. physics.
   d. anthropology.

3. Books in the 636 area deal with
   a. animals.
   b. computers.
   c. marketing.
   d. senior citizens.
4. Books in the 709 area deal with
   a. camping.
   b. science fiction.
   c. art.
   d. poetry.

Magazine File

The magazine file is also known as the *periodicals* file. *Periodicals* (from the word *periodic,* which means "at regular periods") are magazines, journals, and newspapers. In this chapter, the word *magazine* stands for any periodical.

The magazine file often contains recent information about a given subject, or very specialized information about a subject, that may not be available in a book. It is important, then, to check magazines as well as books when you are doing research.

Just as you use the book file to find books on your subject, you use the magazine file to find articles on your subject in magazines and other publications. There are two files in particular that should help: *Readers' Guide to Periodical Literature* and the *Magazine Index.*

Readers' Guide to Periodical Literature: The familiar green volumes of the *Readers' Guide,* found in just about every library, list articles published in almost two hundred popular magazines, such as *Newsweek, Health, People, Ebony, Redbook,* and *Popular Science.* Articles are listed alphabetically under both subject and author. For example, if you wanted to learn the titles of articles published on the subject of child abuse within a certain time span, you would look under the heading "Child abuse."

Here, for example, is a typical entry from the *Readers' Guide:*

Subject heading   Title of article   Author of article   Illustrated

Children
Do We Care About Our Children? N. Gibbs. il *Time*
     136: 42-46 O 8 '90

Volume   Page   Date   Name of magazine
number   numbers

Note the sequence in which information is given about the article:

1 Subject heading.
2 Title of the article. In some cases, there will be bracketed words [like these] after the title that help make clear just what the article is about.
3 Author (if it is a signed article). The author's first name is always abbreviated.
4 Whether the article has a bibliography (*bibl*) or is illustrated with pictures (*il*). Other abbreviations sometimes used are shown in the front of the *Readers' Guide.*
5 Name of the magazine. A short title like *Time* is not abbreviated, but longer titles are. For example, the magazine *Popular Science* is abbreviated *Pop Sci.* Refer to the list of magazines in the front of the *Readers' Guide* to identify abbreviations.
6 Volume number of the magazine (preceding the colon).
7 Page numbers on which the article appears (after the colon).
8 Date when the article appeared. Dates are abbreviated: for example, *Mr* stands for *March, Ag* for *August, N* for *November.* Other abbreviations are shown in the front of the *Readers' Guide.*

The *Readers' Guide* is published in monthly supplements. At the end of a year, a volume is published covering the entire year. You will see in your library large green volumes that say, for instance, *Readers' Guide 1990* or *Readers' Guide 1993.* You will also see the small monthly supplements for the current year.

The *Readers' Guide* is also now available in a much more useful form, on a computer. I was amazed to see at my local library that I could now sit down at a terminal and quickly search for an article on almost any subject published in the last seven years. Searching on the computer was much easier than having to go through seven or so different paper volumes of the *Readers' Guide.*

Magazine Index: The *Magazine Index* is an automated system that lists articles in about four hundred general-interest magazines. Given a choice, you should always use this system rather than the *Readers' Guide:* it lists articles from twice as many sources as the *Guide* and is both fast and easy to use.

You sit in front of what looks like a large television screen that is already loaded with a microfilmed index. By pushing the first of two buttons, you quickly advance the film forward from A to B to C and so on. By pushing the other button, you move in the opposite direction. It really is as simple as that! The entries on the screen look just like the entries in the *Readers' Guide.* You'll note that the most recent articles on a topic are given first. This machine is an excellent research tool that is finding its way into more and more libraries.

Activity 1

At this point in the chapter, you know the two basic steps in researching a topic in the library. What are the steps?

1. _____

   _____

2. _____

   _____

Activity 2

Use the excerpt below from the *Readers' Guide* to answer the questions on the following page.

EXERCISE
    See also
    Aerobics
    Bodybuilding
    Boxercise
    Exercising equipment
    Eye exercises
    Flo-Motion
    Gymnastics
    Health clubs
    Leg exercises
    Periodization (Athletic training)
    Running
    Sports
    Stretching exercises
    Tape recording — Exercise use
    Walking
    Water exercises
    Weight lifting
    Yoga
Abdominal showman. R. Brody. il *Men's Health* 6:24-5 Je '91
Build your back through your belly. G. Gutfeld. il *Prevention (Emmaus, Pa.)* 43:58-64 Jl '91
Exercises fit for a princess [exercise routine used by Princess Diana] L. Webb. il pors *Good Housekeeping* 213:92+ S '91
Fitness. See issues of *Men's Health*
Get fit fast [40 minute workouts] D. Bensimhon. il *Men's Health* 6:66-71 Ag '91
Growing fitter. S. Levin. il *New Choices for the Best Years* 31:42-4 Je '91
I want a flat stomach, fast! [special section] il *Glamour* 89:146-51 Je '91
Making love better with exercise [research by Phillip Whitten] J. S. Chou. il *McCall's* 118:20 S '91
Rear view: exercises and tips to improve your bottom line. il *Redbook* 177:16 S '91
The rewards of total transformation; ed. by Stephanie Ebbert. S. Miller. il pors *Prevention (Emmaus, Pa.)* 43:87-8+ Jl '91
Shape up! [cover story; special section] R. Sutton. il *American Health* 10:37-51 Je '91
Summer slimmers: take off 6 inches in 60 days. S. Lally. il *Prevention (Emmaus, Pa)* 43:33-41+ Jl '91

Tuning up your body for summer fitness & fun. il *Ebony* 46:118+ Jl '91
When should you exercise? M. J. Schnatter. il *McCall's* 118:14 Jl '91
Workout wonders right at home. *'Teen* 35:49 Je '91
    Physiological effects
The athlete's dilemma [metabolic ceiling] J. M. Diamond. il *Discover* 12:78-83 Ag '91
Cruise control [antidizzines or seasickness exercises] il *Prevention (Emmaus, Pa.)* 43:10+ Jl '91
Daily exercise fights hypertension, clots. K. Fackelmann. *Science News* 139:342 Je 1 '91
Effects of exercise on the human immune system. L. D. Caren. bibl f il *BioScience* 41:410-15 Je '91
Exercise! P. D. Wood. il *Word health* p25-7 My/Je '91
Exercise is hip [reducing risk of hip fractures; research by Annlia Paganini-Hill] il *Prevention (Emmaus, Pa.)* 43:12 Je '91
Pump down high blood pressure. G. Gutfeld. il *Prevention (Emmaus, Pa.)* 43:60-4+ Je '91
Putting an end to sore muscles. S. Y. Lee. il *McCall's* 118:18 Ag '91
Regular exercise cuts diabetes risk. K. Fackelmann. *Science News* 140:36 Jl 20 '91
Twofold path to saving again bones [calcium and exercise; research by Miriam E. Nelson] *Science News* 139:367 Je 8 '91
    Psychological aspects
A bridge too far: confessions of a fitness agnostic. R. Lipsyte. il *American Health* 10:26-7 Je '91
The burnout factor. S. Levin. il *Women's Sports & Fitness* 13:12-13 Jl/Ag '91
Don't be an exercise dropout. S. Browder. il *Reader's Digest* 139:168-9+ Ag '91
The never-ending workout [exercise addition] *Mademoiselle* 97:88+ Je '91
EXERCISE CLUBS *See* Health clubs
EXERCISE STRESS TESTS *See* Physical fitness — Testing
EXERCISE TESTING *See* Physical fitness — Testing
EXERCISES, MILITARY *See* Military maneuvers
EXERCISING EQUIPMENT
    Working in [home gym] S. Omelianuk. il *Gentlemen's Quarterly* 61:183+ S '91

1. Who is the author of an article titled "Don't Be an Exercise Dropout"?

   _____

2. What is the title of an article by S. Levin?

   _____

3. How many articles are listed that deal with the psychological aspects of exercise?

   _____

4. In what issue of *McCall's* is there an article about exercise?

   _____

5. On what pages of *World Health* is the article "Exercise!"?

   _____

Activity 3

1. Look up a recent article on smoking in the *Readers' Guide* or the *Magazine Index* and fill in the following information:

   a. Article title

      _____

   b. Author (if given)

      _____

   c. Name of magazine

      _____

   d. Pages _____   e. Date _____

2. Look up a recent article on divorce in the *Readers' Guide* or the *Magazine Index* and fill in the following information:

   a. Article title

      _____

   b. Author (if given)

      _____

   c. Name of magazine

      _____

   d. Pages _____   e. Date _____

Specialized Indexes: Once you know how to use the *Readers' Guide* and the *Magazine Index,* you will find it easy to use some of the more specialized indexes in most libraries. Here are three helpful ones:

■ *New York Times Index.* This is an index to articles published in the *New York Times.* After you look up a subject, you'll get a list of articles published on that topic, with a short summary of each article.

■ *Business Periodical Index.* The articles here are from over three hundred publications that generally treat a subject in more detail than it would receive in the popular magazines indexed in the *Readers' Guide.* At the same time, the articles are usually not *too* technical or hard to read.

■ *Social Sciences Index.* This is an index to articles published by journals in the areas of anthropology, environmental science, psychology, and sociology. Your instructors in these areas may expect you to consult this index while doing a research project on any of these subjects.

Other specialized indexes that your library may have include the following:

Art Index	*General Science Index*
Applied Science and Technology Index	*Humanities Index*
	Nursing Index
Biological and Agricultural Index	*Religious Periodical Literature Index*
Book Review Digest	
Education Index	

Depending on the subject area you are researching, you may want to consult the appropriate index. Some libraries have most of these indexes on a computer.

Activity

1. Examine the magazine area in your library. (It might be known as the *periodicals* area.) Check off each of the indexes it includes:

   _____ Readers' Guide Index   _____ Business Periodicals Index

   _____ Magazine Index   _____ Social Sciences Index

   _____ New York Times Index

2. Are any of these indexes available on a computer as well as in paperbound volumes? _____ If so, which ones? _____

   _____

3. What are two other indexes in this area of your library besides the five mentioned above? _____

   _____

A Note on Other Reference Materials: Every library has a reference area, often close to the place where the *Readers' Guide* is located, in which other reference materials can be found. Such general resource materials include dictionaries, encyclopedias, atlases, yearbooks, almanacs, a subject guide to books in print (this can help in locating books on a particular subject), anthologies of quotations, and other items.

You may also find in the reference area a series of filing cabinets called the *pamphlet file.* This will consist of a series of file cabinets full of pamphlets, booklets, and newsletters on a multitude of topics. One file drawer, for example, may include all the pamphlets and the like for subjects that start with "A." I looked in the "A" drawer of the pamphlet file in my library and found lots of small pieces about subjects like abortion, adoption, and animal rights, along with many other topics starting with "A." On top of these filing cabinets may be a booklet titled "Pamphlet File Subject Headings"; it will quickly tell you if the file includes material on your subject of interest.

Activity

1. What is one encyclopedia that your library has?

   _____

2. What unabridged dictionary does your library have?

   _____

3. Where is your library's pamphlet file located?

   _____

4. Is there a booklet or small file that tells you what subject headings are included

   in the pamphlet file? _____ Where is it? _____

Magazine Storage Area

Near your library's *Readers' Guide* or *Magazine Index,* you'll probably notice slips of paper. For instance, at the top of the opposite page is a copy of the slip used in my local library:

As you locate each magazine and journal article that you would like to look at, fill out a slip. When you are done, take the slips to a library staff person working nearby. Don't hesitate to do this: helping you obtain the articles you want is part of his or her job.

> **PERIODICAL REQUEST**
>
> Name of Magazine _____
>
> Date of Magazine _____
>
> (For your reference: Title and pages of article:)
>
> _____

Here's what will probably happen next:

- If a magazine that you want is very recent, it may be on open shelves in the library. The staff member will tell you, and then you can go find it yourself.

- If the magazine you want is up to a year or so old, it may be kept in a closed area of the library. In that case, the staff person will go find it and bring it to you.

- Sometimes you'll ask to see an article in a magazine that the library does not carry. You'll then have to plan to use other articles, or go to a larger library, or take advantage of interlibrary loan. However, most college libraries or large county libraries should have what you need.

- Very frequently, especially with older issues, the magazine will be on micro-film or on microfiche. (*Microfilm* is a roll of film on which articles have been reproduced in greatly reduced size; *microfiche* is the same thing, but it is on easily handled sheets of film rather than on a roll.) The staff person will bring you the film or fiche and at your request will then show you how to load this material onto a microfilm or microfiche machine nearby, so that it can be read.

Faced with learning how to use a new machine, many people are intimidated and nervous. I know I was. What is important is that you ask for as much help as you need. Have the staff person demonstrate the machine and then watch you as you try it. (Remember that this person is being paid by the library to help you learn how to use the resources in the library, including the machine.) While the machine may seem complex at first, in fact most of the time it turns out to be easy to use. Don't be afraid to insist that the person give you as much time as you need to learn how to use the machine.

After you are sure you can use the machine to look up any article, check to see if the machine will make a copy of the article. Many will. Make sure you have some change to cover the copying fee, and then go back to the staff person and ask him or her to show you how to use the print option on the machine. You'll be amazed at how quickly and easily you can get a printed copy of almost any article you want.

Activity

1. Use the *Readers' Guide* or *Magazine Index* to find an article on date rape that was published in the last three months. Write the name of the magazine and the date on a slip of paper and give it to a library staff person. Is the article available in the actual magazine? _____ If so, is it on an open shelf or is it in a closed area where a staff person must bring it to you? _____

    _____

2. Use the *Readers' Guide* or *Magazine Index* to find an article on date rape that was published more than one year ago. Write down the name of the magazine and the date on a slip of paper and give it to a library staff person. Is the article available in the actual magazine, or is it available on microfiche or microfilm?

    _____

    _____

3. Check off each of the following if your library has it.

    _____ Microfiche machine   _____ with a print option
    _____ Microfilm machine   _____ with a print option

A Summary of Library Areas

You now know the five areas of the library that will be most useful to you in doing research:

1 *Main desk.*
2 *Book file.* In particular, you can use the *subjects* section of the card file to get the names of books on your subject, as well as suggestions about other subject headings under which you might find books. It is by exploring your general subject in books and then in magazine articles that you will gradually be able to decide upon a subject limited enough to cover in your research paper.
3 *Book stacks,* where you will get the books themselves.
4 *Magazine files and indexes.* Once again, you can use the *subjects* sections of these files to get the names of magazine and journal articles on your subject.
5 *Magazine storage area,* where you will get the articles themselves.

PRACTICE IN USING THE LIBRARY

Activity

Use your library to research a subject that interests you. Select one of the following areas or (with your instructor's permission) one of your own choice:

Marriage contracts	New remedies for allergies
Food poisoning (salmonella)	Censorship in the 1990s
Greenhouse effect	New prison reforms
Medical care for the aged	Drug treatment programs
Pro-choice movement	Sudden infant death syndrome
Pro-life movement	New treatments for insomnia
Health insurance reform	Organ donation
Drinking water pollution	Safe sex
Problems of retirement	Voucher system in schools
Cremation	Sexual harassment in business
Day care programs that work	Gambling and youth
Noise control	Nongraded schools
Drug treatment programs for adolescents	Earthquake forecasting
Fertility drugs	Ethical aspects of hunting
Witchcraft in the 1990s	Euthanasia
New treatments for AIDS	Recent consumer frauds
Changes in immigration policy	Stress reduction in the workplace
Video display terminals—health aspects	Sex on television
Hazardous substances in the home	Everyday addictions
Air bags	Toxic waste disposal
Capital punishment	Self-help groups
Prenatal care	Telephone crimes
Acid rain	Date rape
New aid for the handicapped	Heroes for the 1990s

Research the topic first through the *subjects* section of the book file and then through the *subjects* section of one or more magazine files and indexes. On a separate sheet of paper, provide the information indicated in the list on the following page.

1. Topic.

2. Three books that cover the topic directly or at least touch on the topic in some way. Include these items:

   Author
   Title
   Place of publication
   Publisher
   Date of publication

3. Three articles on the topic published in 1990 or later from the *Readers' Guide* or the *Magazine Index.* Include these items:

   Title of article
   Author (if given)
   Title of magazine
   Date
   Page(s)

4. Three articles on the topic published in 1990 or later from other indexes (such as the *New York Times Index, Business Periodical Index, Social Sciences Index,* or *Humanities Index.*) Include these items:

   Title of article
   Author (if given)
   Title of magazine
   Date
   Page(s)

5. Finally, include a photocopy of one of the six articles. Note whether the source of the copy was the article on paper, on microfiche, or on microfilm.

PART THREE

A BRIEF GUIDE TO IMPORTANT WORD SKILLS

PREVIEW

In Part Three, the chapter ''Understanding Word Parts'' will help you review sixty of the most common word parts used in forming English words. The explanations and activities in ''Using the Dictionary'' will explain the most important kinds of information about words that a good dictionary provides. ''Word Pronunciation'' describes several basic rules you can use to pronounce unfamiliar words, including the specialized terms you will meet in your different college subjects. ''Spelling Improvement'' suggests techniques and provides spelling rules and a word list to make you a better speller. Finally, ''Vocabulary Development'' explains three approaches that can increase your word power.

AN IMPORTANT NOTE

Part Three provides a concise review of important word skills, some of which you may remember from earlier school years. All these skills can be supplemented by the extensive materials usually available in college learning centers. With the basic information in Part Three, you can quickly brush up on word skills or refer to them when needed. You can also discover which skills you may want to work on at greater length in your school learning center.

UNDERSTANDING WORD PARTS

This chapter will help you recognize and spell:

- Twenty common prefixes
- Twenty common suffixes
- Twenty common roots

One way to improve your pronunciation and spelling of words is to increase your understanding of common word parts. These word parts—also known as *prefixes, suffixes,* and *roots*—are building blocks used in forming many English words. The activities in this section will give you practice in sixty of the most common word parts. Working with them will help your spelling, for you will realize how many words are made up of short, often-recurring, easily spelled parts. Increasing your awareness of basic word parts will also help you pronounce many unfamiliar words and, at times, unlock their meanings.

PREFIXES

A *prefix* is a word part added to the beginning of a word. The prefix changes the meaning of some words to their opposites. For example, when the prefix *in-* is added to *justice,* the result is *injustice;* when the prefix *mis-* is added to *understanding,* the result is *misunderstanding.* A prefix need not change a word to its opposite, but it will alter the meaning of the word in some way. For instance, when the prefix *re-* (meaning *again*) is added to *view,* the result is *review,* which means *to view again.* When the prefix *mal-* (meaning *bad*) is added to *practice,* the result is *malpractice,* which means *bad* or *improper practice.*

In the following activities, look carefully at the meanings of the two prefixes presented. Then add the appropriate prefix to the base word (the one in *italics*) in each of the five sentences *a* to *e*. Write your word in the space provided. You will know which prefix to choose in each case if you consider both its meaning and the general meaning of the sentence. Next, you'll see two groups of words separated by a slash line (/). In the spaces provided, write a sentence using one word from the first group and a sentence using one word from the second group.

1 mono   alone, one
2 trans   across, over, beyond

In sentences *a* to *e*, add the appropriate prefix to each base word given in parentheses.

    Example: After the full moon rose, Lawrence Talbott was (. . . *formed*)
    <u>transformed</u> into the Wolfman.

a. All the subway and bus lines were shut down during the recent (. . . *it*)
    _____ strike.

b. The instructor's (. . . *tonous*) _____ voice never seemed to vary in pitch; the entire class was falling asleep.

c. The station has a weak (. . . *mitter*) _____; it can't be heard more than five miles away.

d. Because the hotel prefers long-term guests, there are only a few rooms reserved for (. . . *ients*) _____.

e. The traditional Western hero was a man of few words; his usual response to a question was a (. . . *syllabic*) _____ ''yup'' or ''nope.''

Now write a sentence using one of the words before the slash line and a sentence using one of the words that appear after the slash.

monologue monotony mononucleosis / transplant transition transparent

_____

_____

3 **dis** apart, away
4 **pre** before

a. After changing jobs and moving a thousand miles away, Ted felt (. . . *oriented*) _____.

b. Lisa's favorite method of (. . . *writing*) _____ is to brainstorm and jot down her ideas on a large sheet of drawing paper.

c. If I'm (. . . *tracted*) _____ while I'm studying, it can take me a half hour to get back to work.

d. The instructions on the frozen dinner read, "Step 1: (. . . *heat*) _____ oven to four hundred degrees."

e. Before leaving on the trip, Marion took the (. . . *caution*) _____ of checking her car's oil.

discard   disinfect   disdain   /   prediction   prerequisite   prejudice

_____

_____

5 **inter** between, among
6 **sub** under, below

a. As soon as the floodwaters (. . . *side*) _____, people will be able to return to their homes.

b. The corner of Seventh and Main Streets is a dangerous (. . . *section*) _____; five accidents have happened there in the last two weeks.

c. I was so involved in the epic movie that I resented the ten-minute (. . . *mission*) _____ that interrupted the film.

d. That outlet store seems to carry only (. . . *standard*) _____ merchandise, not high-quality goods.

e. When the spy found out that his message had been (. . . *cepted*) _____ by the enemy, he made plans to leave the country.

interfere   interview   interruption   /   subdue   sublease   subconscious

_____

_____

7 ex   out
8 mis   badly, wrong

a. Our club treasurer was removed from office after we discovered that she had

(. . . *managed*) _____ the funds.

b. Although the inside of my car looks fine, the (. . . *terior*)

_____ is badly rusted.

c. Don't wear that striped tie with those checked pants—that's a real (. . . *match*)

_____.

d. The swimming instructor taught the students to (. . . *hale*)

_____ underwater and then take a deep breath on the next
stroke.

e. Joe was (. . . *informed*) _____ about the date of the exam, so
he wasn't prepared to take the test on Friday.

excavate   exception   export   /   misfortune   misgivings   misleading

_____

_____

9 con   together, with
10 post   after, following, later

a. My parents decided not to buy a (. . . *dominium*) _____ because
they didn't like the idea of living so close to so many other people.

b. If the team members make a (. . . *certed*) _____ effort, they
may be able to land a spot in the play-offs.

c. As soon as the outdoor restaurant opened, dozens of office workers began to

(. . . *gregate*) _____ there for lunch.

d. Registration for the new semester was (. . . *poned*) _____ owing to the heavy snowfall.

e. At the bottom of my daughter's letter was the (. . . *script*)

_____ "Please send me ten dollars if you can."

conference   congenial   consensus   /   postoperative   postgraduate   postwar

_____

_____

11 **anti**   against
12 **pro**   before; for (in favor of)

a. It took three (*. . . aircraft*) _____ guns to bring down the fighter plane.

b. My boyfriend isn't (*. . . social*) _____; he's just very shy at parties.

c. The best way to (*. . . long*) _____ your life is to stop smoking.

d. Several (*. . . ponents*) _____ of a nuclear arms freeze chained themselves to the White House fence.

e. The doctor put an (*. . . septic*) _____ dressing on my daughter's skinned knee to guard against infection.

antidote   antiwar   antibiotic   /   proclaim   propaganda   prophet

_____

_____

13 **un**   not, reverse
14 **ad**   to, toward

a. Anyone who comes late to that instructor's class will not be (*. . . mitted*)

_____ to the room.

b. The weather has been so (*. . . predictable*) _____ lately that farmers are afraid to start the spring planting.

c. The heart attack victim was (*. . . conscious*) _____ and had started to slip into a coma.

d. In his speech, the conservative candidate (*. . . vocated*)

_____ less government interference in business.

e. When I pointed out all the dents in the used car, the salesperson grudgingly

(*. . . justed*) _____ the price to a lower figure.

unaccustomed   uninhibited   unavoidable   /   additive   adjoining   advance

_____

_____

15 in   not, within
16 extra   more than

a. My mother must have (. . . *sensory*) _____ perception; she always seems to know what I am thinking.

b. Since your Visa card expired last month, it is now (. . . *valid*)

_____ .

c. The (. . . *competent*) _____ waiter was fired after he dropped three dinners in one night.

d. In the movie, some (. . . *terrestrials*) _____ from a dying planet had decided to colonize earth.

e. That instructor has the reputation of being (. . . *sensitive*)

_____ to a student's problems.

inactive incurable installation / extracurricular extramarital extraordinary

_____

_____

17 re   again, back
18 mal   bad

a. If you purchase the hair dryer by the end of the month, you'll get back a $3

(. . . *bate*) _____ from the manufacturer.

b. The parents of the little girl who died on the operating table are suing the

surgeon for (. . . *practice*) _____ .

c. A major auto company has had to (. . . *call*) _____ thousands of its compact cars to repair a steering-wheel defect.

d. With a (. . . *icious*) _____ grin, the arrogant mugger forced the woman to hand over her wallet.

e. Because he was born with a (. . . *formed*) _____ foot, he has to wear special corrective shoes.

reciprocate   recuperate   renovate   /   malnutrition   malady   malice

_____

_____

19 com   with, together with
20 de   down, from

a. Because I have a bad cold, I have to take a (. . . *congestant*)

    _____ in order to breathe.

b. Elena couldn't decide what to order, so she settled for a (. . . *bination*)

    _____ platter with five kinds of seafood.

c. If the foundation continues to (. . . *teriorate*) _____, the building will have to be torn down.

d. Chuck hates being put on (. . . *mittees*) _____; he'd rather work by himself.

e. To explain the seasons, the ancient Greeks said that every fall the goddess of

    spring (. . . *scended*) _____ into the underworld for six months.

    compete   compile   component   /   decline   denounce   decrease

    _____

    _____

SUFFIXES

A *suffix* is a word part added to the end of a word. While a suffix may affect a word's meaning slightly, it is more likely to affect how the word is used in a sentence. For instance, when the suffix *-ment* is added to the verb *measure,* the result is the noun *measurement.* When the suffix *-less* is added to *measure,* the result is the adjective *measureless.* Very often, one of several suffixes can be added to a single word. Understanding common suffixes is especially helpful when you are learning new words. If you note the suffixes that can be added to a new word, you will learn not just a single word but perhaps three or four other forms of the word as well.

In the following activities, decide from the context which suffix in each pair should be added to the base word (the one in *italics*) in sentences *a* to *e*. Then write the entire word in the space provided. Alternative forms of some suffixes are shown in parentheses, but you will not have to use alternative forms to complete the spelling of any of the base words. Next, you'll find two groups of words separated by a slash line (/). In the spaces provided, write a sentence using one word from the first group and a sentence using one word from the second group.

1 ion (tion)
2 less

In sentences *a* to *e*, add the appropriate suffix to each word shown in parentheses.

a. With my new (*cord* . . .) ———————— telephone, I can talk to people from my backyard.

b. After three (*revis* . . . *s*) ————————, I was satisfied with my essay.

c. The (*tens* . . .) ———————— of modern life seems to be the cause of many stress-related diseases.

d. Some (*child* . . .) ———————— couples have waited over ten years for an adoption agency to find sons and daughters for them.

e. My cocker spaniel is absolutely (*fear* . . .) ————————; he will attack dogs three times his size.

Now write a sentence using one word from the group before the slash line and a sentence using one word from the group after the slash.

pollution   reduction   indication   /   friendless   lifeless   timeless

————————————————————————————

————————————————————————————

3 ant (ent)
4 ness

a. Most of my mail comes addressed to (''*Occup* . . .'') ————————.

b. Some people fill their spare time with television to make up for the (*empti* . . .) ———————— in their lives.

c. After the dentist injected Novocain into my jaw, it took hours for the (*numb* . . .) ———————— to wear off.

d. Sally's (*fond* . . .) ———————— for animals makes her want to adopt every stray cat and dog she sees.

e. Because humans are the (*domin* . . .) ———————— species of life on Earth, we have a responsibility to protect other life-forms.

intolerant   adjacent   sufficient   /   vividness   rudeness   selfishness

————————————————————————————

————————————————————————————

5   en
6   ize (ise)

a. My assignment was to read a three-page magazine article and (*summar . . .*)

_____ it in a short paragraph.

b. It takes a clock radio, a bell, and the smell of coffee to (*awak . . .*)

_____ me in the morning.

c. Ned must be nervous; he keeps getting up to (*sharp . . .*)

_____ his pencil.

d. If you wait for the glue to (*hard . . .*) _____, you won't be able to set the tiles properly.

e. Although my sister sometimes loses her temper, she never fails to (*apolog . . .*)

_____ minutes afterward.

lengthen   brighten   freshen   /   criticize   patronize   familiarize

_____

_____

7   age
8   ist

a. We put our furniture in (*stor . . .*) _____ until our new house was completed.

b. The doctor told me to support my sprained wrist by wearing an elastic

(*band . . .*) _____ on it.

c. After class, Pat works as a (*typ . . .*) _____ in the registrar's office.

d. Brenda dreams of being a (*vocal . . .*) _____ with a rock band, even though she can't carry a tune.

e. My new car, which runs on diesel fuel, gets much better (*mile . . .*)

_____ than my old one.

coverage   shrinkage   wreckage   /   journalist   optimist   dentist

_____

_____

9 ment
10 ful

a. Because water had soaked through the cartons, the entire (*ship* . . .)
    _____ of typing paper was ruined.

b. Tony wants to get married, but Lola says she isn't ready to make a permanent
    (*commit* . . .) _____.

c. Joanne keeps herself looking (*youth* . . .) _____ by eating prop-
    erly, exercising regularly, and tinting her hair.

d. My father says that some television shows should carry labels warning viewers
    that the program is (*harm* . . .) _____ to their mental health.

e. When I learned the apartment I wanted had just been rented to somebody
    else, I tried to hide my (*disappoint* . . .) _____.

judgment   argument   measurement   /   unfaithful   thankful   doubtful

_____

_____

11 ship
12 able (ible)

a. Nobody would claim (*owner* . . .) _____ of the dilapidated old
    Maverick that had been parked at the corner for two weeks.

b. Because I bought the stereo at a final clearance sale, it isn't (*return* . . .)
    _____.

c. The catcher was accused of poor (*sportsman* . . .) _____ after
    he bit the umpire.

d. The weather has been so (*change* . . .) _____ lately that I never
    know what to wear when I go out.

e. Helen Keller, who was deaf and mute, was thought to be (*unteach* . . .)
    _____ until a woman named Annie Sullivan gave her the gift
    of sign language.

championship   courtship   censorship   /   terrible   sensible   uncomfortable

_____

_____

13 ence (ance)
14 ify (fy)

a. When the (*audi...*) _____ would not laugh at his routine, the comedian stalked off the stage in disgust.

b. How can I ever land my first job if every want ad asks for someone with (*experi...*) _____?

c. Nobody could (*ident...*) _____ the two culprits who had robbed the elderly newsdealer of his day's profits.

d. Since I did not (*spec...*) _____ what color I wanted, the store could not deliver my new refrigerator.

e. The lawyer brought in over a dozen witnesses to (*test...*) _____ that her client was innocent.

resemblance   convenience   maintenance   /   simplify   classify   modify

_____

_____

15 ate
16 ly

a. Joanne bought a Volvo because she thinks it will not (*depreci...*) _____ in value as fast as an American car.

b. Children rarely (*appreci...*) _____ what their parents do for them until they grow up and become parents themselves.

c. The five-mile race wore me out; I (*bare...*) _____ made it to the finish line.

d. My cat had never seen such a large spider before, so she approached it (*timid...*) _____.

e. Nick called (*loud...*) _____ up the stairs to Fran that she was wanted on the telephone.

educate   associate   indicate   /   awkwardly   probably   suddenly

_____

_____

17 ious (ous)
18 or (er)

a. My brother is so (*stud*...) _____ these days that he even brings a textbook to the dinner table.

b. Nick was (*fur*...) _____ when he learned that Fran had invited her boss to dinner without consulting him.

c. I once was trapped for two hours in an (*elevat*...) _____ that had gotten stuck between floors.

d. When he comes to visit, my father carries a large stick in case the (*vic*...) _____ dog downstairs tries to attack him.

e. The (*tail*...) _____ told me that the old jacket would need a new lining.

prosperous   suspicious   conscious   /   intruder   conductor   governor

_____

_____

19 ism
20 ery (ary)

a. We accused the instructor of (*favorit*...) _____ when we realized that the athletes in the class always got high grades.

b. I can't walk past a (*bak*...) _____ without going in and buying chocolate chip cookies.

c. Even after he lost his job, his savings, and his wife, Bert still held on to his (*optim*...) _____ and hoped things would improve.

d. Paula is taking a (*journal*...) _____ course because she wants to be a sports reporter.

e. Did you hear about the unemployed machinist who won a million dollars in the state (*lott*...) _____?

hypnotism   vandalism   patriotism   /   burglary   surgery   hereditary

_____

_____

ROOTS

A *root* is a basic word part to which prefixes, suffixes, or both are added. For example, to the root word *port* (meaning *carry*), the prefix *trans-* (meaning *across*) could be added; the resulting word, *transport,* means *to carry across.* Various suffixes could also be added, among them *-ed* (*transported*), *-able* (*transportable*), and *-ation* (*transportation*).

In the following activities, decide from the context which root in each pair should be added to the word part or parts in italics in sentences *a* to *e*. Then write the entire word in the space provided. Some common roots at times change their spelling slightly, especially in the last one or two letters. Alternative spellings of such roots are shown in parentheses. Note, however, that you will need an alternative spelling for only two of the following sentences.

Next, you'll find two groups of words separated by a slash line (/). In the spaces provided, write a sentence using one word from the first group and a sentence using one word from the second group.

1   duc (duct)   take, lead
2   mit (miss)   send, let go

In sentences *a* to *e*, add the appropriate root to each word in parentheses.

a. When Fred fills out his income tax form, he takes every (*de . . . tion*)

________________ in sight.

b. Harold lives in constant fear of getting a (*dis . . . al*) ________________
notice from his moody boss and having to go out looking for another job.

c. I find that listening to soft music is (*con . . . ive*) ______________ to
sleep; it takes all the tension out of me.

d. My daughter can't wait to get her learner's (*per . . .*)

________________ so that she can get behind the wheel and go places.

e. No matter what (*in . . . ements*) ______________ you offer, nothing will
lead me to accept the job.

productive   induction   conduct   /   missive   transmitter   emission

____

____

3 port   carry
4 voc (vok)   call

a. People who have good (. . . *abularies*) _____ are never at a loss for words.

b. On the wall was a beautiful rug that had been (*im . . . ed*)
    _____ from Denmark.

c. In his (*in . . . ation*) _____, the minister called on God to bring peace to the world.

d. When I went back to school, my children gave me (*sup . . .*) _____.

e. My decision is (*irre . . . able*) _____; there is no way that I will change what I have said.

transportation   porter   export   /   vocational   evoke   invoke

_____

_____

5 tract (trac)   draw
6 auto   self

a. Does the airplane really fly by itself when it's on (. . . *matic*)
    _____ pilot?

b. It took all the dentist's strength to (*ex . . .*) _____ my impacted wisdom teeth.

c. Vince bought a set of steel-belted radial tires because he wanted more (. . . *ion*)
    _____ on icy roads.

d. After the show, fans waited outside the star's dressing room, hoping she would (. . . *graph*) _____ their programs.

e. The smiling (. . . *mobile*) _____ salesman convinced me I needed power windows and a stereo system.

subtract contraction tractable / autonomy automatic autobiographical

_____

_____

7   path   feeling
8   cept (capt)   take, seize

a. The science fiction movie was about a (*tele . . .*) _____ who knew exactly what everyone was feeling and thinking.

b. My little daughter is (*. . . ivated*) _____ by *Sesame Street*; when it's on, she can't take her eyes off the screen.

c. Dick has an (*anti . . . y*) _____ for cats; he can't stand being in the same room with one.

d. The union leaders refused to take the company's offer, saying it would be (*unac . . . able*) _____ to the rank and file.

e. We accused the store manager of (*de . . . ive*) _____ advertising when we discovered that he had no $9.95 barbecues in stock.

psychopathy   empathy   apathy   /   perception   exceptional   caption

_____

_____

9   dict (dic)   say, tell, speak
10 script (scrib) write

a. We ordered a (*sub . . . ion*) _____ to *Better Homes and Gardens* so that we could get some decorating ideas.

b. My doctor's (*pre . . . ions*) _____ are hard to get filled because very few pharmacists can read them.

c. As the service was about to end, the minister pronounced a (*bene . . . ion*) _____ on the congregation.

d. Nobody in the office likes to take (*. . . ation*) _____ from Ms. Ackerman because she speaks so quickly.

e. The astrologer (*pre . . . ed*) _____ that an earthquake would destroy Los Angeles next year.

dictionary   edict   diction   /   scriptural   description   inscribe

_____

_____

11 vers (vert)   turn
12 tang (tact)   touch

a. After Vera washes her long hair, she uses a special rinse to get the (... *les*)

_____ out.

b. Each duelist was told to walk five paces, turn, face his (*ad ... ary*)

_____, and shoot.

c. The appeals court, in a dramatic (*re ... al*) _____, set the
prisoner free.

d. The family had few (... *ible*) _____ assets, but they had a
wealth of love and affection.

e. Hitler's views on race were a (*per ... ion*) _____ of the legitimate science of genetics.

extrovert   aversion   subversion   /   intangible   tactile   tactful

_____

_____

13 cess (ced)   go, move, yield
14 sist   stand

a. It took five police officers to handcuff the 280-pound suspect, who was

(*re ... ing*) _____ arrest.

b. I've had to work overtime for six (*suc ... ive*) _____ nights,
but I refuse to stay for seven nights in a row.

c. The obnoxious patron (*in ... ed*) _____ on being served right
away and threatened to stand in the kitchen until he was waited on.

d. During the economic (*re ... ion*) _____, many steelworkers
lost their jobs.

e. I always need (*as ... ance*) _____ in the library; card catalogs
are a mystery to me.

concession   secede   cessation   /   consist   persistent   resistance

_____

_____

15 gress   go
16 pend (pens)   hang, weigh

a. I am making good (*pro . . .*) _____ in English; my grades have gone from C's to B + 's.

b. With every swing of the (*. . . ulum*) _____, the grandfather clock ticked noisily.

c. Mitch was told to play more (*ag . . . ively*) _____; he wasn't scoring enough points.

d. The huge hot-air balloon hung (*sus . . . ed*) _____ in the air like a colorful Christmas ornament.

e. The mental patient had (*re . . . ed*) _____ to an infantile state; she huddled in a corner like a helpless baby.

transgression progressive digress / pensive appendage compendium

_____

_____

17 psych   mind
18 vid (vis)   see

a. Stanley has been in (*. . . otherapy*) _____ for two years, but he still doesn't know why he gets angry so often.

b. The blinking lights of (*. . . eo*) _____ games have been known to trigger attacks of epilepsy.

c. My roommate is going to visit the school (*. . . ologist*)

_____ to get some suggestions on how to cope with stress.

d. The (*. . . edelic*) _____ drugs of the 1960s, such as LSD, induced hallucinations.

e. The (*e . . . ence*) _____ collected at the scene of the kidnapping was clear enough to ensure the criminal's conviction.

psychiatrist   psychic   psychotic   /   vista   visitation   adviser

_____

_____

19 spec (spic)   look
20 graph   write

a. The description of the haunted basement was so (. . . *ic*)

    _____ that I found myself shivering as I read it.

b. Disappointments will often seem less important to us if we put them in

    (*per . . . tive*) _____.

c. As soon as Jill finished writing her paper, she (*in . . . ted*)

    _____ it for sentence errors.

d. At the end of her term paper, Nora added a (*biblio . . . y*)

    _____ listing the books and articles she had consulted.

e. When we got to the top of the hill and looked down, a (. . . *tacular*)

    _____ view met our eyes.

    inspection conspicuous spectacle / photographer biographical seismograph

    _____

    _____

PRACTICE IN UNDERSTANDING WORD PARTS

Activity 1

Draw a single line under the prefix and a double line under the suffix in each of the following words:

revitalize	untruthful	monopolize
recommendation	transference	submission
depression	subscription	postponement
disengagement	subordination	adventurous
predominant	relationship	intermittent

Activity 2

Your instructor will give you a spelling test on all the words used in the prefix activities on pages 252–257. You will be expected to spell correctly the *prefix part of the word* and to do your best with the spelling of the rest of the word. (The word will be marked wrong only if the prefix is spelled incorrectly.) Study carefully, then, the spelling of the twenty prefix parts. You will find that knowing the spelling of a prefix will help you considerably in the spelling of an entire word.

Activity 3

The same instructions apply that were given for Activity 2, except that the test will be on the twenty suffixes on pages 258–262.

Activity 4

The same instructions apply that were given for Activity 2, except that the test will be on the twenty roots on pages 263–268.

USING THE DICTIONARY

This chapter will help you use the dictionary to:

- Look up the spelling of words
- Find the syllable divisions in a word
- Pronounce an unfamiliar word
- Obtain other information about words

The dictionary is a valuable tool. To take advantage of it, you need to understand the main kinds of information that a dictionary gives about a word. Look at the information provided for the word *disdain* in the following entry from *The American Heritage Dictionary*, paperback edition.*

Spelling and syllabication   *Pronunciation*   *Parts of speech*

dis•dain (dĭs•dān´) *v.* 1. To show contempt for. 2. To refuse aloofly. —*n.* Mild contempt and aloofness. [< Lat. *dedignari.*] —**dis•dain´ful** *adj.* —**dis•dain´ful•ly** *adv.* } ← *Meanings*

Other forms of the word

* Dictionary excerpts in this chapter and in the Mastery Tests © 1983 by Houghton Mifflin Company. Reprinted by permission from *The American Heritage Dictionary of the English Language,* paperback edition.

SPELLING

The first bit of information, in the boldface (heavy-type) entry itself, is the spelling of *disdain*. At times you may have trouble looking up words that you cannot spell. Be sure to pronounce each syllable in the word carefully and write it down the way you think it is spelled. If you still cannot find it, proceed as follows:

1   Try the other vowels. For example, if you think the vowel is *e*, try *a, o, i, u,* and *y*.

2   Try doubling consonants. If you think the letter is one *c*, try *cc*; if one *m*, try *mm*; if one *t*, try *tt*; and so on. On the other hand, if you think the word has double letters, try a single letter.

3   If you think a word has the letter or letter combination in the first column of each group that follows but you can't find the word in the dictionary, try looking at the letter or letters in the second column of each group.

c	k, s	g, j	j, g	s	c, z, sh
er, re	re, er	ie, ei	ei, ie	sh, ch	ch, sh
f	v, ph	k	c, ch	shun	tion, sion
		oo	u	y	i, e

Use your dictionary and the preceding hints to correct the spelling of the following words.

acquaintence	_____	assisstant	_____
courtasy	_____	cemetary	_____
anounce	_____	conshious	_____
boundery	_____	sollitary	_____
practicaly	_____	femanine	_____
casheir	_____	envellope	_____
ernest	_____	librerian	_____
decieve	_____	intreview	_____

SYLLABICATION

The second bit of information that the dictionary gives, also in the boldface entry, is the syllabication of *disdain*. Note that a dot separates each syllable (or part) in the word. The syllable divisions help you pronounce a word and also show you where to hyphenate a word as needed when writing a paper.

Use your dictionary to mark the syllable divisions in the following words. Also indicate how many syllables are in each word.

w r i n k l e   (_____ syllables)

d e l i c a t e   (_____ syllables)

e l e c t r o n i c   (_____ syllables)

h i p p o p o t a m u s   (_____ syllables)

PRONUNCIATION

The third bit of information in the dictionary entry is the pronunciation of *disdain:* (dĭs-dān'). You may already know how to pronounce *disdain,* but if you didn't, the information within the parentheses would serve as your guide. Use your dictionary to complete the following exercises that relate to pronunciation.

Vowel Sounds

You will probably use the pronunciation key in your dictionary mainly as a guide to pronouncing different vowel sounds (vowels are the letters *a, e, i, o,* and *u*). Here is the pronunciation key that appears on every other page of the paperback *American Heritage Dictionary:*

> ă pat ā pay â care ä father ĕ pet   ē be ĭ pit ī tie î pier ŏ pot ō toe ô paw,
> for oi noise oo took o͞o boot ou out th thin *th* this ŭ cut û urge
> y͞oo abuse zh vision ə about, item, edible, gallop, circus

The key tells you, for example, that the sound of the short *a* is pronounced like the *a* in *pat,* the sound of the long *a* is like the *a* in *pay,* the sound of the short *i* is like the *i* in *pit,* and so on.

Now look at the pronunciation key in your dictionary. The key is probably located in the front of the dictionary or at the bottom of every page. What common word in the key tells you how to pronounce each of the following sounds?

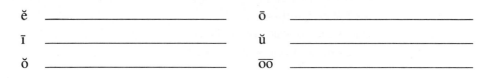

ĕ _____   ō _____

ī _____   ŭ _____

ŏ _____   o͞o _____

(Note that the long vowel always has the sound of its own name.)

The Schwa (ə)

The symbol ə looks like an upside-down *e*. It is called a *schwa,* and it stands for the unaccented sound in such words as *ago, item, edible, gallop,* and *circus.* More approximately, it stands for the sound *uh*—like the *uh* speakers may make when they hesitate in their speech. Perhaps it would help to remember that *uh,* as well as ə, could often be used to represent the schwa sound.

Here are some of the many words in which the sound appears: *recollect* (rĕk′ə-lĕkt′ *or* rĕk′uh-lĕkt′); *hesitate* (hĕz′ə-tāt *or* hĕz′uh-tāt); *courtesy* (kûr′tə-sē *or* kûr′tuh-sē). Open your dictionary to any page and you will almost surely be able to find three words that make use of the schwa in the pronunciation in parentheses after the main entry. Write each of the three words and their pronunciations in the following spaces:

1. _____   (_____)

2. _____   (_____)

3. _____   (_____)

Accent Marks

Some words contain both a primary accent, shown by a heavy stroke (′), and a secondary accent, shown by a lighter stroke (′). For example, in the word *discriminate* (dĭs krĭm′ ə-nāt′), the stress, or accent, goes chiefly on the second syllable (krĭm′) and to a lesser extent on the last syllable (nāt′).

Use your dictionary to add accent marks to the following words:

repulse (rĭ pŭls)
chameleon (kə mēl yən)
perspective (pər spĕk tĭv)
mercenary (mûr sə nĕr ē)
evacuation (ĭ văk yoo ā shən)
sociopolitical (sō sē ō pə lĭt ĭ kəl)

Full Pronunciation

Here are ten pronunciations of familiar words. See if you can figure out the correct word in each case. Confirm your answers by checking your dictionary. One is done for you as an example.

kwĭz	*quiz*	kwĕs′chən	
tĭk′əl		ĕg′zĭt	
wûr′ē		kē′bôrd′	
dĭ-zûrt′		fĭk-tĭsh′əs	
mēt′bôl′		lŭg′zhə-rē	

Now use your dictionary to write out the full pronunciation (the information given in parentheses) for each of the following words:

1. curtail _____
2. adamant _____
3. expedite _____
4. subservient _____
5. dissipate _____

6. coalition _____
7. permeate _____
8. specious _____
9. caricature _____
10. accentuate _____

Now practice *pronouncing* each word. Use the pronunciation key in your dictionary as an aid to sounding out each syllable. Do *not* try to pronounce a word all at once; instead, work on mastering *one syllable at a time.* When you can pronounce each of the syllables in a word successfully, say them in sequence, add the accent, and pronounce the entire word.

OTHER INFORMATION ABOUT WORDS

Parts of Speech

The next bit of information that the dictionary gives about *disdain* is *v*. This label, as the key in the front of your dictionary explains, indicates the *part of speech* and is one of the abbreviations given in the dictionary.

Fill in any meanings that are missing for the following abbreviations:

v. = verb

n. = _____

adj. = adjective

pl. = _____

sing. = _____

Principal Parts of Irregular Verbs

Disdain is a regular verb and forms its principal parts by adding *-ed, -ed,* and *-ing* to the stem of the verb. When a verb is irregular, the dictionary lists its principal parts. For example, with the verb *write* the present tense comes first (the entry itself, *write*). Next comes the past tense (*wrote*) and then the past participle (*written*), the form of the verb used with such helping words as *have, had,* and *was.* Then comes the present participle (*writing*) — the *-ing* form of the verb.

Look up the parts of the following irregular verbs and write them in the spaces provided. The first one has been done for you.

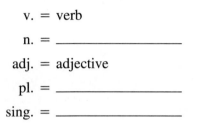

Present	Past	Past Participle	Present Participle
write	wrote	written	writing
break			
grow			
give			

Plural Forms of Irregular Nouns

The dictionary supplies the plural forms of all irregular nouns (regular nouns form the plural by adding -*s* or -*es*). Give the plurals of the following nouns. If two forms are shown, write both.

echo   _____

knife   _____

phenomenon   _____

alumna   _____

sister-in-law _____

Meanings

When a word has more than one meaning, the meanings are numbered in the dictionary, as with *disdain*. In many dictionaries, the most common meanings are presented first. The introductory pages of your dictionary will explain the order in which meanings are presented.

Use the context to try to explain the meaning of the italicized word in each of the following sentences. Write your definition in the space provided. Then look up and record the dictionary meaning of the word. Be sure you find the meaning that fits the word as it is used in the sentence.

1. After opening clams all summer, Joe's *calloused* hands were tough and hard.

   Your definition: _____

   Dictionary definition: _____

2. The police officers were shocked by the *callous* attitude of the bystanders who had witnessed the stabbing and failed to call for help.

   Your definition: _____

   Dictionary definition: _____

3. A wide scratch in the dresser's walnut *veneer* revealed the plywood beneath.

   Your definition: _____

   Dictionary definition: _____

4. A *veneer* of self-confidence couldn't hide Ruth's basic insecurity.

   Your definition: _____

   Dictionary definition: _____

Etymology

Etymology refers to the history of a word. Many words have origins in foreign languages, such as Greek (Gk) or Latin (L). Such information is usually enclosed in brackets and is more likely to be present in a hardbound desk dictionary than in a paperback one. Good desk dictionaries include the following:

American Heritage Dictionary
Random House College Dictionary
Webster's New Collegiate Dictionary
Webster's New World Dictionary

A good desk dictionary will tell you, for example, that *maverick* derives from the name of a Texas rancher who refused to brand his calves. The word is now a general term used to describe someone who does not conform or "follow the herd."

See whether your dictionary gives the origins of the following words:

boycott _____ chauvinism _____

Usage Labels

As a general rule, use only standard English words in your writing. If a word is not standard English, your dictionary may give it a usage label such as *informal, nonstandard,* or *slang.* Look up the following words and record how your dictionary labels them. Note that a recent hardbound desk dictionary will be the best source of information about usage.

push (meaning "promote or sell")

_____

gag (meaning "joke")

_____

nowheres

_____

picky

_____

creep (meaning "obnoxious person")

_____

PRACTICE IN USING THE DICTIONARY

Activity 1

Use your dictionary to write the full pronunciation for the following words.

1. ennui _____   6. pejorative _____

2. vacillate _____   7. loquacious _____

3. charisma _____   8. inexorable _____

4. felicitous _____   9. disparage _____

5. sinecure _____   10. misanthrope _____

Activity 2

Refer to the excerpt on the opposite page, from the paperback *American Heritage Dictionary*, to answer the questions that follow.

1. How many syllables are in the word *corpuscle?*_____

2. Where is the primary accent in the word *correspondingly?* _____

3. Where is the primary accent in the word *correlational?* _____

4. What word in the pronunciation key tells you how to pronounce the *a* in *correlation?* _____

5. In the word *corral,* the *a* is pronounced like the *a* in
   a. pat.
   b. pay.
   c. father.
   d. care.

6. In the word *corpus,* the *o* is pronounced like the *o* in
   a. toe.
   b. for.
   c. pot.
   d. gallop.

7. In the word *corpulence,* the first *e* is pronounced like a
   a. short *e*.
   b. long *e*.
   c. short *i*.
   d. schwa.

Extract for Activity 2

corps (kôr, kōr) *n., pl.* corps (kôrz, kōrz). **1.** A specialized section or branch of the armed forces. **2.** A group of persons under common direction. [Fr.]

corpse (kôrps) *n.* A dead body, esp. of a human being. [< Lat. *corpus.*]

cor•pu•lence (kôr′pyə-ləns) *n.* Fatness; obesity. [< Lat. *corpulentia.*] **—cor′pu•lent** *adj.* **—cor′pu•lent•ly** *adv.*

cor•pus (kôr′pəs) *n., pl.* **-po•ra** (-pər-ə). **1.** *Anat.* A structure constituting the main part of an organ. **2.** A large collection of specialized writings. [Lat.]

cor•pus•cle (kôr′pə-səl, -pŭs′əl) *n.* **1.** A cell capable of free movement in a fluid or matrix as distinguished from a cell fixed in tissue. **2.** A minute particle. [Lat. *corpusculum,* little particle.] **—cor•pus′cu•lar** (-pŭs′kyə-lər) *adj.*

corpus de•lic•ti (də-lĭk′tī′) *n.* **1.** *Law.* Evidence of the fact that a crime has been committed. **2.** The victim's corpse in a murder case. [NLat., body of the crime.]

cor•ral (kə-răl′) *n.* An enclosure for confining livestock. *—v.* **-ralled, -ral•ling. 1.** To drive into and hold in a corral. **2.** *Informal.* To seize; capture. [Sp.]

cor•rect (kə-rĕkt′) *v.* **1.** To remove the errors or mistakes from. **2.** To mark the errors in. **3.** To admonish or punish in order to improve. **4.** To remedy or counteract. *—adj.* **1.** True or accurate. **2.** Conforming to standards; proper. [< Lat. *corrigere.*] **—cor•rect′•a•ble** or **cor•rect′i•ble** *adj.* **—cor•rec′tive** *adj. & n.* **—cor•rect′ly** *adv.* **—cor•rect′ness** *n.*
  Syns: correct, amend, mend, rectify, remedy, right v.

cor•rec•tion (kə-rĕk′shən) *n.* **1.** The act or process of correcting. **2.** Something offered or substituted for a mistake or fault. **3.** Punishment intended to improve. **4.** A quantity added or subtracted to improve accuracy. **—cor•rec′tion•al** *adj.*

cor•re•la•tion (kôr′ə-lā′shən, kŏr′-) *n.* A complementary, parallel, or reciprocal relationship: *a direct correlation between recession and unemployment.* [Med. Lat. *correlatio.*] **—cor′•re•late′** *v. & adj.* **—cor′re•la′tion•al** *adj.*

cor•rel•a•tive (kə-rĕl′ue-tĭv) *adj.* **1.** Related; corresponding. **2.** Reciprocally related. *—n.* **1.** Either of two correlative entities. **2.** A correlative word or expression, as *neither* and *nor.* **—cor•rel′a•tive•ly** *adv.*

cor•re•spond (kôr′ĭ-spŏnd′, kŏr′-) *v.* **1.** To be in agreement, harmony, or conformity. **2.** To be similar or equal (to). **3.** To communicate by letter. [< Med. Lat. *correspondēre.*] **—cor′re•spond′ing•ly** *adv.*

ă pat ā pay â care ä father ĕ pet ē be ĭ pit ī tie î pier ŏ pot ō toe ô paw, for oi noise ŏŏ took
ōō boot ou out th thin *th* this ŭ cut û urge yōō abuse zh vision ə about, item, edible, gallop, circus

---

8. *True or false?* _____ You should not pronounce the letter *p* in the word *corps.*

9. *True or false?* _____ *Corral* can be used as a verb.

10. What is the plural form of *corpus*? _____

WORD PRONUNCIATION

This chapter will help you:

- Review the two major rules for dividing words into syllables
- Apply the two rules to specialized terms in different subjects
- Review other rules relating to word division and pronunciation

WHY YOU NEED TO LEARN PRONUNCIATION

You will meet many specialized terms in your various academic subjects. Knowing how to *pronounce* the terms will help you master their meanings. You can often locate difficult-to-pronounce words in the dictionary. But in other cases the words may be too technical to appear in a desk dictionary—or you will simply not have the time to look up every pronunciation.

Another problem related to word pronunciation is that there are probably more words in your *listening* vocabulary than in your *sight* vocabulary. That is, you probably recognize more spoken words than written ones. Learning how to sound out and pronounce unfamiliar words will help narrow any gap between your listening and sight vocabularies.

Using the two major rules provided in this section, you should be able to divide most unfamiliar words into syllables—and so pronounce them without having to refer to the dictionary. The rules hold true most of the time; with them, you will never be far from correct word pronunciation.

BACKGROUND INFORMATION

Before looking at the rules, be sure you understand the necessary background information that follows. First of all, remember that the vowels are *a, e, i, o, u,* and sometimes *y;* the consonants are all the other letters.

It is also important to remember that each syllable is a different general sound in a word. If a word has two syllables, it has two sounds; three syllables, three sounds; and so on. For example, in the word *impacted* (as in "impacted wisdom tooth"), there are three syllables (im pact ed) and three sounds. How many syllables (and sounds) are there in the following words?

nostril   (_____ syllables)

Frankenstein   (_____ syllables)

contemporary   (_____ syllables)

After you use the rules below to divide a word into syllables, work on pronouncing *one syllable at a time.* Only when you can pronounce each syllable in a word separately should you put the sounds together in succession. Then, when you can correctly pronounce all the sounds in the word in succession, you should add the accent (stress) where it sounds right. If the word doesn't "sound right," or if it is hard or awkward to say, change the accent or the pronunciation (or both) slightly until it does sound right to your ear. Remember that the rules given below will get you close to the correct pronunciation, but they are not always exact. You may have to make final adjustments.

THE TWO MAJOR RULES FOR DIVIDING WORDS INTO SYLLABLES

Rule 1: Divide between Double Consonants

Here are examples of rule 1:

mes/sage   dis/tance   fun/gus

In each case the division is between the double consonants: the *ss* in *message,* the *st* in *distance,* and the *ng* in *fungus.*

At times, the division will occur between a consonant and a *consonant blend*— two or more consonants that blend together to form one sound. Here are examples:

mor/phine   con/struct   sub/stance

The syllable division in *morphine* is between the consonant *r* and the consonant blend *ph;* in *construct,* between the consonant *n* and the consonant blend *str;* in *substance,* between the consonant *b* and the consonant blend *st.*

Activity

Use a slash line to divide the following words into syllables at the point where double consonants occur.

1. kidney
2. lemming
3. morbid
4. rampant
5. parlor

6. urbane
7. lambent
8. hostel
9. plasma
10. haggard

11. horror
12. vellum
13. vestry
14. collate
15. dormant

Pronunciation Hint: The vowel before double consonants usually has a short sound. For example, the *u* in *umber* has a short sound, like the *u* in *cut.*

Rule 2: Divide before a Single Consonant

Here are examples of rule 2:

    lo/cal   vi/per   bla/tant

In each case, the syllable division is before the single consonant: before the *c* in *local,* before the *p* in *viper,* and before the first *t* in *blatant.*
    At times, the division will occur before a consonant blend. For example, in the word *preclude,* the division occurs before the consonant blend *cl: pre/clude.*

Activity

Use a slash line to divide the following words into syllables before single consonants.

1. malign
2. pagan
3. climax
4. tripod
5. vapid

6. biped
7. supine
8. evince
9. nadir
10. putrid

11. primeval
12. deduce
13. brazen
14. eject
15. votary

Pronunciation Hint: The vowel before a division at a single consonant usually has a long sound. For example, the *o* in *cogent* has a long sound, like the *o* in *go.*

■ **Review Test**

Divide these words into syllables by applying either or both of the two rules.

1. vertex	6. turbulent	11. conjecture
2. seduce	7. solon	12. germicide
3. doldrums	8. vulpine	13. bovine
4. arbiter	9. stringent	14. wanton
5. cajole	10. lethargic	15. somnolent

OTHER HELPFUL RULES FOR DIVIDING WORDS INTO SYLLABLES

Rule 3: Always Divide Compound Words between the Words That Form the Compound

Divide the following words:

moonshine	keyhole	breakfast
molehill	ringmaster	snowshoe

Rule 4: Divide between Prefixes and Suffixes

Common prefixes include: *anti, trans, non, re, post, con, mis, ex, de, inter, sub, ad, dis, ante, ultra, bi, syn, ab, tri, in, pre.* Common suffixes include: *en, ize, ess, ism, able, ible, ward, ment, ry, ic, ist, less, ship, ance, age, ful, ness, ier, ious, ition, ion, ing.*
Divide the following words at prefix or suffix divisions:

alarming	expunge	synthesis
interjection	disinherit	submission
disgrace	perversity	antebellum

Rule 5: Two Vowels Together May Represent Separate Sounds and Be in Separate Syllables

Use this rule to divide and pronounce the following words:

chaos	duet	mortuary
envious	corporeal	reiterate

PRACTICE IN WORD PRONUNCIATION

Activity 1

Divide the words in items 1–25 below into syllables. You should then be able to sound out and pronounce each separate syllable and then the whole word.

Remember that the chief rules for syllable division are to (1) divide between double consonants and (2) divide before a single consonant.

> **Example:** dis/con/so/late
> (The word has four syllables. The first two divisions are between double consonants—*sc* and *ns*; the third division is before the single consonant.)

Note: After you divide a word into syllables, place the stress, or accent, on the syllable that makes the word easier to pronounce. The stress that sounds the most natural is generally the correct one. For instance, the word *disconsolate* is most easily emphasized on the second syllable—*dis **con** so late*—and that accent is the correct one.

1. impute
2. regressive
3. contingent
4. rotunda
5. admonition
6. distortion
7. pristine
8. masticate
9. concave
10. corrosive
11. salvo
12. refract
13. portico
14. invective
15. cognizant
16. fresco
17. grimace
18. infidel
19. perfidy
20. malignant
21. ruminate
22. jubilation
23. dilemma
24. apropos
25. terrapin

Activity 2

The following lists consist of specialized terms you can expect to encounter in your various academic courses. You should be able to divide the words into syllables and pronounce them correctly (or come close to the correct pronunciation) using chiefly the two basic rules for syllable division.

Terms from Psychology

1. bipolar
2. temporal
3. somatic
4. egocentrism
5. locus
6. hippocampus
7. narcolepsy
8. endomorph
9. perceptor
10. puberty

Terms from Sociology

1. ethnocentric
2. ghetto
3. cognitive
4. mutation
5. integration
6. exponential
7. patrilocal
8. diffusion
9. subculture
10. collective

Terms from Biology and Other Sciences

1. follicle
2. chromosphere
3. centipede
4. proton
5. micturition
6. corona
7. rotifer
8. mollusk
9. convection
10. electron

Terms from Business and Economics

1. accumulator
2. interface
3. chattel
4. franchise
5. compensation
6. directorate
7. syndicate
8. micromotion
9. prototype
10. endowment

SPELLING IMPROVEMENT

This chapter will show you how to improve your spelling by using:

- A dictionary
- Electronic aids
- A personal spelling list
- Lists of specialized words
- A list of common English words
- Four basic spelling rules

Poor spelling often results from bad habits developed in early school years. With work, such habits can be corrected. If you can write your name without misspelling it, there is no reason why you can't do the same with almost any word in the English language. Six steps you can follow to improve your spelling are discussed here.

USING THE DICTIONARY

Get into the habit of using the dictionary. When you write a paper, allow yourself time to look up all those words whose spelling you are unsure about. Do not overlook the value of this step just because it is such a simple one. Through using the dictionary, you will probably improve your spelling 95 percent almost immediately.

USING ELECTRONIC AIDS

There are three electronic aids that may help you with spelling. First, many *electronic typewriters* on the market today will automatically beep when you misspell or mistype a word. They feature built-in dictionaries that will then give you the correct spelling. Smith-Corona, for example, has a series of portable typewriters with an "Auto-Spell" feature that start at around $150 at discount stores.

Second, a *computer with a spell-checker* will identify incorrect words and suggest correct spellings. If you know how to write on a personal computer, you will have no trouble learning how to use the spell-check feature.

Finally, *electronic spell-checkers* are pocket-size spelling aids. They look much like the pocket calculators you may carry to your math class, and they are the latest example of how technology can help the learning process. Electronic spellers can be found in the typewriter or computer section of any discount store, at prices in the range of $100. The checker has a tiny keyboard on which you type out a word the way you think it is spelled; the checker then quickly provides you with the correct spelling of related words. Some of the checkers even *pronounce* the word for you.

KEEPING A PERSONAL SPELLING LIST

Either in a separate notebook for spelling or in a specific section within your notebook for English or reading and study skills, keep a list of words that you misspell.

To master such words, do the following:

1   Look at the first word, say it, and spell it. Then look away and try to spell it. When you can, go on and work on the next word until you can spell it without looking at it. Then go back and test yourself on the first word. After learning each new word, go back and review all the preceding ones. *This review and repeated self-testing are the keys to effective learning.*

2   As a reinforcement, you may want to write out difficult words several times or "air-write" them with your finger in large, exaggerated motions. Also, when you write a word out, you may want to capitalize the letters you confuse in it. For example, if you tend to spell *resources* as *resorces,* you might want to write *resoURces.*

3   With long words, divide the word into syllables and try to spell the syllables. For example, *misdemeanor* can be spelled easily if you can hear and spell in turn its four syllables: *mis de mean or*. Again, the word *formidable* can be spelled easily if you hear and spell in turn its four syllables: *for mi da ble*. Even a very long word like *antidisestablishmentarianism* becomes simple if you first break it down into syllables: *an ti dis es tab lish men tar i an is m*. Remember, then: Try to see, hear, and spell long words in terms of their syllable parts.

Activity

Use the space below as a starter for words that you misspell. As you accumulate additional words, you may want to jot them down on a back page of this book or your English or reading notebook.

Incorrect Spelling	Correct Spelling	Points to Remember
alot	a lot	two words
writting	writing	one "t"
alright	all right	two words

LEARNING KEY WORDS IN MAJOR SUBJECTS

Make up lists of words central to the vocabulary of your major subjects. For example, a list of key words in business might include *economics, management, resources, scarcity, capitalism, decentralization, productivity, enterprise,* and so on; in psychology: *behavior, investigation, experimentation, frustration, cognition, stimulus, response, organism,* and so on. Set aside a specific portion of your various course notebooks to be used only for such lists and study them using the method for learning words described on page 288.

Activity

Write in the space below the name of one of your subjects and fifteen repeatedly used terms which you should learn to spell for that subject.

Subject _____

1. _____
2. _____
3. _____
4. _____
5. _____
6. _____
7. _____
8. _____
9. _____
10. _____
11. _____
12. _____
13. _____
14. _____
15. _____

STUDYING A BASIC WORD LIST

Master the spellings of the words in the following list. They are some of the most often used words in English. Your instructor may assign twenty-five or fifty words for you to study at a time and give you a series of quizzes until you have mastered the list.

ability	attempt	chief	education
absent	attention	children	either
accept	awful	church	English
accident	awkward	cigarette	enough
across	back	clothing	entrance
address	balance	collect	everything
advertise	bargain	color	examine
advice	beautiful	comfortable	exercise
after	because	company	expect
again	become	condition	family
against	been	conversation	flower
all right	before	daily	foreign
almost	begin	danger	friend
a lot	being	daughter	from
also	believe	death	garden
always	between	deposit	general 100
although	bottom	describe	grocery
among	brake	different	guess
amount	breathe	direction 75	handkerchief
angry	building	distance	happy
animal	business	does	heard
another	came 50	doubt	heavy
answer	careful	dozen	himself
anxious	careless	during	holiday
apply 25	cereal	each	house
approve	certain	early	however
argue	change	earth	hundred
around	cheap	easy	hungry

instead	noise	ready	thought
intelligence	none	really	thousand
interest	nothing 150	reason	through
interfere	number	receive	ticket
kindergarten	ocean	recognize	tired
kitchen	offer	remember	today
knowledge	often	repeat	together
labor	omit	restaurant	tomorrow 225
language	only	ridiculous	tonight
laugh	operate	right	tongue
learn	opportunity	said	touch
length	original	same	travel
lesson 125	ought	sandwich	truly
letter	pain	sentence	under
listen	paper	several	understand
loneliness	peace	should	until
making	pencil	since	upon
marry	people	sleep 200	usual
match	perfect	smoke	value
matter	period	something	vegetable
measure	person	soul	view
medicine	picture	state	visitor
middle	place	straight	voice
might	pocket	street	warning
million	possible	strong	weather
minute	potato	student	whole
mistake	president	studying	window
money	pretty 175	suffer	without
month	promise	summer	would
morning	psychology	sweet	writing
mountain	public	teach	written
much	quick	telephone	yesterday
needle	quiet	than	your 250
neither	quite	there	
newspaper	raise	thing	

LEARNING BASIC SPELLING RULES

A final way to improve your spelling is to learn and practice the four often-used rules that follow. While the rules have exceptions, they usually hold true.

Rule 1: *I* before *E*

Use *i* before *e* except after *c*. For example:

believe	deceive	yield
chief	receive	receipt
field	perceive	piece
grief	ceiling	priest
cashier	conceited	deceit

Activity

Fill in *ie* or *ei* in each of the following words:

1. th_____f
2. dec_____t
3. rel_____f
4. pr_____st
5. y_____ld
6. dec_____ve
7. handkerch_____f
8. br_____f
9. v_____w
10. repr_____ve

Note: Here are some exceptions to the rule: *height, either, leisure, seize, weird, neighbor, efficient, science.*

Rule 2: Final *E*

Drop a final *e* when adding a suffix that begins with a vowel. Keep the final *e* when adding a suffix that begins with a consonant. Some background information will help make this rule clear to you.

- There are two kinds of letters in the alphabet: vowels (*a, e, i, o, u,* and sometimes *y*) and consonants (all the other letters).
- Suffixes are common endings on many English words. Here are some suffixes that begin with vowels: *en, ize, ess, ism, able, ible, ic, ist, ance, age, ier, ation, ition, ion, ing, ed.* Here are some suffixes that begin with consonants: *ward, ment, ry, ship, ful, ness.*
- In the following examples, the final *e* is dropped before a suffix beginning with a *vowel:*

hope	+ ing	= hoping	sense	+ ible	= sensible
excite	+ ed	= excited	create	+ ive	= creative
believe	+ able	= believable	fine	+ est	= finest

- In the following examples, the final *e* is retained before a suffix beginning with a *consonant:*

hope	+ less	= hopeless	use	+ ful	= useful
excite	+ ment	= excitement	life	+ like	= lifelike
extreme	+ ly	= extremely	apprentice	+ ship	= apprenticeship

Activity

Use the *final e* rule with the following words:

1. amuse + ing = _____
2. write + er = _____
3. recite + ing = _____
4. definite + ly = _____
5. aware + ness = _____
6. approve + al = _____
7. desire + able = _____
8. force + ful = _____
9. creative + ity = _____
10. measure + ment = _____

Rule 3: *Y to I*

When a word ends in a consonant plus *y*, change the *y* to *i* when you add a suffix. Here are some examples:

reply + es	= replies	carry + age	= carriage
angry + ly	= angrily	marry + es	= marries
lazy + ness	= laziness	defy + ed	= defied
happy + er	= happier	penny + less	= penniless

■ *Complete this sentence:* The letter before *y* in all the preceding examples is a _____. Therefore, you change the _____ to _____ before adding the suffix.

Activity

Use the *y*-to-*i* rule with the following words:

1. sky   + es   = _____
2. carry   + ed   = _____
3. lonely + ness   = _____
4. fancy   + er   = _____
5. cry   + ed   = _____
6. party   + es   = _____
7. merry   + ment   = _____
8. city   + es   = _____
9. copy   + er   = _____
10. mercy + less   = _____

Note: Do not worry about the following exceptions. They are here simply to make the rule complete. One exception is that you do not change the *y* when you add *-ing*. For example, *play + ing = playing*. A second exception is that you do not change the *y* when a word ends in a vowel plus *y* (rather than a consonant plus *y*). For example, *employ + ed = employed*.

Rule 4: Doubling

Double the final consonant of a word when all of the following apply:

1   The word is one syllable or is accented on the last syllable.
2   The word ends with a consonant preceded by a vowel.
3   The suffix you are adding begins with a vowel.

Here are some examples:

■   If you are adding *-ing* to *drop*, you double the final consonant because:

  Drop is one syllable.
  Drop ends with a consonant preceded by a vowel.
  The suffix (*ing*) being added begins with a vowel.

■   If you are adding *-able* to *control*, you double the final consonant because:

  Control is accented on the last syllable.
  Control ends with a consonant preceded by a vowel.
  The suffix (*able*) being added begins with a vowel.

■   If you are adding *-ed* to *happen*, you do *not* double the final consonant, because *happen* is accented on the first rather than the last syllable.

Activity

Use the doubling rule with the following words.

   1. plan   + ing   = _____
   2. stop   + ed   = _____
   3. grab   + ing   = _____
   4. omit   + ed   = _____
   5. begin   + er   = _____
   6. cup   + ful   = _____
   7. big   + est   = _____
   8. occur   + ence = _____
   9. prefer   + ed   = _____
10. commit + ment = _____

■ **Final Activity**

Use the four rules to spell the following words.

1. trap   + ing = _____

2. slip   + ed = _____

3. conc_____ t

4. duty   + es = _____

5. sincere + ly = _____

6. comply + ed = _____

7. refuse + al = _____

8. conc_____ve

9. transmit + er = _____

10. nerve   + ous = _____

On the lines below, explain which rule you applied to spell each word.

1. _____

2. _____

3. _____

4. _____

5. _____

6. _____

7. _____

8. _____

9. _____

10. _____

VOCABULARY DEVELOPMENT

This chapter will explain how you can develop your vocabulary by:

- Regular reading
- Using context clues
- Systematically learning new words

A good vocabulary is a vital part of effective communication. A command of many words will make you a better writer, speaker, listener, and reader. In contrast, a poor vocabulary can seriously slow your reading speed and limit your comprehension. Studies have shown that students with strong vocabularies and students who work to improve limited vocabularies are more successful in school. And one research study found that *a good vocabulary, more than any other factor, was common to people enjoying successful careers in life.*

The question, then, is not whether vocabulary development is helpful but what the best ways are of going about it. This section will describe three related approaches you can take to increase your word power. Remember from the start, however, that none of the approaches will help unless you truly decide in your own mind that vocabulary development is an important goal. Only when you have this attitude can you begin doing the sustained work needed to improve your word power.

- *Complete the following sentence:* Most people who enjoy successful careers in life have in common a _____.

REGULAR READING

The best way to learn words is by experiencing them a number of times in a variety of sentences. Repeated exposure to a word will eventually make it a part of your working language. This method of learning words requires that *you make reading a habit.*

You should, first of all, read a daily newspaper. You do not have to read it from first page to last. Instead, you should read the features that interest you. You might, for instance, read the movie and television pages, the sports section, columns on consumer tips, and any news articles or features that catch your eye. Second, you should subscribe to one or more weekly magazines such as *Newsweek, Time,* or *People,* as well as monthly magazines suited to your interests. Among monthlies, you might choose from such magazines as *Sports Illustrated, Cosmopolitan, Science Digest, Consumer Reports, Ladies' Home Journal, Ebony, Personal Computing, Glamour, Redbook,* and many others. Finally, you should, if possible, try to fit reading for pleasure into your schedule. A number of interesting books are listed starting on page 537. You may find such reading especially difficult when you also have textbooks to read. Try, however, to redirect half an hour to one hour of your recreational time to reading books on a regular basis instead of watching television, listening to music, or the like. By doing so, you may eventually reap the rewards of an improved vocabulary *and* discover that reading can be truly enjoyable.

■ *Complete the following sentence:* The best way to learn a word is by seeing it in several different _____.

■ Check off each step below that you can realistically take to make reading a part of your life.

_____ Begin a subscription to a daily newspaper. What newspaper would be a good choice for you? _____

_____ Begin a subscription to a weekly magazine. What magazine might you want to subscribe to? _____

_____ Go to the library or bookstore and pick out a book that you will read for pleasure. (You may want to look at the list of recommended books on page 537.) What book might you want to try first?

_____

_____ Find a time and place that will be suitable for quiet reading. (I, for example, read in bed for a half hour or so before I go to sleep. That's an ideal quiet time for me.) What is one possibility?

_____

Activity 1

Read through a daily newspaper. Record below the name and date of the paper and the titles and authors (when their names are given) of five different features or articles that you found interesting to read.

Name of newspaper: _____ Date: _____
Articles read:

1. _____

2. _____

3. _____

4. _____

5. _____

Bring one of the articles to class and give a three-minute talk on it to a small group of other students. Do not read the article to them. Instead, explain what you felt was the main point of the article (the title will often provide a clue). Also, express in your own words some of the details used to support or develop the main point.

Activity 2

Go through a weekly or monthly magazine and read at least five articles that seem interesting to you. Record the following information:

Name of magazine: _____ Date: _____
Articles read (title and author):

1. _____

2. _____

3. _____

4. _____

5. _____

Prepare a three-minute report on one of the articles, to be presented to a small group of students.

In your report for Activity 2, do the following:

- Explain briefly the main point of the article (again, the title often provides a clue to the author's main idea).
- Then present to the group the chief details that are used to support or develop that point.
- As you provide details, quote several sentences (no more than three) from the article.

Activity 3

Obtain one of the books listed on pages 537–542. Fill in the following information about the book:

Title: _____ Author: _____

Place of publication: _____ Publisher: _____ Year: _____

Read a minimum of fifty pages in the book. Prepare a ten-minute oral report on the fifty-odd pages for a small group of your peers. Your purpose in this report is to give them a good sense of the flavor of the book. To do this, you should explain and summarize in your own words how the book begins, who the main people or characters are, and what specific problems or conflicts are developed. Read at least two passages you like from the book as part of your report. The passages you read should be no more than 20 percent of your entire report.

Alternatively, prepare a written report that you will hand in to your instructor. Follow the same instructions that were given for the oral report. Set off quoted passages longer than three sentences by single-spacing them and by indenting them ten spaces in from the left margin of your paper.

Some Final Thoughts about Regular Reading

Keep in mind that you cannot expect to make an instant habit of reading newspapers, magazines, and books. Also, you should not expect such reading to be an instant source of pleasure. You may have to work at becoming a regular reader, particularly if you have done little reading in the past. You may have to keep reminding yourself of the enormous value that regular reading can have in developing your powers of language, thinking, and communication. Remember that if you are determined and if you persist, reading can become a rewarding and enjoyable activity.

USING CONTEXT CLUES

When asked how they should deal with an unknown word they meet in reading, many people answer, "Use the dictionary." But stopping in midsentence to pull out a dictionary and look up a word is seldom practical—or necessary. You can often determine the meaning of an unknown word by considering the context in which the word appears. The surrounding words and sentences frequently provide clues to the meaning of the word. Notice the italicized word in the following selection:

> A poll showed that the senator's *candor* was appreciated even by the voters who did not agree with him. "I don't go along with some of his views," one voter said. "But it's refreshing to have a politician tell you exactly what he believes."

Even if you do not know the meaning of *candor,* the context helps you realize that it means *openness* or *honesty.* Much of the time, such context clues in surrounding words or sentences will help you make sense of unknown words in your reading.

If you are a regular reader, you will use context clues on repeated occasions to determine the meaning of a word. Perhaps another time you will read:

> Tony appreciated Lola's *candid* remark that his pants were baggy. And he was pleased with himself for not getting upset when faced with an unflattering truth.

Again, context helps you understand and learn the word. And through repeated use of such context clues to understand an unfamiliar word, you will make that word a natural part of your working vocabulary.

In combination with regular reading, the use of context clues is an excellent means to vocabulary improvement. Unfamiliar words that are encountered often enough in context eventually become part of one's natural working vocabulary. If you develop the habits of reading regularly and using context clues to guess the meanings of unknown words, you will turn many unfamiliar words into familiar ones.

- ■ Complete the following sentence: Instead of using a dictionary, you can often determine the meaning of an unknown word by looking at

_____.

Activity 1

Read each of the following sentences carefully. Then decide which of the five choices provided comes closest in meaning to the word in italic type. Circle the letter of your choice.

1. The *stringent* regulations of the maximum-security prison prohibit the reading of newspapers and magazines.
   a. recent
   b. basic
   c. strict
   d. many
   e. frustrating

2. The team's *euphoria* ended quickly when the winning touchdown was disallowed.
   a. joy
   b. disappointment
   c. cooperation
   d. surprise
   e. depression

3. For a suspected murderer to be freed on a technicality is a *travesty* of justice.
   a. example
   b. model
   c. mockery
   d. advancement
   e. show

4. The manager's *adroit* handling of the crisis situation led to her promotion.
   a. careless
   b. matter-of-fact
   c. emotional
   d. indifferent
   e. skillful

5. Be sure to *scrutinize* the lease carefully before signing it to make sure there is nothing objectionable in the fine print.
   a. remember
   b. examine closely
   c. ignore
   d. copy
   e. memorize

6. Most of us were offended by the *facetious* remark he made at the funeral.
   a. humorous
   b. respectful
   c. confusing
   d. incoherent
   e. snobbish

7. The children responded with *alacrity* when their parents suggested dinner at McDonald's.
   a. boredom
   b. severity
   c. hysteria
   d. humor
   e. eagerness

8. This wilderness area will be kept in its *pristine* condition; nothing will be built, changed, or destroyed here.
   a. fussy
   b. improved
   c. prim
   d. original
   e. expensive

9. The *moribund* downtown area of our city will be revitalized by new shops and businesses.
   a. unattractive
   b. busy
   c. crowded
   d. bankrupt
   e. dying

10. One of our psychology instructor's *idiosyncrasies* is sticking a piece of chalk behind his ear as he lectures.
    a. favorite sayings
    b. odd habits
    c. faults
    d. tricks
    e. major problems

Activity 2

Use the context to try to explain the italicized word in each of the following sentences. Then check your answers in a dictionary.

1. The *archaic* language in Shakespeare's plays makes them difficult for many modern readers to understand.

   Your definition: _____

   Dictionary definition: _____

2. All the solid-looking buildings on the movie set were merely *facades* supported from the rear by wooden props.

   Your definition: _____

   Dictionary definition: _____

3. The majority of the Asian immigrants to our city are forced to work at *menial* jobs until they learn to speak English.

   Your definition: _____

   Dictionary definition: _____

4. Gold is so *malleable* that it can be spun into cloth or pounded into leaf-thin sheets.

   Your definition: _____

   Dictionary definition: _____

5. The *credulous* child believed the stranger at the door when he told her he was a long-lost relative.

   Your definition: _____

   Dictionary definition: _____

Activity 3

The ten sentences that follow were taken from college textbooks. They should dramatize to you how context clues are a practical tool for helping you identify the meanings of words you may not know in your college work. Read each sentence carefully. Then decide which of the five choices provided comes closest in meaning to the italicized word. Circle the letter of your choice.

1. Mozart, a *precocious* genius, composed his first symphony at age seven and his first opera at twelve.
   a. strange
   b. obnoxious
   c. unusually advanced
   d. adolescent
   e. very aggressive

2. Even an *abstemious* person would have been tempted by the abundant display of food and drink that graced the dining rooms of the prewar luxury liners.
   a. greedy
   b. selfish
   c. cheap
   d. sympathetic
   e. moderate

3. A change in the fruit fly gene may cause a short stumplike *appendage* to form (instead of a wing) that is useless for flying.
   a. sleeve
   b. necklace
   c. leg
   d. limblike organ
   e. handle

4. A *coalition* of foreign enemies—including every great European power except Russia—began a war with France in 1792.
   a. army
   b. alliance
   c. clump
   d. troop
   e. club

5. You may be able to *assuage* an irate customer by issuing a prompt, courteous refund.
   a. annoy
   b. get rid of
   c. lose
   d. bribe
   e. soothe

6. These economic crises resulted in unpredictable price *fluctuations,* from high to low and back again.
   a. irregularities
   b. reductions
   c. misunderstandings
   d. revisions
   e. inflation

7. The state government used budget cutting and attempts at curriculum control as *cudgels* against the state college system.
   a. incentives
   b. tricks
   c. taxes
   d. weapons
   e. orders

8. Some gods were thought to exert their powers in *malignant* ways unless appeased by offerings or magic.
   a. unexpected
   b. evil
   c. beneficial
   d. repellent
   e. mystical

9. Under the *auspices* of agencies like the Job Corps and Head Start, a great number of new federal programs were initiated in the early 1960s.
   a. patronage
   b. titles
   c. threats
   d. suspicions
   e. names

10. The novel describes a society where jobs, social benefits, and social obligations are *capriciously* distributed on the sole basis of a lottery.
    a. quickly
    b. unhappily
    c. fairly
    d. unpredictably
    e. unjustly

SYSTEMATICALLY LEARNING NEW WORDS

Learning Technical Words

Some of the most important words you must learn and remember are the technical terms used in specific subjects. In a psychology course, for instance, you need to understand such terms as *behaviorism, stimulus, regression, cognition, neurosis,* and *perception.* With an introductory course in particular, you must spend a good deal of time learning the specialized vocabulary of the subject. Mastering the language of the subject will be, in fact, a major part of mastering the subject.

Textbook authors often define a technical word at the same time as they introduce it to you. Here are several examples:

> *Catharsis,* the release of tension and anxieties by acting out the appropriate emotions, has long been recognized as helpful to one's health.

> A *capitalist,* then, is an individual who invests money or other assets in a business, hoping to make a profit.

> The word *ulcer* is used to designate an open sore in the skin or in the alimentary canal.

If you come upon a technical word that is not explained, look for its definition in the glossary that may appear in the back of the book. Or look for the word in the index that will probably be included in the back of the book. Once introduced and explained, many technical words may then recur frequently in a book. If you do not learn such words when they are first presented, it may be impossible for you to understand later passages where the words are used again. To escape being overwhelmed by a flood of unfamiliar terms, you should mark off and master important technical words as soon as they appear.

Your instructor may be your best source of information about technical terms. He or she will probably introduce a number of these terms to you in class and provide definitions. You should write down each definition and clearly set it off in your notes by underlining the term and perhaps writing *def* beside it in the margin. If you are responsible for textbook material, you should mark off and then write down definitions and other important ideas, as described on page 319. (If an instructor's definition of a term differs in wording from a text definition of the same term, you should study the one that is clearer for you.)

Some students find it helpful not only to set off definitions in their class and text notes but also to keep a list of such definitions at the back of their course notebooks. What is crucial is that you realize the importance of noting and mastering the definitions of key words in a subject. If you do not do this, you cannot expect to understand the subject fully or master it.

The activities on pages 320–325 will give you practice in locating and writing down definitions of technical terms.

■ Complete the following sentences:

Courses such as sociology, psychology, and biology have their own specialized _____.

Technical terms are often _____ when they are first introduced; they may also be defined in a _____ or an _____ at the back of a textbook.

You may find it helpful to keep a list of important definitions at the back of _____.

Learning General-Interest Words

General-interest words are not technical terms; they are words you might come upon in your everyday reading. While reading a magazine, for example, you might encounter the following sentence: "People who vacation in resort towns often have good reason to feel exploited." You may be able to guess the meaning of the word *exploited* from the context and so feel no need to consider this word any further. However, perhaps *exploited* is a word you have seen and been slightly puzzled about before, and a word you think it would be useful for you to master. You should have an organized method of learning words such as this so that you can not only recognize them but also use them in speaking and writing.

A Method of Learning New Words: To build your vocabulary, first mark off in your reading words that you want to learn thoroughly. If you are reading a newspaper or magazine, tear out the page on which the word appears and put the page in a file folder. If you are reading a book, jot down the word and the page number on a slip of paper which you have tucked into the book for that purpose. Then, every so often, sit down with a dictionary and look up basic information about each word. Put this information on a vocabulary word sheet like the one on the opposite page.

Study each word as follows:

■ First, make sure you can correctly pronounce the word and its derivations. (Page 272 explains the dictionary pronunciation key that will help you pronounce each word properly.)

■ Second, study the main meanings of the word until you can say them without looking at them.

■ Finally, spend a moment looking at the example of the word in context.

Vocabulary Word Sheet

1 Word: _____ *exploit* _____ Pronunciation: _____ *(eks ploit')* _____

Meanings: _____ *v.* _ *1 To take advantage of* _____

_____ *2 To make use of selfishly* _____

_____

Other forms of the word: ____ *exploiter   exploitable   exploitative* ____

Use of the word in context: ____ *People who vacation in resort* ____

towns often have good reason to feel exploited.

Your own sentence using the word: ____ *I tried to exploit the fact*

that my boss was my father-in-law by asking for a raise.

2 Word: _____ Pronunciation: _____

Meanings: _____

_____

_____

Other forms of the word: _____

Use of the word in context: _____

_____

Your own sentence using the word: _____

_____

3 . . .

You should follow the same process with every word. After testing yourself on the first word, go on to the second word. After testing yourself on the second word, go back and retest yourself on the first. After you learn each new word, continue going back and testing yourself on all the words you have studied. Such repeated self-testing is the key to effective learning.

An Alternative Method of Accumulating Words: Some people can effectively use three- by five-inch cards, rather than a word sheet, to accumulate words. In this method, you prepare a card for each word, using the following format.

1   *Front of the card:* word; pronunciation; part of speech; forms of the word; example of the word in context.

```
exploit      (eks ploit') v.

exploiter   exploitable   exploitative

People who vacation in resort towns
often have good reason to feel exploited.
```

2   *Back of the card:* different meanings of the word; check (√) beside the meaning that fits the context in which you found the word; sentence using the word.

```
√   1 To take advantage of
    2 To make use of selfishly

    I tried to exploit the fact that my
    boss was my father-in-law by asking
    for a raise.
```

An advantage of this method is that the cards can be shuffled so that the words can be studied in any order. A drawback of the method is that some people do not find it practical or convenient to keep a pack of vocabulary cards handy. Use whichever method you think will work for you.

Activity

Locate five words in your reading that you would like to master. Enter them on your vocabulary word sheet and fill in all the needed information. Your instructor may then check your word sheet and perhaps give you a quick oral quiz on selected words.

You may receive a standing assignment to add five words a week to a word sheet and to study the words. Note that you can create your own word sheets using loose-leaf paper, or your instructor may give you copies of the word sheet that follows.

1. Word: _____ Pronunciation: _____

    Meanings: _____

    _____

    _____

    _____

    Other forms of the word: _____

    Use of the word in context: _____

    _____

2. Word: _____ Pronunciation: _____

    Meanings: _____

    _____

    _____

    _____

    Other forms of the word: _____

    Use of the word in context: _____

    _____

3. Word: _____ Pronunciation: _____

   Meanings: _____

   _____

   _____

   _____

   Other forms of the word: _____

   Use of the word in context: _____

   _____

4. Word: _____ Pronunciation: _____

   Meanings: _____

   _____

   _____

   _____

   Other forms of the word: _____

   Use of the word in context: _____

   _____

5. Word: _____ Pronunciation: _____

   Meanings: _____

   _____

   _____

   _____

   Other forms of the word: _____

   Use of the word in context: _____

   _____

Learning through Vocabulary Study Books

A final systematic way of learning new words is to use vocabulary study books. The most helpful of these books present words in more than one sentence context and then provide several reinforcement activities for each word. The more you work with a given word in actual sentence situations, the better your chances of making it part of your permanent word base.

There may also be materials in your college learning center that take a ''word in context'' approach. The regular use of vocabulary study books and materials, combined with regular reading and with your own ongoing vocabulary word sheets, is a solid way to improve your vocabulary.

PART FOUR

READING COMPREHENSION SKILLS

PREVIEW

Part Four explains and offers practice in seven key reading comprehension skills. All these skills will help you read and take notes on your textbooks and other college materials. The first five skills involve the ability to recognize and use: (1) definitions and examples of definitions, (2) enumerations and their headings, (3) the relationship of headings to subheadings, (4) emphasis words and other signal words, and (5) main ideas in paragraphs and short selections. The last two skills involve the ability to outline and to summarize material you have read.

READING COMPREHENSION

One mistaken idea that some students have about reading is that comprehension should happen all at once. They believe that a single reading of a textbook selection should result in satisfactory understanding of that selection. What such students do not realize is that good comprehension is usually a *process*. Very often, comprehension is achieved gradually, as you move from a general feeling about what something means to a deeper level of understanding.

SEVEN KEY SKILLS

The purpose of Part Four is to help you learn seven key skills that will increase your understanding of what you read. The first five skills include the ability to recognize and use important elements of written material; the last two skills are techniques that will help you take effective study notes:

1 Recognizing definitions and examples
2 Recognizing enumerations
3 Recognizing headings and subheadings
4 Recognizing signal words
5 Recognizing main ideas in paragraphs and short selections
6 Knowing how to outline
7 Knowing how to summarize

Your mastery of the seven basic skills will enable you to read and understand the important ideas in articles and textbook chapters.

■ *Complete the following statements:*
Good comprehension seldom happens all at once but is usually a

_____.

There are seven skills you can learn to improve your

_____.

COMPREHENSION AND RAPID READING

Another mistaken idea that students sometimes have about reading is that an increase in reading *rate*—the purpose of the much-advertised speed-reading courses—means an automatic increase in reading comprehension. Speed-reading courses *may* increase the number of words your eyes take in and "read" per minute. And comprehension may improve because you tend to concentrate more as you read at a faster rate. However, with difficult material, understanding is likely to *fall* as the rate rises. The surest way to improve both speed *and* comprehension is to develop reading comprehension skills. Speed will automatically follow as you learn how to identify main ideas and then go quickly over lesser points and supporting details. Speed will also result as you learn how to vary your reading rate according to the nature of the material and your purpose in reading. In summary, by emphasizing comprehension rather than sacrificing it, you will make yourself a more efficient reader, and therefore a faster reader.

■ What are two mistaken ideas that students sometimes have about reading?

_____

_____

■ What is a drawback of speed-reading courses?

_____

■ What is the surest way to develop reading speed *and* comprehension?

_____

SKILL 1: RECOGNIZING DEFINITIONS AND EXAMPLES

Definitions are often among the most important ideas in a selection. They are particularly significant in introductory courses, where much of your time is spent mastering the specialized vocabulary of the subject. You are, in a sense, learning the "language" of sociology or biology or whatever the subject might be.

Most definitions are abstract, and so they are usually followed by one or more examples that help clarify their meaning. Always select and mark off at least one example that helps make an abstract definition clear for you.

In the following passage from a sociology textbook, underline the definition. Also, locate the two examples and write *ex* in the left-hand margin beside each of them.

INTUITION

Galen, a famous Greek physician of the second century, prepared an elaborate chart of the human body showing exactly where it might be pierced without fatal injury. How did he know the vulnerable spots? He just *knew* them. True, he had learned a good deal of human anatomy through his observations and those of his associates, but beyond this, he relied on his intuition to tell him which zones were fatal. *Intuition* is any flash of insight (true or mistaken) whose source the receiver cannot fully identify or explain. Hitler relied heavily on his intuition, much to the distress of his generals. His intuition told him that France would not fight for the Rhineland, that England would not fight for Czechoslovakia, that England and France would not fight for Poland, and that England and France would quit when he attacked Russia. He was right on the first two insights and wrong on the last two.

You may have realized that the first lines of this passage are not a definition of *intuition* but an example. The definition ("*Intuition* is any flash of insight") is found midway through the paragraph. The examples (Galen and Hitler) are found at the beginning and end of the paragraph. Underlining the definition and writing *ex* in the margin beside the examples will be helpful later, when you are taking study notes on the passage.

■ How should you mark off definitions? _____

_____

_____

■ Why should you mark off examples? _____

_____

_____

■ If a text gives several examples of a definition, which one should you mark off, write down, or both? Why? _____

_____

_____

Activity 1

Read quickly through the following selections, underlining each definition and writing *ex* in the left-hand margin beside an example of the definition. Some definitions will have several examples, but you need mark off only the example that makes the definition clear for you.

Note that textbook authors often call attention to terms they are defining by setting them off in *italic* or **boldface** type.

1.   Our self-concept is the product of learning. This learning goes on every day, usually without our being aware of it. *Learning* may be defined as a relatively permanent psychological change that occurs in us as a consequence of experience. Through the experience of falling in the bathtub and getting his nose full of water, a boy may learn to fear the water. The same principle operates in the learning of the self-concept. A fat girl, through the experience of listening to her classmates poke fun at her body, learns that being fat is bad and therefore that she is bad. In the learning of the self-concept, there are three important factors that must be considered: association, consequences, and motivation.

2.   Questions which do not have answers in the empirical world—answers that cannot be obtained through observations—are "nonanswerable questions." For example, if someone asks you whether this book is good or not, no amount of observation of the book, no amount of looking at it, touching it, feeling it, or counting pages will give you the answer. Your answer will be based on your personal taste and values. The question "Does God exist?" is a nonanswerable question. It cannot be answered through observations. It is answered in many ways, but the answers come from the symbolic world. They come from the particular religious values people have agreed to share. Different people will arrive at different answers—thus we have hundreds of religions. "Is premarital sex wrong?" is a nonanswerable question. Different people give it different answers. Total agreement is difficult because you are not dealing with an answerable question.

3.   **Mixtures** are combinations of two or more elements, or of elements and compounds, or of two or more compounds. The combination is merely a physical mixing. Therefore, the components of a mixture can be separated by physical means. For example, consider a mixture of iron filings (element) and salt (a compound). We know this combination is a mixture because we can separate the components by a physical process. We can use a magnet to attract the iron away from the salt. Or we could place the mixture in water (which dissolves the salt) and filter, thereby separating the iron filings. The salt solution is also a mixture. The mixed compounds, salt and water, can be separated by the physical change of boiling the water away and thereby leaving the salt behind.

4.   A crowded bus winding through a rain-soaked city stops at a corner to pick up a load of passengers. One of the people who gets on is a frail, elderly woman loaded down with parcels and bags, beads of water dripping from her plastic rain bonnet. She looks for an empty seat, but there is none. Shrewdly, she next looks for someone who might stand up so that she can sit down. The rest of the scene is easy to imagine: She makes her way with ostentatious difficulty to where a healthy-looking college student is sitting, and she plops her bags down right in front of him. The student knows what's expected, but he's comfortable. Other people on the bus begin to eye him with disapproval. The woman sitting next to him clears her throat loudly. The student no longer feels comfortable. Reluctantly, but with a flourish, he surrenders his seat. The situation offers a straightforward illustration of *informal social control,* unofficial pressure to conform to norms and values that are not fully internalized. All of us try to live up to the expectations of others, even in ways we don't always consciously recognize. The fear of ostracism, ridicule, verbal and physical threats, and other negative sanctions, and our desire for such positive sanctions as a smile, a pat on the back, or a kiss, influence the way we sit in class, the way we talk, the clothes we wear, and much else besides.

Activity 2

Mark off definitions and examples in the following selections. In addition, on separate paper take brief study notes on each selection. Your study notes should consist of the definition or definitions plus one example that makes the definition or definitions clear to you. In each case, try to summarize your example—that is, condense it into the fewest words possible that are still complete and clear. One selection is done for you as an example.

Example

The stock-in-trade of the propagandist is _loaded words_—words that evoke strong emotional reactions, usually negative. An unfavorable attitude can be created in people by calling an opponent a "Communist," "dictator," "militant," or "revolutionary." In the early 1950s, Senator Joseph McCarthy succeeded in casting suspicion *ex* on reputable citizens by calling them Communists. George Wallace, in his campaign for reelection as governor of Alabama in 1970, subtly evoked prejudice by campaigning against the "bloc" vote. And some anti-Nixon politicians in the 1972 campaign called him a "dictator."

Loaded words—words that evoke strong emotional reaction, usually negative.

Ex.—Senator J. McCarthy in 1950s called decent citizens "Communists."

1. One device for helping slum dwellers better their lives was the settlement house. This was a new kind of community center right in the slum which offered services to the poor, especially immigrants. One of the first of such centers was Hull House, founded in Chicago in 1889 by Jane Addams. At Hull House she started classes in sewing, child care, and English. There was help for working mothers with babies. There were free medical clinics and gymnasiums and singing clubs to keep youngsters off the streets. The goal was to give not just charity but a helping hand in adjusting to American urban life.

2. In order to overcome the constraints of the nine-to-five schedule and to grant workers increased autonomy, more than two thousand companies have experimented with flexible work-hour schedules, or _flextime_. With flextime, workers set their own schedules as long as the hours are compatible with company needs and the hours are sufficient to complete assignments. Thus one worker may work from seven to three, while another works from ten to six. One variation of flextime is the compressed workweek, in which workers put in four ten-hour days rather than five eight-hour days. When possible, employees are allowed to choose their day off, with many choosing three-day weekends.

3.   Influence also may be increased by using special persuasion techniques. One of the most widely studied of these is the foot-in-the-door technique, in which someone first asks for a small favor and then asks for a larger one. To demonstrate the effectiveness of this, investigators varied the kinds of favors they asked of suburban housewives. Identifying themselves as members of a safe-driving committee, they first asked the women to do a small favor—display the committee's small sign in the front window of their homes. Later the investigators contacted the women again and asked permission to place a large safe-driving sign on their lawns. Women in a control group were not asked to do the initial favor. Of the women who had agreed to the small request, 76 percent also agreed to the larger one. In contrast, only 16 percent of the control group agreed to show the large sign.

4.   There are disadvantages associated with advancement on the basis of merit. When a supervisor needs to fill positions, he or she will naturally choose people who are good at their present jobs. If people who have been moved up then prove capable of handling the new assignment, they will be advanced again and again—until they finally reach their level of incompetence! A very good teacher, for instance, may not make a good principal. But a good teacher who becomes a good principal might then be promoted to district superintendent. If this same teacher performs poorly at that level, that is where he or she will remain, with unhappy consequences. For instance, people who know that their performance is substandard often try to alleviate their anxiety by burying themselves in rules and regulations, which further decreases the quality of their work. The process we have been describing is so widely in evidence that it has become something of a household word, the *Peter principle:* "In a hierarchy, every employee tends to rise to his (or her) level of incompetence."

Activity 3

Working with a chapter or chapters in one of your textbooks, find five definitions *and* examples. Choose only definitions for which there are examples. Also, make sure each example is one that helps make the meaning of a definition clear to you. Use separate paper for this activity. Include the number of the page on which you find each definition and example, in case your instructor wants to refer to the text in reviewing your answers.

Here is a model for Activity 3:

Textbook: *Understanding Psychology*   Author(s): *Feldman*

Definition: *Personal stressors—major life events that have immediate negative consequences that generally fade with time.*

Example: *Death of a family member*

■ Review Test

Read the following selections, noting definitions and examples of the definitions. In the space provided, write the number of the sentence that contains a definition. Then write the number of the *first* sentence that provides an example of the definition.

1. [1]One-way communication occurs when a listener tries to make sense out of a speaker's remarks without actively taking part in the exchange of a message. [2]A term that describes this style of communication is *passive listening*. [3]Probably the most familiar examples of passive listening occur when students hear an instructor lecture or when viewers watch television. [4]One-way communication also takes place in interpersonal settings, as when one person dominates a conversation while the others fall into the role of audience members, or when some parents lecture their children without allowing them to respond.

   Definition: _____   Example: _____

2. [1]There is some point between the ages of thirty-five and forty-five when most of us realize that life may be more than halfway over, that there may be more to look back on than forward to. [2]The dreams of youth will never be realized. [3]We'll never be president or chairperson of the board. [4]We'll never play shortstop for the Dodgers or dance for the New York City Ballet. [5]The middle-level, middle-aged businessperson looking ahead to another ten to twenty years of grinding out accounts in a Wall Street cubbyhole may experience a severe midlife depression. [6]The housewife with two teenagers, an empty house from eight to three, and a fortieth birthday on the way may feel she is coming apart at the seams. [7]Both are experiencing the *midlife crisis,* a feeling of entrapment and loss of purpose that afflicts many and propels some into extramarital affairs just to prove that they are still physically attractive.

   Definition: _____   Example: _____

3. [1]Behaviorist theory, or operant learning theory, essentially states that animals (including human ones) learn when they are rewarded (by an "operant conditioner," or reinforcer) for taking the right steps toward a solution. [2]A white rat can be taught to press a bar, then wait ten seconds for one of two lights to go on, then do one of two different tasks, depending on which light appears—the operant conditioner or reward being a food pellet. [3]The experimenter can thereby build complex chains of acts by rewarding the rat for each part of the chain (usually beginning with the last step and working backward). [4]So, we are told, the baby acquires complex social patterns, for at each step toward such a set of acts (speaking, eating at the table, going to the toilet), the infant is rewarded with smiles, hugs, food, and praise.

   Definition: _____   Example: _____

4. [1]The ancient Hebrews had a custom that is noteworthy in this context. [2]During the days of atonement, a priest placed his hands on the head of a goat while reciting the sins of the people. [3]This symbolically transferred the sin and evil from the people to the goat. [4]The goat was then allowed to escape into the wilderness, thus clearing the community of sin. [5]The animal was called a scapegoat. [6]In modern times the term *scapegoat* has been used to describe a relatively powerless innocent who is made to take the blame for something that is not his or her fault. [7]Unfortunately, such scapegoats are not allowed to escape into the wilderness but are usually subjected to cruelty or even death. [8]Thus, if people are unemployed, or if inflation has depleted their savings, they can't very easily beat up on the economic system—but they can find a scapegoat. [9]In Nazi Germany, it was the Jews; in the rural South, it was black people.

Definition: _____   Example: _____

SKILL 2: RECOGNIZING ENUMERATIONS

Like definitions, enumerations are keys to important ideas. Enumerations are lists of items. Such items may actually be numbered in the text. More often, however, a list of items is signaled by words such as *first of all, second, moreover, next, also,* and *finally.* Typical phrases that introduce enumerations are: "There are three reasons why . . ."; "The two causes of . . ."; "Five characteristics of . . ."; "There are several ways to . . ."; and so on.

Activity

In the following selection, number 1, 2, and 3 the guidelines for constructive criticism. Note that each of the guidelines will be indicated by a signal word.

> At times people need help so they can perform better. A necessary and yet far too often misused response is constructive criticism. *Constructive criticism* is evaluation of behavior—usually negative—given to help a person identify or correct a fault. Because criticism is such an abused skill, we offer several guidelines that will help you compose criticism that is both constructive and beneficial. First, make sure that the person is interested in hearing the criticism. The safest rule to follow is to withhold any criticism until it is asked for. It will be of no value if a person is not interested in hearing it. Another guideline is to make the criticism as specific as possible. The more detailed the criticism, the more effectively the person will be able to deal with the information. Finally, show the person you are criticizing what can be done to improve. Don't limit your comments to what a person has done wrong. Tell him or her how what was done could have been done better.

You should have written 1 in front of "make sure that the person is interested in hearing the criticism" (signaled by *First*), 2 in front of "make the criticism as specific as possible" (signaled by *Another guideline*), and 3 in front of "show the person you are criticizing what can be done to improve" (signaled by *Finally*). Develop the habit of looking for and numbering all the enumerations in a textbook chapter.

When you take study notes on enumerations, be sure to include a heading that explains what a list is about. For example, because the following list does not have a descriptive heading, the notes are not very clear:

1: Make sure the person is interested in hearing the criticism

2: Make the criticism as specific as possible

3: Show the person you are criticizing what can be done to improve

Your notes will be clear and helpful if they include, as the following notes do, a heading describing what the list is about:

Guidelines for Constructive Criticism

1: Make sure the person is interested in hearing the criticism

2: Make the criticism as specific as possible

3: Show the person you are criticizing what can be done to improve

■ Why should you look for and number enumerations? _____ _____

_____

_____

_____

_____

■ What do phrases such as *Two effects of, Three important results are,* and *Five factors to note* tell you? _____

_____

_____

_____

The activities that follow will give you practice in the skill of locating and marking off enumerations.

Activity 1

In the selections that follow, number 1, 2, 3, and so on, the items in each list or enumeration. Remember that words such as *first, another, also,* and *finally* often signal an enumeration. Also, in the space provided, write a heading that explains what each list is about. Look first at the example and the hints.

Example

Heading: _____*Rewards of Schooling*_____

In strictly pragmatic terms, schooling yields three rewards, and the amount of each reward increases in proportion to the amount of schooling. First, the individual who is well schooled stands the [1]best chance of getting any job, other things being equal. Thus, the chance of unemployment is reduced. Second, the individual with a good background is the [2]one chosen for advancement and promotion; this enables him or her to earn more over the long run. Third, because of rewards one and two, the educated individual has [3]more personal freedom. Such a person will have more job opportunities from which to choose, is less threatened with unemployment, and can be freer economically because of his or her higher earning power. The decision in favor of further schooling needs to be encouraged if only for the pragmatic reasons listed above.

Hints

a   A selection often contains a phrase that introduces the enumeration. The introductory phrase in the passage above is "schooling yields three rewards." Look for such introductory phrases; they will help you write your heading.

b   Every heading that you write should begin with a word that ends in *s*, as in "Reward*s* of Schooling." As a reminder, the *s* has been added to each of the heading spaces that follow.

1.   Heading: _____*s*_____

In dealing with problems in your day-to-day life, there are at least three types of situations in which you may need some outside help. One of these occurs when you can't identify what is troubling you. You may be suffering from a symptom that bothers you a great deal—anxiety, insomnia, or depression, for example—but you find yourself unable to determine what causes it. Another situation occurs when you have an idea of what your problem is but can't figure out how to solve it. For instance, you know that you're having trouble with your parents because you fight with them almost every time you see them, but you can't find a way to stop this misery. In the third type of situation, you may have identified your problem and you may even have an idea of how to solve it, but you find yourself unable to do so. Let's say that you're working and going to school at the same time, and many nights you're so tired that you can't sleep. You take a sleeping pill, but then you have trouble getting started in the morning, and so you resort to more pills, different pills. These enable you to get through the day, but you're still "hyped up" at night—and so on. Here you know that you should break this cycle, but you can't seem to do it.

2. Heading: _____

There are numerous advantages associated with franchising. One of the most important is the training and guidance given by the franchisor. One of the best-known training programs is that offered by McDonald's, which sends the owner to "Hamburger U." Here the individual learns how to make hamburgers, control inventory, keep records, handle human relations problems, and manage the unit.

Another advantage is the customer appeal associated with buying a well-known name. Many franchisors advertise on television and radio and have catchy jingles that attract customers to the unit. Just think of some you have heard during this past week from Pizza Hut, Holiday Inn, and Kentucky Fried Chicken.

A third advantage is that the franchise, assuming it is an established one, is a proven idea. There is no need to worry about whether people will like the food being sold or the auto service being provided. There are many other successful franchised units selling the same goods and services.

Finally, there is the financial assistance angle. Some bankers will not be willing to lend money to get a small business started but will change their mind when they find that it is an Aamco franchise, a Holiday Inn, or a Jack-in-the-Box.

3. Heading: _____

Water pollution takes two forms. The first occurs when garbage and chemicals are thrown into the water. These waste materials upset the natural environment and often prove dangerous to the fish and other life in the water. To prevent further deterioration of our waters, business is now treating its wastes before putting them into the water or is looking for other, safer ways to dispose of them.

A second common problem is thermal, or warm-water, pollution. Hydroelectric power plants, in particular, tend to cause this type of pollution. In creating electricity, utilities take water from a nearby lake or river, convert it to steam for turning the plant's turbine engines, change the steam back to water, and then return it to the original lake or river. The problem is that the water is often returned at five to ten degrees above the original temperature. This causes a change in the environment of the lake or river and can be harmful to the aquatic life there.

4. Heading: _____ 5 _____

But none of these theories can be proved or disproved unless power can be measured in some way. In what ways do you calculate a person's or group's sway over events? One measure of power is the offices people hold. We can reasonably assume that the president of a big corporation or the mayor of a large city has more power than ordinary people. But what about the people who work behind the scenes, who don't appear on official rosters? We can measure their influence by reputation. If people are asked to identify the influential members of their community, we can conclude that persons who are named on many different lists belong to the local elite. But how do we verify the judges' opinions? Yet another measure of power is participation in key decisions. Who attends the crucial meetings? Who speaks for what groups? Who has lunch with whom? Who seems to have the final word? Although this may seem the best method, in-depth analyses of key decisions require almost unlimited time and effort and the combined skills of a psychologist and a detective.

Activity 2

In the following selections, number 1, 2, 3, and so on, the items in each list, and underline the words that introduce the list. In addition, on separate paper take brief study notes on each selection. Your notes should consist of numbered lists of items and an accurate heading for each list. Try to summarize the items in each list—that is, condense them to the fewest words possible that are still complete and clear. One selection is done for you as an example.

Example

Studies have indicated a number of values to reading and reciting, as opposed to reading alone. For one thing, when you read something with the knowledge that you must soon recite what you have read, you are more likely to be [1]motivated to remember and less likely to become inattentive. Moreover, recitation provides [2]immediate knowledge of results, so that you can see how well you are doing and adjust and modify your responses accordingly. Finally, recitation provides [3]active practice in recalling the material you wish ultimately to retain.

Values of Reading and Reciting

1. More motivation to remember

2. Immediate knowledge of results

3. Active practice in recalling material

1.   Even short-term hospital stays can, of course, be disturbing to small children. Bowlby found that hospitalized fifteen- to thirty-month-old infants went through three fairly well-defined stages of what Bowlby termed *separation anxiety*. In the protest stage, infants actively try to get their mothers back by crying, shaking the crib, and throwing themselves about; they continually expect their mothers to return. In the despair stage, infants diminish active movements, cry monotonously or intermittently, and become withdrawn and inactive; because they are so quiet, it is often assumed that they have accepted the situation positively. In the detachment stage, children accept care from a succession of nurses and are willing to eat, play with toys, smile, and be sociable; when their mothers visit, the children remain apathetic and even turn away. Children between six months and four years are most likely to react this way, but even within this age range not all children show this degree of disturbance.

2.   Scholars distinguish at least three generations in the development of modern computers. First-generation computers (generally available by 1955) were large, clumsy, and noisy, and they required special atmospheric conditions to operate properly. Their circuitry was based on vacuum tubes. The next generation featured the development of small transistors by 1960. Speed was greatly increased; space requirements were reduced; and new techniques were employed which resulted in less noise and an increased capacity to do all types of data processing. By 1965 we had the third generation of computers. Their circuitry was based on miniaturized circuits that could handle millions of instructions per second to reach speeds measured in billionths of a second. In 1970 silicon chips were introduced, representing a new development in computer techniques. These computers have a greater capacity to accumulate information, can use more sophisticated and business-oriented languages, and have a greater potential for instant communication. Speed is now measured in trillionths of a second, and such computers have reduced the cost of large data-processing projects. With each of these advances in technology, we have found more and better ways to use computers. Even now, research is under way to further improve the capacity of computers to serve our needs.

3.   According to Abraham Maslow, work helps us meet a number of important needs. His theory of human motivation assumes that human needs are arranged along a hierarchy. When the needs at one level of the hierarchy are satisfied, the next set of needs begins to seem more important and to press for satisfaction. At the base of the hierarchy lie our most primitive needs—hunger and thirst. While these physiological needs are relatively simple and self-centered, they are also the most potent, for they support life itself. The next level of the hierarchy is associated with our need for safety. After we feel assured of three meals a day, we work to secure warmth and comfort, protection from harm, and a stable future. The third set of needs, which becomes our greatest concern after we have established the necessary security, is that of "belongingness" and love. Working with others provides us with opportuni-

ties for friendships, validation, identification with a group, and a sense of mutual purpose. We need to know that our identities, beliefs, and problems are shared and validated by special groups within our culture. Besides work colleagues, such groups might include our neighbors, church, a women's group, fraternity brothers, Young Democrats, or Weight Watchers. Esteem emerges as the fourth level of the hierarchy. Through work efforts and other personal commitments, we strive for a sense of competence, worth, and prestige. The fifth level of need, that of self-actualization, is more complex. It involves using work to realize our creativity and values to experience a sense of personal meaning and integrity. Our work and other life activities allow us the chance to know and understand the world around us and to share wisdom and feel a part of something greater than ourselves.

4.   It's likely that in these and other cases you respond to criticism in one of three ways. Perhaps you are one of those people who withdraw when judged negatively by others. Sometimes this withdrawal takes the form of accepting the attack silently, even though you don't agree with or appreciate it. In other cases the withdrawal is physical: you might leave the presence of the critic temporarily or even permanently if the criticism is harsh enough. Although such a response does maintain peace and quiet, it takes a toll on your self-respect, for in addition to silently accepting the other's judgment of your behavior, you now must also suffer from the loss of self-esteem that comes from failing to stand up for your rights.

A second possible response to criticism is to justify yourself. While this alternative has the advantage of at least maintaining your self-respect, it has two drawbacks. First, the criticism you are resisting may be valid. Compulsive justifiers will defend against any attack and in so doing fail to learn much valuable information about themselves. A second shortcoming of justification is that the critic seldom accepts your explanation. "You can defend yourself all day long," the other might seem to say, "but I still think you're wrong." In such cases justification is hardly worth the effort.

A third typical response to criticism is to counterattack—to reduce the pressure on yourself—by pointing out some fault of the speaker. Although this strategy often shifts the spotlight away from your faults, it also has the undesirable consequence of generating ill will between you and the critic, thus weakening the relationship. In this sense counterattacking can sometimes result in your winning a battle and losing a friendship.

Activity 3

Using one of your textbooks, find and record (on your own paper) five separate enumerations. Write a heading for each list. There should be at least three items under each heading.

At the top of your first sheet of paper, give the name of the textbook you are using and the authors. Also include the number of the page on which you find each enumeration, in case your instructor wants to refer to the text in reviewing your answers. A model is given below.

Model

Textbook: _Alive and Well_   Authors: _A. & H. Eisenberg_

Heading: _Problems of the Elderly_   Pages: _542–544_

(1) Retirement

(2) Health

(3) Finances

▪ Review Test

Locate and number the enumeration in each selection that follows. Then, in the space provided, summarize the points in each enumeration. Also, write a heading that accurately describes what the enumeration is about.

1.   *Parapsychology* is the study of psychic phenomena (also known as *psi phenomena*). Psi events are those that lie outside normal experience and seem to defy accepted scientific laws. Modern parapsychologists are seeking answers to the questions raised by psi phenomena. The major areas of psi investigation are:

Clairvoyance: Ability to perceive events or gain information in ways that appear unaffected by distance or normal physical barriers.

Telepathy: Extrasensory perception of another person's thoughts, or more simply, an ability to read someone else's mind.

Precognition: Ability to perceive or accurately predict future events. Precognition may take the form of prophetic dreams which foretell the future.

Psychokinesis: Ability to exert influence over inanimate objects by willpower ("mind over matter"). If you can influence which face of a flipped coin comes up or move an object without touching it, you have psychokinesis.

Heading: _____

(1) _____

(2) _____

(3) _____

(4) _____

2. Human beings are biological organisms. They possess the ability to respond to stimulation, to move, to regulate inputs and outputs of energy, and to reproduce. They proceed physically through the process of development (that is, over time, they move from simple to complex levels of organization). In the *embryonic stage* (the first two months after conception) the organism increases in size from about 0.14 millimeter in diameter to about $1\frac{1}{2}$ inches. Cell layers that become the nervous, circulatory, skeletal, muscular, digestive, and glandular systems are formed and continue to develop. During the *fetal stage* (third month after conception until birth), the organism continues developing in such a manner that it has all the biological equipment necessary to survive at birth. During the *neonatal stage* (roughly the first four weeks after birth), the organism "breaks in" its biological equipment. It begins to breathe, to digest, to circulate the blood, and so on. By the beginning of *infancy* (about the first two or three years of life), the organism is well designed for sleeping, eating, and eliminating. It is during infancy that the organism truly begins to become human. The process of maturation defines the blank tablet so that experience may imprint a unique identity on it.

Heading: _____

(1) _____

(2) _____

(3) _____

(4) _____

3. There are several reasons why children involved in the divorce situation often live disrupted lives. First, they must deal with the trauma of their parents' separation and of one parent's leaving home. "I remember it was near my birthday when I was going to be six that Dad said at lunch he was leaving," one eight-year-old recalled. "I tried to say, 'No, Dad, don't do it,' but I couldn't get my voice out. I was much too shocked." In addition, the child of divorce now has only one parent to turn to on a day-to-day basis, and that parent—usually the mother—may often be too busy with work, housekeeping, or finding a social life to offer sufficient support and guidance to the child. Children of divorce must also often deal with the continuing conflict between warring parents. This conflict is especially traumatic in cases of child custody battles, in which the parents vie with each other for custody of the child while the child awaits the outcome.

Heading: _____

(1) _____

(2) _____

(3) _____

4.   There are several characteristics that appear to be most important in determining whether or not a person will, in our eyes, constitute a model—that is, whether we will imitate him or her. First, we tend to choose as models people who appear to have power, people who control rewards and punishments. In a gang of neighborhood friends, for example, the leader—the child who somehow always decides who will play shortstop and who will play first base—is the one whom the others are most likely to imitate. Another determinant of modeling is *rewardingness*, the extent to which the model actually has provided rewards to the observer. When a person has supplied us with attention, affection, money, or any other reward, we are more likely to imitate him or her. The last decisive characteristic is the model's similarity to the observer. One important dimension of similarity is sex. Boys tend to imitate boys, and girls tend to imitate girls. But even similarities that seem trivial can promote modeling. In one experiment, subjects were more likely to imitate another subject's choice of nonsense syllables when they thought that this subject's mistakes were similar to their own.

Heading: _____

(1) _____

(2) _____

(3) _____

SKILL 3: RECOGNIZING HEADINGS AND SUBHEADINGS

Headings and subheadings are important visual aids that give you a quick idea of how the information in a chapter is organized. The model below shows a typical use of heads in a selection.

CHAPTER TITLE

The chapter title is set off in the largest print in the chapter. The title represents the shortest possible summary of what the entire chapter is about.

THIS IS A MAIN HEADING

Appearing under the chapter title are a series of main, or major, headings. Main heads may be centered or may start at the left margin; they are often set off with capital letters and, sometimes, a different color of ink. They represent a breakdown of the main topics covered in the chapter.

This Is a Subheading

Set off under the main headings are subheadings, or minor headings. They are in smaller type; sometimes they are underlined, italicized, or set in from the left margin. The subheadings represent a breakdown of the different ideas that are explained under the main headings.

Activity

1. Look at the first chapter of this book (pages 11–19).

   How many main heads are there in the chapter? _____

   How many subheads are there? _____

   How do the main heads differ from the subheads? _____

   _____

   _____

   _____

   _____

2. Look at a chapter in one of your other textbooks.

   How many main heads are there in the chapter? _____

   How many subheads are there? _____

   How do the subheads differ from the main heads? _____

   _____

   _____

   _____

   _____

USING HEADINGS TO LOCATE IMPORTANT IDEAS

There are two methods for using headings to locate key ideas. Each method is explained and illustrated on the following pages.

Method 1: Change Headings into Basic Questions

Changing a heading into one or more basic questions is one good way to locate key ideas. A basic question can be general, starting with the word *What, Why,* or *How.* Or it can be specific, starting with the word *When, Where,* or *Who.* Use whatever words seem to make sense in terms of the heading and the passage that follows it.

Consider, for example, the following textbook selection:

DECLINE OF THE PURITAN WORK ETHIC

The Puritan concept of work as necessary for survival and as a duty and virtue in and of itself long dominated our culture. Work, obedience, thrift, and the delay of gratification were valued highly, and people's righteousness was often judged according to how hard they worked and how much they accomplished.

These views have changed, however, at an accelerated pace. Today's workers, particularly young workers, demand much more of themselves and their jobs than simply "filling a slot" and earning a living. The search for a meaningful, fulfilling job has become crucial. Workers increasingly desire to have responsibility and autonomy, to have a voice, and to demand not merely good physical working conditions but also good psychological working conditions. Rigid, authoritarian work structures are increasingly rejected as workers look to their jobs as a significant source of creative self-expression.

■   What are two questions that could be made out of the heading "Decline of the Puritan Work Ethic"?

_____

_____

The title could be changed into two basic questions: "What is the Puritan work ethic?" "Why has the Puritan work ethic declined?" The answer to the second question especially (the Puritan work ethic has declined because today's workers want meaningful, personally fulfilling jobs) forms the main idea of the passage. This technique of turning headings into basic questions often helps you cut through a mass of words to get to the heart of the matter. Develop the habit of using such questions.

Method 2: See How Subheads Relate to Main Heads

If subheads follow a main head, determine how they are related to the main head; this is a second way to locate key ideas. For example, suppose you noted the following main head and subheads spaced out over three pages of a business text:

ADVANTAGES OF THE PRIVATE ENTERPRISE SYSTEM

Freedom of Choice by Consumers
Decentralized Decision Making
High Productivity

Without having read a word of the text, you will have found one of the main ideas: The private enterprise system has three advantages—(1) freedom of choice, (2) decentralized decision making, and (3) high productivity.

Often the relationship between headings and subheads will be as clear and direct as in this example. Sometimes, however, you must read or think a bit to see how a heading and its subheads are related. For instance, in the excerpt from a psychology text on pages 112–113, following the main head "Defense Mechanisms" are the subheads "Repression," "Intellectualization," "Projection," "Displacement," and "Rationalization." When you realize that the subheads are a list of the kinds of defense mechanisms, you have found one of the most important ideas on those pages—without having read even a word of the text. Occasionally there will be no clear relationship between a heading and its subheads. You want to be ready, though, to take advantage of a relationship when it is present.

■ Why should you change headings into a basic question or questions?

_____

_____

■ Why should you check to see how subheads relate to the main heads?

_____

_____

■ Look at the excerpt from the communications text starting on page 120. How many subheads appear under the heading "The Elements of Communication"? _____ What is the relationship between "The Elements of Communication" and the subheads?

_____

_____

■ Look at the excerpt from the business text starting on page 114. How many subheads appear under the heading "The Job of Building a Business"? _____ What is the relationship between "The Job of Building a Business" and the subheads?

_____

_____

Activity 1

Read the following selections to find the answer or answers to the basic question or questions. Write your answer or answers in the space provided.

1. *Question:* How does TV violence affect children?

TV VIOLENCE AND CHILDREN

What effect does the routine portrayal of violence on television have on growing children? Numerous experiments and field studies suggest that a child who has watched a violent video sequence is more likely to engage in subsequent aggressive acts than one who has not. According to one study, a preference for violent TV shows is a more accurate predictor of aggressiveness than socioeconomic background, family relationships, IQ, or any other single factor. It is difficult to say which comes first, the aggressive disposition or the preference for violent shows, but the relationship between the two stands. A steady diet of TV assaults and murders may also make kids numb. One eleven-year-old said, "You see so much violence that it's meaningless. If I saw someone really get killed, it wouldn't be a big deal. I guess I'm turning into a hard rock."

Answer: _____

_____

2. *Question:* Why is marriage universal?

THE UNIVERSALITY OF MARRIAGE

Since all societies practice male-female marriage as we have defined it, we can assume the custom is generally adaptive. But saying that does not specify exactly how it may be adaptive. Several interpretations have traditionally been offered to explain why all human societies have the custom of marriage. Each suggests that marriage solves a problem found in all societies: how to share the products of a division of labor by sex, how to care for infants dependent for a long time, and how to minimize sexual competition. To evaluate the plausibility of these interpretations, we must ask whether marriage provides the best or the only reasonable solution to each problem. After all, we are trying to explain a custom that is presumably a universal solution. The comparative study of other animals, some of which have something like "marriage," may help us to evaluate these explanations.

Answer: _____

_____

3. *Question:* In what ways can job boredom be overcome?

OVERCOMING JOB BOREDOM

A major problem in the production process is the fact of job boredom. We know from research in industry that many people are bored with their jobs. For example, assembly line workers who spend their entire day doing the same operation over and over complain that the work is painfully dull and unrewarding. Many of them have no pride in their jobs. On the other hand, without this division of labor in which everyone performs a simple task, industry could never achieve high production. How can the workers and the work be brought together in a meaningful way? Today a number of methods are being tried, including job enlargement and job enrichment. *Job enlargement* involves giving the workers added duties, such as having them perform more operations or move from job to job on an assembly line. By making the work less routine, the company tries to break down the boredom factor. *Job enrichment* involves changing the jobs so as to build into them things that motivate the workers. These include increased responsibility, challenging work, opportunity for advancement and growth, and a greater feeling of personal achievement.

Answer: _____

_____

4. *Question:* What kind of self-concept do middle-aged people have?

SELF-CONCEPT DURING MIDDLE AGE

How do middle-aged people view themselves? On the whole, quite positively, especially as judged by a survey of one hundred well-educated, successful men and women aged forty to sixty. They are more sensitive to their position in society and become wrapped up in assessing themselves and evaluating their lives. They see middle age as a unique time of life, qualitatively different from other ages. People look at different aspects of themselves in their self-assessments—how they are in their families, in their careers, and in their bodies. They see themselves as neither young nor old, but rather as a "bridge between the generations." Middle-aged people feel a responsibility to the younger generation and feel closer to the older one.

Answer: _____

_____

Activity 2

Following are chapter and section headings taken from a variety of college texts. Change each into a *meaningful* basic question or questions, using words like *what, why, who, which, when, in what ways, how.* Note the example.

Example: Alternatives to Conflict

a. *What are alternatives to conflict?*

b. *Which is the best alternative?*

Sociology

1. Childhood Isolation

a. _____

b. _____

2. The Nature of Urban Life

a. _____

b. _____

3. Problems of the Elderly

a. _____

b. _____

4. Attitudes toward Poverty

a. _____

b. _____

Psychology

5. Changing the Self-Concept

a. _____

b. _____

6. The IQ Controversy

a. _____

b. _____

7. Personality Types

a. _____

b. _____

8. Remembering and Forgetting

a. _____

b. _____

History and Political Science

9. The New Deal
   a. _____
   b. _____

10. Congressional Limitations of Presidential Power
    a. _____
    b. _____

11. Impact of the Media on Politics
    a. _____
    b. _____

12. The Industrial Revolution
    a _____
    b. _____

Business and Economics

13. Computers in Retail Stores
    a. _____
    b. _____

14. Short-Term Financing
    a. _____
    b. _____

15. Labor Unions
    a. _____
    b. _____

16. The United States and International Trade
    a. _____
    b. _____

Biology and Other Sciences

17. Disorders of the Skeletal System
    a. _____
    b. _____

18. The Neanderthal Period
    a. _____
    b. _____

19. Marine Ecosystems
    a. _____
    b. _____

20. Predicting Inheritance
    a. _____
    b. _____

Form for Activity 4

A. _____

   1. _____

   2. _____

   3. _____

   4. _____

B. _____

   1. _____

   2. _____

   3. _____

   4. _____

C. _____

   1. _____

   2. _____

   3. _____

   4. _____

D. _____

   1. _____

   2. _____

   3. _____

   4. _____

E. _____

   1. _____

   2. _____

   3. _____

   4. _____

Activity 3

Using a chapter from one of your textbooks, change five headings into basic questions. Then read the sections under the headings to find accurate and concise answers to the questions. On separate sheets of paper, indicate the headings, the questions you asked about the headings, and the answers to the questions. At the top of your first sheet, give the name of the textbook, the author or authors, and the pages. Turn this activity in to your instructor.

Activity 4

Scrambled together in the list that follows are five textbook headings and four subheadings for each of them. Using the form on the opposite page, write the headings in the lettered blanks (A, B, C, D, E) and write the appropriate subheadings in the numbered blanks (1, 2, 3, 4).

Trial by Jury	Body	Bank Officer
Kinds of ESP	Precognition	Psychokinesis
Credit Manager	Actuary	Stages in the
Tundra	Greeting	Judicial Process
Conclusion	Tropical Rain Forest	Grassland
Claims Representative	Careers in Finance	Clairvoyance
Mental Telepathy	Preliminary Hearing	Introduction
Parts of a Speech	Terrestrial Ecosystems	Plea Bargaining
Setting Bail		Desert

Activity 5

Using one of your textbooks, find five sets of main heads and subheads that have a clear relationship to each other. Each main head that you choose should have at least two subheads. Be sure to number the subheads. Also, include the numbers of the pages on which you find your main heads and subheads, in case your instructor wants to refer to the text in reviewing your answers. A model follows.

Model

Textbook: _____*Business Today*_____ Authors: _____*Rachman and others*_____

Main Head: _____*The Marketing Mix*_____ *(pages 298–301)*

Subheads: _____*1. Product*_____

_____*2. Price*_____

_____*3. Place*_____

_____*4. Promotion*_____

A Note on Activity 5: Following the main head "The Marketing Mix" are four subheads—titles in smaller print under the main heading. Each subhead, it is clear, is one of the ingredients in a marketing mix. By recognizing the relationship between the main head and the subheads, the reader has found an important idea—without having yet read a word of the text!

■ Review Test

1. Answer the basic questions that are asked about the selection below.

   Questions: What is the myth of acceptance? Why is it a myth?

THE MYTH OF ACCEPTANCE

The myth of acceptance states that the way to judge the worth of one's actions is by the approval they bring. Communicators who subscribe to this belief go to incredible lengths to seek acceptance from people who are significant to them, even when they must sacrifice their own principles and happiness to do so. Adherence to this irrational myth can lead to some ludicrous situations:

Remaining silent in a theater when others are disturbing the show for fear of "creating a scene"

Buying unwanted articles so that the salespeople won't think you have wasted their time or think you are cheap

In addition to the obvious dissatisfaction that comes from denying your own principles and needs, the myth of acceptance is irrational because it implies that others will respect and like you more if you go out of your way to please them. Often this simply isn't true. How is it possible to respect people who have compromised important values only to gain acceptance? How is it possible to think highly of people who repeatedly deny their own needs as a means of buying approval? While others may find it tempting to use these people to suit their ends or amusing to be around them, genuine affection and respect are hardly due such characters.

Answers: _____

_____

2. Using words such as *what, why, who, which, in what ways,* and *how,* write two meaningful questions for each of the textbook heads that follow:

Real and Ideal Culture
a. _____
b. _____

Psychoactive Drugs
a. _____
b. _____

Explanations of Deviance
a. _____
b. _____

The Consequences of Overpopulation
a. _____
b. _____

3. Scrambled together in the list that follows are three textbook headings and three subheadings for each of the headings. Write the headings in the lettered blanks (A, B, C) and write the appropriate subheadings in the numbered blanks (1, 2, 3).

Nurse   The School   Physician
Agents of Social Control   Occupational Therapist   Government
Properties of Gases   Volume   Pressure
The Family   Members of the Health   Temperature
                             Team

A. _____
    (1) _____
    (2) _____
    (3) _____
B. _____
    (1) _____
    (2) _____
    (3) _____
C. _____
    (1) _____
    (2) _____
    (3) _____

SKILL 4: RECOGNIZING SIGNAL WORDS

Signal words help you, the reader, follow the direction of a writer's thought. They are like signposts on the road that guide the traveler. Common signal words show emphasis, addition, comparison or contrast, illustration, and cause and effect.

EMPHASIS WORDS

Among the most valuable signals for you to know are *emphasis words,* through which the writer tells you directly that a particular idea or detail is especially important. Think of such words as red flags that the author is using to make sure you pay attention to an idea. Look over the following list, which contains some typical words showing emphasis.

important to note	especially valuable	the chief factor
most of all	most noteworthy	a vital force
a significant factor	remember that	above all
a primary concern	a major event	a central issue
the most substantial issue	the chief outcome	a distinctive quality
a key feature	the principal item	especially relevant
the main value	pay particular attention to	should be noted

Activity

Circle the one emphasis signal in each of these selections. Note the example.

Example

The (safest and most effective solution) to the various approaches to sex education is obviously a course of compromise. Certain sexual needs should be permitted expression; unadorned information about the physiological and psychological aspects of sex should be presented to all; and the Judeo-Christian traditions within which we live must be understood and dealt with sensibly in the framework of present-day society.

1. The narrowing of the pathways through the arteries by atherosclerotic plaque is our nation's most serious health problem. It can lead to a number of disorders.

2. One other factor of great significance to the effectiveness of punishment is its severity or restrictiveness. A severe or restrictive punishment can be extremely frustrating; because frustration is one of the primary causes of aggression, it would seem wise to avoid using frustrating tactics when trying to curb aggression.

3. In order to capture as large a share of this market as possible, each firm attempts to distinguish its products from those of the competition. To do this, it relies on the use of sales representatives, advertisements, credit terms, and company reputation for service. This ability to differentiate products is very important because with so many competitive producers, no one has much control over the price.

4. Maslow says further that these needs are hierarchical; that is, one need will not declare itself until the previous one is satisfied. The key point to remember here is that, according to Maslow, it does little good to talk to hungry people about being respected because they have other needs that must be met first. Respect will not be one of their motives.

ADDITION WORDS

Addition words tell you that the writer's thought is going to continue in the same direction. He or she is going to add on more points or details of the same kind. Addition words are typically used to signal enumerations, as described on pages 326–335.

Look over the following addition words.

also	first of all	last of all	and
another	for one thing	likewise	second
finally	furthermore	moreover	the third reason
first, one	in addition	next	

Activity

Read the selections that follow. Circle the *three* major addition words in the first passage and the *four* major addition words in the second passage.

1.   Involving the community and the larger society in combating child maltreatment means getting people other than parents to help with child rearing. One form of relief for abused and neglected children is to remove them from their parents' homes and place them in foster care. Another alternative being pursued is the use of "supplemental mothers" who are available regularly to baby-sit with potentially maltreated children. Moreover, there are community-based "crisis nurseries" where parents can take their children when they feel the need to get away for a few hours. Ideally, crisis nurseries are open twenty-four hours a day and accept children at any hour without prearrangement in order to relieve or divert a crisis in the parent-child relationship.

2.   The quality of our decisions is affected by the information we use in making them. For one thing, if we fail to consider carefully all available information, we can limit the number of alternatives we consider or make a premature choice. Furthermore, the information we use may be distorted because it is outdated or misrepresented by its source. Also, we ourselves can unwittingly distort information because of our personal beliefs, attitudes, and values. Finally, new information may change our decisions. Suppose you were planning to spend your summer working at a camp, for example, only to find out after talking to your academic adviser that you will need to take classes during the summer to graduate on schedule. Instead of facing the single decision of how to obtain a camp job, you would now need to decide between camp and graduation.

COMPARISON OR CONTRAST WORDS

Comparison words signal that the author is pointing out a similarity between two subjects. They tell you that the second idea is like the first one in some way. Look over the following comparison words.

like	just as	in the same way	similarly
likewise	in like manner	alike	equally
just like	in a similar fashion	similarity	as

Contrast words signal a change in the direction of the writer's thought. They tell you that the author is pointing out a difference between two subjects or statements. Look over the following contrast words.

but	yet	variation	on the other hand
however	differ	still	conversely
in contrast	difference	on the contrary	otherwise

Activity

Circle the *one* comparison and the *one* contrast signal in each passage.

1. In one stage of the development of their motor skills, young infants display bursts of rapid, repeated movements. Such movements may seem to have no purpose. However, they provide a foundation for the more skilled behaviors that come later. Rhythmical patterns that involve the legs peak just before a child begins to crawl. Likewise, rhythmical hand and arm movements appear before complex manual skills.

2. Gathering materials for a speech is just like gathering information for any project. Many resources are available—you only have to take advantage of them. When you have a personal experience or more than average knowledge about a topic, you can use yourself as a resource. But most of the time, you will need outside information, which you can get in one or more of three ways. You can interview people with specialized knowledge about your topic. You can write away for information. You can do research in the library.

3. At first, most American companies approached the growing foreign markets from bases here in the United States. But as international business became an increasingly important source of profits, American companies began to open foreign branches and sales offices, staffed by local workers. The ownership of some companies became increasingly international. Gradually, these "American" companies became multinational corporations, with operations in several countries. In a similar fashion, large corporations in other countries have become multinational.

4.   Americans typically think of men as naturally better suited to perform the most strenuous physical labor. Not all peoples of the world, however, hold the same view. The rulers of the African Dahomeyan kingdom used women as bodyguards because they believed women to be especially fierce fighters. Similarly, Tasmanians assumed that women were perfectly well suited to the most dangerous hunting tasks. These examples suggest that there are no universal, inborn characteristics of gender in regard to skills and general abilities to do various types of work.

ILLUSTRATION WORDS

Illustration words tell you that an example or illustration will be given to make an idea clear. Such words are typically used in textbooks that present a number of definitions and examples of those definitions (see pages 319–323). Look over the following illustration words.

for example	specifically	for instance
to illustrate	once	such as

Activity

Circle the one illustration signal in each selection below.

1.   Test markets are usually selected as being typical American cities with a good cross section of income and ethnic groups. Columbus, Ohio, for example, has long been known as an excellent city in which to test new products and learn consumers' reactions.

2.   The qualities of leadership in human societies are not as clear-cut and easy to see as they are in animal societies. Most people, for instance, have certain qualities that allow them to be leaders at one time or another or in one situation or another.

3.   Purchases that require more thought fall into the category of "shopping goods." These are fairly important things that a person doesn't buy every day, such as a stereo, a washing machine, a good suit, or—in the service area—an interior decorator, a tax service, and a college. One reason a purchase requires more thought is the differences among brands in price or features. The existence of these differences prompts comparison shopping.

4.   At home and in school, children are always subordinate to adults to some extent. But peers, on the other hand, are social equals. Among peers, there are opportunities to learn the meaning of give-and-take that do not exist in the same sense in adult-child interactions. To illustrate, children can teach their friends new skills or help them solve problems, opportunities they rarely have with adults. Adults know the rules and have the power and authority to enforce them; among their peers, children can participate in the creation and enforcement of standards.

CAUSE-AND-EFFECT WORDS

Cause-and-effect words signal that the author is going to describe results or effects. Look over the following cause-and-effect words.

because	reason	since
therefore	effect	as a result
so that	thus	if . . . then
cause	consequently	result in

Activity

Circle the *one* cause-and-effect word in each of the following passages.

1.   Most people are comfortable in familiar situations with persons who are similar to themselves. A person who wears unusual native dress or has different cultural customs can seem to be a threat. As a result, prejudices are sometimes formed. Studies have found that the attitudes of preschool children toward the elderly vary. Children who are unfamiliar with older people show clear prejudices.

2.   Vision dominates information from the other senses. You may have seen a skillful ventriloquist in action and wondered how he or she could make sounds come from the dummy. Close your eyes while a ventriloquist is talking, and you will be aware that both voices come from the same place. But when your eyes are open and you see the dummy's mouth moving, what you see becomes more important than what you hear. This characteristic, by which visual information assumes more importance in our minds than information from the other senses, is called *visual capture*. It is one reason why we can't alway trust the "evidence of our own senses."

3.   Corporate power today rests with chief executives, who themselves have little financial stake in the firms they manage. The firms pile rewards on executives who achieve quick profits. Consequently, managers show an excessive concern for short-run profits. They look for an immediate return on the money they expend. Sometimes too little money is provided for research and technology, and the long-term success of the company may suffer.

4.   Piaget calls middle childhood the *period of concrete operations*. He refers to it as *concrete* because children are bound by immediate physical reality and cannot go beyond the here and now. During this period children still have difficulty dealing with remote, future, or hypothetical matters.

PRACTICE IN RECOGNIZING SIGNAL WORDS

Activity 1

Below are some of the signal words that are most often used by writers. Place each word under its proper heading.

for example	in addition
therefore	for instance
moreover	just as
most important	consequently
but	most significant
also	however
differ	such as
alike	similarly
as a result	especially valuable

Emphasis   *Addition*

_____   _____

_____   _____

_____   _____

Comparison   *Contrast*

_____   _____

_____   _____

_____   _____

Illustration   *Cause and Effect*

_____   _____

_____   _____

_____   _____

Activity 2

Circle the signal words in the selections that follow. The number and kind of signal words you should look for are indicated at the start of each selection.

1. One emphasis signal; one contrast signal; one addition signal; two cause-and-effect signals.

   All of us desire approval, most of all from people we love and respect. But too much reliance on the approval of others can do great damage to the self-concept. We can never really know what other people think of us. Furthermore, their opinions change. Therefore, waiting for their approval to start liking ourselves may doom us to wait eternally, since their approval will never be absolute or final.

2. Two cause-and-effect signals; one contrast signal; one addition signal.

   Surveys of college students have shown that from 30 to 50 percent of first-year students will change their majors at least once by graduation. Changing one's mind *is* a pervasive experience for students. The belief in irreversible choices stems from the idea that because most academic programs have lockstep requirements, a person will lose time and credits if he or she gets out of step with other students in the program. It is true that there is a risk of losing time and having to make up credit, and it does cost money to postpone graduating. However, the hidden costs of not leaving a major or occupation one is uncomfortable with are also great in terms of job dissatisfaction, personal stress, and poor performance. Therefore, short-term avoidance of inconvenience can lead to long-range heartaches.

3. Two cause-and-effect signals; two addition signals; one contrast signal.

   There are several cultural reasons why the aged are stigmatized and oppressed in American society. First, the members of our society are obsessed with youth. We have traditionally associated a number of highly valued traits with youth: beauty, health, sexual vigor, happiness, usefulness, and intelligence. As a result of this association, those considered old are typically believed to be physically unattractive, sickly, asexual, useless, and incompetent. Second, in our rapidly changing, highly technical society, old people are considered to be unnecessary. Their wisdom represents an age that now is irrelevant in the United States. On the other hand, in simpler societies where tradition is paramount, the elderly are highly respected, admired, and even revered as the repositories for the group's accumulated wisdom.

4. Two contrast signals; two cause-and-effect signals; one illustration signal; one addition signal.

   Until about ten thousand years ago, all human beings lived in hunting-and-gathering societies. In some remote regions, a few such societies still exist today, but they are fast disappearing. Because hunters and gatherers must usually move their settlements in search of food, their way of life cannot support large concentrations of people. The typical hunting-and-gathering band is consequently very small. In contrast to the distribution of labor in our own society, there are no specialists in hunting-and-gathering societies—everyone performs the same jobs and has the same responsibilities. The family is the only subgroup. It assumes many of the economic, political, and educational responsibilities of our large formal organizations. For instance, the family is the group in which children learn most of their skills. It is also the group that cares for the sick, disabled, and elderly.

■ **Review Test**

Signal words have been removed from each of the following textbook excerpts and placed above it. Fill in the missing signal word or words in the answer spaces provided. Note that you will have to read each passage carefully to see which word or words will fit logically in each answer space.

1. *In addition   most vital   Yet   however   for instance*

   We take plants for granted. The carpet of greenery that blankets the earth

   is, to us, an ordinary and everyday thing. Plants, _____, are the
   only living things on earth capable of producing life-sustaining oxygen.

   _____, plants release moisture into the atmosphere, which contri-
   butes to the climate conditions we know today. Unfortunately, human beings continue

   to destroy this _____ element of their environment. In the Amazon

   jungle, _____, vast tracts of rain forest are being leveled; without
   the moisture-producing plants, the climate there is already undergoing dangerous
   changes. People are constantly learning more about the delicate interrelation of life

   on this planet. _____ they persist in these suicidal actions.

2. *Yet   most effective   Therefore   For example   reason*

   A bureaucracy is a complicated system of administration that follows definite
   rules and methods. The word *bureaucracy* usually carries negative connotations in

   everyday speech. _____, it brings to mind images of "red tape,"
   forms in triplicate, lost files, incorrect bills, unanswered letters, counter clerks blinded

   by petty regulations, "runarounds," and "buck passing." _____

   the bureaucratic form has thrived for the simple _____ that, on

   the whole, it works well. It is the _____ means ever devised of

   making a large organization work. _____, sociologists use the
   word in a neutral sense, without the overtones it generally has in ordinary usage.

3. *effect   In addition   But   First of all   because*

   While dozens of men's-dress-shoe companies have sold out or folded up under the onslaught of foreign competition, E. T. Wright & Co. of Rockland, Massachusetts, has grown at a rate of about 6 percent per year. _____ five years ago, the picture was not as rosy. Demand for Wright's durable conservative shoes was weak _____ every pair of Wright's shoes was built to last . . . and last. Ironically, the shoes' high quality had the _____ of slowing sales. The company's aging, prosperous customers could boast that they had worn the same pair of Wright's shoes for years. The company's retailers complained that boxes of Wright's shoes were collecting dust in their stockrooms. One possible solution to Wright's slump would have been to cheapen the product, but that idea did not set well with the company's owners. They decided on other solutions instead. _____, they raised the price on their basic dress shoe and, at the same time, introduced new products aimed at a younger, more style-conscious consumer. _____, they later added a new channel of distribution—catalog sales.

4. *in contrast   such as   Thus   For instance   But*

   Symbols vary in the range of meanings that are assigned to them. At one extreme are *multivocal symbols,* which carry a great many different meanings. _____, an American flag conveys any number of meanings in most people's minds (freedom, democracy, capitalism, military power, and so forth). The word *green,* _____, is linked to a much more restricted range of meanings. Some symbols have just one meaning; they are *univocal symbols.* A univocal symbol allows very precise expression of the concept it represents. This is desirable in certain situations, _____ when drafting a legal contract. _____ what they gain in precision, univocal symbols lose in flexibility and richness. _____ most of our emotionally charged symbols are multivocal ones.

SKILL 5: RECOGNIZING MAIN IDEAS IN PARAGRAPHS AND SHORT SELECTIONS

THE TWO BASIC PARTS OF A PARAGRAPH

Almost every effective communication of ideas consists of two basic parts: (1) a point is made, and (2) evidence is provided to support that point. The purpose of textbooks is to communicate ideas, and they typically do so by using the same basic structure: a point is advanced and then supported with specific reasons, details, and facts. You will become a better reader by learning to look for and take advantage of this basic structure used in textbooks.

Activity

To make sure that you understand the concept of two basic parts in the communication of ideas, take a few minutes to do the following. Make a point about anything at all and then provide at least two bits of specific evidence to support that point.

Here are examples.

Point: I dislike the fast-food restaurant in my town.

Support: (1) The roast beef sandwiches have a chemical taste.

(2) Prices are high—for example, 80 cents for a small soda.

Point: My neighbors are inconsiderate.

Support: (1) They allow their children to play on my lawn.

(2) They often have their stereo on loud late at night.

Point: There are many inexpensive ways to save energy.

Support: (1) Install a water-saver plug in your shower head.

(2) Turn down the thermostat of your hot water heater to 120 degrees.

Point: Marijuana should not be legalized.

Support: (1) Some people who don't use it now will begin using it because of its availability.

(2) Legalization will give a stamp of social approval that no mind-altering drug deserves.

Now write your own point and support for that point:

Point: _____

Support: (1) _____

_____

(2) _____

_____

Many textbook paragraphs that you read will be made up of the same two basic parts. The point is usually expressed in one sentence called a *main-idea,* or *topic, sentence.* The other sentences in the paragraph contain specific details that support or develop the main-idea sentence. Learning how to recognize these two basic parts quickly is sure to increase your reading comprehension.

Activity

Read the following textbook paragraph and see if you can identify the two major parts. Underline the main idea and write a number (1, 2, 3) in front of each reason that supports the main idea.

> Changes are occurring in the traditional nine-to-five workday. Many employers are exploring new options, such as flextime, compressed workweeks, and job sharing. With flextime, employees have a choice of starting and stopping times for their workdays. As long as they are present during a midday core period of six hours, they can choose to arrive any time between 7 and 9 A.M. and leave any time between 3 and 5 P.M. Compressed workweeks are another option. In this scheme, employees work longer shifts but fewer days. In one bank's computer department, employees work three twelve-hour days, at the end of which they have a four-day "weekend." Shared jobs are also becoming more popular. Two employees split the hours, work, and benefits of a single full-time job—a situation ideal for parents of young children and others who do not want a full-time job. Alternatives such as these may soon help solve the problems of rush-hour commuting and child care as well as increase employee morale.

The main idea is expressed in the first sentence, and the supporting ideas follow. The outline that follows shows clearly the two basic parts of the paragraph:

> Changes are occurring in the traditional nine-to-five workday.
> (1) Flextime
> (2) Compressed workweeks
> (3) Job sharing

THE VALUE OF FINDING THE MAIN IDEA

Finding the main idea is a key to understanding a paragraph or short selection. Once you identify the main idea or general point that an author is making, everything else in the paragraph should click into place. You will know what point is being made and what evidence is being provided to support that point. You will see the parts (the supporting material in the paragraph) in relation to the whole (the main idea).

If the main idea is difficult and abstract, you may want to read all the supporting details carefully to help increase your comprehension. If the main idea is easily understood, you may be able to skip the supporting details or read them over quickly, since they are not needed to comprehend the point.

The main idea is often located in the first sentence of a paragraph. You should thus pay special attention to that sentence. However, the main-idea sentence may also be at the end, in the middle, or any other place in the paragraph. On occasion, the main idea of a paragraph may appear in slightly different words in two or more sentences in the paragraph—for example, in the first and last sentences. In other cases, the main idea in one paragraph will serve as the central thought for several paragraphs that follow or precede it. Finally, at times the main idea will not be stated directly at all, and the reader will have to provide it by combining parts of several sentences or by looking closely at the evidence presented.

■ *Complete the following sentences:* One way to help yourself understand a paragraph or short selection is to look for two basic parts:

(1) _____. (2) _____. The main idea most

often appears in the _____ sentence of a paragraph.

PRACTICE IN FINDING THE MAIN IDEA

Activity 1

Locate and underline the main idea in each of the paragraphs that follow. The paragraphs are taken from a variety of articles and college textbooks.

To find the main idea, look for a general statement. Then ask yourself, *"Does most of the material in the paragraph support or develop the idea in this statement?"* Get into the habit of using this question as a test for a main idea.

1.   The decision to leave college is often a positive step. Many students gain more by working for a while, enrolling at a more compatible institution, or just allowing themselves time to mature than they would have gained by remaining at the original school. Colleges need to make dropping out more acceptable by making it easier for students to take leaves of absence, to study part time, and to earn more credit for independent study, life experiences, and work done at other institutions. Some educators want the college door to revolve freely to let students enter and exit at appropriate times—to reassess, to lower tension, to get married, to relax, to play, on the one hand; and to return, to think, to study, to learn, on the other.

2.   The clearest single statement we can make is that women who smoke during pregnancy are likely to have infants with lower birth weight. This finding has been reported again and again and seems to be reliable. In addition, there are some indications from studies of smoking during pregnancy that women who smoke are more likely to have infants with some kind of malformation or stillborn infants. Some recent research also points to long-term consequences for the infants: in three different studies seven- to eleven-year-old children whose mothers smoked during pregnancy had more difficulties in school and were more likely to be hyperactive. It seems pretty clear that smoking is harmful not only to the smoker but also to the fetus.

3.   In our society a person who wishes to marry cannot completely disregard the customary patterns of courtship. If a man saw a woman on the street and decided he wanted to marry her, he could conceivably choose a quicker and more direct form of action than the usual dating procedure. He could get on a horse, ride to the woman's home, snatch her up in his arms, and gallop away with her. In Sicily, until recently, such a couple would have been considered legally "married," even if the woman had never met the man before or had no intention of marrying. But in the United States any man who acted in such a fashion would be arrested and jailed for kidnapping and would probably have his sanity seriously challenged. Such behavior would not be acceptable in our society; therefore, it could not be considered cultural.

4.   To many parents, the infant's crying may be mainly an irritation, especially if it continues for long periods and the infant is not easily consoled. But crying serves important functions for the child as well as for the parent-child pair. For the child, crying helps to improve lung capacity (since the baby gulps in more air between cries) and helps to organize the workings of the heart and respiratory system. So it is quite literally physically good for a child to cry at least a little. Perhaps more important, the cry serves as a signal of distress and is one of the important "attachment behaviors" in the child's repertoire. When babies cry, they signal that they are hungry or in pain or otherwise agitated, and this is important information for parents.

Activity 2

Below each of the paragraphs that follow are four general statements. Decide which statement best expresses the main idea of the paragraph. Remember that the statement you choose should be supported by all or most of the material in the paragraph. Circle the letter of that statement.

1.   How do adolescents become underachievers? Many underachieving adolescents have had poor parent-child relationships. For example, their parents may reject them, fail to encourage them to be independent, treat them inconsistently, and rarely model achievement orientation. Generally, the parents of underachievers are not happy with themselves as parents and show high levels of anxiety. The school environment itself may be the culprit—underachieving adolescents may simply find school boring. When both home and school situations are modified, a remedial program is more likely to be effective in changing the adolescent's achievement behavior.

   a. Modifying an underachiever's school environment is important.
   b. There are several possible reasons why an adolescent becomes an under-achiever.
   c. Poor parent-child relationships influence students' performance in school.
   d. The parents of underachievers treat their children inconsistently.

2. It is realistic to assume that oral communication will probably play a larger role in future business communication than it has in the past. However, it is just as important to realize that writing will always be with us. Certainly the telephone is personal, immediate, and two-way, and it provides an opportunity to discuss questions or interpretations as they arise. In many instances, also, telephoning is less expensive than writing. On the other hand, a written communication leaves a permanent record to be referred to; that is why, even when oral methods of communication are used, we so often conclude by saying, "I wish you'd put that in writing" and "I'd like to see it in black and white." A written business communication gives its writer a chance to consider and to organize thoughts; it provides the chance to reread and to revise; and it offers a choice of various forms and styles in which the message can be couched. It is foolish to think, therefore, that reports or memos or letters will be replaced as integral parts of the communication process in business, and it is absurd to use the cost of the letter, for instance, as the sole reason for considering it obsolete.

    a. Oral communication has many advantages over written materials.
    b. Written communication will always be important in business.
    c. The telephone is rapidly replacing the business memo and letter.
    d. Written communications cost more than using the telephone.

3. When a spouse dies, legalistics are minimal, but after a divorce a ream of documents and interminable waiting periods may seem to be required. When someone dies, the rest of the family remains intact, but in divorce children and others commonly choose up sides and assign blame. For the parent who does not attain custody of the children, divorce signals major changes in the parental role as well as the marital role. After a death people receive compassionate leave from work and are expected to be less productive for a while, but after a divorce people are commonly criticized. Death is final, but divorced people may nourish many "what ifs?" and vacillate in their emotions.

    a. The death of a spouse is more stressful than a divorce.
    b. Outsiders are kinder to a bereaved spouse than they are to a divorced person.
    c. There are legal matters to deal with after death or divorce.
    d. Divorce, in many ways, requires a more difficult adjustment than does the death of a spouse.

4.   Perhaps the most difficult question for the manager, however, is what motivates people. All sorts of factors can be listed, including money, good working conditions, interesting work, a chance to do something one likes, and an opportunity for growth and development. Depending on the individual, of course, our list could contain hundreds of factors. Yet if we were to look for one overriding theme in motivation, it might well be need satisfaction. By this we mean that people have desires or needs that require satisfaction. If the company provides the means for meeting these needs, it can motivate its employees. For example, if a firm has a job that pays $500 a day, some workers for whom money is a high priority may be willing to take it. The fact that the job involves driving a truck carrying dynamite is of no importance to these people. For them, the high daily wage justifies the risk. In this case we would say that the worker's need for money is greater than his or her need for safety.

a. Motivation to work involves many factors.
b. Need satisfaction is the predominant factor in motivation.
c. Dangerous jobs will be performed by workers who need money.
d. Knowing what motivates people is important to a manager.

Activity 3

Do one or both of the following assignments, as directed by your instructor.

1. In the model textbook chapter on pages 149–186, locate four different paragraphs in which the main idea is clearly expressed in one sentence. On a separate sheet of paper, write down the page of this book on which each paragraph appears, the first five words of each paragraph you have chosen, and the full sentence within the paragraph that expresses the main idea.
2. In an article or textbook, locate four different paragraphs in which the main idea is clearly expressed in one sentence. Make copies of the paragraphs (using the copying machine in your library), underline the main-idea sentences, and hand in the paragraphs to your instructor.

■ Review Test

Locate and underline the main-idea sentence in each selection on the opposite page. Then write the number of each main-idea sentence in the space provided at the left.

_____ 1.   [1]Little in American society remained untouched by war. [2]Family ties loosened as millions of men left their homes for military duty and women moved from the household to the factory. [3]The housing shortage became critical in many areas, especially near military installations. [4]Gasoline rationing sharply reduced travel in private automobiles. [5]As one observer remarked, "You could have fired a bazooka down any Main Street in the country without hitting a vehicle." [6]Colleges and universities were deeply affected. [7]Faculty members joined the armed services; student enrollments dropped sharply as only women and young or physically disqualified men remained. [8]The government used college and university facilities for some training programs. [9]Higher education suffered because of the war, but religion flourished. [10]Churches were filled with worshipers, and between 1940 and 1946 membership in all religious bodies rose by some six million. [11]Moreover, religion became more personal and emotional as wives and parents prayed for their loved ones abroad.

_____ 2.   [1]Whenever we want a copy of something, we go to a photocopy machine (usually a Xerox machine) and make a duplicate. [2]In fact, photocopying has become so prevalent in the United States that few people bother to copy anything in longhand anymore. [3]This has resulted in an epidemic known as "Xeromania." [4]In 1975 there were 2.3 million copying machines in this country emitting an estimated 78 billion copies. [5]This is enough paper, if laid end to end, to girdle the globe 546 times at its widest point. [6]And these copying machines are everywhere, from the local public library to the nearby business office. [7]Furthermore, this Xeromania seems to be going on worldwide.

_____ 3.   [1]Almost every American community pays for its public schools by taxing real estate. [2]This procedure is discriminatory because rich school districts can spend more money on each student at a lower taxing rate than poor ones. [3]In Kansas, for example, property owners in the Moscow school district paid in 1972 a tax levy of $7.53 for every $1,000 of assessed property valuation to finance their schools. [4]This raised enough money for the town to spend $1,742 per pupil. [5]In Galena, Kansas, a community not blessed like Moscow with oil and gas fields, the tax rate was $36.68 for every $1,000 of assessed valuation. [6]Although this rate was five times greater than in Moscow, it raised only enough to spend $509 per pupil (less than one-third the money spent for pupils in Moscow).

_____ 4.   [1]Theorists have suggested that people often are unsure of their exact capabilities. [2]Sometimes people succeed, and sometimes they fail, and therefore they seldom can be certain of their true strengths. [3]Uncertainty can lead people to handicap themselves when put to the test—that is, they may do something to make good performance more difficult. [4]Then, if they fail, they don't have to face the possibility that they really aren't capable. [5]And if they succeed, they have proof that they are truly skilled. [6]For example, a student who gets drunk the night before a big exam may be engaging in self-handicapping. [7]Failure the following morning can be blamed on the alcohol, not on low intelligence. [8]If the student passes the exam with flying colors, he or she can feel superior, having overcome the handicap of the evening's drinking.

SKILL 6: KNOWING HOW TO OUTLINE

The five skills already discussed will help you locate and understand the main ideas in your textbooks. Outlining is another skill that will improve your reading comprehension as well as provide additional benefits. Outlining is an organizational skill that develops your ability to think in a clear and logical manner. It will help as you prepare textbook and classroom notes. It will also help as you plan speeches that you have to give or papers that you have to write. You have already learned a good deal about outlining in marking enumerations, noting relationships between heads and subheads, and identifying main ideas in paragraphs. You will now receive some direct practice in this important skill.

A SAMPLE OUTLINE

In an outline, you reduce the material in a selection to its main points, supporting points, and details. Special symbols are used to show how the points and details relate to one another.

To understand the outlining process, read the following selection and study the outline of the selection. Then look carefully at the comments about it.

All homeowners can take action if they are serious about saving on energy costs. Those with more than $100 to spend should consider any of the following steps. First, the sidewalls and especially the ceiling should be fully insulated. Proper insulation can save 30 percent or more of a heating or cooling bill. Next, storm windows and doors should be installed. They provide an insulating area of still air that may reduce energy loss by 10 percent or more. Finally, a homeowner might consider installing a solar water-heating system. Four factors in such a decision are geographic location, sunlight available, energy costs in the area, and the construction of the house.

Homeowners with less than $100 to spend can take many energy-saving steps as well. To begin with, two kinds of inexpensive sealers can be used to reduce energy leaks around the house. Caulking will seal cracks around outside windows and door frames and at corners of the house. Weather stripping can be applied to provide a weathertight seal between the frame and moving parts of doors and windows. Another inexpensive step is to check that a home heating or cooling system is clean. A dirty or clogged filter, for example, can make a furnace or an air conditioner work much harder to heat or cool a house. Next, a "low-flow" shower head can be used to reduce hot water use. A special shower head can be purchased or a small plastic insert available at a hardware store can be added to a regular head to limit water flow. Finally, blinds and draperies can be used to advantage throughout the year. In winter they can be closed at night to reduce heat loss. In summer they can be closed during the day to keep the house cooler. These and other relatively inexpensive steps can produce large savings.

Title ——————→ Ways to Save on Home Energy Costs

Main points at the margin

Supporting ideas indented under main points

Details indented under supporting ideas

A. Spending more than $100
 1. Insulate sidewalls and ceiling
 2. Add storm windows and doors
 3. Consider solar water-heating system depending on:
  a. Geographic location
  b. Sunlight available
  c. Energy costs
  d. Construction of house
B. Spending less than $100
 1. Sealers
  a. Caulking
  b. Weather stripping
 2. Clean heating or cooling system
 3. "Low-flow" shower head
  a. Special shower head
  b. Plastic insert
 4. Blinds and draperies
  a. Winter—close at night
  b. Summer—close during day

POINTS TO NOTE ABOUT OUTLINING

First: The purpose of an outline is both to summarize material and to show the relationships between different parts of the material. An outline is a summary in which letters and numbers are used to mark the main and supporting points and details.

In outlining, a sequence of symbols is used for the different levels of notes. In the outline above, capital letters (A and B) are used for the first level, numbers (1, 2, 3 . . .) are used for the second level, and small letters (a, b, c . . .) are used for the third level.

Second: Put all the headings at any particular level at the same point in relation to the margin. In the outline above, A and B are both at the margin; 1, 2, and 3 are all indented an equal amount of space from the margin; and a, b, and c are all indented an equal, greater amount of space from the margin.

Third: Most outlines do not need more than two or three levels of symbols. In textbook note-taking, two levels will often do. Use a sequence like the following, with subpoints indented under main points.

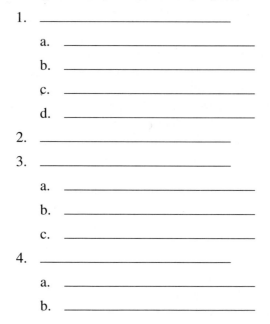

Fourth: Every outline should have a title (such as "Ways to Save on Home Energy Costs") that summarizes the information in the outline.

Activity

To check your understanding of outlining, answer question 1 and complete the statements in items 2 and 3.

1. Why do you think you should always begin main ideas at the margin?

    _____

    _____

    _____

    _____

    _____

2. Supporting ideas must always be _____
    main ideas.

3. The material that appears in an outline is summarized in its _____

    _____.

DIAGRAMING

Many students find it helpful at times to use *diagraming* (also known as *mapping*) rather than outlining. In diagraming, you create a visual outline of shapes as well as words. Diagrams usually use circles or boxes that enclose major ideas and supporting details. The shapes are connected with lines to show the connections between ideas.

On the following page are two diagrams of the selection "Ways to Save on Home Energy Costs."

Notice that in the balloon diagram, the main idea is written in the large circle that anchors the entire outline. Each supporting idea occupies one of the balloons attached to the main idea. In the box diagram, the main idea is written in the long box at the top. Below the long box are smaller boxes that contain the supporting ideas.

Activities in this chapter will ask you to use diagrams as well as outlines in order to make relationships between ideas visually clear. Then, in your own note-taking, you will be able to use either diagrams or outlines, whichever you find more helpful.

Balloon Diagram

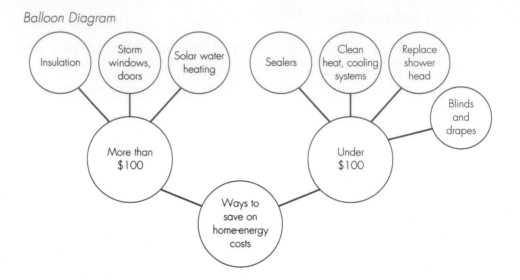

Box Diagram

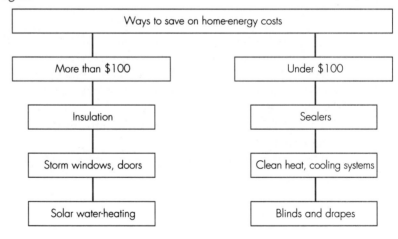

PRACTICE IN OUTLINING AND DIAGRAMING

The following pages provide a series of exercises that will develop your ability to outline and diagram effectively.

Activity 1:
Completing Outlines

Read each of the following selections. Then complete the outline that comes after each selection. Certain items in some outlines have already been added.

Note: In the chapter "Recognizing Enumerations," you practiced making one-level outlines. Here you will practice making two-or-more-level outlines as well.

Selection 1

Population in the South, which totaled about eleven million on the eve of the Civil War, fell into rather distinct social and economic classes. At the top of the scale stood the small aristocracy of large planters. In 1860 there were 2,292 planters who owned more than a hundred slaves and 10,658 who held over fifty. However, the wealth of this small group gave them social prestige and political power far beyond their numbers. Slightly below the large planters in social and economic status were the lesser planters who had fewer slaves and farmed less land; in 1860 there were 35,616 planters who had twenty to fifty slaves. Professionals and the few business and industrial leaders were also in this general class. Most of the people in the old South were in the middle or lower middle class and were mainly yeoman farmers, skilled mechanics, and tradespeople. The so-called plain people of the old South owned very few slaves, in many cases none at all. They raised a wide variety of crops and livestock and were largely self-sufficient. Below the yeoman farmers were the poor whites and free blacks. And at the bottom of the southern class structure stood the slaves.

_____

1. _____

2. _____

3. _____

4. _____

5. _____

Selection 2

When deciding to go to a professional for psychological help, there are several steps you can take. Begin by asking for recommendations. Talk with your instructor; also confer with someone in your school's counseling service. Other good sources for recommendations are physicians and members of the clergy. After you have one or two names, try to check out reputations through the professional sources available to you. For instance, if your priest gives you a name, you might check it out with your school counselor. Next, call the professionals and ask about their training, degrees, and experience; a good therapist will not hesitate to give you this information. You might also want to find out what approach they follow and what goals they aim for in treating people. Finally, make your first visit to the professional an exploratory one: learn as much as you can about how he or she does therapy and how your own problems might be dealt with. If you aren't satisfied, go to someone else. One visit to a professional doesn't commit you to further visits. This approach to selecting a professional, while initially somewhat time-consuming, will be well worth it in terms of the quality of help you receive.

Getting Psychological Help

1. _____

    a. _____

    b. _____

    c. _____

    d. _____

2. _____

3. _____

    a. _____

    b. _____

4. _____

Selection 3

The schools perform several vital functions for the maintenance of the prevailing social, political, and economic order. Education, along with the institutions of the family and religion, has a primary responsibility for the socialization of newcomers to the society. A second function of education is the shaping of personalities so that they are in basic congruence with the demands of the culture. In other words, one goal of the educational system of any society is to produce people with desired personality traits (for example, competitiveness, altruism, bravery, conformity, or industriousness, depending on the culture of the society). A third function is to prepare individuals for their adult roles. In American society this means the preparation of individuals for the specialized roles of a highly complex division of labor. It also means the preparation of youngsters for life in a rapidly changing world. In early American history the primary aim of schooling was teaching the basics of reading, writing, spelling, and arithmetic. These were needed to read the Bible, write correspondence, and do simple accounting—the required skills for adults in an agrarian society. Modern society, on the other hand, demands people with specialized occupational skills, with expertise in narrow areas. The educational system is saddled with providing these skills in addition to the basics. Finally, the schools have taken over the teaching of skills and knowledge that were once the explicit duty of each family to transmit to its offspring. These include citizenship skills, cooking, sewing, and even sex education.

The Role of Education in Corporate Society _____

1. _____

2. _____

3. _____

    a. _____

    b. _____

4. _____

    a. _____

    b. _____

    c. _____

    d. _____

Activity 2:
Completing Diagrams

Read each of the following selections. Then complete the diagram that appears opposite each selection.

Selection 1

Despite the rigors of class exclusivity, most Americans claim social mobility as an ideal. People do move upward or downward from class to class, and they do it in one of two ways. *Career mobility* is social mobility through the course of one's work. A person who advances from factory worker to supervisor, from mail room to boardroom, or, conversely, from engineer to skid row bum illustrates this concept. *Generational mobility,* another type of social mobility, takes place from one generation to another. The carpenter son of a professional couple is downwardly mobile; the stewardess daughter of a shoemaker is upwardly mobile. As we will see, people's attitudes toward social mobility often reflect their own class backgrounds.

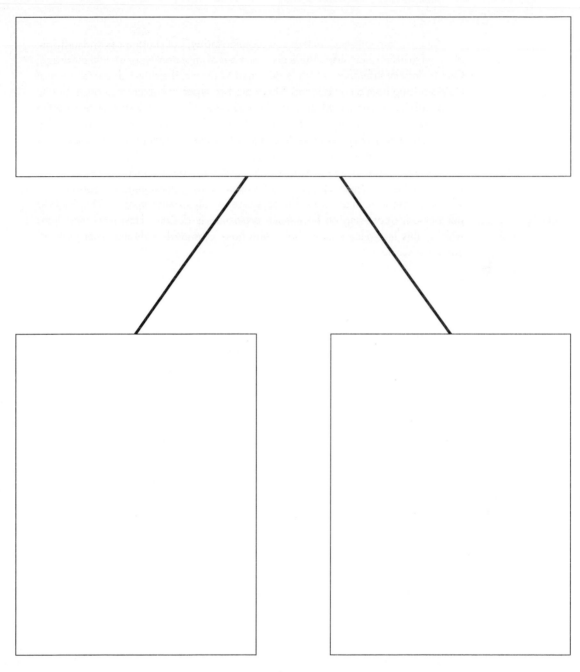

Selection 2

Since automobile accidents are so common today, both businesses and individuals need to insure their autos. There are a number of important types of auto coverage. One is *liability insurance,* which is designed to protect the driver or owner against claims arising from auto accidents. There are two types of liability insurance: bodily injury liability insurance, which provides coverage of anyone inside or outside the car who suffers bodily injury because of the driver, and property damage liability insurance, which provides protection against claims or damage to other people's property during an accident. Additionally, most drivers also have some form of *medical payments insurance,* which is designed to meet the medical needs of the persons in the car. Medical payments insurance covers the occupants regardless of who was at fault in an accident. The coverage usually extends from $250 to $5,000 per person, depending on how much protection is desired. However, most firms will sell this insurance only to those who have already bought the other types of liability insurance.

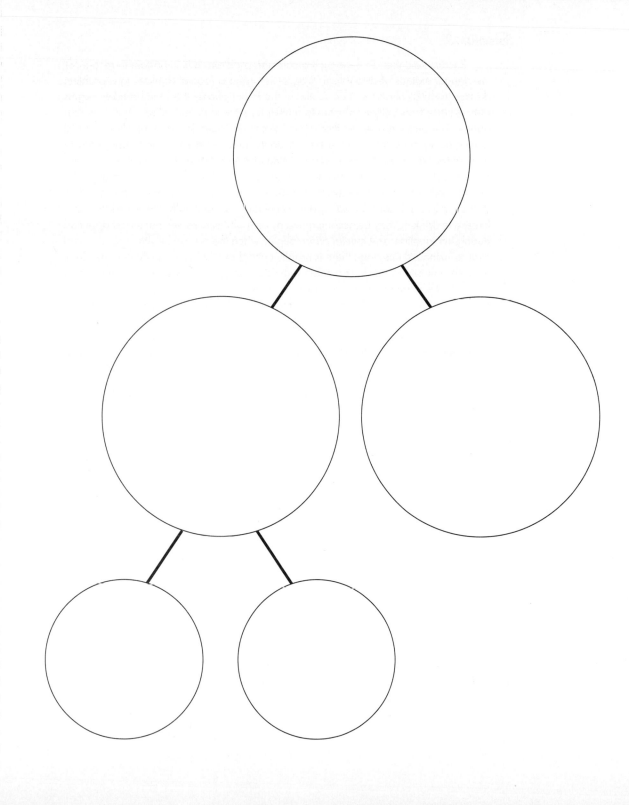

Selection 3

Because alcohol abuse is such a common problem, it is important to recognize the danger signals of alcoholism. Progression from a "social drinker" to a problem drinker to an alcoholic is often subtle. In the *initial phase*, the social drinker begins to turn more frequently to alcohol to relieve tension or to feel good. There are four danger signals in this period that signal excessive dependence on alcohol. The first is increasing consumption. The person drinks more and more and may begin to worry about drinking. The second is morning drinking. Morning drinking is a dangerous sign, particularly when it is used to combat a hangover or to "get through the day." Next is regretted behavior. The person engages in extreme behavior while drunk that leaves him or her feeling guilty or embarrassed. Finally, there are blackouts. Excessive drinking may be accompanied by an inability to remember what happened during intoxication. The *crucial phase* begins when the person begins to lose control over drinking. At this stage there is usually control over when and where a first drink is taken, but one drink starts a chain reaction leading to a second and a third, and so on. In the *chronic phase*, the alcoholic drinks compulsively and continuously. He or she eats infrequently, becomes intoxicated from far less alcohol than before, and feels a powerful need for alcohol when deprived of it. Work, family ties, and social life all deteriorate. Self-drugging is usually so compulsive that when there is a choice, the bottle comes before friends, relatives, employment, and self-esteem. The drinker is now an addict.

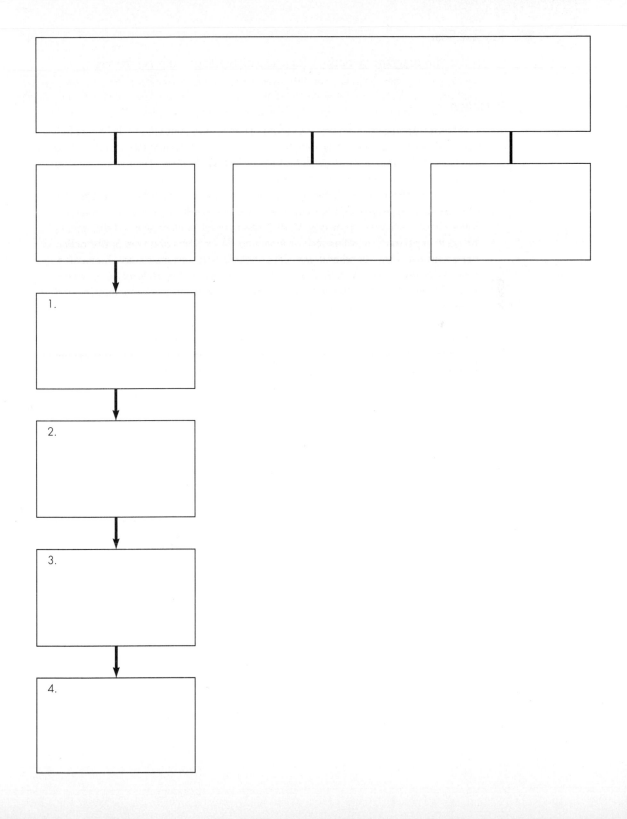

■ **Review Test**

Complete the diagram or outline for each of the following selections.

Selection 1

Nonasserters pay in several ways for not expressing themselves. The most obvious costs are social ones. Shy people make few new acquaintances and have a hard time building friendships with those people they do meet. Even when they do mingle with others, nonexpressive people are often misunderstood.

Nonassertiveness also takes a psychological toll on its victims. Three attitudes often develop in people who are not able to express the full range of their feelings. Some simply withdraw from any kind of meaningful contact with others, taking refuge in impersonal activities such as watching TV for hours at a time or distracting themselves with liquor or other drugs. Other people deal with their inept communications by becoming cynics, claiming that people aren't worth caring about anyway. A third group of nonasserters react to the condition with despair at themselves and at an imperfect world where life is not worth living.

Besides social and psychological consequences, nonassertion also has physiological costs, in the form, first of all, of psychosomatic illnesses. Such illnesses are real, differing in no physical way from organically caused ones. Nonassertive people often develop stress-related diseases as well as psychosomatic illnesses. Hypertension, or high blood pressure, often has its roots in chronic stress.

---

1. _____

2. _____

    a. _____

    b. _____

    c. _____

3. _____

    a. _____

    b. _____

Selection 2

The early stages of illness are the *"symptom experience" stage* and the *"assumption of the sick role"* stage. During the former period patients come to believe something is wrong. Either a person close to them mentions that they look unwell, or patients experience some symptoms, which can appear insidiously.

There are three aspects of this "symptom experience" stage: the physical experience of symptoms, such as pain or fever; the cognitive aspect, that is, the interpretation of the symptoms in terms that have some meaning to the person; and the emotional response of fear or anxiety relative to the experience.

The next stage is called *assumption of the sick role*. This stage can be referred to as the state of acceptance of the illness. At this time people decide that their symptoms or concerns are sufficiently severe to suggest that they are sick. During the beginning of this stage, some people seek professional help quickly, but others continue self-treatment, often following the suggestions of family members and friends.

At the end of this stage, sick people will experience either one or two outcomes. They may find that the symptoms have changed and that they are feeling better. Still, they will seek confirmation of this from the family, and if family members support the patients' perceptions, they will no longer be considered or consider themselves sick. As a result, they must then resume normal obligations such as returning to work or attending a school concert. On the other hand, if the symptoms persist or increase and if this is validated by family members or significant others, then sick people know that they should seek a physician's advice.

1. _____

    a. _____

    b. _____

    c. _____

2. _____

    a. _____

        (1) _____

        (2) _____

    b. _____

        (1) _____

        (2) _____

Selection 3

The people who own the business are called *partners*. However, there are various types of partners. Some may run the business while others play no active role. Some have unlimited liability; others do not.

General partners have unlimited liability and are usually very active in the firm's operations. Every partnership must have at least one general partner who assumes ultimate responsibility for all the firm's obligations and is empowered to enter into contracts in the name of the business. If all the partners fall into this category the organization is known as a *general partnership*.

Under the Uniform Limited Partnership Act, currently adopted by most states, people who want to invest in a partnership but do not want to risk all their assets can do so as *limited partners*. These individuals have their liability limited to the amount of money they have invested in the company. Such partners do not play an active role in the operation of the firm. It should be noted, however, that if these limited partners do enter into contracts for the partnership by passing themselves off as general partners, they can become liable for any losses resulting from their action.

While the general and limited partners are the most common types, there are also other partners. They can be broken down into four categories, including silent, secret, dormant, and nominal. *Silent partners* are those who are known as owners in the business but who take no active role in managing the operations. They have no voice in the matter, hence the term *silent*. *Secret partners* do take an active role in running the business, but they are not known as partners by the public. *Dormant partners* take no active role in running the firm, nor are they known as partners by the general public. *Nominal partners* are individuals who lend their names to the enterprise but invest no money in the firm and play no role in its management.

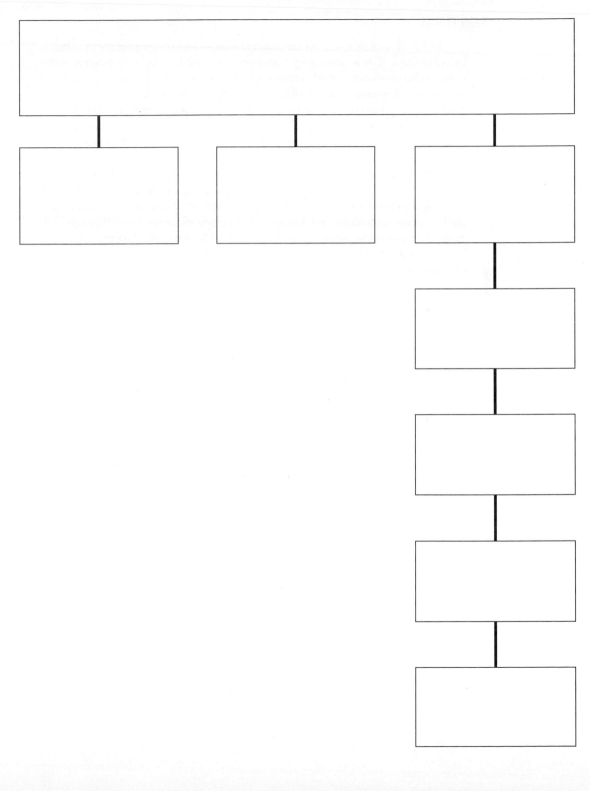

Selection 4

Self-disclosure deepens the attachment between two persons simply by virtue of being rewarding. It is rewarding both to the receiver and in various ways to the giver. To the receiver, the disclosure is a gift of trust; the receiver is hearing privileged information. It is also a gift of affection; the receiver is special. To the giver, self-disclosure is rewarding in several ways. First, it relieves emotional loneliness; the private self, revealed and accepted, no longer shivers in isolation. Also, self-disclosure relieves guilt and fear. As long as we conceal our mental bogeys, they will continue to howl and cackle in the dark corridors of the mind. Once we reveal them, they look (and feel) much less threatening. Third, human beings seem to have a need to tell. This need probably accounts, in part, for the popularity of psychotherapy. It certainly accounts for the so-called stranger-on-the-train phenomenon, whereby people lay bare their souls to total strangers, particularly strangers whom they are fairly certain of never seeing again. Self-disclosure to a friend satisfies the same need, and it has the added advantage of creating a bond of trust with a person who (unlike the stranger or the psychotherapist) may still be part of your life ten years from now.

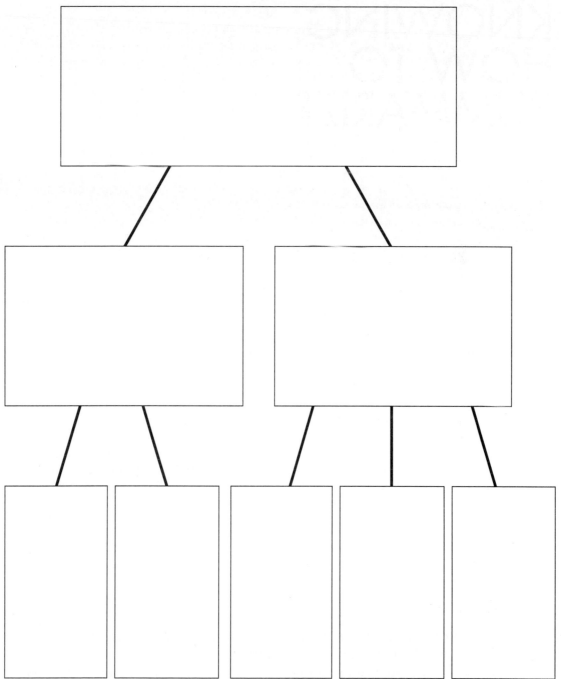

SKILL 7: KNOWING HOW TO SUMMARIZE

To understand the summarizing process, first read the following selection and summary. Then study the points about summarizing that follow.

> In another kind of coping behavior, *rationalization,* an acceptable motive is substituted for an unacceptable one. Put another way, we "make excuses"—we give a different reason from the real one for what we are doing. Rationalization is a common defense mechanism for avoiding the anxiety connected with an unacceptable motive. A student who has sacrificed studying to have a good time may blame his or her failing grades on bad teaching, unfair examinations, or too heavy a work load. A father may beat his child just because he is angry but rationalize it by saying that he is acting for the child's good.

Summary

Rationalization—a kind of coping behavior in which an acceptable motive is substituted for an unacceptable one.

Ex.—father rationalizes beating child by saying it's for child's good.

POINTS TO NOTE ABOUT SUMMARIZING

1 A *summary,* like an outline, is a reduction of a large quantity of information to the most important points. Unlike an outline, however, a summary does not use symbols such as A, 1, a, and so on, to indicate the relationships among parts of the original material. The preceding summary includes the most important points—the definition of rationalization and an example that makes the definition clear—but the other material is omitted.

2 Summarizing is helpful because it requires that you thoroughly *understand* the material you are reading. You must "get inside" the material and realize fully what is being said before you can reduce it to a few words. Work in summarizing material will help build your comprehension power. It will also markedly improve your ability to take effective classroom and textbook notes.

3 The length of a summary depends on your *purpose* in summarizing. The shortest possible summary is a title. If your purpose requires more information than that, a one-sentence summary might be enough. Longer passages and different purposes might require longer summaries. For example, in writing a report on an article or book, you might often want to have a summary that is a paragraph or more in length.

In the following practice activities you will be writing title summaries, single-sentence and several-sentence summaries, and one-paragraph summaries. After such varied practice, you should be prepared to write whatever kind of summary you might need.

■ *Complete the following sentences:* A summary _____ a large quantity of material to the most important points. Unless you fully

_____ the material you are reading, you will not be able to summarize it.

PRACTICE IN SUMMARIZING

Activity 1

The shortest possible summary of a selection is its title or heading. For this activity, circle the letter of the title that best summarizes each selection on the following pages. You should select the title that best answers the question "What is this about?" The title should be as specific and descriptive as possible and at the same time account for all the material in the selection.

1.   Chances are you've always been told, "Don't swim after eating. Wait an hour, or you'll get a cramp." The advice is one of the most widely believed bits of folk wisdom around. In fact, however, it is far better to swim on a partly full stomach than on an empty one. When you feel hungry, it means that your body, muscles included, needs refueling. The myth was probably based on the observation that digestion draws a large amount of blood to the stomach, decreasing the supply to the muscles. It does take time for the body to completely convert food into glucose, the form in which muscles can use it. But some of the glucose becomes available right away. By the time you've finished your picnic and are ready to swim, your energy-starved muscles will already be sufficiently fortified to perform normally. This does not mean it's advisable to jump right in after a heavy banquet, especially if the repast included wine or other alcoholic drinks. Such a meal makes most people drowsy, slows reflexes, and dims general alertness. But if you're hungry, eat a moderate meal first, then take the plunge.

What would be an accurate title for this selection?

a. Folk Wisdom

b. Digestion and Energy

c. Eating and Swimming

d. Refueling Your Body

2.   Suppose a man works six or seven days a week in a factory, trying to support his family, but never seems to be able to make ends meet. If he analyzed his situation rationally, he would probably blame the well-to-do generally and his employers specifically for failing to pay him an adequate wage. But these people have the power to cut off his income; to oppose them openly would be self-destructive. He could also blame himself for his financial problems, but this too makes him uncomfortable. Instead, he looks to the Mexican immigrants who have begun working in his factory. He doesn't really know them, but he suspects they're willing to work for low wages and that many other Mexicans are eager to take his job. By a process of twisted logic, he blames the Mexicans for his poverty. Soon he is exchanging rumors about "them" with his cronies and supporting efforts to close the border. Hating Mexicans makes the man and his friends feel a little better.

What would be an accurate title for this selection?

a. The Psychology of Prejudice

b. Prejudice against Mexicans

c. Discrimination in the Factory

d. Twisted Logic

3.   Reading about an occupation and talking with people about it are two important ways of gathering occupational information. If you really want to explore an occupation, however, we encourage you to try to get some "hands-on" opportunities in it. Some corporations provide tours for the public to explain how they produce their products. You may be able to arrange a tour in a setting that employs people in the field you are interested in. If you have the time and the motivation, you may be able to persuade an employer to allow you to work as a voluntary apprentice for one or several days as a way of exploring an occupation and your reactions to it. It may also be possible to find part-time or summer work in the field or in related fields. Finally, you can take advantage of the cooperative education, internship, and externship opportunities that may be available on your campus. Through such programs, you will be able to work part-time in settings that relate to your degree program. An advantage of this, as well as any of the other hands-on opportunities you can participate in, is that in addition to being able to gather occupational information, you will be building skills for securing a full-time job at graduation. In fact, many employers use volunteer and internship programs to evaluate and groom potential employees.

What would be an accurate title for this selection?
a.   Investigating Career Choices
b.   Part-Time Job Programs
c.   Internship Programs
d.   Volunteering to Work

4.   Many athletes in universities are bound to become cynical about their education. Coaches proclaim that their athletes are students first and athletes only secondarily. This is the typical recruiting speech to prospects and their parents. But in practice, the reverse is often true. The athlete has signed a contract and is paid for his or her athletic services. The athlete is an employee, and the relationship between a coach and the athlete is essentially employer-employee. Athletes are often counseled to take easy courses, whether or not those courses fit their educational needs. Because of the enormous demands on their time during the season, athletes frequently must take a somewhat reduced course load, and thus they will not usually graduate in the normal amount of time. Study halls and tutors are frequently available, even required, for college athletes, but the primary function of these adjuncts is to ensure athletic eligibility, not necessarily the education of the athlete. If the athlete achieves an education in the process, it is incidental to the overriding objective of big-time sport. As a former University of Virginia football coach honestly put it: "We've stopped recruiting young men who want to come here to be students first and athletes second."

What would be an accurate title for this selection?
a.   The Educational Needs of College Athletes
b.   Corruption in College Sports
c.   College Recruiting Practices
d.   Priorities in College Sports

Activity 2

Write an accurate heading or title for each of the paragraphs that follow. Each heading should be only a phrase—not a complete sentence. The heading should condense into several words the essential thoughts of each selection. It will be the shortest possible summary of the selection. A good way to proceed is to try to find the fewest words that will answer accurately the question "What is this about?"

Note that you will be doing exactly the kind of summarizing that textbook authors do when they write headings and subheads. The experience of "writing labels" should help you appreciate—and take advantage of—the headings given to you by textbook authors.

1. Heading: _____

Of all possible ways to eat, skipping breakfast and eating a big lunch is the worst. You're probably aware that going without breakfast is bad for you, but you probably don't know that a big midday meal doesn't even the score. Lunch is not a pick-me-up; it actually pulls your energy down. A recent study found that a group of people who ate a large lunch lost as much efficiency when they returned to work as if they'd gone without a whole night's sleep. On the other hand, a separate ten-year study found that eating breakfast increases efficiency. Another study, of adolescents, found that kids do better in school when they eat breakfast. Why is breakfast so important? When you wake up in the morning, you haven't eaten for eight to twelve hours. Your blood sugar and stored carbohydrates are low, and you may be short of other nutrients as well. Your morning meal "breaks" the "fast" and replaces the calories and nutrients you need to help keep you going all day. The calories are burned up quickly—more quickly than at any other time of the day.

2. Heading: _____

The British approach to heroin addiction (heroin maintenance) is fundamentally different from the American approach. The object of the American model is to get addicts "off" heroin by drying up their supplies and imprisoning them. Narcotics control, under this plan, is placed under the jurisdiction of law enforcement authorities. The British plan, in sharp contrast, places control in the hands of medical authorities. Instead of treating addicts as criminals, the British allow doctors to administer drugs to addicts under two conditions: when their complete withdrawal cannot be accomplished and when they can perform satisfactorily if given a controlled dosage. The doctors must notify the British Home Office of all patients under this treatment. When properly registered, those addicts are entitled to receive maintenance doses of heroin; however, if an addict commits a crime, then he or she is treated the same as any other offender. Moreover, if not registered but in possession of opiates, the individual is prosecuted for illegal possession of a dangerous drug.

3. Heading: _____

For centuries people assumed that the differences between the sexes were inborn or "natural," that biology decreed different interests and abilities for women and men. Men were thought to be instinctively aggressive; a woman caring for a child was supposedly fulfilling her "maternal instinct." Generations of husbands told their wives not to worry their "pretty little heads" about politics or business and gallantly protected the "weaker sex" from education. It was not until researchers discovered societies in which men are passive and vain and women domineering, and societies in which there are few differences between the way men and women behave, that people began seriously to question the biological basis of masculinity and femininity. Anatomy was not destiny after all. Feminists especially, but male thinkers as well, began to argue that the differences in behavior between males and females were learned, not innate. Little girls are given dolls, little boys are given trucks and guns, and few of us escape the "blue and pink" tyranny. Rather quickly people divided into two camps: those who maintained that sex differences were innate (the "nature" argument) and those who argued emphatically that they were not (the "nurture" argument).

4. Heading: _____

When Captain Cook asked the chiefs in Tahiti why they always ate apart and alone, they replied, "Because it is right." If we ask Americans why they eat with knives and forks, or why their men wear pants instead of skirts, or why they may be married to only one person at a time, we are likely to get similar and very uninformative answers: "Because it's right." "Because that's the way it's done." "Because it's the custom." Or even "I don't know." The reason for these and countless other patterns of social behavior is that they are controlled by *social norms*—shared rules or guidelines which prescribe the behavior that is appropriate in a given situation. Norms define how people "ought" to behave under particular circumstances in a particular society. We conform to norms so readily that we are hardly aware they exist. In fact, we are much more likely to notice departures from norms than conformity to them. You would not be surprised if a stranger tried to shake hands when you were introduced, but you might be a little startled if he or she bowed, curtsied, started to stroke you, or kissed you on both cheeks. Yet each of these other forms of greeting is appropriate in other parts of the world. When we visit another society whose norms are different, we quickly become aware that things we do this way, they do that way.

Activity 3

Your instructor may ask you to condense into a sentence the essential thought of each of the preceding four selections. To do this, first see if there is a sentence that expresses the main idea of the selection. In some cases, it might be all the summary you need. In other cases, you should outline before you summarize. That is, you should locate and number the series of points that back up the main idea. Then put the main idea and the main supporting points into your summary sentence.

Use separate sheets of paper for this activity.

Activity 4

Read the article on the opposite page and then write a one-paragraph summary of 100 to 125 words. Here are some guidelines for summarizing an article:

a   Think about the title for a minute or so. The title often summarizes what the article is about.

b   Consider any subtitle that may appear. The subtitle, the caption, or other words in large print under or next to the title will often provide a quick insight into the meaning of an article.

c   Note any subheadings that appear in the article. Subheadings provide clues to the article's main points and give an immediate sense of the content of each section.

d   Make an outline of the article before beginning to write.

e   Express the author's ideas in your own words—not in the words of the article itself.

f   Do not write an overly detailed summary. Remember that the purpose of a summary is to reduce the original material to its main ideas and essential supporting points.

g   Do not begin your sentences with expressions like "the author says"; equally important, do not introduce your own opinions into the summary with comments like "another good point made by the author." Instead, concentrate on presenting the author's main points directly and briefly.

HELPING YOUR CHILD LEARN TO BE A BETTER READER

The Need for a Home Reading Program

Years ago, parents and children would often read together after dinner. Now, that time is generally spent watching TV. According to a report from the New York State Senate Education Committee, "Children spend five thousand hours watching TV before they reach first grade. Many high school graduates have logged fifteen thousand hours of television but only eleven thousand hours in the classroom."

Today many parents and educators are asking, "Why can't Johnny read?" And the answer has to do with the shift in the family activities at home. According to research, the best reading instruction in school can be virtually wasted without reading practice at home. And the child who starts school with little preparation at home is already playing "catch-up." Greta Kipnis, Director of Reading for the Commack, New York, schools, says, "We need parents to help children build a reading habit."

Kipnis and other reading experts advise parents to begin a "reading readiness" program at home—before the child even starts kindergarten. Educators in several states (New York, Idaho, Maryland, Massachusetts, Ohio, and Pennsylvania) are now encouraging parents to spend fifteen minutes a day reading with their child, whether from books, magazines, or newspapers.

Setting Up Your Child's Reading Program

Even before your children are ready to read, you can prepare them to develop reading skills. Begin with conversation by encouraging your children to talk. Speak to them one to one at the earliest possible age, and let them hear conversations. The first words your children read will be those they have heard or spoken.

Once your children are ready for books, their reading should be based on real-life experiences and observations. Call their attention to the things you *see* together: rain, snow, clouds, animals, plants, cars, buses, and trains. "Then, when children start to read about these things," says Dr. Arthur Kelly, a Long Island, New York, elementary school principal, "they will do so with more interest because they will relate to the stories."

Start with picture books at first and encourage your children to tell stories about the pictures. Drawing and coloring pictures is helpful, too, but don't force it if your children are not interested. When they progress from pictures to written words, look up several words a day with them in the dictionary (there are versions for children). Make a game of using the new words.

If buying books becomes too costly, let the children select books from the library. Another good idea is temporary exchanges of books with friends or relatives.

James Donovan, chairman of the New York State Senate Education Committee, reports that the new emphasis on reading at home has fostered improved reading skills and increased children's pleasure in reading. "You can participate without spending a cent," he said. "All you have to do is spend fifteen minutes a day reading with your children." And this kind of activity also strengthens feelings of family togetherness.

Activity 5

Write a one-paragraph summary of an article in a weekly or monthly magazine. Identify at the start of the summary the title and author of the work. Also, include in parentheses the date of publication. Here is an example: "In an article titled 'The Power of Talk' (*Newsweek,* February 8, 1993), Howard Fineman states . . ."

Then, in your own words, summarize the main point of the article and the key details used to support or develop that point.

Finally, be sure to clip out the article or make a copy of it and attach it to your summary.

Activity 6

Watch a television show of special interest to you. Then prepare a one-paragraph summary of the show. In your first sentence, give basic information about the show by using a format such as the following: "The January 9, 1994, broadcast of CBS's *Sixty Minutes* examined . . . ."

Activity 7

Write a one-paragraph summary of an important concept from one of your text-books. Try to choose a general-interest subject such as psychology or sociology rather than a highly specialized field such as anatomy or electronics.

In your summary, first provide identifying information. For example, "In the chapter 'Basic Facts' in *Drugs: A Factual Account,* 5th ed. (McGraw-Hill, 1993), Dorothy E. Dusek and Daniel A. Girdano discuss . . . ." Then present the important idea in the chapter, along with key details that support or develop that idea.

■ Review Test

Circle the letter of the title that best summarizes each of the selections on the following pages. Remember that the title should be as specific and descriptive as possible and at the same time account for all the material in the selection.

1.   There's a time to get angry, and it's best for your child if you do. Let's say your preschooler hits a playmate with a toy—hard enough to make the other child cry. How can you teach yours to feel sorry so he or she won't do it again? Researchers say the best way for parents to react is to show their anger and to let the child know exactly why they are mad. Many parents believe that it is best to control their emotions, to wait until they're calm and collected before reprimanding their youngsters. But the mother or father who explains reasonably to a youngster, "Peter was crying because you hit him," is not likely to make much of an impression. Young children need to be told off swiftly, and strongly, before they'll take criticism to heart. When your youngster misbehaves, scold him or her vigorously at once. At the same time be sure to tell the child clearly what he or she has done wrong. An angry response without an accompanying explanation does little good. Physically restraining a child or taking away television privileges as a punishment can also be effective—but only when combined with explanation. Make certain your child understands that although his or her behavior has upset you, you still love him or her. Use simple, direct words such as, "You hurt Peter. How would you feel if he hit you? You must never, never hurt people." If your tone of voice communicates intense feeling, your message will carry conviction.

What would be an accurate title for this selection?
a. Theories of Discipline
b. How to Discipline Your Child
c. The Benefits of Anger
d. The Value of Punishment

2.   In traditional Eskimo society, hospitality to a traveler was highly valued. A host was obliged to do everything possible to make a traveler comfortable, even if he found the man personally offensive. There was even a norm requiring a host to offer his wife to a guest for the night. This culture trait of obligatory hospitality is an unusual one, entirely unknown in urban, industrial societies. But it was highly functional in Eskimo culture. Travel through snows and Arctic blizzards would be utterly impossible unless the traveler could rely on the certainty of food, warmth, and rest at the next settlement, and the host in turn could expect the same hospitality when he traveled. Without this norm, communication and trade among various groups might have been too hazardous to undertake. A similar norm does not exist in the United States today, where it would make no sense. We have other arrangements, such as restaurants and motels, to serve the same function, and the need for shelter from the environment is not so pressing.

What would be an accurate title for this selection?
a. Eskimo Life
b. Eskimo Hospitality
c. Travel in the Arctic
d. Sexual Norms in Eskimo Society

3.   The immunological system, which protects the body against infection, seems to function less effectively when a person is under stress. Sometimes the body doesn't respond to infection quickly enough; at other times it responds incorrectly, as in the case of allergic reactions. Stress has even been diagnosed as one cause of the common cold. It is important to realize that stress or anxiety alone is not sufficient to cause these disorders. There must also be a source of infection present. But as research by Swiss physiologist Hans Selye suggests, people subjected to stress have an increased chance of contracting infectious diseases. As Selye asks, "If a microbe is in or around us all the time and yet causes no disease until we are exposed to stress, what is the cause of our illness, the microbe or the stress?" Medical researchers now suspect that cancers are caused by a malfunction in the body's system of immunities and thus may also be linked to stress.

What would be an accurate title for this selection?
a.   Selye's Theory
b.   Stress and the Immunological System
c.   Stress as a Cause of Cancer
d.   Infectious Diseases and the Immunological System

4.   Perhaps the myth of the perfect communicator comes from believing too strongly in novels, television, or films. In these media we are treated to descriptions of such characters as the perfect mate or child, the totally controlled and gregarious host, and the incredibly competent professional. While these images are certainly appealing, it's inevitable that we will come up short when compared with them. Once you accept the belief that it's desirable and possible to be a perfect communicator, the thought follows that people won't appreciate you if you are imperfect. Admitting one's mistakes, saying "I don't know," or sharing feelings of uncertainty or discomfort become social defects when viewed in this manner. Given the desire to be valued and appreciated, it is a temptation to try at least to appear perfect. Thus, many people assemble a variety of social masks, hoping that if they can fool others into thinking that they are perfect, perhaps they'll find acceptance. The costs of such deception are high. If others ever detect that this veneer of confidence is a false one, then the actor is seen as a phony and regarded accordingly. Even if the unassertive actor's role of confidence does go undetected, such a performance uses up a great deal of psychological energy and thus makes the rewards of approval less enjoyable.

What would be an accurate title for this selection?
a.   Being a Perfect Communicator
b.   The Myth of the Perfect Communicator
c.   Psychological Costs of Social Masks
d.   Acting with Confidence

PART FIVE

SKIM READING AND COMPREHENSION

PREVIEW

Part Five shows you how to do skimming, or selective reading. You will read quickly through a series of selections, looking for and writing down what seem to be important ideas. To locate the important ideas, you will be asked to apply several of the comprehension skills that you learned in Part Four. Each article or textbook chapter that you skim-read and take notes on will be timed, and you will check your performance by answering questions on the selections afterward. Through a progress chart, you will be able to measure both your skim-reading rate and your comprehension score for each selection.

SKIM READING

One of the chief myths that students believe about reading is that they must read every word. Consider, though, that the average textbook contains about six hundred pages, or more than 350,000 words. If students have several textbooks and try to read every word of every assignment, they are likely to have little time left to study what they have read—let alone to attend to the essentials of their every-day lives!

Fortunately, not every word in a book must be read, nor must every detail be learned. The purpose of Part Five is to give you practice in *skimming,* or selective reading. In skimming, you do not read every word; instead, you go quickly and selectively through a passage, looking for and marking off important ideas but skipping secondary material. You can then go back later to read more closely and take notes on important points.

Skim reading will help you when you do not need to read every word of every assignment. Skim reading will also help make you a flexible reader, which should be your final reading goal. Flexible readers, depending on their purpose in reading and the nature of the material, are able to practice several different kinds of reading: study reading (using the skills learned in Part Four), rapid reading (the concern of Part Six), and skim reading—the subject of this part of the book.

HOW TO SKIM-READ

To skim-read effectively, you must be able to apply several of the comprehension skills you learned in Part Four. You must know how to do the following things:

1   *Find definitions:* Remember that definitions are often signaled by special type, especially *italics*. Look also for one example that makes a definition clear to you.

2   *Locate enumerations:* And remember that it does not help to locate a numbered series of items if you do not know what *label* the series fits under. So be sure to look for a clear heading for each enumeration.

3   *Look for relationships between headings and subheadings:* Such relationships are often the key to basic enumerations. And when it seems appropriate, you will also want to *change headings into questions* and find the answers to the questions.

4   *Look for emphasis words and main ideas:* If time permits, look for points marked by emphasis words and for main ideas in what seem to be key paragraphs.

■   What is one of the chief myths about reading? _____

_____

■   What is often a real alternative to reading every word of a selection? _____

_____

■   What are four skills to practice when skim reading?

    1.   _____

    2.   _____

    3.   _____

    4.   _____

The four reading selections that follow will give you practice in skim reading. You will have a limited amount of time to (1) read and (2) take notes on each selection. At the end of a time period, you will be asked questions about important ideas in the selection, and you can use your notes to answer the questions. You should do well on the quizzes if you have been able to identify and write down main ideas quickly.

The timed practice will have several benefits. It will teach you skim reading, improve your note-taking and handwriting efficiency, and help you solidify the comprehension skills you practiced in Part Four. By using the progress chart on page 416, you will be able to measure your performance as you move through the selections.

SELECTION 1

You have five minutes to skim the following selection for its main points and to take notes on those points. Be sure to time yourself or have your instructor time you as you read and take notes on the selection.

Hint: Definitions and a major enumeration are the keys to the important points in this selection.

VISUAL ELEMENTS IN ASSERTIVE COMMUNICATION

"Actions speak louder than words" may be an overworn phrase, but it's still true. If you mean what you say, your nonverbal behavior will back up your statements. On the other hand, the most assertive words will lose their impact if expressed in a hesitant, indirect manner. All the following visual elements can be part of assertive communication.

Eye Contact

Inadequate eye contact is usually interpreted in a negative way as anxiety, dishonesty, shame, boredom, or embarrassment. Even when they are not aware of a person's insufficient eye contact, others will often react unconsciously to it by either avoiding or taking advantage of the person exhibiting it. Don't go overboard and begin to stare down everyone you meet—this will be just as distracting as the other extreme—but do be sure to keep your gaze direct.

Distance

Choosing the correct distance between yourself and another person is an important ingredient of assertion. Anthropologist Edward Hall has outlined four distinct distances used by Americans in differing situations. *Intimate distance* ranges from the surface of the skin to about eighteen inches. As its name implies, it is appropriately used for private purposes: expressions of affection, protection, and anger. *Personal distance* runs from eighteen inches to approximately four feet and is used with people we know well and feel relaxed with. As Hall states, this is the range at which we keep someone "at arm's length," suggesting that while there is relatively high involvement here, the immediacy is not as great as that which occurs within intimate distance. *Social distance* ranges from four to twelve feet and is generally appropriate in less personal settings: meeting strangers, engaging in impersonal business transactions, and so on. This is the range at which job interviews are often conducted, customers are approached by salespeople, or newcomers are introduced to us by a third party. We often accuse someone who ought to be using social distance but instead moves into our personal space of being "pushy." Finally, Hall labels as *public distance* the space extending outward from twelve feet. As its name implies, public distance is used in highly impersonal settings and occasions involving larger numbers of people: classrooms, public performances, and so on. Be sure you are using the appropriate range for the messages you want to express.

Facial Expression

In the typical assertiveness training group, one or two participants will express confusion as to why they have such trouble being taken seriously. They claim to use the appropriate language, keep eye contact, stand at the proper distance, and so on. When asked to demonstrate how they usually express themselves, the problem often becomes apparent: the facial expression is totally inappropriate to the message. Many communicators, for example, verbally express their dissatisfaction while smiling as if nothing were wrong. Others claim to share approval or appreciation while wearing expressions more appropriate for viewing a corpse.

Gestures and Posture

Like facial expressions, your movements and body positioning can either contribute to or detract from the immediacy of a message. Fidgeting hands, nervous shifting from one foot to another, or slumped shoulders will reduce or even contradict the impact of an assertive message. On the other hand, gestures that are appropriate to the words being spoken and a posture that suggests involvement in the subject will serve to reinforce your words. Watch an effective storyteller, an interviewer, an actor, or some other model and note the added emphasis he or she gives to a message.

Body Orientation

Another way of expressing your attitude is through the positioning of your body in relation to another person. Facing someone head on communicates a much higher degree of immediacy than does a less direct positioning. In fact, a directly confronting stance in which the face, shoulders, hips, and feet squarely face the other is likely to be interpreted as indicating an aggressive attitude. (To verify this impression, think of the stance used by a baseball player who is furious with an umpire's decision or a Marine drill instructor facing a recruit.) Observation for assertive models will show that the most successful body orientation for most settings is a modified frontal one, in which the communicators are slightly angled away from a direct confrontation — perhaps ten to thirty degrees. This position clearly suggests a high degree of involvement, yet allows occasional freedom from total eye contact, which you have already learned is not to be desired.

When the five minutes are up, try to answer the questions on page 417 by referring to your notes but *not* referring to the text.

SELECTION 2

You have ten minutes to take notes on the main ideas in the following selection. You will then be asked questions dealing with main points in the selection. You will be able to refer to your notes, but not to the text, in answering the questions.

Hint: A major enumeration and a minor enumeration are the keys to the important points in this selection.

TWO FACTORS IN THE SUCCESS OF A MARRIAGE

Maturity

As David Knox points out, age itself is probably not the key variable in determining the likelihood a marriage has of succeeding. But age is associated with *maturity,* and he isolates four elements of maturity that he does consider to be critical. These are emotional, economic, relationship, and value maturity.

Emotional Maturity: The emotionally mature person has high self-esteem, which permits a greater degree of intimacy and interdependence in a relationship. Emotional maturity allows people to respond appropriately to situations. When conflict arises, they aim to resolve it, rather than becoming defensive or threatening to end the relationship.

Economic Maturity: Economic maturity implies the ability to support oneself and a partner if necessary. Especially for teenagers who have had little formal training or other job preparation, economic problems can put heavy strains on a marriage. Without a decent wage, people's physical and emotional energy can be drained as they try to scrape together enough to live on. Developing a loving relationship under those conditions is extremely difficult; trying to live on love makes people cross and irritable.

Relationship Maturity: Relationship maturity involves the skill of communicating with a partner. People with this kind of maturity are able to (1) understand their partner's point of view, (2) make decisions about changing behavior a partner doesn't like, (3) explain their own points of view to their partner, and (4) ask for changes in the partner's behavior when they believe this is appropriate. Without the willingness and skills to understand each other and to make themselves understood, it is difficult or impossible for a couple to maintain intimacy.

Value Maturity: Value maturity allows people to recognize and feel sure and comfortable about their own personal values. By their mid-twenties, most people have developed a sense of their own values. A high school senior or a first-year college student, however, may still have a number of years of testing and experiencing before he or she reaches value maturity.

Other factors in the success of a marriage are more subjective, for they relate to the explanations people give of why they marry a certain person. Although they are harder to measure objectively, the reasons people choose to marry are also associated with the success of a relationship.

Reasons for Marrying

Everyone's reasons for marrying are far more complex than "because we were in love." It is a combination of many complicated situations and needs that motivates people to marry. We'll look at several common reasons—first, those that are, in our opinion, negative, or less likely to lead to a stable marriage; and second, positive reasons—and see how each relates to the probability of a marriage's success.

Negative Reasons: *Rebound.* One negative reason for marrying is rebound. Marriage on the rebound occurs when a person marries very shortly after breaking up another relationship. To marry on the rebound is undesirable because the wedding occurs in deference to one's previous partner, rather than because one really loves the partner being married.

Rebellion. Marriage for rebellion results when young people marry primarily because their parents disapprove. Social-psychological theory and research show that parental interference can increase feelings of romantic attraction between partners. This has been called the *Romeo and Juliet effect.* As with marriage on the rebound, the wedding occurs in deference to someone else (one's parents) rather than to one's partner.

Escape. Some people marry to escape an unhappy home situation. The working-class, noncollege male, for instance, may reason that getting married is the one way he can keep for himself any money he makes, instead of handing it over to his parents; or, denied the opportunity to go away to college, working-class young people often use marriage as an escape from parental authority.

Physical appearance. Marrying solely because of the physical attractiveness of one's partner seldom leads to lifelong happiness. For one thing, beauty is "in the eye of the beholder," and if the "beholder" finds he or she really doesn't like the partner, that "beauty" is certain to diminish. Second, the physical beauty of youth changes as partners age. The person who married for beauty often feels she or he has been cheated. After a time, there is little left to be attracted to and love.

Loneliness. Sometimes people, especially older adults, marry because they don't want to grow old alone. Marrying is not always the solution, for people can be lonely within marriage if the relationship isn't a strong one. In other words, it is the relationship rather than the institution that banishes loneliness.

Pity and obligation. Some partners marry because one of them feels guilty about terminating a relationship: a sense of pity or obligation substitutes for love. Sometimes this pity or obligation takes the form of marrying in order to help or to change a partner, as when a woman marries a man because she believes that her loyal devotion and encouragement will help him quit drinking and "live up to his potential." Such marriages don't often work: The helper finds that his or her partner won't change so easily, and the pitied partner comes to resent being the object of a crusade.

Social pressure. Parents, peers, and society in general all put pressure on singles to marry. The expectations built up during courtship exert a great deal of social pressure to "go through with it." As engagements are announced or as people become increasingly identified as a "couple" by friends and family members, it becomes increasingly difficult to "back out." Still, breaking an engagement or a less formal commitment is probably less stressful than divorcing later or living together unhappily.

Positive Reasons: We have seen that rebound, rebellion, escape, appearance, loneliness, obligation, and social pressure are all unlikely bases for a happy marriage. What are some positive reasons? Knox lists three: companionship, emotional security, and a desire to parent and raise children.

Marriage is a socially approved union for developing closeness with another human being. In this environment, legitimate needs for companionship—to love and be loved by someone else—can be satisfied. Marrying for emotional security implies that a person seeks the stable structure of marriage to help ensure the maintenance of a close interpersonal emotional relationship over time. Although most people do not marry only to have children (and this alone may *not* be a positive reason for marrying), many regard children as a valuable part of married life. "The benefits of love, sex, companionship, emotional security, and children can be enjoyed without marriage. But marriage provides the social approval and structure for experiencing these phenomena with the same person over time."

When the ten minutes are up, try to answer the questions on page 418 by referring to your notes but *not* referring to the text.

SELECTION 3

You have ten minutes to skim the following selection for its main points and to take notes on those points.

CLASSIFICATIONS OF ABNORMAL BEHAVIOR

Abnormal behavior takes many forms. Some deviations from the normal are so slight that they are popularly termed mere *quirks*—strange little habits like eccentricities in dress or speech. People who have somehow picked up such habits may seem a bit queer at times, but they are not seriously discomforted or prevented from functioning effectively. At the other extreme are the serious forms of mental disturbance that render their victims out of touch with reality and incapable of conducting the ordinary affairs of life. These drastic forms of abnormal behavior, called *psychoses,* are relatively rare. Yet, in a nation as large as the United States, it has been estimated that on any given day they afflict about a million people, two-thirds of whom are being treated in mental hospitals.

In a sort of twilight zone between normal behavior and the extreme abnormality of psychosis lie the conditions known as *neuroses* (or sometimes *psychoneuroses*). These are long-lasting emotional disturbances characterized by high levels of stress and anxiety. Their victims usually manage to get along in school, hold jobs, and conduct more or less successful family and social relationships. But their chronic feeling of being anxious and distressed interferes with their effectiveness and their zest for life. They are the people who are most likely to seek relief through psychotherapy. Estimates of how many people are neurotic vary widely. One study found that fully 30 percent of big-city residents were mildly to seriously neurotic. Other studies have placed the figure for the population as a whole as low as about 8 percent. Attempts to determine the number are handicapped by the difficulty of setting a dividing line between what is normal and what is not.

In a sense, every neurosis is unique. Each person experiences an individual pattern of stressful situations and responds to them in individual ways dictated by an individual set of biological, psychological, and environmental factors. Thus any attempt to classify the symptoms of neurosis has to be somewhat arbitrary. One classification system used by many psychotherapists includes anxiety states, obsessive-compulsive reactions, and hysteria.

Anxiety States

Anxiety, of course, is characteristic of most forms of abnormal behavior. But sometimes it is such an obvious and outstanding symptom that it constitutes what has been termed an *anxiety state*. Many neuroses fall into this category, which takes a number of forms. Two of the most common anxiety states are the following.

Anxiety Reaction: The symptoms of an *anxiety reaction* are a chronic and relatively unfocused feeling of uneasiness and vague fear. People displaying anxiety reaction feel tense and jumpy, are afraid of other people, doubt their ability to study or work, and sometimes suffer from actual panic. They may experience such physical symptoms as palpitation of the heart, cold sweats, and dizziness.

Phobic Reaction: Anxiety states sometimes become attached to a specific object or event. The victim is then said to be suffering from a *phobic reaction*—in other words, displaying an unreasonable fear. Two common phobias are *claustrophobia* (fear of confinement in small places, which makes some people unable to ride in elevators) and *acrophobia* (fear of high places, which affects some people when they have to climb to the top of a theater balcony). Phobias can be acquired through simple classical conditioning in childhood, but they can also develop in more complex ways and may be attached to any object at all. Some people are thrown into panic by a snake, an ambulance, or even a toy balloon.

Obsessive-Compulsive Reactions

Obsessions are thoughts that keep cropping up in a persistent and disturbing fashion. Some neurotics are obsessed with the idea that they have heart trouble or that they are going to die by a certain age. A common and mild form of obsession is the feeling of people starting out on a trip that they have left the door unlocked or the stove turned on.

Compulsions are irresistible urges to perform some act over and over again, such as washing one's hands dozens of times a day. The hostess who cannot bear to see a knife or fork out of line at the table and keeps emptying her guests' ashtrays is exhibiting mild forms of compulsion. So is the businesswoman who cannot get any work done unless her papers are arranged in neat piles on her desk and she has a half dozen freshly sharpened pencils waiting all in a line. So is the child who steps on every crack in the sidewalk.

Obsessive-compulsive reactions seem to represent an attempt to substitute acceptable thoughts or actions for unacceptable desires that are causing conflict and anxiety. In particular, they may be an attempt to cover up feelings of hostility.

Hysteria

As used to describe neuroses, the word *hysteria* has a different meaning from the usual one. It refers specifically to the following two conditions.

Conversion Reaction: This form of hysteria results in strange and often dramatic physical symptoms though nothing is physically wrong. People who display conversion reaction may suffer paralysis of the arms or legs and even blindness or deafness. They may lose all sensitivity in one part of the body. In one type of conversion reaction, called *glove anesthesia,* they lose all sensitivity in the hand, as if it were covered by a glove. They cannot feel a pinprick or even a severe cut anywhere from fingertips to wrist.

Dissociative Reactions: People with dissociative reactions set themselves apart in some manner from the conflicts that are troubling them. One type of dissociative reaction is *amnesia,* or loss of memory. Another takes the rare form called *multiple personality*—in which the victims seem to be split into two or more completely different selves, representing aspects of the personality that they have been unable to integrate into a unity. (One of the selves may express the motive for affiliation by being kind and pleasant, while the other shows extreme hostility and aggression.) *Sleepwalking,* in which people move about and perform acts while asleep that they cannot remember after they wake up, is also a dissociative reaction.

■

Anxiety states, obsessive-compulsive reactions, and hysteria are not the only neuroses. There are many others. It might even be said that there are as many different neuroses, some of which defy classification, as there are neurotics. All are characterized by high levels of stress and anxiety lasting over a considerable period of time, but different individuals display different symptoms. Neuroses may be mild and cause little trouble, or they may be so severe as to verge on the psychotic.

When the ten minutes are up, try to answer the questions your instructor gives you by using your notes but *not* referring to the text.

SELECTION 4

You have ten minutes to skim the following selection for its main points and to take notes on those points.

THE JOB SEARCH

Unless you inherit the family business or invent a best-selling product while you are still in college, you will eventually have to search for your first full-time, career-field job. Getting a job is a process you must work hard at, not a task you accomplish on one odd Thursday afternoon. This process can be broken down into four stages: making contact, preparing the essential written materials, going out on interviews, and following up on the interview.

Making Contact

The first step in getting a job is making contact with potential employers in the field in which you are interested. Somewhere out there is a company you will be happy with and a job you are capable of performing well. You must begin early—months before you finish school, in most cases—to find prospective employers.

There are several sources to investigate for information on employers in your career field.

College Placement Bureaus: Every college has an office dedicated to helping students like you find jobs. The people who work there make contact with many employers in the area, and they know where the job openings are. In addition, the office maintains a library of career-oriented publications, including the *College Placement Annual* (a listing of firms seeking college graduates, along with names of people to contact); the *Dun and Bradstreet* directories of companies (which include information on many firms' products, number of employees, and key executives); and *Poor's Register of Directors and Executives* (which also supplies specifics about a great number of businesses). In addition to these publications, the placement bureau will have copies of the latest *Occupational Outlook Handbook,* an important career guide published by the federal government. This book is a treasure trove of information on how to prepare for a job and on which career fields will boom in the future.

Want Ads and Employment Agencies: Many job openings are never advertised, so you may not find what you are looking for in the want ads. Still, the want ads are one place to check. And newspaper listings, especially in large-city dailies, can tell you what kinds of jobs are available in your field and what the starting salaries are like. Employment agencies are also sources of job information. There are federal, state, and private agencies, all listed in your local phone book. Private agencies usually charge a fee, so know what you are getting into before signing anything.

Information-Gathering Calls and Interviews: One good approach to finding out where the jobs are is to call some employers in your field, *not to ask for a job* but simply to obtain information about the company. You might prepare a *brief* list of questions and then call the company; ask for the manager or the head of the appropriate department. Your questions might be, for example, "How large is your department?" or "What is the approximate starting salary for a (fill in the job title you are interested in)?" or "What are the main duties of a _____?" Sometimes, visiting the company in person is better: you are there and so cannot be brushed off; you also get a chance to make a good impression. Your visit may lead to a later interview; at the least, you will find out more about your field and that particular company.

Personal Connections: We've all heard the saying "It's not what you know; it's who you know," and this is often true in making contact with a potential employer. You have a network of acquaintances. If you multiply each person by all the people he or she knows, you can send a message out to hundreds of people. Make absolutely certain that your circle of relatives, friends, and associates knows that you are job hunting. Tell classmates, instructors, church members, fellow employees—everyone you can think of. You may get a name, a lead, or an invitation to an interview—possibilities you can't afford to ignore.

Preparing the Essential Written Materials

The second step in getting a job is preparing a résumé (sometimes called a *data sheet*) and cover letters. A *résumé* is a one- or two-page summary of your qualifications for a job. A *cover letter* (sometimes called a *letter of application*) is a letter tailored to a specific company explaining why you are the best candidate for a particular job. You will send off these documents each time you reply to a want ad and bring them with you on arranged interviews. You may also need résumés and appropriate cover letters if you decide to send out unsolicited applications to the companies you have discovered in your initial search. Some people send out hundreds of unsolicited mailings, but such a project can be very expensive and time-consuming. You may, however, want to send out a dozen or two to the companies that interest you most; you may receive one or two invitations to come for an interview.

There are several general points to remember about writing résumés and cover letters.

- Appearance is crucial. Both must be typed on good-quality letter paper and must be *error-free*. This means no strikeovers, no messy erasures, no fingerprints, and so on. Employers believe that anyone who does not take the trouble to make a cover letter and résumé perfect will most likely be equally careless on the job. (Résumés may be duplicated by photocopying, but all cover letters should be individually typed.)

- Both a résumé and a cover letter should be brief—one page each if possible.

- Finally, the language in both should be flawless—no mistakes in spelling, grammar, or punctuation—so have someone else proofread your work if necessary.

Key Details about the Résumé: A résumé should be a digest of personal and work-related information. It should begin with your name, address, and phone number at the top; it should include your educational history, work history, any special training you have, and the information that references are available on request. A section of a résumé showing an appropriate format appears on the following page. Note that both educational background and work experience begin with the most recent information and work backward in time.

Key Details about the Cover Letter: A cover letter should be included along with every résumé you submit. Your résumé and cover letter should complement each other. The résumé presents the facts about you in concise form, while the cover letter allows you to emphasize your strong points and offer persuasive evidence as to why you are suited to the job.

Following is a checklist of key features of a cover letter:

- A cover letter should be addressed to a specific person, if possible (unless you are answering a "blind" ad with a post-office box number), at a particular company. In the first paragraph, you should make clear which position you are applying for and how you heard about the opening.

- In the body of the cover letter, you have an opportunity to make your "voice" heard, to stand out from the other candidates who may be applying for the job. You should state—briefly—your qualifications for the job, referring to your résumé. Highlight the job experience or personality traits you have that would help you succeed in the job you are applying for.

- In your final paragraph, indicate that you will gladly come for an interview. State that you will call the employer (mention a specific day a week or so from the day your letter will probably arrive) to discuss your qualifications.

- The cover letter is *not* the place to discuss salary or potential problems (your child-care difficulties, for example). Emphasize, instead, that you are motivated, energetic, ambitious, and more interested in what you can do for the company than in what the company can do for you.

A sample section of a good cover letter is shown on page 413.

Résumé

JOANNE MORELLI
52 West Avenue
Norwood, New Jersey 08080
609-555-7896

OBJECTIVE

A career in the health administration field.

EDUCATION

School: Stockton State College, Pomona, New Jersey 08040 (1991–present)
Major: Allied health, specializing in administration
Additional Coursework: Twenty credit hours in computer programming
Grade-Point Average: An overall B

JOB EXPERIENCE

Position: Assistant manager at Brannigan's, South River Road, Elmwood, N.J. 08507
(1992–present)
Responsibilities: As evening-shift manager at a 150-seat restaurant, my responsibilities
include employee scheduling, inventory control, ordering, and customer relations.
Some of this work is done on an IBM PC computer.
Position: Waitress and head waitress at Brannigan's (1990–1992)
Responsibilities: Serving customers, scheduling waitresses, interviewing and training
new waitresses

Cover Letter

52 West Avenue
Norwood, New Jersey 08080
April 30, 1993

Ms. Elaine Hunter
Community Hospital
100 Butler Pike
Monroeville, Pennsylvania 17901

Dear Ms. Hunter:

I learned through the Placement Office at Stockton State College of an opening for an assistant administrator at Community Hospital. I feel I am an excellent candidate for the job.

I will earn my bachelor of science degree in Allied Health from Stockton this June. Because I specialized in administration, I have studied management, public relations, accounting, systems analysis, and business writing. In addition, I have studied health-related courses in the history of medicine, medical law, and ethics. But beyond that, I feel I have prepared myself well for a job in administration by taking as many courses in computer programming as I could. I have also learned to handle responsibility and to organize effectively through my assistant manager's post at Brannigan's.

I am aware that Community Hospital is expanding rapidly and will soon be adding a . . .

Going Out on Interviews

When a company calls you in for an interview, be prepared. You have done a great deal of work to get to this point, so treat the interview as a crucial step toward achieving your goal. For a successful interview, you must:

Pay Attention to "Interview Etiquette": First, arrive on time and bring a copy of your résumé. Being late can strike you off an interviewer's list before you get in the door. Next, dress appropriately. Don't wear jeans, running shoes, T-shirts, sandals, sexy skirts or dresses, or anything rumpled, stained, or torn. Your goal is not to look as if you're ready to wash the car or visit a disco; instead, you want to look neat and professional. For this reason, you should never chew gum, smoke, or sprawl casually in the chair while you are being interviewed. You should shake hands with the interviewer when you meet. When you leave, offer your hand again and thank the interviewer for his or her time.

Prepare Some Responses to Typical Interview Questions: Treat an interview like a test and be prepared to answer questions. At a minimum, prepare solid answers for each of the following questions. Write out your answers and go over them repeatedly until you feel comfortable and confident with your responses.

1. Why are you interested in this job?
2. What are your greatest strengths and weaknesses?
3. Tell me about yourself. (Note that this is an invitation to discuss your work experience, not your childhood.)
4. Why should we hire you?

You should also prepare some questions of your own for the interviewer to show that you have thought seriously about both the job and the company. You might ask about any special challenges the job poses, or how the job fits into the organization's overall goals. This is *not* the time to ask about overtime, promotions, or benefits—you will appear money-hungry. Save those questions until after you've been offered the job.

Come Across to the Interviewer as a Competent Person: Interviewers give poor recommendations to candidates who appear to be too self-important or painfully shy. Try to come across as a confident person but not as a know-it-all. Be willing to listen, but don't act terror-stricken. You should strive to present a balanced personality and to appear calm and secure during the interview session.

Follow-Up on the Interview

Once you walk out the door of the interviewer's office, you have one more chance to make a good impression. Go a step further than the majority of job applicants do by writing a brief thank-you note to the interviewer. In the note, remind the interviewer of the date you came in and the job you applied for. You might also want to reaffirm your enthusiasm for the job and reemphasize the qualities that make you the best candidate for the job. Be sure that the note is short—no more than one page—and typed as cleanly and carefully as your résumé. Send the note within a week of your interview. A sample thank-you note is shown below. Taking the time to write a thank-you note often clinches the job for a prospective employee.

Thank-You Note

Dear Ms. Hunter:

Thank you for your tour of Community Hospital and for the privilege of an interview. Now that I know more about Community and its goals, I am eager to join the skilled people who are working there. The position of administrative assistant sounds challenging, but I know that I am well-prepared to handle the responsibilities involved. The work I have done both in college and in my managerial position would seem to confirm this.

Again, thank you for your time and helpful information. I hope to hear from you soon.

In Conclusion . . .

Many people have stated that getting a job is a job in itself. Although it is true that the job search requires time and effort, you should not lose sight of your goal. The job you find will be an important factor in your future contentment and financial security. You might remember, too, that discouragement is inevitable at times, for rejection is part of the job hunt. Virtually everyone has been rejected for one or more jobs. Rejections, however, will soon be forgotten when an employer finally says, "When can you start?"

When the ten minutes are up, try to answer the questions your instructor gives you by using your notes but *not* referring to the text.

SKIM-READING PROGRESS CHART

On the chart below, there are skim-reading speeds for the selections in Part Five. The abbreviation WPM here refers to the number of words *processed* per minute. (You have not been able to literally *read* every word in the limited time involved.) The reading speeds assume that you have taken one-quarter of your time to read each selection and three-quarters of your time to take notes on what you have read.

Selection	WPM	Comprehension
1 Visual Elements in Assertive Communication	505	
2 Two Factors in the Success of a Marriage	480	
3 Classifications of Abnormal Behavior	435	
4 The Job Search	570	

Note: Reading speed will vary depending on the nature and difficulty of the material. In the four skim-reading selections, the highest speed is for "The Job Search," an article taken from a popular magazine. Because the three other selections contain more information to process, slightly lower skim-reading rates are suggested.

QUESTIONS ON THE SKIM-READING SELECTIONS

■ **Skim-Reading Selection 1**

1. Name any four visual elements in assertive communication.

   _____

   _____

   _____

   _____

2. What are the four distinct distances that are used by Americans in differing situations?

   _____

   _____

   _____

   _____

Score: Number correct (_____) × 12.5 = _____%

■ **Skim-Reading Selection 2**

1. What are two factors in the success of a marriage?

    _____

    _____

2. What is economic maturity? _____

    _____

3. What are four negative reasons for marrying?

    _____

    _____

    _____

    _____

4. What is one positive reason for marrying? _____

    _____

Score: Number correct (_____) × 12.5 = _____%

■ **Skim-Reading Selection 3**

Your instructor will refer to the Instructor's Manual to give you the questions for Selection 3.

■ **Skim-Reading Selection 4**

Your instructor will refer to the Instructor's Manual to give you the questions for Selection 4.

PART SIX

RAPID READING AND COMPREHENSION

PREVIEW

Part Six is concerned with developing your comprehension and increasing the number of words that your eyes take in and "read" per minute. Poor perception habits that may slow down your reading rate are explained, and an activity is provided to show you how your eyes move when they read. You then learn how a conscious effort to increase your speed is a key to overcoming careless perception habits and achieving a higher reading rate. A series of timed reading selections and sets of questions give you practice in building up your reading speed and comprehension. Through a progress chart, you will be able to compare your reading and comprehension scores as you move through the selections.

RAPID READING

This section will give you further practice in developing comprehension skills. At the same time, the section will help you work on increasing the number of words that your eyes take in and "read" per minute. You should remember, however, that while an increase in reading rate can be valuable, it is no cure-all for reading problems. If you feel you are reading your college assignments too slowly or ineffectively, factors other than reading speed are probably responsible. For example, perhaps you don't know where and how to look for main ideas and key supporting details in a textbook chapter. You may need to work on the reading comprehension and skim-reading skills presented in Parts Four and Five of this book. Also, you may need to learn more about such study skills as textbook previewing, marking, and note-taking, which are described in Part Two. And you may have to learn how to read more flexibly. This means that you adjust your speed and style of reading to accommodate your purpose as well as the level of difficulty of the material. In summary, there is much more to effective reading than an increase in speed alone. It is equally true, however, that rapid or speed reading can at times be a helpful skill. The activities in this part of the book will show you how to acquire that skill.

■ *Complete the following sentence:* _____ reading is only one part of effective reading.

POOR PERCEPTION HABITS

If you read material of average or less than average difficulty slowly, you can probably significantly increase your present reading speed. In all likelihood, poor perception habits are slowing down your reading. Such habits include *subvocalizing* (pronouncing words silently to yourself as you read); slow and stilted *word-for-word reading;* unnecessary *regressions* (returns to words you have already read); and *visual inaccuracy* (the tendency to misread letters and words on the page). Poor concentration habits often cause this last problem.

■ How many bad perception habits are mentioned in the preceding paragraph?

———————

HOW THE EYES READ

You will understand more clearly how the eyes work during reading when you perform the following experiment. Punch a hole with a pen or pencil through the black dot that follows this paragraph. Hold the page up for another person to see and have him or her read a paragraph or two silently. As the person reads, put your eye close to the hole and watch his or her eye movements. In the space provided here, write down your observations, including a description of how the reader's eyes moved across the lines of print.

●

————————————————————————————————

————————————————————————————————

In performing this activity, you probably observed that the reader's eyes did not move smoothly across the printed lines. Instead, they moved in jerks, making stop-and-go motions across the lines of print. These stops, which you may have been able to count as you peeked through the hole, are called *fixations,* and only during such fixations do you actually read. You may remember as a child trying—and failing—to catch your eyes moving as you looked in a mirror. You never saw them move because the eyes go too quickly between fixations for any clear vision. The eye must fixate, or stop, in order to see clearly. In summary, then, the eye reads by making a number of fixations or stops as it proceeds across a line of print.

In addition to the stops, you probably also noted the sweep of the eyes, like the carriage return of a typewriter, back and down to the beginning of each new line. Possibly you also noticed an occasional backward eye movement, or regression, when the eyes skipped back to reread words or phrases a second time.

Eye reading speed can be increased, in part, by reducing the number of fixations per line. Persons who make eight stops per line are not reading as quickly as those who make four. To read more quickly, they should learn to take in several words at each stop rather than only one or two. And as this is done, the tendencies to subvocalize and to read one word at a time will also be minimized. In addition, speed can be increased by reducing the duration of each pause or stop, by increasing the speed of the return sweep, and by cutting down on the number of backward eye movements or regressions. Finally, with improved concentration, the eyes can be made to read with greater accuracy as well as speed.

THE KEY TO RAPID READING

Eye speed can be increased and bad perception habits overcome through practice with timed passages in which you consciously *try to read faster.* As you read for speed in the situations that follow, remember that your *mind* is probably not slowing you down; your *eyes* are slowing you down. The mind is an incredible, computerlike instrument that can process words at an extraordinary rate of speed. What holds it back is the limited rate at which your eyes feed in words for it to process. Consciously force your eyes to move and work at ever higher and higher speeds. Your deliberate effort to "turn on" speed through practice should yield surefire results.

On the following pages are six selections to use in increasing your reading speed. You should read only the first selection at your normal rate of speed. You can then use this rate to measure later increases in speed. As you finish each selection, get your time from your instructor—or time yourself—and record it in the space provided. Then, without looking back at the passage, answer the comprehension questions.

Afterward, find your reading rate with the help of the table on pages 452–454. Also, check your answers with the instructor and fill in your comprehension score in the space provided. Finally, record both your reading rate and your comprehension score in the progress chart on page 451.

■ Many people have paid hundreds of dollars for speed-reading courses whose message or "secret" can be reduced to four simple words. What are the words? _____

SOME THOUGHTS AS YOU BEGIN RAPID READING

You are about to practice rapid reading—making your eyes and brain work together to process words at a high rate of speed. When you finish, you will probably be a faster reader than you were when you started, as your initial and final reading rates may show. If you want to maintain and even increase your rate of speed, you must practice on a regular basis. You can, for example, work on increasing your speed by rapidly reading newspaper columns, magazine articles, or other material of average difficulty.

At the same time, be sure to keep rapid reading in perspective. It is different from slow and leisurely reading, in which your purpose is pleasure. It is different from skim reading, in which your purpose is to locate the main points in an article or chapter. It is different from the kind of slow study reading that you do to increase your understanding of a difficult selection. It is but one of the many skills of an effective reader, and it is useful at certain times for certain reading purposes.

SELECTION 1

Remember to read this selection at your present comfortable rate of speed. You can then use the difference in speeds between this selection and the ones that follow to measure any advances in your reading rate.

WHY SO MANY PEOPLE IGNORE TRAFFIC LAWS

Some of the hard realities of negotiating the nation's streets and highways won't   1
be found in a driver-education manual. For instance:

Disregard of traffic laws in New York City has reached the point where many
parents are walking their children to school.

Turning right on a red light without stopping is so common in the nation's most
populous state that the practice is called "the California stop."

In Boston, a yellow light is considered by many drivers to mean speed up to
beat the change to red.

It all adds up to what traffic officials see as a gross disregard for the rules of   2
the road. Whether the cause is fewer police officers to enforce the laws or a general
surliness brought on by an ailing economy, observers say the problem is growing
in many cities.

Being ignored more frequently are stop signs, signal lights, and laws on yielding   3
the right-of-way. The National Safety Council says such violations cause more than
a quarter of the eighteen million traffic accidents annually.

"Today, it's a fifty-fifty toss-up whether people will stop for a red light," asserts   4
Robert J. McGuire, police commissioner of New York City. The number of tickets for
running red lights jumped 47 percent when police monitored seventeen of New
York's busiest intersections.

A similar complaint is heard in Boston. "I've never been in a city where as many   5
people run red lights and make illegal turns," says Heidi Foreman, a businesswoman there.

Violations Made Easy

Others say approval of right turn on red in many states and cities has made it   6
easier for people to ignore red lights altogether.

Some driving practices seem to defy common sense. Motorists reading and   7
shaving have been observed in Chicago. On an expressway near Washington,
one driver cut across three lanes of traffic five times within a mile before causing
an accident.

"Driving pretty much the way you want is a relatively new phenomenon—   8
something we've seen happen in the last four or five years," says Commissioner
Anthony R. Ameruso of the New York City Transportation Department.

Most alarming is the low flash point of some motorists' tempers. "We're seeing   9
more obscene gesturing and shouting when people get cut off in traffic," says Paul
Fowler of the Automobile Club of Southern California.

Traffic disagreements don't always end with verbal abuse. A stretch of Houston's   10
Westheimer Avenue is called "Altercation Avenue" because of the fights that often
break out. The worst violence recorded by Houston police left one man dead and
another wounded from gunfire after a car bumped a pickup truck a year ago.

In Dallas, Don Smerek, a football player with the Cowboys, was shot and   11
wounded as he pounded on the roof of a car during a right-of-way argument.

Even police are attacked. An officer in Texas was shot at while trying to calm   12
a motorist who was losing his temper in a traffic jam. So worried are police that
"drive friendly" signs dot Texas roadsides, and Houston's police psychologist advises
drivers to handle disputes by being "very apologetic."

Paradoxically, the upswing in unruly behavior behind the wheel comes at a time   13
when traffic fatalities are dropping in many cities. But, says Joseph Schofer of the
Northwestern University Transportation Institute, ignoring traffic laws increases the
likelihood of accidents.

Shower of Tickets

Statistics support his observation. Traffic fatalities are up in Boston. Accidents   14
have increased in New York even though police issued a record one million tickets for
moving violations in 1982. In Los Angeles, accidents involving pedestrians are rising.

Such figures have brought appeals for help. Residents of neighborhoods in   15
Southern California are pushing for more stop signs and speed bumps. San Francisco
officials asked the California Legislature to double to $100 the maximum fine for
running red lights and stop signs.

In New York, citizens' groups such as STOP—Safety Traffic Offenses Program—   16
are demanding more police on traffic patrol. "There are too many corners and not
enough cops," says Lisa Kaplan, who tells of drivers who honk at her for not running
red lights.

But the police are strained by budget cutting. The Boston police force, reduced   17
by five hundred since 1980, issued 18,385 tickets for moving violations during a
four-month period of 1982—6,600 fewer than in the same time a year earlier.

Tight budgets also have kept many jurisdictions from upgrading their road sys- 18
tems, adding to urban traffic snarls and the growing pothole epidemic. The resulting
delays and damage to cars leave drivers testy and impatient.

Some motorists, too, are affected by the economy. "A guy who gets behind the 19
wheel worried about losing his job or whether he can afford presents for the kids
will not have his mind on the road," says Art Conrad, director of Chicago's Driver
Improvement School.

But New York Police Commissioner McGuire sees a more general cause: "People 20
today do pretty much what they feel like doing, whether it's drugs, shoplifting, or
running red lights."

Time: _____   *Reading Rate (see page 452):* _____ *WPM*

■ Check Your Understanding

1. Tight budgets in many states have led to
   a. fewer traffic signs.
   b. more traffic tickets to increase revenue.
   c. fewer police on patrol.
   d. faulty traffic lights.

2. The "California stop" is a
   a. protest group.
   b. name for a traffic violation.
   c. type of stop sign.
   d. traffic law.

3. In Texas,
   a. violence and death have resulted from disputes between drivers.
   b. parents are walking their children to school.
   c. citizens always speed up for yellow lights.
   d. driver fatalities are very low.

4. *True or false?* _____ Traffic fatalities are dropping in many cities.

5. Right-turn-on-red laws have
   a. increased fuel consumption.
   b. been passed by all fifty states.
   c. made it easier for some people to ignore red lights.
   d. caused problems for New York taxis.

6. According to the passage, one reason for increased traffic violations is
   a. the ailing economy.
   b. poor driver-education training.
   c. high gas prices.
   d. alcohol abuse.

7. To handle drivers' aggression, one psychologist suggests
   a. suing a person who hits you.
   b. being apologetic.
   c. getting rid of your anger by shouting.
   d. ignoring the other person.

8. Which sentence best expresses the main idea of the passage?
   a. Disregard for the rules of the road is increasing.
   b. Budget cutting is causing problems on our highways.
   c. Ignoring driving laws is an old phenomenon.
   d. Traffic fatalities are increasing in many cities.

Number Wrong: _____   *Score:* _____

0 wrong = 100%	2 wrong = 75%	4 wrong = 50%	6 wrong = 25%
1 wrong = 88%	3 wrong = 63%	5 wrong = 38%	7 wrong = 13%

SELECTION 2

Your purposes here are to understand the selection and, in addition, *to try to increase your reading speed significantly.*

Do not be alarmed if, over the next several passages, your comprehension drops. This often happens when you try not only to understand but to read quickly as well. Your comprehension should "catch up with" your reading rate as you continue to practice.

CAFFEINE: ALL-AMERICAN DRUG

1   Did you start out your day with a cup of coffee, tea, or cocoa? Have you drunk any cola or eaten any chocolate today? Perhaps you had a headache and took an Anacin or Midol tablet to ease the pain. If you did any of these things, you gave yourself a dose of America's most-used drug: caffeine. Caffeine is a stimulant that can be harmful in large doses, yet it is freely available in a wide variety of drinks, food, and over-the-counter medications. Our nation, as a result, is hooked on caffeine.

2   People have used caffeine for centuries. Tea was harvested in Asia as early as 700 A.D. and shortly afterward made its way to Europe. The coffee plant was first grown in Arabia about a thousand years ago; by the end of the seventeenth century, coffee was in use in America as both a stimulating beverage and a medication. Today, the average American consumes over one hundred cups of tea and 450 cups of coffee per year.

3   The effect of caffeine on the body—whether from tea, coffee, chocolate, cola, or an over-the-counter drug—is the same. The caffeine is absorbed immediately and, within ten minutes, directly affects the central nervous system, especially the areas that govern heart rate, muscular coordination, and respiration. This produces the familiar caffeine "jitters"—a faster pulse rate and heartbeat, a feeling of wakefulness and nervousness. In addition, caffeine relaxes the kidneys; this increases urine output and may cause dehydration.

Caffeine is not completely harmful, however. A cup or two of coffee or tea per   4
day seems reasonably safe for most people. In fact, caffeine in small doses can help
people who must drive all night or work at monotonous jobs. Caffeine is also used
to treat hyperactive children since, for some unexplained reason, the stimulant calms
them down. But the dangers of caffeine mount as the dosage increases. Caffeine
causes acid to form in the stomach and promotes heartburn and indigestion. It may
cause ulcers. Large amounts of caffeine have been linked to heart disease and high
blood pressure. Caffeine has especially damaging effects on women. Heavy caffeine
users have a greater chance of developing fibrocystic disease, in which benign lumps
form in the breast. In a study done at Ohio State University, forty-seven patients with
this disease were advised to eliminate all caffeine from their diets. Twenty women
followed the advice; of these, thirteen were completely cured. Of the twenty-seven
women who continued to use caffeine, only one was cured. Pregnant women also
face some danger from caffeine. Heavy coffee drinking has been connected with
high risks of miscarriage, stillbirth, premature birth, and birth defects such as cleft
palate. The Food and Drug Administration warns all pregnant women and those
who want to become pregnant to avoid caffeine.

A high dose of caffeine can have negative psychological effects as well. One   5
study showed that psychiatric patients who consumed large amounts of caffeine
tended to be more depressed than other patients. People who drink many cups of
strong brewed coffee every day can show symptoms that resemble anxiety attacks—
insomnia, shakiness, upset stomach, and irregular heartbeat. Workers with all-day
access to strong coffee, such as restaurant workers, nurses, and office personnel,
are vulnerable to such caffeine-induced anxiety attacks.

How much caffeine is too much caffeine? The answer depends on how much   6
and what kind of caffeine you consume daily. More than one thousand milligrams
of caffeine per day is almost certainly damaging. Even five hundred milligrams per
day can lead to symptoms of chronic caffeine poisoning: restlessness, headaches,
insomnia, heart irregularities, and diarrhea. A cup of brewed ground roast coffee
contains from one hundred to 150 milligrams of caffeine; instant coffee has up to
one hundred milligrams.

Tea also varies in the amount of caffeine it may contain. In one analysis of   7
domestic tea brands, the figures ranged from twenty milligrams for a weak brew of
Tetley to ninety milligrams for a strong brew of Red Rose. (Leaving a tea bag immersed
in water for one minute yields a weak brew; leaving it in for three minutes or more
produces a strong brew.) A twelve-ounce cola has up to seventy-five milligrams of
caffeine. Six ounces of cocoa contains ten milligrams of caffeine, as does eight
ounces of chocolate milk.

The presence of caffeine in colas and chocolate has special significance for   8
children, who are heavy users of both substances. Children weigh less than adults
and may be many times more sensitive to a dose of caffeine than an adult would
be. One can of cola can have the same effect on a child that four cups of coffee
would have on an adult. A couple of sodas and a chocolate bar can be a caffeine
overdose for a child.

Withdrawing from a caffeine addiction isn't easy. Drinking even as little as three   9
cups of coffee a day can make a person psychologically and physically dependent
on the drug. Cutting out caffeine completely through a "cold turkey" withdrawal can
lead to tiredness, depression, drowsiness, irritability, headache, and nausea. For
this reason, a caffeine user should break the habit gradually. Cutting down on caffeine
consumption by stages gives the body a chance to wean itself away from the drug.
Substituting instant decaffeinated coffee for regular will also help, since a cup of
decaffeinated contains only about three milligrams of caffeine. Brewed-coffee lovers
can mix decaffeinated and regular coffee in the brewing basket, thus reducing the
amount of caffeine in the finished product. Tea drinkers may want to try decaffeinated
tea or herbal teas (be cautious, though, and read the label, for some herbal teas
contain caffeine). Caffeine-free sodas are widely available now and should be substituted for cola drinks. Children, especially, should avoid the cola drinks that lead to
caffeine addiction at an early age.

Instead of zapping your body with daily hits of caffeine, consider kicking the   10
habit. The drawbacks of caffeine use far outweigh the benefits. A healthy diet,
combined with sufficient sleep and exercise, will give your body all-day energy
without the harmful side effects caffeine causes. The price of that temporary caffeine
jolt is too high to pay.

Time: _____   *Reading Rate (see page 452):* _____ *WPM*

■ Check Your Understanding

1. *True or false?* _____ Small amounts of caffeine appear to present little risk
   to the general public.
2. Caffeine
   a. affects the central nervous system.
   b. causes cancer.
   c. can cause mental illness.
   d. does not affect children.
3. Children usually consume caffeine in the form of chocolate and _____.
4. Caffeine
   a. is a relatively new discovery.
   b. has little effect on children.
   c. has been used for centuries.
   d. is not a drug.
5. The author considers the following amount to be too much caffeine:
   a. one soda per day
   b. more than two cups of coffee per day
   c. two cups of tea per day
   d. six ounces of chocolate milk per day

6. Which of the following treatments does the author recommend for caffeine addiction?
    a. medication
    b. self-help group
    c. "cold turkey" withdrawal
    d. gradual withdrawal

7. One group that should definitely minimize caffeine intake is
    a. the elderly.
    b. teenagers.
    c. children.
    d. office workers.

8. Which sentence best expresses the main idea of the passage?
    a. Manufacturers want customers to become addicted to caffeine.
    b. Large doses of caffeine can be harmful.
    c. Children are more susceptible to caffeine's effects than adults.
    d. Withdrawing from a caffeine habit is very difficult.

Number Wrong: _____   *Score:* _____

| 0 wrong = 100% | 2 wrong = 75% | 4 wrong = 50% | 6 wrong = 25% |
| 1 wrong = 88% | 3 wrong = 63% | 5 wrong = 38% | 7 wrong = 13% |

SELECTION 3

Once again, you should make a deliberate effort to read at a rapid rate of speed. You must *will* your eyes to move faster, and you must *will* your brain to process the incoming facts, ideas, and details rapidly.

If you are not already doing so, sit up straight, put your feet flat on the floor, and hold the book at a comfortable angle. Consciously force your eyes to move at a higher rate of speed. Make the decision that you are going to read faster, and do it!

CHILD ABUSE

1   Tommy, age three, was playing in the backyard with his brothers and a couple of friends. Perhaps he was making too much noise, or perhaps he did not clean up when his mother first asked. In any case, his mother said he had been "bad," dragged him into the house, and took him to the basement. There, she put him in his playhouse and set it afire. Tommy suffered burns over 95 percent of his body but survived. He required extensive plastic surgery and is now living with his father.

2   Two-year-old Nancy was not fully toilet-trained, and each time she wet herself, her mother placed her in a bathtub of hot water—to teach her a lesson, the mother said. One afternoon, the water was too hot. Nancy suffered second-degree burns from her waist down. Nancy was hospitalized; her mother is receiving counseling. They are now at home together.

3   These are not isolated examples of parents' conscious or unwitting cruelty to their children. Such cruelty goes on, in some cases with even greater ferocity and physical injury, every day, year after year. Nationally, an estimated two million cases of child abuse occurred in 1978, and more than 500,000 of them were reported to health social services agencies.

4   Child abuse is a phenomenon that knows no social, geographic, or racial boundaries. It occurs in the best of families in wealthy suburbs and in rural areas as well. It is, in fact, a national plague that experts say is likely to create another generation of child abusers in the United States from among those being abused today.

For years, the problem was hidden behind the closed doors of houses or apart-   5
ments. But, since the passage of laws in the 1970s requiring health and other
professionals to report all cases of suspected abuse, a quiet revolution has been
occurring. More cases of child abuse are being reported, and social-welfare agencies
are getting help for both the children and their parents. That is not to say, however,
that the reporting is in any way complete. More than five thousand cases are reported
annually to the Philadelphia County Children and Youth Agency, but a spokeswoman
said, "There's a lot more out there that goes unreported." Schools are just now
beginning to focus on abuse, the spokeswoman said. "Out of the quarter million
kids within the Philadelphia schools, we received only three hundred reports last
year. However, the schools are making strides in this area," she said. To increase
the frequency of reporting, institutions that come into contact with injured children
are training staff members to recognize abuse. The tremendous amount of stress in
today's society—both within and outside the home—is considered one of the main
factors in the rise of child abuse.

Poor marital relationships, single parenthood, social and economic problems,   6
unemployment, and social isolation add undue stress to our lives. The problem of
social isolation is critical. Today people are moving around and finding themselves
living farther away from their families and the emotional support which they provide.
Mothers find themselves living either in large city apartment complexes or in suburban
communities in which they know absolutely no one. In this lonely atmosphere, they
try to deal with the pressures of being the parent of one, two, or three children.

Dr. Benjamin Price, who sees at least one case of child abuse a week in Einstein   7
Hospital's pediatric clinic or emergency room, believes that "parenting" should be
a compulsory subject within the educational system. "If people were fully prepared
to cope with the emotional demands of fatherhood or motherhood, many of these
problems would slowly decrease," he said. "We can't forget emotional abuse. It is
harder to diagnose but can be just as destructive to the child as any of the more
dramatic cases involving burns, bruises, or broken bones."

Most physicians and social workers who were interviewed agreed that child   8
abuse and neglect are on the upswing. Though it is without a doubt more visible
and more publicized today, child abuse is not a new phenomenon. Infanticide,
abandonment, beatings, mutilation—all are a part of the history of child abuse.
During the industrialization of the United States, children as young as five years old
worked twelve to sixteen hours a day in factories and sweatshops. Such working
conditions inspired the first welfare efforts to stem child abuse. In 1871, the first
formally documented case of child abuse was recorded, in New York City. Until
then, no intervention had legally been possible. Between 1962 and 1967, all fifty
states passed laws requiring identification, reporting, and treatment of child abuse
by designated social service agencies. It was discovered, however, that these laws
were not sufficient. During the 1970s, they were revised to legally bind all professionals who work with children, including doctors, nurses, and teachers, to report any
suspected case of child abuse or neglect.

Low incomes and unemployment increase the chances of violence, and child   9
abuse is 45 percent higher among blue-collar parents of either sex than among white-
collar parents. There are no significant differences between black and white parents
in the rate of abusive violence. However, Jewish parents have the lowest rate of
violence. Members of minority religions have the highest. The likelihood of child
abuse is lowered when both parents are of the same religion.

According to several physicians and social workers, dealing with the courts and   10
the red tape involved with the backlog of cases frustrates them and adds tension to
an already explosive situation. Price cited as an example a case with which he
was involved several years ago. "An eighteen-month-old boy was brought into the
emergency room with lesions which were definitely associated with child abuse. This
was not the first time he had been examined and treated with these lesions," Dr.
Price said. It was suspected that the mother's boyfriend had beaten the child. The
welfare department was notified, and the child was allowed to return home—if the
mother's boyfriend moved out. "The day the child was released, both mother and
boyfriend took him home," Price said. Several days later, the child appeared in the
emergency room with identical lesions. This time, he was removed from the home
and temporarily placed with foster parents. A family court trial for the mother was
scheduled. "I can still remember how the mother appeared in the courthouse the day
of the trial. She dressed the little boy and his three-year-old sister in their Sunday
best. The little girl had on a long dress and even had bows in her hair," Price said.
After a wait of several hours at the courthouse, the trial was postponed. A few days
later the little girl was rushed to the emergency room—dead on arrival, the victim
of child abuse.

Time: _____   *Reading Rate (see page 452):* _____ WPM

■ Check Your Understanding

1. *True or false?* _____ Since the 1970s, fewer cases of child abuse are be-
    ing reported.
2. According to the passage, the tremendous amount of _____
    in today's society is considered one of the main factors in the rise of child
    abuse.
3. Dr. Price believes that one compulsory subject within the educational system
    should be
    a. first aid.
    b. parenting.
    c. dealing with stress.
    d. child psychology.

4. The first formally documented case of child abuse was recorded in
   a. 1961.
   b. 1776.
   c. 1898.
   d. 1871.

5. *True or false?* _____ All fifty states have laws requiring the reporting and treatment of child abuse.

6. In trying to prevent and deal with cases of abuse, physicians and social workers are hampered by
   a. the federal government.
   b. exhausted hospital staffs.
   c. the red tape involved with court cases.
   d. all of the above.

7. The likelihood of child abuse is increased by
   a. race.
   b. low income.
   c. both of the above.
   d. neither of the above.

8. Which sentence best expresses the main idea of the passage?
   a. Child abuse is a growing problem in the United States.
   b. Child abusers must be punished more severely.
   c. Courts must be quicker to prosecute abusers.
   d. Unemployment is a major cause of child abuse.

Number Wrong: _____   *Score:* _____

| 0 wrong = 100% | 2 wrong = 75% | 4 wrong = 50% | 6 wrong = 25% |
| 1 wrong = 88% | 3 wrong = 63% | 5 wrong = 38% | 7 wrong = 13% |

SELECTION 4

With this selection, you may want to try the following technique. As you read, lightly underline each line of print with your index finger. Do not rest your hand on the page, and do not point to individual words with your finger. Hold your hand slightly above the page and use your finger as a pacer, moving it a little more quickly than your eyes can comfortably follow. Try to glide your finger smoothly across each line of print, and to make your eyes follow just as smoothly. If the technique helps you attend closely and read rapidly, use it in other selections as well.

THE SMART WAY TO BUY A NEW CAR

"I'm really sorry," said the saleswoman to Rick, who was glancing at a big, beautiful red car. "Joe over there just told me this car is spoken for." 1

Seeing Rick's forlorn expression, she went on. "Look, we're holding it for a woman who said she might not be able to raise the down payment. Let me go check with the manager and see what the situation is." 2

As she walked off toward the office, Rick gazed at the luxurious upholstery and the space-age dashboard of his dream car. His old clunker had been stalling at stoplights for the past six months, and the last repairs had cost as much as the car was worth. He knew he needed a new car, but he hadn't known until he had taken this shiny beauty for a ten-minute test drive that he could no longer be happy without this particular car. He realized it was a bigger car than he needed and got fewer miles to the gallon than he wanted, but still 3

"You're in luck." The saleswoman interrupted his reverie. "My boss says we can't hold it any longer. It's all yours—let's sit down and do the paperwork." 4

The paperwork, it turned out, needed some doing. When Rick balked at the initial price, objecting that it was far higher than he could afford, the saleswoman said, "You give me a price. What do you think is a good price?" Rick said, "I'd just like a fair shake. The sticker price posted on the car is $12,300. I bet if I shopped around I could get a lower price." The saleswoman said, "Let me try something. Let me go back and see if I can persuade my boss to give you an extra $150 for your trade-in. Would that clinch it?" Rick said, "Make it $200 and you have a deal." The saleswoman disappeared for ten minutes, and when she reappeared, she was smiling. "He agreed," she said. "You drive a hard bargain." Rick then signed the sales agreement, feeling pleased that he had negotiated a good deal. 5

Rick, however, had been taken for a ride, just as many people who buy new 6
cars are taken every day by salespeople who sell cars for many hundreds, even
thousands, of dollars more than they are worth. Rick had violated rules one, two,
three, and four for buying new cars: he held on to his old car too long before
shopping for a new one, fell in love with a new model, did no homework before
visiting a car dealer, and combined negotiating for a new car with trading in his
old one.

Rick had waited to shop for a new car until he was unprepared to continue 7
driving the one he already owned. His car was ready to expire, so he hardly had
the time it might take to go about making a wise purchase on a new one. Also, he
was psychologically unable to deal any longer with the troubles of his old clunker;
he desperately wanted it out of his life, at any cost. As a result, he felt a sense of
longing as soon as he entered the showroom—a feeling intensified by his spin around
the block in the new, smooth-riding model. Consider, though, that his brief test drive
told Rick almost nothing except how pleasant it would be to drive away from the
dealership behind the wheel of a new car.

Clearly, Rick hadn't given much thought to what he really wanted. He bought 8
on impulse, falling in love with one of the first cars he saw. Once his emotions
overcame his judgment, he lost the only source of leverage a customer has in such
negotiations—a willingness to walk away from the deal. Car salespeople often
become amazingly pliant when they see a potential customer leaving the showroom.
Unfortunately, Americans are conditioned to fall in love with cars. Many believe
what the ads tell them—that a particular car will make them seem more attractive,
richer, and sexier. They forget that the main reason for getting a car is transportation.
As a result, many car buyers do not control their emotions enough to walk away
from the "dream" car sitting in front of them. But customers who lose their hearts to
a car may also lose many of their hard-earned dollars.

To decide what kind of car he really wanted and how much it was actually 9
worth, Rick should have done some homework. Instead of evaluating his needs in
the privacy of his home, he trusted that chance would guide him to the right make
and model. As a result, he bought a car better suited to an upper-middle-class family
of five than to a single person on a tight budget. Rick also had no idea how the car
would perform, what kind of repair record it had, if it would stand up in a crash,
and other vital information.

To find out, he should have consulted one of two sources before visiting an auto 10
showroom: the latest April issue of the monthly magazine *Consumer Reports* or *The
Car Book,* an annual publication by Jack Gillis that is available at any local bookstore.
If the April issue of *Consumer Reports* is not in a nearby library, one can obtain it
by sending $4 to the Back Issue Department, Consumer Reports, P.O. Box 2485,
Boulder, Colorado 80322. The April issue is almost entirely devoted to cars and is
particularly valuable, since it provides detailed information on such matters as cost,
performance, comfort, safety, reliability, and options.

After finding out what cars appealed to him, Rick should then have visited some 11
auto showrooms for more information gathering. When a salesperson approached,
he should have said, "Hi, you have a Ford Taurus GL that I'd like to test-drive." At
the same time, Rick should make it crystal-clear that while he seriously intends to buy
a car, he is not ready to commit to a deal. Rick might say, for example, "It's my
policy never to decide anything right away. This is a major purchase, and I intend
to sleep on it for several days before doing anything." There is a high probability
that Rick will get some pressure from the salesperson, who is likely to ask something
like, "What can I do to sell you this car today?" Rick should make it clear there is
nothing the salesperson or the manager can do; he will not agree to even a supposedly
fabulous, cannot-be-repeated, once-in-a-lifetime offer.

After learning what model he wanted, Rick could then have found out the dealer's 12
cost. *Discovering what the dealer paid for a car is extremely useful, even invaluable
in negotiating the lowest price, and this information is easy and inexpensive to get.*
There are at least two good sources for this information. First, available for about
$4 at local bookstores is *Edmund's New Car Prices,* with separate booklets for
domestic and foreign cars.

Second, for $11, *Consumer Reports* will provide a complete computer printout 13
with information on any car model. Information on two cars costs $20, and on three
cars it costs $27. Printouts for each additional car cost $7. A copy of the following
order form can be used:

Consumer Reports Auto Price Service	Please send me a Consumer Reports price and options printout for each model listed below.		
Please print	**Make**	**Model**	**Style**
Name _____	Example BUICK	CENTURY LIMITED	SEDAN 4-DOOR
Address _____	1 st car _____		
_____	2 nd car _____		
City _____	3 rd car _____		
State _____ Zip _____			
Mail with payment to: Consumer Reports, Box 8005 Novi, Michigan 48050	PRICES: $11 for 1 car. $20 for 2 cars. $27 for 3 cars $7 for each additional printout after 3.		

Each printout gives detailed information on standard and optional equipment 14
as well as the dealer's cost and list price for the basic model and all available
options. Having this information means one can go to a dealer well equipped to
negotiate. Here, for example, is the basic price information for a Ford Taurus GL
four-door given in a recent edition of *Consumer Reports:*

	Dealer cost	Sticker price (on the side window of the car)
Basic car	$9,981	$11,622

At this point, Rick is ready to negotiate, and he should do this *without even* 15
going to a showroom. He should check the telephone yellow pages and get the
numbers of five or so car dealers in his area that carry the car he wants to buy. He
should then call and ask for a salesperson and say, "Hi, I'm going to buy a Taurus
GL and want to get a good price. I know from a *Consumer Reports* printout that your
cost for the car is $9,981. What is the lowest price you can quote me above that
cost?" In most cases, the salesperson will want to call Rick back. Rick should make
it clear that he is shopping around, but that he will be waiting for the salesperson's
call. In this situation, Rick is clearly in the driver's seat. Because he knows the dealer's
cost, all the power in the situation belongs to him, the customer.

While some salespeople may be irritated by a customer who is not interested 16
in paying for a huge markup, others will take the opportunity to make a legitimate
profit of about $200 to $400. A profit of $200 on the above Ford Taurus, for
instance, would mean a savings of $1,581 off the sticker price for the consumer.
That's a fair markup for the dealership too, considering that all a salesperson must
then do is write up the sale, a matter of about fifteen minutes' work. As the dealer
will also receive a "holdback," about 3 percent of the car's invoice price given by
the manufacturer, he or she will make enough on the sale to cover advertising costs
and other overhead and make a decent profit as well.

After Rick gets the best price, he should visit the dealer to get the dealer's price 17
on his trade-in. If the price does not seem good enough, Rick should take his car to
the dealer with the next lowest price for the new car. When he gets the lowest
combination of new car price plus credit for his trade-in, he is ready to do one final
bit of homework: getting the lowest interest rate on a new-car loan.

Car loans are expensive, and a knowledgeable consumer will shop around, 18
trying to find the best deal. The price of borrowing money may vary, but whatever
the cost of the loan, the price of the car itself should remain the same. While factory-
subsidized loans are often among the best deals, low-interest dealer-subsidized loans
may be tied to a higher price for the car. A wise shopper keeps the two items separate.

With the trade-in price and the loan interest rate taken care of, Rick is ready to sit 19
down with the dealer he has chosen and get everything in writing. Some unscrupulous
dealers will try to add on costs, such as a dealer's preparation fee, even *after* you've
agreed on a price. Dealers will also try to sell service contracts, which generally
make sense only for high-risk cars—ones likely to have a number of mechanical
problems as predicted by ratings in the April issue of *Consumer Reports.* Except, of
course, for such legitimate charges as sales tax, initial gas and oil charges, and title
and inspection fees, a buyer should respond to any additions to the price by saying,
"That's not acceptable. I am buying the car on the basis of our original verbal
agreement."

In paying too much for a hastily chosen car, Rick was not alone. Because they 20
fail to do any homework and allow their emotions to hamper their judgment, most
people are poor car buyers. This situation is unfortunate because, next to a home,
a car is the most expensive purchase for most people. The consumers who do a little

research are likely to be well rewarded for the time they spend. They will also have the satisfaction of knowing that they have acted wisely and aggressively. Instead of being a car dealer's victims, they will have taken the steps needed to put themselves in the driver's seat.

Time: _____   *Reading Rate (see page 452):* _____ *WPM*

■ Check Your Understanding

1. *True or false?* _____ It is impossible for the consumer to learn the dealer's actual cost for a car.

2. According to the article, the time to establish a trade-in price for your old car is
   a. before doing anything else.
   b. when you test-drive a new car.
   c. after you have learned the dealer's cost.
   d. after you have agreed on a price for the new car.

3. *True or false?* _____ Buyers of new cars should generally buy service contracts only for high-risk cars.

4. Which sentence best expresses the main idea of paragraph 8?
   a. People shouldn't be emotional when buying a car.
   b. Americans spend too much money on their cars.
   c. Americans believe what car ads tell them.
   d. Rick didn't really know what kind of car he wanted.

5. Which sentence best expresses the main idea of paragraph 19?
   a. Rick was ready to get everything in writing.
   b. Some car dealers are dishonest.
   c. The April issue of *Consumer Reports* predicts how many mechanical problems a car will have.
   d. Buyers should not permit dealers to change their original verbal agreements.

6. The author implies that many car salespeople
   a. help their customers find the best buy.
   b. do not hesitate to take advantage of their customers.
   c. prefer not to pressure their customers.
   d. make more money from knowledgeable customers than from uninformed ones.

7. *True or false?* _____ In paragraph 18, the author implies that the cost of a car loan can add a great deal to the price of a car.

8. Which sentence best expresses the central point of the selection?
   a. Car dealers often treat buyers unfairly.
   b. With some research and know-how, you can get a fair deal on a new car.
   c. Because he had not planned well, Rick bought the wrong car.
   d. New cars are more expensive than people think.

Number Wrong: _____   *Score:* _____

0 wrong = 100%	2 wrong = 75%	4 wrong = 50%	6 wrong = 25%
1 wrong = 88%	3 wrong = 63%	5 wrong = 38%	7 wrong = 13%

SELECTION 5

Remember that it is your *deliberate effort to read faster,* along with extensive practice, that will make you a speed reader. Keep this crucial fact in mind as you read this selection.

NESTING: ADULT CHILDREN AT HOME

Bruce B. moved back to his parents' house after his roommate decided to move out of the apartment they shared. Bruce had been paying half of the $500-a-month rent on the New Jersey apartment. With his roommate gone, however, Bruce could no longer afford to stay there. As a result, twenty-nine-year-old Bruce now lives in his old room in his parents' home.   1

Tony S., thirty-two, recently lost his job, and he too returned to his parents' house. So did Patty B., twenty-five, a recently divorced mother of two small children. Owing to financial or personal problems, grown children are flocking home to the shelter of the family nest. As might be expected, families find that there are advantages—and problems—when adult children live at home.   2

The trend toward "nesting" has increased dramatically over the years. In 1970, according to the Census Bureau, 13.7 million people age eighteen or over were living with their parents. In 1980, that figure had risen to 18.3 million. (Interestingly, more males than females have become nesters, even though the number of adult males is almost the same as the number of adult females.) One reason for the increase to 18.3 million is the fact that there are more young people in the population now than in previous years. Still, the number of nesters, as a percentage of the growing pool of young adults, has gone up sharply.   3

443

Returning children are often ones facing some kind of emotional crisis: a broken   4
marriage or romantic relationship, an argument with a roommate, or an inability to
cope with independence. But the main reason for the nesting phenomenon is probably
an economic one. High school graduates who do not go on to college often face
discouraging job prospects and are forced to remain at home. In addition, the
unemployment rate among all young people is high. According to the U.S. Bureau
of Labor Statistics, the rate of unemployment for Americans between eighteen and
twenty-four is almost 18 percent. And the rate for adults between twenty-five and
thirty-four is 11 percent. Today's high cost of living and high interest rates on home
mortgages are probably the most decisive factor in the migration home. For example,
rents in major cities can be $400 and up for a one-room apartment. And buying a
house is rarely a solution. Young people often lack the hefty down payment, good
credit record, and stable income needed to purchase a house. As one university
economist has said, "A growing proportion of young people are finding that independence is beyond their means."

In many cases, nesting can benefit both children and parents. Nesters who have   5
gotten themselves into financial trouble by running up charge accounts or utility bills
can often ease the financial crunch by moving back home. In fact, some credit
counselors recommend a move home as a way to untangle oneself from a financial
mess. A grown child who contributes to room and board costs can help out his or
her parents as well. Bruce B.'s father, a retired widower living on a pension, feels
more secure with his son contributing to pay for household expenses.

Grown children at home can help in other ways, too. They can perform household   6
chores, tend younger siblings, and provide company for a single parent. In turn, the
nesters—especially ones who had been holding down two jobs to make ends meet—
have more time for leisure and hobbies. Barbara M., for example, was moonlighting
as a waitress while she worked as a secretary in a bank. Since she returned home,
she has had time to indulge in her two passions: playing softball and singing with
a choral group.

As might be expected, however, there are many problems associated with   7
nesting. In *The Not So Empty Nest,* Phyllis Fuerstein writes, "The major discontent
we found was lack of breathing space." One thirty-year-old nester who moved home
after nine years of marriage said, "There are touchy situations. Sometimes I think,
'Why did she put that picture over there?' But it's not my place to say anything."
Adult children can clash with their parents over privacy rights, eating habits, spending
habits, or choice of friends or music. It's difficult for both parents and children to
give up the old parent-child patterns.

The change in sexual mores over the last few decades also creates problems   8
for parents and nesters. For the grown child, living at home means being unable to
bring a date to his or her room. Explains George, twenty-nine, a carpenter, "Your
parents may know you do those things, but they would not like to be confronted with
them personally." A New Jersey mother whose grown daughter has returned home
twice says, "When Kate's away, I don't worry about what she's doing or who she's
with. When she's here, I find myself staying up at night when Kate is out. It's as
though the clock is set back years."

Parents and children, in addition, may disagree over financial arrangements.   9
Some nesters feel that they should not have to pay room and board at home; they
still expect their parents to feed and shelter them. Parents, in turn, can feel awkward
about asking their children to contribute to household expenses, even though another
adult at home can place a significant burden on parents.

Besides making adjustments at home, nesters must deal with society's view of   10
living at home and the resulting blow to their own egos. Tony S. says, "When I meet
a woman, there's no way I'm going to tell her I live at home." Nesters often feel that
they have somehow failed as adults and must return to being children in their parents'
home. They face negative reactions from their friends as well: "How can you stand
it?" and "You must be miserable living with your parents" are typical reactions.
Donna P., a contented nester, says that young people need a strong sense of self to
deal with the people who equate adulthood with living outside the family home.

It is possible to deal with the problems nesting presents if both parents and   11
children treat each other as adults. Family therapists say that the most important
ingredient of a successful nesting situation is that the grown children not be totally
dependent. They need to earn their keep and contribute to the household. For the
unemployed young adult, this can mean cleaning the house or maintaining the family
car. Another way of avoiding difficulties is to create clear house rules in advance.
When firm agreements are reached, there is less room for misunderstandings to
develop. Eating schedules, space arrangements, and cleanup responsibilities should
be discussed. In addition, a target date for departure should be set. Even if it changes,
it gives everyone a sense of limits and an opportunity to bring up the subject.

Nesting situations, if handled properly, can strengthen family ties. As one parent   12
said, "When David leaves again, I'll probably regret it more than I did the first time."

Time: _____   *Reading Rate (see page 452):* _____ *WPM*

■ Check Your Understanding

1. According to the passage, the most recent unemployment figure for people
   between the ages of eighteen and twenty-four is
   a. 18 percent.
   b. 11 percent.
   c. 25 percent.
   d. 9 percent.

2. *True or false?* _____ Besides making adjustments at home, nesters must
   also face society's view of returning to the roost.

3. Between 1970 and 1980, the number of people age eighteen or older living
   with their parents increased from 13.7 million to
   a. 20 million.
   b. 25 million.
   c. 18.3 million.
   d. 30.6 million.

4. *True or false?* _____ More males than females have become nesters.

5. One woman quoted in the article stated that successful nesters need a strong sense of
   a. optimism.
   b. humor.
   c. self.
   d. love.

6. *True or false?* _____ Credit counselors never recommend that young adults move home to solve their financial problems.

7. According to the passage, all of the following cause disagreements between parents and nesters *except*
   a. sexual mores.
   b. eating habits.
   c. spending habits.
   d. tastes in clothing.

8. Which statement best expresses the main idea of this selection?
   a. The unstable economy has created an increase in nesters.
   b. There are both benefits and problems when young adults move back home.
   c. The generation gap causes problems when adult children live with their parents.
   d. Peer pressure prevents adult children from returning home.

Number Wrong: _____   *Score:* _____

| 0 wrong = 100% | 2 wrong = 75% | 4 wrong = 50% | 6 wrong = 25% |
| 1 wrong = 88% | 3 wrong = 63% | 5 wrong = 38% | 7 wrong = 13% |

SELECTION 6

This is the last selection you will read. Try to make your speed here your fastest. Think of yourself as a runner ready to jump from the starting line at the shot of the gun. Make up your mind to go through the selection at the highest speed of which you are capable without losing comprehension.

STUDENTS IN SHOCK

1   If you feel overwhelmed by your college experiences, you are not alone—many of today's college students are suffering from a form of shock. Going to college has always had its ups and downs, but today the "downs" of the college experience are more numerous and difficult, a fact that the schools are responding to with increased support services.

2   Lisa is a good example of a student in shock. She is an attractive, intelligent twenty-year-old college junior at a state university. Having been a straight-A student in high school and a member of the basketball and softball teams there, she remembers her high school days with fondness. Lisa was popular then and had a steady boyfriend for the last two years of school.

3   Now, only three years later, Lisa is miserable. She has changed her major four times already and is forced to hold down two part-time jobs in order to pay her tuition. She suffers from sleeping and eating disorders and believes she has no close friends. Sometimes she bursts out crying for no apparent reason. On more than one occasion, she has considered taking her own life.

4   Dan, too, suffers from student shock. He is nineteen and a freshman at a local community college. He began college as an accounting major but hated that field. So he switched to computer programming because he heard that the job prospects were excellent in that area. Unfortunately, he discovered that he had little aptitude for programming and changed majors again, this time to psychology. He likes psychology but has heard horror stories about the difficulty of finding a job in that field without a graduate degree. Now he's considering switching majors again. To help pay for school, Dan works nights and weekends as a sales clerk at K-Mart. He doesn't get along with his boss, but since he needs the money, Dan feels he has no choice but to stay on the job. A few months ago, his girlfriend of a year and a half broke up with him.

Not surprisingly, Dan has started to suffer from depression and migraine head- 5
aches. He believes that in spite of all his hard work, he just isn't getting anywhere.
He can't remember ever being this unhappy. A few times he considered talking to
somebody in the college psychological counseling center. He rejected that idea,
though, because he doesn't want people to think there's something wrong with him.

What is happening to Lisa and Dan happens to millions of college students each 6
year. That means that roughly one-quarter of the student population at any time will
suffer from symptoms of student shock. Of that group, almost half will experience
depression intense enough to warrant professional help. At schools across the country,
psychological counselors are booked up months in advance. Stress-related problems
such as anxiety, migraine headaches, insomnia, anorexia, and bulimia are epidemic
on college campuses.

Suicide rates and self-inflicted injuries among college students are higher now 7
than at any other time in history. The suicide rate among college youth is 50 percent
higher than among nonstudents of the same age. It is estimated that each year more
than five hundred college students take their own lives.

College health officials believe that these reported problems represent only the 8
tip of the iceberg. They fear that most students, like Lisa and Dan, suffer in silence.

There are three reasons why today's college students are suffering more than 9
earlier generations. First is a weakening family support structure. The transition from
high school to college has always been difficult, but in the past there was more family
support to help students get through it. Today, with divorce rates at a historical high
and many parents experiencing their own psychological difficulties, the traditional
family is not always available for guidance and support. And when students who
do not find stability at home are bombarded with numerous new and stressful experiences, the results can be devastating.

Another problem college students face is financial pressure. In the last decade 10
tuition costs have skyrocketed—up about 65 percent at public colleges and 90 percent at private schools. For students living away from home, costs range from
$8,000 to as much as $20,000 a year and more. And at the same time that tuition
costs have been rising dramatically, there has been a cutback in federal aid to
students. College loans are now much harder to obtain and are available only at
near-market interest rates. Consequently, most college students must work at least
part time. And for some students, the pressure to do well in school while holding
down a job is too much to handle.

A final cause of student shock is the large selection of majors available. Because 11
of the magnitude and difficulty of choosing a major, college can prove to be a time
of great indecision. Many students switch majors, and some do so a number of times.
As a result, it is becoming commonplace to take five or six years to get a degree. It
can be depressing to students not only to have taken courses that don't count toward
a degree but also to be faced with the added tuition costs. In some cases these costs
become so high that they force students to drop out of college.

While there is no magic cure-all for student shock, colleges have begun to 12 recognize the problem and are trying in a number of ways to help students cope with the pressures they face. For one thing, many colleges are upgrading their psychological counseling centers to handle the greater demand for services. Additional staff is being hired, and experts are doing research to learn more about the psychological problems of college students. Some schools even advertise these services in student newspapers and on campus radio stations. Also, juniors and seniors are being trained as peer counselors. These peer counselors may be able to act as a first line of defense in the battle for students' well-being by spotting and helping to solve problems before they become too big for students to handle.

In addition, stress-management workshops have become common on college 13 campuses. At these workshops, instructors teach students various techniques for dealing with stress, including biofeedback, meditation, and exercise.

Finally, many schools are improving their vocational counseling services. By 14 giving students more relevant information about possible majors and career choices, colleges can lessen the anxiety and indecision often associated with choosing a major.

If you ever feel that you're "in shock," remember that your experience is not 15 unique. Try to put things in perspective. Certainly, the end of a romance or failing an exam is not an event to look forward to. But realize that rejection and failure happen to everyone sooner or later. And don't be reluctant to talk to somebody about your problems. The useful services available on campus won't help you if you don't take advantage of them.

Time: _____   *Reading Rate (see page 452):* _____ WPM

■ **Check Your Understanding**

1. *True or false?* _____ A college student is more likely to commit suicide than a nonstudent of the same age.

2. According to paragraph 12, which of the following methods is *not* being used by colleges to reduce stress?
   a. upgraded psychological counseling
   b. lowered tuition
   c. research into the psychological problems of students
   d. peer counseling

3. The main idea for paragraphs 9, 10, and 11 is
   a. the first sentence of paragraph 9.
   b. the first sentence of paragraph 10.
   c. the first sentence of paragraph 11.
   d. unstated.

4. The author supports his point that college life has become more difficult for students with
   a. anecdotes, statistics, and reasons.
   b. quotations from experts.
   c. information taken from a survey of college dropouts.
   d. personal experiences.

5. *True or false?* _____ From the essay we can conclude that students who can turn to their families for support are less likely to suffer from "student shock."

6. The author implies that some students who suffer from extreme depression
   a. should drop out of college.
   b. are reluctant to get professional help.
   c. can always handle it on their own.
   d. have never done well in school.

7. The author concludes his essay by
   a. making a frightening prediction.
   b. quoting an expert on psychology.
   c. asking a tough question.
   d. giving advice.

8. Which sentence best expresses the central point of the selection?
   a. Going to college is a depressing experience for many students.
   b. College life has become more stressful, so schools are increasing support services.
   c. Lisa and Dan have experienced too much stress at school to enjoy college life.
   d. Colleges should increase their counseling services.

Number Wrong: _____   *Score:* _____

| 0 wrong = 100% | 2 wrong = 75% | 4 wrong = 50% | 6 wrong = 25% |
| 1 wrong = 88% | 3 wrong = 63% | 5 wrong = 38% | 7 wrong = 13% |

RAPID READING PROGRESS CHART

Reading Selection	Speed (WPM)	Comprehension (%)
1 Traffic Laws		
2 Caffeine		
3 Child Abuse		
4 New Car		
5 Nesting		
6 Students in Shock		

Initial Reading Rate ("Traffic Laws")

Speed _____ WPM; comprehension _____%

Final Reading Rate ("Students in Shock")

Speed _____ WPM; comprehension _____%

READING RATE TABLE

You can use the following table to find the number of words you read per minute in each of the six selections in Part Six and in the mastery test on page 513. Suppose, for example, that you read selection 5 in three minutes and thirty seconds (3:30). To locate your WPM, go across the 3:30 column until you come to column 5. The place where the two columns meet gives your WPM—in this case, 337.

Enter your WPM and your comprehension score for a selection into the progress chart on the preceding page.

Time	1 Traffic Laws	2 Caffeine	3 Child Abuse	4 New Car	5 Nesting	6 Student Shock	Mastery Test
1:00	833	1022	1186	2027	1180	1445	1202
1:10	718	881	1022	1747	1017	1246	1036
1:20	626	768	892	1524	887	1086	904
1:30	555	681	791	1351	787	963	801
1:40	502	616	714	1221	711	870	724
1:50	455	558	648	1108	645	790	657
2:00	416	511	593	1013	590	722	601
2:10	386	473	549	938	546	669	556
2:20	357	439	509	870	506	620	516
2:30	333	409	474	811	472	578	480
2:40	313	384	446	762	444	543	452
2:50	294	361	419	716	417	511	425

Time	1 Traffic Laws	2 Caffeine	3 Child Abuse	4 New Car	5 Nesting	6 Student Shock	Mastery Test
3:00	278	341	395	676	393	482	400
3:10	264	323	375	641	374	457	380
3:20	250	307	356	609	354	434	361
3:30	238	292	339	579	337	413	343
3:40	227	279	324	554	322	395	328
3:50	217	267	309	529	308	377	314
4:00	208	255	296	507	295	361	300
4:10	200	246	285	487	284	347	289
4:20	192	236	274	468	272	334	277
4:30	185	227	263	450	262	321	267
4:40	179	219	254	435	253	310	258
4:50	172	211	245	420	244	299	249
5:00	167	204	237	405	236	289	240
5:10	161	198	230	393	229	280	233
5:20	156	192	223	380	221	271	225
5:30	151	186	216	369	214	263	218
5:40	147	180	210	358	208	255	212
5:50	143	175	204	348	202	248	206
6:00	139	170	198	338	197	241	200
6:10	135	166	193	329	191	235	195
6:20	131	161	188	320	186	228	189

(Continued)

Time	1 Traffic Laws	2 Caffeine	3 Child Abuse	4 New Car	5 Nesting	6 Student Shock	Mastery Test
6:30	128	157	183	312	181	222	185
6:40	125	153	178	304	177	217	180
6:50	122	150	174	297	173	212	176
7:00	119	146	170	290	168	206	172
7:10	116	143	166	283	165	202	168
7:20	114	139	162	277	161	197	164
7:30	111	136	158	270	157	193	160
7:40	109	133	155	265	154	189	157
7:50	106	130	151	259	151	185	153
8:00	104	128	148	253	147	181	150
8:10	102	125	145	248	145	177	147
8:20	100	123	142	243	142	173	144
8:30	98	120	139	238	139	170	141
8:40		118	137	234	136	167	139
8:50		116	134	230	134	164	136
9:00		113	131	225	131	161	133
9:10		111	129	221	129	158	131
9:20		109	127	217	126	155	129
9:30		107	125	213	124	152	126
9:40		106	123	210	122	150	124
9:50		104	121	206	120	147	122
10:00		102	118	203	118	145	120

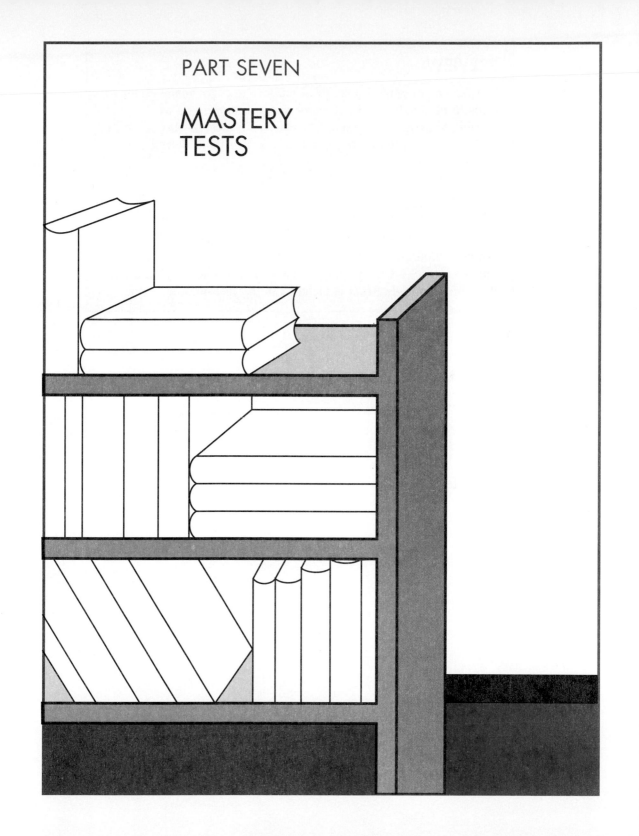

PART SEVEN

MASTERY
TESTS

PREVIEW

Part Seven consists of a series of mastery tests for many of the skills in the book. Your instructor may use these tests as homework assignments, supplementary activities, in-class quizzes at the end of a section, or review tests at any point during the semester.

NOTE TO INSTRUCTORS

As much as possible, the mastery tests are designed so that they can be scored objectively, using the special box at the bottom of each test page. Another complete set of mastery tests for use with *Reading and Study Skills* is included in the Instructor's Manual.

MOTIVATIONAL SKILLS

■ Mastery Test

Answer the following questions. Some of them are multiple-choice and others true-false questions.

1. Jean Coleman's five survival strategies are "Be realistic," "Get organized," "Be positive," "Persist," and
   a. "Think."
   b. "Grow."
   c. "Finish school quickly."
   d. "Earn as you learn."

2. *True or false?* _____ You should know the names and phone numbers of some students in each of your classes.

3. Your college placement office can help you
   a. set career goals.
   b. get good grades.
   c. solve personal problems.
   d. get organized.

4. *True or false?* _____ You should establish a work area at home for all your school materials.

5. Students who say "I'm bored with the subject" as a way of avoiding work
   a. are disorganized.
   b. procrastinate.
   c. sleep instead of doing the work.
   d. have unrealistic expectations for college courses.

6. The *Occupational Outlook Handbook*
   a. is published by the Federal government.
   b. contains valuable information about current jobs.
   c. describes the best job prospects in the future.
   d. All of the above are true.

7. *True or false?* _____ The author of this textbook had a successful first semester of college.

8. According to Jean Coleman, students should take mostly (though not only)
   a. study skills courses.
   b. career-related courses.
   c. liberal-arts courses.
   d. courses which "expand" their minds.

9. To achieve a long-term career goal, a person must first set and work toward

a continuing series of _____ goals.

10. Students with personal problems
    a. can still succeed in college.
    b. should temporarily drop out of school.
    c. have an acceptable excuse for poor grades.
    d. are entitled to skip some classes.

Score: Number correct (_____) × 10 = _____%

TAKING CLASSROOM NOTES

■ **Mastery Test**

Some of the questions that follow are true-false or multiple-choice questions, and some require you to write short answers.

1. You should take extensive notes during class because in two weeks you may forget how much of what you learn?
   a.   20 percent
   b.   40 percent
   c.   60 percent
   d.   80 percent

2. *True or false?* _____ You should listen to the details that connect or explain main points, but you need not write these details down.

3. What is one way an instructor might signal that a certain idea is

   important? _____

   _____

4. One aid in taking class notes is to
   a.   use a small, easy-to-carry notebook for each class.
   b.   write on both sides of a page.
   c.   use white space to indicate shifts from one idea to another.
   d.   use as many indentations as possible.

5. A list of items that fits under a heading is called
   a.   a definition.
   b.   an example.
   c.   an enumeration.
   d.   an emphasis signal.

6. If an idea is confusing, you should
   a.   ask the instructor about it during class.
   b.   try to find it in the textbook.
   c.   ask a student about it after class.
   d.   forget about it.

7. What is the advantage of writing down any examples your instructor

   provides? _____

   _____

   _____

8. When writing notes in outline form, you should
   a.   start main points at the margin.
   b.   start definitions at the margin.
   c.   indent secondary ideas.
   d.   do all of the above.

9. *True or false?* _____ Instructors sometimes use discussion periods to introduce important ideas in a course.

10. How would you abbreviate the term *extended family* during a fast-moving lecture? _____

Score: Number correct (_____) × 10 = _____%

TIME CONTROL AND CONCENTRATION

■ Mastery Test

Some of the questions that follow are true-false or multiple-choice questions, and some require you to write short answers.

1. A large monthly calendar
   a. allows you to see upcoming exams and paper deadlines at a glance.
   b. should be hung in a prominent place.
   c. should have large blocks of white space.
   d. All of the above are true.

2. *True or false?* _____ When studying, you should keep track of your lapses in concentration.

3. For each hour of class time, you should plan at least _____ of study time.

4. *True or false?* _____ A reward system defeats the purpose of studying.

5. *True or false?* _____ Team study with friends is always helpful and efficient.

6. Aids to concentration include
   a. physical exercise.
   b. nourishing meals.
   c. a positive attitude.
   d. All of the above are true.

7. Items on a "to do" list should be labeled A, B, or C, depending on how _____ they are.

8. *True or false?* _____ You should try to have one particular place where you do most of your studying.

9. *True or false?* _____ A series of study sessions is more efficient for learning material than a single long session.

10. Show that you have completed an item on a "to do" list by _____ it out.

Score: Number correct (_____) × 10 = _____%

TEXTBOOK STUDY I

■ Mastery Test

Some of the questions that follow are true-false or multiple-choice questions, and some require you to write short answers.

1. When previewing a selection, which of the following should you *not* do?
   a. Study the title.
   b. Read over the first and last paragraphs.
   c. Write down important ideas.
   d. Look for relationships between headings and subheadings.

2. *True or false?* _____ Many students mark off too much material when reading a textbook.

3. *True or false?* _____ Your first reading of a chapter should proceed slowly, and you should stop as often as necessary to reread material until you are sure you understand it all.

4. Examples should be
   a. underlined.
   b. circled.
   c. labeled *ex* in the margin.
   d. underlined and labeled *ex* in the margin.

5. You should set off definitions in the text by _____ them.

6. Use _____ to mark off each point in an enumeration (list of items).

7. *True or false?* _____ Every note that you write down should have a symbol in front of it—A, B, 1, 2, a, b, or the like.

8. To study a textbook chapter, you first *preview* the chapter. Then you _____ it through once, marking off what appear to be important ideas.

9. As the third step in studying a chapter, you reread, decide on the important ideas, and _____ study notes. Finally, you recite the material to yourself, over and over, until you have learned it.

10. Leave space in the margin of your notes so that you can write key _____ to help you study the notes.

Score: Number correct (_____) × 10 = _____%

TEXTBOOK STUDY II

■ **Mastery Test**

Complete the four-step study process that follows this selection from a sociology textbook.

CROWDS

A *crowd* is a temporary collection of people in close physical proximity. The social structure of a crowd is very simple, rarely consisting of more than a distinction between leaders and others, but crowds are always more than just aggregates of individuals. Physical closeness leads to social interaction, even if the members of the crowd actually try to avoid interpersonal contact. The mere awareness of the presence of others leads to a subtle but rich interchange of impressions, based on the establishment or avoidance of eye contact, facial expressions, gestures, postures, and even styles of clothing.

Characteristics of Crowds

Crowds vary greatly in character and behavior. A crowd of one type—say, a crowd of football spectators—can be quickly transformed into a crowd of a quite different type, such as a rampaging mob. Most crowds, however, have certain characteristics in common:

Suggestibility: People in a crowd tend to be more suggestible than usual. They are more likely to go along with the opinions, feelings, and actions of the rest of the crowd.

Anonymity: The individual feels relatively insignificant and unrecognized in a crowd. The crowd often appears to act as a whole, and its individual members are not and do not feel readily identifiable.

Spontaneity: Members of a crowd tend to behave in a more spontaneous manner than they would on their own. They do not reflect on their actions as much as usual and are more likely to let their behavior be guided by their emotions.

Invulnerability: Because members of crowds feel anonymous, they are inclined to feel that they cannot be personally "got at." They may behave in ways that would be less likely if they felt social-control mechanisms could be applied to them as individuals.

Step 1: Preview. Take about fifteen seconds to preview the passage above. The title tells you that the passage is about crowds. What term is set off in italics in the passage? What does the subhead tell you about the organization of the passage? _____

_____

Step 2: Read and Mark.   Read the passage straight through. As you do, underline the one definition you find. Also, number the items in the enumeration in the passage.

Step 3: Write.   Complete the following study notes on "Crowds":
Crowd— _____

_____

Characteristics of crowds:

1. _____

_____

2. _____

_____

3. _____

_____

4. _____

_____

Step 4: Recite.   To remember the four characteristics of crowds, create a *catchword:* a word made up of the first letters in the four characteristics of crowds. Write your catchword here: _____

Jot down in the spaces below the recall words that could help you recite the material to yourself.

_____   _____

Score: Number correct (_____) × 12.5 = _____%

TEXTBOOK STUDY III

■ Mastery Test

Complete the four-step study process that follows this selection from a psychology textbook.

FRUSTRATION AND ITS SOURCES

Things often happen that prevent us from reaching the goals toward which we are driven. The term *frustration* refers to the blocking of behavior that is directed toward a goal. Although there are many ways in which motives may be frustrated— that is, prevented from being satisfied—conflict among simultaneously aroused motives is perhaps the most important reason why goals are not reached. This and two other sources of frustration will be considered below.

Environmental Frustration

By making it difficult or impossible for a person to attain a goal, *environmental obstacles* can frustrate the satisfaction of motives. An obstacle may be something physical, such as a locked door or a lack of money. Or it may be people—parents, teachers, or police officers, for example—who prevent us from achieving our goals. In general, environmental obstacles are the most important sources of frustration for children; what usually prevents children from doing what they are motivated to do is some restraint or obstacle imposed by their parents or teachers.

Personal Frustration

As children grow up and move toward adulthood, *unattainable personal goals* become increasingly important as sources of frustration and anxiety. These are largely learned goals that cannot be achieved because they are beyond a person's abilities. For instance, a boy may learn to aspire to high academic achievement but lack the ability to make better than a mediocre record. He may be motivated to join the school band, play on the football team, be admitted to a certain club, or take the lead in a play, but he may be frustrated because he does not have the necessary talents. Thus people are often frustrated because they aspire to goals beyond their capacity to perform.

Conflict-Produced Frustration

The adult, as well as the child, is faced with environmental obstacles and unattainable goals, but the most important source of frustration is likely to be a *motivational conflict*—a conflict of motives. In expressing anger, for example, people are often caught in such a conflict. On the one hand, they would like to give vent to their rage; on the other, they fear the social disapproval which would result if they did. The anger motive is thus in conflict with the motive for social approval. In some societies, sexual motivation is often in conflict with society's standards of approved sexual behavior. Other common conflicts pit needs for independence against affiliation needs, or career aspirations against economic realities. Life is full of conflicts and the frustration arising from them.

Step 1: Preview.   Take about thirty seconds to preview the passage above. The title tells you that the passage is about the sources of frustration. How many subheads are there in the passage? _____

Step 2: Read and Mark.   Read the passage straight through. As you do, underline the definitions you find. Write *ex* in the margin beside any example that helps make a definition clear. Also, number the items in the enumeration in the passage.

Step 3: Write.   Complete the following study notes on "Frustration and Its Sources":

Frustration— _____

_____

Sources of frustration:

1. _____

_____

Ex.— _____

_____

2. _____

_____

Ex.— _____

_____

3. _____

_____

Ex.— _____

_____

Step 4: Recite.   To remember the three sources of frustration, create a *catchword:* a word made up of the first letters in the three sources of frustration. Write your catchword here: _____

Jot down in the spaces below the recall words that could help you recite the material to yourself.

_____   _____

Score: Number correct (_____) × 10 = _____%

BUILDING A POWERFUL MEMORY

■ **Mastery Test**

Some of the questions that follow are true-false or multiple-choice questions, and some require you to write short answers.

1. *True or false?* _____ The first step in the memory process is to organize in some way the material to be learned.

2. An important aid to memory is
   a. remembering isolated ideas and details.
   b. mechanical repetition
   c. memorizing items at random.
   d. deciding to remember.

3. After you learn each new item in the material you are trying to remember, you should go back and _____ yourself on all the previous items.

4. Which of the following is *not* a memory technique?
   a. using key words
   b. self-hypnosis
   c. catchwords
   d. using several senses

5. Remembering a key word will help you remember the entire _____ that goes with it.

6. *True or false?* _____ There is no particular value to going over several times material that you have already learned perfectly.

7. Effective memory work
   a. should be spaced over several sessions.
   b. involves single, long sessions of repeated self-testing.
   c. should be done only on the evening before an exam.
   d. involves "pushing out" old ideas.

8. *True or false?* _____ After memorizing material, you should watch a late movie or engage in other activities to relax before going to bed.

9. Write a catchword that will help you remember these principles of behavior modification: nonreinforcement, shaping, punishment, and extinction.

   _____

10. Write a catchphrase that will help you remember the psychological components of "habit": drive, cue, response, and reward.

Score: Number correct (_____) × 10 = _____%

TAKING OBJECTIVE EXAMS

■ **Mastery Test**

All the questions that follow have been taken from actual college tests. Answer the questions by using the specific hints for multiple-choice and true-false questions that are listed below. Also, in the space provided, give the letter of the hint used to determine the correct answer.

Test-Taking Hints

a The longest multiple choice answer is often correct.

b A multiple-choice answer in the middle, especially one with the most words, is often correct.

c Answers with qualifiers, such as *generally, probably, most, almost, often, may, some,* and *sometimes,* are usually correct.

d Answers with absolute words, such as *all, always, everyone, everybody, never, no one, nobody, none,* and *only,* are usually incorrect.

Hint _____ 1. The withdrawal of love is more effective than ordinary punishment because it
    a   is more painful.
    b. is immediately effective.
    c. requires a change of behavior before loving interaction is renewed.
    d. requires atonement.

Hint _____ 2. *True or false?* _____ The Heisenberg principle says that people always look for other people like themselves.

Hint _____ 3. *True or false?* _____ Environmental impact statements must be prepared for actions proposed by all state-supported agencies.

Hint _____ 4. Alcoholism may best be prevented by
    a. more treatment centers.
    b. better educational programs to enable people to make their own decisions.
    c. voluntary health agencies.
    d. federal legislation.

Hint _____ 5. The cult experience is
    a. usually transient.
    b. permanent.
    c. secondary to the church.
    d. more intense for Catholics than Protestants.

Hint _____ 6. *True or false?* _____ Marketing principles have application only within business organizations.

Hint _____ 7. *Hypovolemia* refers to
    a. salt concentration.
    b. cellular dehydration.
    c. water retention.
    d. low volume of the fluid portion of the blood.

Hint _____ 8. *True or false?* _____ Processing symbols can be used only to represent arithmetic operations.

Hint _____ 9. A person who suffers damage to the middle portion of the somatosensory cortex will
    a. die.
    b. experience paralysis.
    c. probably experience numbness in one hand.
    d. feel tingling sensations in one foot.

Hint _____ 10. The Task Force Report on Violence suggests that riots
    a. have at times been effective means of collective bargaining.
    b. are abnormal.
    c. are unique.
    d. involve the lower classes.

Score: Number correct (_____) × 10 = _____%

TAKING ESSAY EXAMS

■ **Mastery Test**

Spend a half hour getting ready to write a one-paragraph essay on the subject "Describe six hints to remember when taking classroom notes." Choose what you consider to be six of the most helpful hints from the thirteen presented on pages 41–48.

Study Hint: First summarize each of the six hints in the spaces below. Then study the hints by following the advice given in step 2 on pages 224–225.

Hints to Remember When Taking Classroom Notes

1. _____

_____

_____

2. _____

_____

_____

3. _____

_____

_____

4. _____

_____

_____

5. _____

_____

_____

6. _____

_____

_____

When the half hour is up, write your essay answer on the other side of this sheet.

_____

_____

_____

_____

_____

_____

_____

_____

_____

_____

_____

_____

_____

_____

_____

_____

_____

_____

_____

_____

_____

_____

_____

Score: Number correct (_____) $\times$ 16.6 = _____%

TAKING OBJECTIVE AND ESSAY EXAMS

■ Mastery Test

You have five kinds of questions to answer on this quiz: following directions, matching, fill-ins, true-false, and multiple-choice.

Following Directions: Write your full name, last name first, above the line on the right-hand side below. Print your full name, first name last, through the line on the left-hand side below.

1. _____   2. _____

Matching: Enter the appropriate letter in the space next to each definition.

3. Explain by giving examples. _____   a.   Enumerate

4. List points and number them (1, 2, 3, etc.) _____

b.   Describe

c.   Illustrate

d.   Trace

Fill-Ins: Write the word or words needed to complete each of the following sentences.

5. On an objective exam, answer all the _____ questions first.

6. To prepare for an essay exam, think of probable essay questions and prepare an informal _____ answer for each question.

True or False: Write the word *true* or *false* to the left of the following statements.

_____ 7. When you receive an essay exam, you should get an overview of it by reading all the questions on the test.

_____ 8. Never go back and change the first answers you have put down on an objective test.

Multiple-Choice: Circle the letter of the answer that best completes each of the following statements.

9. The main secret to doing well on an exam is to
   a.   study the night before.
   b.   be well prepared.
   c.   budget your time.
   d.   use outlines.

10. On an essay exam, you should *not*
    a. start with the easiest question.
    b. budget your time.
    c. leave out transition words.
    d. use the margins of the exam to jot down main points.
    e. do any of the above.

Score: Number correct (_____) × 10 = _____%

USING THE LIBRARY

■ Mastery Test

1. Books placed on reserve by instructors are often shelved near the
   a. stacks.
   b. main desk.
   c. periodical area.
   d. reference section.

2. A card catalog usually indexes books according to
   a. author.
   b. title.
   c. subject.
   d. all of the above.

3. To locate a book in the stacks, you need to know its _____.

4. Periodicals are
   a. books.
   b. card files.
   c. magazines.
   d. all of the above.

5. *True or false?* _____ To find out whether a library has the specific issue of the magazine you want, you should check the file of periodical holdings.

6. *True or false?* _____ If you were looking up books about Truman Capote, you would look under *T* in the *Authors* section of the card catalog.

Items 7–10:   Below is an entry from the *Readers' Guide to Periodical Literature.* Answer the questions about the entry that follow it.

> **Love**
> The chemistry of love. P. Gray
> il *Time* 141:46–51 F 15, '93

7. What is the title of the article? _____

8. What is the name of the magazine? _____

9. On what pages of the magazine does the article appear? _____

10. In what month and year did the article appear in the magazine? _____

Score: Number correct (_____) × 10 = _____%

UNDERSTANDING WORD PARTS

■ Mastery Test

Complete the italicized word in each sentence by adding the correct word part. Use the meaning of the word part and the sentence context to determine the correct answer in each case.

pre—before	*ad*—toward
script—write	*re*—again, back
ex—out	*miss*—send
port—carry	*un*—not
com—with, together	*dis*—apart

1. The personnel manager asked me to send a (*tran . . .*) _____ of my college grades to her office.

2. As the soldiers (*. . . vanced*) _____ on the city, the sound of gunfire became louder.

3. During the murder investigation, the corpse was (*. . . humed*) _____ from the grave so that an autopsy could be performed.

4. A voice on the store loudspeaker said, "Would a (*. . . er*) _____ with a mop and bucket please report to aisle 3?"

5. A (*. . . mission*) _____ of seven people was appointed to study the problem of the toxic dump site in our town.

6. After the play, several students began to (*. . . mantle*) _____ the scenery and pack it in large crates.

7. On New Year's Day, the newspaper published the (*. . . dictions*) _____ of several psychics.

8. Because alcohol makes people feel (*. . . inhibited*), _____ they often do things they wouldn't ordinarily do.

9. The instructor told me that I could (*. . . vise*) _____ my essay and submit it for a better grade.

10. After a new round of radiation treatments, the boy's bone cancer went back into (*re . . . ion*) _____.

Score: Number correct (_____) × 10 = _____%

USING THE DICTIONARY

■ Mastery Test

Part A: Refer to the following excerpt from the paperback *American Heritage Dictionary* to answer the questions that follow.

---

ad•mit•tance (ăd-mĭt′ns) *n.* Permission or right to enter.

ad•mit•ted•ly (ăd-mĭt′ĭd-lē) *adv.* By general admission.

ad•mix•ture (ăd mĭks′chər) *n.* **1.** A mixture or blend. **2.** Something added in mixing. **ad-mix′** *v.*

ad•mon•ish (ăd mŏn′ish) *v.* **1.** To reprove mildly. **2.** To warn, urge, or caution. [< Lat. *admonere*.] —**ad′mo•ni′tion** (-mə-nĭsh′ən) or **ad•mon′ish•ment** *n.* —**ad•mon′i•to′ry** (-ə-tôr′ē, -tōr′ē) *adj.*
    Syns: admonish, rebuke, reprimand, reproach, reprove v.

ad nau•se•am (ăd nô′zē-əm) *adv.* To a disgusting or ridiculous degree. [Lat., to nausea.]

a•do (ə-doo′) *n.* Fuss; trouble. [ME.]

a•do•be (ə-dō′bē) *n.* **1. a.** Sun-dried, unburned brick of clay and straw. **b.** Clay or soil from which such bricks are made. **2.** A structure built with adobe. [< Ar. *attōba*.]

ad•o•les•cence (ăd′l-ĕs′əns) *n.* The period of physical and psychological development between childhood and adulthood. [< Lat. *adolescēre,* to grow up.] —**ad′o•les′cent** *n. & adj.*

A•don•is (ə-dŏn′ĭs, ə-dō′nĭs) *n.* **1.** *Gk. Myth.* A youth loved by Aphrodite for his striking beauty. **2. adonis.** A young man of great physical beauty.

a•dopt (ə-dŏpt′) *v.* **1.** To take (a child) into one's family legally and raise as one's own. **2.** To take and follow by choice or assent. **3.** To take up and use as one's own. [Lat. *adoptare*.] —**a•dopt′a•ble** *adj.* —**a•dopt′er** *n.* —**a•dop′tion** *n.*
    Usage: One refers to an *adopted* child but to *adoptive* parents.

a•dop•tive (ə-dŏp′tĭv) *adj.* Acquired by adoption: *adoptive parents.* —**a•dop′tive•ly** *adv.*

a•dor•a•ble (ə-dôr′ə-bəl, ə-dōr′-) *adj. Informal.* Delightful; lovable; charming. —**a•dor′a•bil′ity** or **a•dor′a•ble•ness** *n.* —**a•dor′a•bly** *adv.*

a•dore (ə-dôr′, ə-dōr′) *v.* **a•dored, a•dor•ing. 1.** To worship as divine. **2.** To love deeply; idolize. **3.** *Informal.* To like very much. [< Lat. *adorare*.] —**ad′o•ra′tion** *n.* —**a•dor′er** *n.* —**a•dor′ing•ly** *adv.*

ă pat   ā pay   â care   ä father   ĕ pet   ē be   ĭ pit   ī tie   î pier   ŏ pot   ō toe   ô paw, for   oi noise   oo took   ōo boot   ou out   th thin   *th* this   ŭ cut   û urge   yoo abuse   zh vision   ə about, item, edible, gallop, circus

---

1. How many syllables are in the word *adolescence?* _____

2. How many syllables are in the word *admittedly?* _____

3. Where is the primary accent in the word *adorable?* _____

4. Where is the primary accent in the word *admonishment?* _____

5. What word in the pronunciation key tells you how to pronounce the *e* in *adobe?* _____

6. What word in the pronunciation key tells you how to pronounce the *au* in *ad nauseam?* _____

7. In the word *admonish,* the *a* is pronounced like the *a* in
   a. pat.
   b. pay.
   c. father.
   d. about.

8. In the word *admittedly,* the *y* is pronounced like
   a. short *e.*
   b. long *e.*
   c. short *i.*
   d. the schwa.

9. In the word *adopt,* the *o* is pronounced like the *o* in
   a. toe.
   b. pot.
   c. for.
   d. out.

10. *True or false?* _____ The word *adore* may be pronounced in two ways.

Score: Number correct (_____) × 10 = _____%

WORD PRONUNCIATION

■ Mastery Test

Using the rules in the box, divide the following words into syllables. And for each word, write the number of the rule or rules that apply. Note the example that is provided. Part A of this test appears below; Part B is on the next page.

> 1 Divide between two consonants.
> 2 Divide before a single consonant.

Example
enigma   _____e-nig-ma_____   _2_   _1_

Part A: General-Interest Words

	Syllable Division	Rule Numbers	
1. specter	_____	_____	
2. lucid	_____	_____	
3. bifocal	_____	_____	
4. exculpate	_____	_____	
5. reprobate	_____	_____	_____
6. impassive	_____	_____	
7. effulgent	_____	_____	
8. mendicant	_____	_____	_____
9. peccadillo	_____	_____	_____
10. circumlocution	_____	_____	_____

Part B: Specialized Words

	Syllable Division	Rule Numbers	
11. peptide	_____	_____	
12. solvency	_____	_____	
13. synthesis	_____	_____	_____
14. dendrite	_____	_____	
15. androgens	_____	_____	_____
16. intravenous	_____	_____	_____
17. supernova	_____	_____	
18. nocturnal	_____	_____	
19. nullification	_____	_____	_____
20. nomenclature	_____	_____	_____

Score: Number correct (_____) × 5 = _____%

SPELLING IMPROVEMENT

■ Mastery Test

Use the four spelling rules on pages 292–296 to spell the following words.

1. defer   + ed   =   _____

2. kindly   + ness =   _____

3. regret   + ed   =   _____

4. th_____f

5. baby   + es   =   _____

6. sense   + ible =   _____

7. grate   + ing   =   _____

8. tidy   + ness =   _____

9. manage   + ment =   _____

10. rel_____ve

11. broke   + en   =   _____

12. repel   + ed   =   _____

13. hope   + ful   =   _____

14. shiny   + est   =   _____

15. leave   + ing   =   _____

16. dec_____ve

17. lively   + hood =   _____

18. worry   + ed   =   _____

19. commit   + ed   =   _____

20. gr_____vance

Score: Number correct (_____) × 5 = _____%

VOCABULARY DEVELOPMENT

■ Mastery Test

Read each of the following sentences carefully. Then decide which of the choices provided comes closest in meaning to the word in *italic* type. Circle the letter of your choice.

1. With great *trepidation,* I boarded the rusty, battered airplane.
   a. care
   b. nervousness
   c. anticipation
   d. relief
   e. animation

2. During the earthquake, several cars were swallowed by large *chasms* that opened up in the ground.
   a. cracks
   b. pipes
   c. tunnels
   d. rocks
   e. mines

3. Our *ostentatious* neighbors have a marble fountain and several life-size statues in their backyard.
   a. lazy
   b. insecure
   c. showy
   d. friendly
   e. mistrustful

4. The union negotiators agreed to accept gradual salary *increments* that will add up to an additional $50 a week per worker.
   a. deductions
   b. bonuses
   c. reductions
   d. scales
   e. increases

5. The little boy tried to *emulate* his father by hammering some bent nails into a piece of scrap lumber.
   a. annoy
   b. help
   c. attract
   d. imitate
   e. ignore

6. At the news conference, one reporter *queried* the president about his frequent vacation trips.
   a. congratulated
   b. questioned
   c. nagged
   d. told
   e. teased

7. During the *arduous* trip west, many pioneers became snowbound in the high mountain passes.
   a. long
   b. rewarding
   c. boring
   d. wintry
   e. difficult

8. The *innocuous*-looking pills were actually filled with a deadly poison.
   a. harmless
   b. unpleasant
   c. tasty
   d. dangerous
   e. healthy

9. The week before the exam, the professor reviewed the *salient* points of all the chapters we had covered.
   a. additional
   b. skipped
   c. important
   d. insignificant
   e. unclear

10. The candidate *vilified* his opponent by calling him a liar and a cheat.
    a. tricked
    b. pacified
    c. debated
    d. rejected
    e. slandered

Score: Number correct (_____) × 10 = _____%

DEFINITIONS AND EXAMPLES

■ Mastery Test

In the spaces provided, write the number of the sentence in each selection that contains a definition. Then write the number of the *first* sentence that provides an example of the definition.

1.   ¹People generally want to do what they are supposed to do, but it isn't always easy or even possible. ²Sometimes people experience difficulty in meeting the demands of a role. ³Role strain may occur when conflicting demands are built into a role. ⁴For example, one part of a line supervisor's role is to maintain good relations with the people working under him or her. ⁵At the same time, he or she is expected to act as a representative of management, enforcing decisions from above. ⁶Robert Merton suggests that such conflicting patterns of expectation are built into many roles in our society.

Definition: _____   Example: _____

2.   ¹*Privileged communication* refers to information that is given to a professional person. ²Historically, under common law a physician who, for example, learned that a patient had a history of mental illness could be made to reveal this in a court. ³As a result, patients withheld some information from their physicians; this was not always in their best interests. ⁴Most states and provinces solved this problem by enacting legislation that overrode the common law and provided that, under certain circumstances, the physician cannot be compelled to reveal confidential information. ⁵Some of these acts were later amended to include the clergy and spouses. ⁶As of 1968, three states—New York, Arkansas, and New Mexico—had extended these statutes to include nurses.

Definition: _____   Example: _____

3.   ¹As we will see in this chapter, organizations include not only profit-making associations such as corporations but also police departments, schools, hospitals, prisons, and tenants' associations. ²One type of organization that is currently growing in popularity in the United States is the voluntary association, a formal organization that people join primarily out of personal interest because they share the organization's goals and norms. ³Members of such fraternal organizations as the Elks and the Masons, for instance, engage in social activities and also undertake philanthropic projects; such a group will sponsor a youth club, for example, or will conduct a fund drive for some local hospital or charity.

Definition: _____   Example: _____

4.   [1]Young children seem to use their early individual words in two ways. [2]First, they use words merely to label objects, such as "cookie" or "doll." [3]Second, they use single words as holophrases—the single word, when combined with the context in which it is used, conveys a whole sentence of meaning. [4]If the baby slams a cup down on a high chair and says, "Milk!" a whole message is involved, such as "Bring me my milk right now." [5]If the baby sees the milk bottle being brought out of the refrigerator and says "milk" in a quieter tone, something like "There's my milk" is conveyed. [6]Patricia Greenfield has argued that these holophrases are the precursors of later, more complex sentences; the child is using gestures, tone of voice, and situations to add the full meaning to the individual words. [7]Later the child learns how to add other words to make longer sentences that will do the same job.

Definition: _____   Example: _____

5.   [1]A mentor is someone who is far enough along in his or her own emotional and career development to guide and help younger workers. [2]The mentor has more experience than younger colleagues have and is usually at a higher occupational level. [3]He or she can provide an informal source of information, influence, and support. [4]This is the way most inexperienced workers refine their skills and learn shortcuts, informal (often unspoken) rules and processes in a particular business environment or career area. [5]The mentor can be a boss or a coworker or someone outside the immediate work environment, even in a different career area. [6]Although mentors are most often of the same sex, cross-gender relationships are becoming increasingly common. [7]This is especially significant for women, who may need the informal tutoring and sponsorship of a mentor but have had difficulty finding one. [8]This was due in the past to the lack of females at the higher levels of many work environments and to the hesitation of many males to mentor a female (because of kidding from other males or sexual overtones). [9]The situation is now changing, and most people, during the years their careers and skills are developing, will have several mentors as they change jobs or advance within a field.

Definition: _____   Example: _____

Score: Number correct (_____) × 10 = _____%

ENUMERATIONS

■ Mastery Test

Locate and number the enumerations in the selections that follow. Then, in the space beneath each selection, summarize briefly the points in the enumeration. Note that headings have already been provided for you.

1.   The psychological process by which children learn their sex roles is a complex one, but it contains three main elements. The first is conditioning through rewards and punishments, usually in the form of parental approval or disapproval. The child who behaves in the "right" way is encouraged, but the boy who plays with dolls or the girl who plays with mud is strongly discouraged. The parents also deliberately arrange conditioning experiences—for example, by giving children sex-related toys. Another example is imitation. Young children tend to imitate older children and adults and are inclined to imitate those whom they regard as most like themselves. Young children thus use other people of the same sex as models for their own behavior. Perhaps the most important element is self-definition. Through social interaction with others, children learn to categorize the people around them into two sexes and to define themselves as belonging to one sex rather than the other. They then use this self-definition to select their future interests and to construct their personalities and social roles. (This is why children who have been assigned to the wrong sex at birth have such difficulty identifying with the correct sex after the age of about three or four. The boy who has been raised as a girl "knows" that he is not a boy and naturally resists attempts to make him into one.)

Psychological Elements in Learning Sex Roles

(1) _____

(2) _____

(3) _____

2.   Why are poor people, on the average, less healthy than affluent people? There is no single reason, but we can make educated guesses about some of the factors which contribute to this result. First, low-income families tend to have less nutritious diets than higher-income families. In particular, low-income diets are often deficient in the amount of protein which they provide. It is likely that many poorer families have some level of malnutrition much of the time, and this may influence their susceptibility to illnesses. Also, the general standard of living among low-income groups is likely to be lower. Their homes are more crowded, more likely to be in disrepair, and more frequently located in dangerous neighborhoods. Another factor is that low-income families usually receive less medical care and lower-quality medical care than wealthier ones do. Failure to have minor ailments cared for may make these people more likely to have major ailments later on. And finally, people with low incomes are probably under a lot of physical and psychological stress, a factor which appears to be related to the onset of illness.

Factors in Health of Poor People

(1) _____

(2) _____

(3) _____

(4) _____

3.   During an interview, an effective listener will use the entire body. The eyes reflect the attitude of the listener. Facial expressions, movements of the head and body, and the use of physical space between speaker and listener all provide signal cues about information feedback. This is how the speaker measures the effectiveness of the communication during the interview. An effective listener will maintain a brief pause after the speaker has finished before beginning his or her response. Furthermore, an effective listener will begin the response with a transitional word, phrase, or thought that will serve as a bridge between what has been spoken and what is about to be spoken. *Now, also, yet, in addition,* and *then* are just a few examples of transition words. *On account of, in summary, by the way,* and *in terms of* are some common transitional phrases. These transitions do not add to the content of the information, but they do guide the direction of the content. In some situations, the brief pause alone will serve as a listening transition.

Characteristics of the Effective Listener

(1) _____

(2) _____

(3) _____

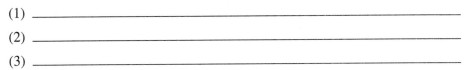

Score: Number correct (_____) × 10 = _____%

HEADINGS AND SUBHEADINGS

■ **Mastery Test**

Part 1:   Answer the questions below about the selection that follows.

Questions: What are two pitfalls in becoming assertive? How should they be handled?

BECOMING ASSERTIVE: TWO PITFALLS

There are two problems that you may encounter in shaping assertiveness, and you should be ready for them. The first is failure—a lapse into nonassertiveness behavior. You are doing very nicely with your experiments—returning things to stores, speaking up in class, complaining about the neighbors' stereo, and so forth—when suddenly someone comes to you with an unreasonable request, and before you know it, you've given in. When this happens, simply accept the fumble as natural. Nonassertive behavior, like any other automatic behavior, cannot be turned off like a faucet. The second problem you may encounter is the occasional unpleasant reaction from a person with whom you are being assertive. This doesn't happen often, but it does happen. For example, when you contest the garage mechanic's bill, you may hear a few words about idiots who don't know cars or about the gall of this younger generation. In such cases, the best response is simply to ignore the zap and stick to your argument.

Answers: _____

_____

_____

Part 2:   Using words such as *what, why, who, which, in what ways,* and *how,* write two meaningful questions for each of the textbook heads that follow.

1.   Applications of Biofeedback   a. _____
                                          b. _____

2.   Critical Periods in Human   a. _____
     Development   b. _____

3.   Common Sleep Problems   a. _____
                                          b. _____

4.   Special-Interest Groups and   a. _____
     Congress   b. _____

Part 3: Scrambled together in the list that follows are three textbook headings and three subheadings for each of the headings. Write the headings in the lettered blanks (A, B, C) and write the appropriate subheadings in the numbered blanks (1, 2, 3). Two items have already been inserted for you.

Economic Security	Health Problems	Payroll Processing
Uses of the Computer	Styles of Conflict	Problems of the Elderly
Direct Aggression	Inventory Control	Indirect Aggression
Record Keeping	Assertion	Negative Stereotypes

A. _____

   1. *Health Problems* _____

   2. _____

   3. _____

B. _____

   1. _____

   2. _____

   3. *Payroll Processing* _____

C. _____

   1. _____

   2. _____

   3. _____

Score: Number correct of possible twenty (_____) × 5 = _____%

SIGNAL WORDS

■ Mastery Test

In the spaces provided, write the major signal words used in the following selections. The number of spaces tells you how many signal words to look for. Selection 1 appears below; selection 2 is on the next page.

Selection 1

Finally, an advertising message can be focused on the product, on the institution, or on some public service. Advertising usually focuses on the product. But it can key in as well on building a good public relations image for the marketer, in which case it is called *institutional advertising*. Pharmaceutical companies thus often emphasize an image of competent research, integrity, and concern for consumers. And when the energy crisis drew attention to the oil industry in the mid-1970s, a rash of advertisements appeared to convince consumers of the oil companies' concern for energy conservation, for providing for future energy needs, and for the general state of the environment. For example, during this period Mobil Oil alone spent $10 million per year telling consumers about its policies regarding ecology and about its involvement with community affairs and interests.

1. _____

2. _____

3. _____

4. _____

5. _____

Selection 2

There is no universally accepted format to use in drawing up a résumé. However, you should probably consider five areas: personal facts, education, extracurricular activities, work experience, and references. These represent major areas most often covered in résumés. It is common to start the résumé with some personal information about yourself and close it with a list of your references. The organization of the data sheet is up to you. Remember, however, that the information should not be crowded onto the page. Space it out so that it looks orderly and neat. Also, stay away from gimmicks. Do not use a fancy typeface. If you are including a picture of yourself in the upper right-hand corner, make it a conservative-looking one. Since you are just starting out, you really will not have that much information on your data sheet. Therefore, keep your résumé short—usually no more than two pages.

6. _____

7. _____

8. _____

9. _____

10. _____

Score: Number correct (_____) × 10 = _____%

MAIN IDEA

■ Mastery Test

Locate and underline the main-idea sentence in each selection that follows. Then, in the space provided in the margin, write the number of the sentence you underlined.

_____ 1.   [1]The eyes themselves can send several kinds of messages. [2]Meeting someone's glance with your eyes is usually a sign of involvement, while looking away signals a desire to avoid contact. [3]As mentioned earlier, this is why solicitors on the street— panhandlers, salespeople, petitioners—try to catch our eye. [4]Once they've managed to establish contact with a glance, it becomes harder for the approached person to draw away. [5]A friend explained how to apply this principle to hitchhiking. [6]"When I'm hitching a ride, I'm always careful to look drivers in the eye as they come toward me. [7]Most of them will try to look somewhere else as they pass, but if I can catch somebody's eye, he or she will almost always stop." [8]Most of us remember trying to avoid a question we didn't understand by glancing away from the instructor. [9]At times like these we usually become very interested in our textbooks, fingernails, the clock—anything but the instructor's stare. [10]Of course, the instructor always seemed to know the meaning of this nonverbal behavior and ended up picking on those of us who signaled our uncertainty.

_____ 2.   [1]Consider the American courtroom. [2]The first thing that strikes your eye as you walk into the courtroom is the judge's seat. [3]Centered, elevated above the other seats, and facing the rest of the courtroom, the seat leaves no doubt as to who's boss in this room. [4]The witness chair is lower than the judge's, but it too faces the rest of the court. [5]This seat puts witnesses on the spot, forcing them to state their evidence while the whole court, including the defendant, looks them straight in the face. [6]The seat is thus a reminder to witnesses of their oath of honesty. [7]Then consider the jury box: off to the side, placed at an angle to the rest of the seats. [8]This placement tells the jury that they are observers, not participants; they are not to take sides. [9]Then consider the seats of the prosecutor and the defense attorney. [10]They are parallel and on the same level. [11]This arrangement tells everyone that the accusing government has no authority or advantage over private citizens and their representatives. [12]The defendant is innocent until proved guilty; the chairs tell us so. [13]In other words, the furniture arrangement guides thought and action; it tells the participants what their roles are and how they should behave. [14]If you placed a band of Aborigines in these seats, they would probably have some idea of what to do.

_____ 3. [1]Alcohol is a relatively safe drug when used in moderation, but if abused it is one of the most dangerous drugs. [2]It is a depressant that directly affects the central nervous system. [3]Alcohol slows brain activity and muscle reactions. [4]Thus, there is an increased probability of accidents if drinkers drive vehicles. [5]Studies have shown that approximately 50 percent of the fatal accidents in the United States involve drivers who have been drinking. [6]Alcohol consumption is related to other problems as well. [7]Although it is impossible to know the exact statistics, experts estimate that very likely the majority of homicides and aggravated assaults, and nearly half of all forcible rapes, are alcohol-related. [8]Moreover, an estimated $25 billion annually is lost through job absenteeism, lost production, medical expenses, and accidents resulting from alcohol. [9]Then there are the intangible and unmeasurable expenses of disrupted families, desertion, and countless emotional problems arising from drinking.

_____ 4. [1]The Middle Colonies, and especially Pennsylvania, differed from New England in another way than the richness of the farmland. [2]They were not founded by tiny groups of fellow believers who discouraged outsiders, as the first Puritans in Massachusetts did. [3]Instead, they prospered by attracting many newcomers of different faiths. [4]Europeans were attracted by Pennsylvania—a place of good land, peace, and no whipping posts or gallows for religious minorities. [5]Thousands of Germans from the Rhine Valley, which was torn by wars and church quarrels, emigrated to Penn's paradise. [6]They first came in 1683 and founded a suburb of Philadelphia that is still called Germantown. [7]By 1760 they made up one-third of the colony's population. [8]After 1700 a number of Presbyterians from northern Ireland came over, too. [9]Some European Jews were attracted by the religious freedom and economic opportunities of New York and Philadelphia. [10]Many English Catholics settled in Maryland, which had been granted in 1632 to Cecil Calvert, Lord Baltimore, a Catholic Englishman.

Score: Number correct (_____) × 25 = _____%

OUTLINING

■ Mastery Test

For Part 1 of this mastery test (below), you are to complete an outline. For Part 2 (on the next page), you are to complete a diagram.

Part 1: Read the selection below and then complete the outline that follows.

In order for an organization to be efficient, three essentials must be present. The first essential ingredient is the presence of *objectives*. These are simply goals that the organization wants to attain. The second essential ingredient of an effective organization is *coordination*, by which individuals work cooperatively in pursuing the objectives of the enterprise. Coordination depends on two things. First, there must be a willingness to cooperate with others. Second, everyone must be given a specific job. The third essential ingredient is the proper *delegation of authority*. Authority is the right to command. In many companies, people far down in the organization make important decisions; these companies are highly *decentralized*. In other businesses, most such decisions are made at the top; such firms are highly *centralized*.

_____

A. _____

B. _____

    1. _____

    2. _____

C. _____

    1. _____

    2. _____

Part 2: Read the selection below and then complete the diagram on the opposite page.

INFLUENCING THE WEATHER

Modern human beings, equipped with a much greater knowledge of climate and weather, have concentrated their attention on trying to influence it in small areas, for specific purposes. One way to influence the weather is making rain. Present techniques focus on ways of encouraging the tiny droplets of water in a cloud to grow large enough so that they will fall to the ground. Four methods are being used: seeding the cloud with dry ice, with silver iodide particles, with microscopic dust particles, or with water drops. All have been successful, it appears, in limited areas.

Another technique for influencing the weather is preventing frost. Late spring frosts wreak havoc in orchards and gardens; losses can rise into millions of dollars. They have been fought fairly successfully for many years by two methods, heaters and smoke generators. Frost is produced when the lower levels of the air are cooled below thirty-two degrees by losing heat to cold ground. The heaters are used to raise the temperature of the lower few feet of the atmosphere. Smoke generators work on a different principle. The layer of smoke intercepts the long-wave radiation from the ground and prevents the earth from cooling to a point where frost is produced in the air.

A final method of weather control is dispersing fog. Fogs are most costly to the airlines; they prevent flights or make them hazardous. Fog dispersal dates back to World War II in England, when pipes were laid on the field and gasoline was burned to disperse the fog. Today fog-dispersal techniques are used successfully by commercial airlines to open their airports for takeoffs and landings.

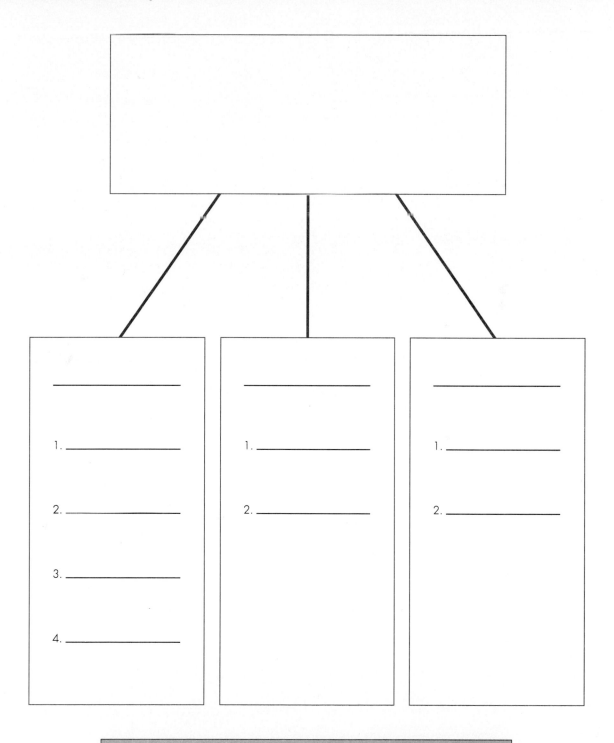

1. _____

2. _____

3. _____

4. _____

1. _____

2. _____

1. _____

2. _____

Score: Number correct (_____) × 5 = _____%

SUMMARIZING

■ **Mastery Test**

Circle the letter of the title that best summarizes each selection. Remember that the title should be as specific and descriptive as possible and at the same time account for all the material in the selection. Item 1 appears below; items 2, 3, and 4 are on the next pages.

1. In order to talk a child to sleep, you can use a simple technique called *toe-to-head relaxation* that children, overactive ones included, seem to enjoy. And once they get the hang of it, they can do it on their own. Bedtime problems are the number one complaint that parents voice to pediatricians. Child psychologists believe the reason is that children, particularly those between two and five years old, are so strongly attached to their mothers that they're reluctant to be separated from them, even to sleep alone. The relaxation technique is reassuring because the mother stays and comforts the youngster until sleep takes over. First, try to get the child to play quietly in bed for about fifteen minutes. Then tell the youngster to lie down with arms at the side. Explain that you're going to make the child's body feel droopy and sleepy. Beginning with the toes and working up to the head, help your child to relax each part of the body. Repeat the following phrase in a soothing monotone: "Your toes are droopy." Touch the toes to assure the child that they feel heavy. Now say "Your feet are droopy" six times, in the same soothing monotone. After two or three body parts, repeat the idea that the parts that you've made droopy are still at rest. By the time you reach the eyes, they should be closed. If not, gently tell your child to shut them. You'll be surprised how much an overactive youngster welcomes sleep. After you use the toe-to-head method regularly, your child will memorize the routine and eventually be able to drop off to sleep without help. And the technique also works for adults.

What would be an accurate title for selection 1?
a. Bedtime Problems
b. Conquering Insomnia
c. Children and Sleep
d. How to Put a Child to Sleep

2.   In 1964 Americans were shocked by the murder of Kitty Genovese in New York City. Murder in the Big Apple was not new, but Genovese had screamed for help repeatedly as her killer stabbed her again and again. About forty neighbors heard the commotion. Many watched. Nobody helped. The impression grew that, as a nation, we were a callous, indifferent bunch who would rather watch than help as others died. It's easy to make a case for not helping. The helper could also have been stabbed. The helper could have been ineffective and looked foolish if the circumstances had not been as serious as they appeared. After all, we hear many arguments in city neighborhoods, but few end in murder. "Getting involved" can also mean having to testify in court or encountering retribution from the criminal. But one experiment suggests that diffusion of responsibility may inhibit helping behavior in groups or crowds. Male subjects performing meaningless tasks in cubicles heard a recording, which they believed was quite real, of a person having an epileptic seizure. When these subjects believed that four other people were also immediately available, only 31 percent made an effort to help the victim. But when a subject thought that he was the only one available, 85 percent attempted to offer aid. When others are not around, we are more willing to help others ourselves.

What would be an accurate title for selection 2?
a. The Story of Kitty Genovese
b. Why People Don't Get Involved
c. Diffusion of Responsibility and Helping Behavior
d. Psychological Studies of Helping Behavior

3.   On the whole, a higher educational credential means higher earnings—simply because the value the job market places on it makes it a major asset in the competition for the best jobs. The most prestigious jobs tend to be those that are known not only to yield the highest incomes but also to require the longest education. A landmark study of social mobility (movement from one status to another) in the United States found that the most important factor affecting whether a son achieved a higher status than his father's was the amount of education the son attained. A high level of education is a scarce and valued resource for which people compete vigorously. According to conflict theorists, the remarkable expansion of American education in recent decades has less to do with the demands of the economy than with competition for power, wealth, and prestige.

What would be an accurate title for selection 3?
a. Education and Status
b. Prestigious Jobs
c. Education and the Competition for Wealth
d. A Major Asset

4.   After the Civil War most landless blacks became sharecroppers. A black family would live on a portion of a former plantation, raise cotton, and give a large share of the harvested crop to the landowner as rent for the land and in return for tools, seeds, and work animals, which the landowner usually provided. There were some white sharecroppers too, but for most black farmers this was the only way of making a living. Black sharecroppers tilled other people's soil with other people's tools. They rarely saw cash. Their diet of fat meat and corn bread kept them in the grip of illness. Their children received almost no education in the inferior, segregated schools provided for blacks. Their children had no future, except as sharecroppers or servants to whites. If they protested politically, the planters might throw them off the land and merchants might refuse credit. Being without money, they were without power. Their condition seemed little improved over slavery times. In some ways it may have been worse, for though free, the sharecroppers were still enslaved by poverty.

What would be an accurate title for selection 4?
a.   Problems of White Sharecroppers
b.   Black Sharecroppers
c.   Life after the Civil War
d.   Segregation in the South

Score: Number correct (_____) × 25 = _____%

SKIM READING

■ Mastery Test

Take five minutes to skim-read the following selection and to take notes on it. Then see if you can answer the questions that follow by referring to your notes but *not* referring to the text.

PRISONS

Prisons are a relatively modern invention. Two hundred and fifty to three hundred years ago, convicted criminals were killed, maimed, branded (for example, with a scarlet A for adultery), or deported (as often as not, to the New World). The idea of locking people up, which began to take hold during the mid-nineteenth century, was based on the assumption that isolation and hard work would make the sinner reconsider his or her errant ways and repent. But once prisons were established, they became institutionalized.

The Control Functions of Prisons

What functions do prisons perform? Most obviously, they punish criminals for their wrongdoing. Clearly, prisoners do suffer, and most people consider this just. Prisons are also supposed to protect the public by taking known deviants off the streets. In addition, they are thought to act as a deterrent, discouraging those on the outside from breaking laws and those on the inside from committing crimes after they are released. Finally, there is much talk of prisons rehabilitating offenders through training programs and counseling, so that when offenders are released, they will approach life in a new, law-abiding frame of mind.

Why Prisons Don't Work

The cost of locking a person up for a year is between $8,000 and $16,000 (as critics of prisons note, this is enough to send a person to college with a summer vacation in Europe). This amounts to nearly $12 billion annually. What does this money buy?

Clearly, prisons don't protect the public. Only 3 percent of the people known to have committed crimes ever go to jail (only 1.5 percent if we include unreported crimes). And most prison officials estimate that, at most, only 15 to 25 percent of inmates are actually dangerous.

Nor do most prisons accomplish anything that might be called *rehabilitation*. After their release, at least a third of former prison inmates end up back in prison. Indeed, prisons may socialize people *to* deviance. Many observers consider them "schools for crime," where first offenders learn the tricks and rationalizations of deviant careers.

And there is little evidence that prisons act as a deterrent to potential lawbreakers. In 1961 the penalty for assault with a deadly weapon in California was one to ten years. In 1966 the California legislature raised the sentence for assaulting a police officer with a deadly weapon to five years to life. That year the rate of attacks on police was 15.8 per 100 officers, compared with 8.4 per 100 officers in 1961.

Proposed Reforms

Are there any alternatives to prisons as we know them? Efforts to reform prisons—whether motivated by humanitarian principles or by the desire to reduce crime—have centered on three general areas: work programs, conjugal visits, and group therapy. In this country, North Carolina has led the way with "work furlough" programs, where inmates are permitted to leave prison for up to sixty hours a week to work outside. More than thirty states launched similar programs during the 1960s, but usually on a small scale. In the Swedish penal system, widely regarded as the most enlightened in the world, providing prisoners with steady, useful jobs and requiring them to support themselves and their families, while paying restitution to their victims, are central to the rehabilitation effort.

Only a few prisons in this country allow conjugal visits, but many other nations permit spouses of prisoners to visit them, and some allow prisoners to visit their families for short periods. The idea behind conjugal visits is that the people who are most likely to discourage a convict from continuing in a criminal career are his or her spouse and children.

Group therapy programs are difficult to assess. Nearly all forms of psychotherapy depend on uninhibited self-revelation and open expression of feelings. But the psychologists who run such programs in prisons are, after all, prison officials. A prisoner's parole may depend on his or her participation in a therapy program, thus making its voluntary nature problematic. The inmate is thus put in a double bind: total openness might well delay his or her parole, but self-concealment renders the program useless.

Questions about the Selection

Answer the following questions by referring to your notes but *not* referring to the selection.

1. What are the four central functions of prisons?

    a. _____

    b. _____

    c. _____

    d. _____

2. What are the three reasons why prisons don't work?

   a. _____

   b. _____

   c. _____

3. What are three proposed reforms?

   a. _____

   b. _____

   c. _____

Score: Number correct (_____) × 10 = _____%

RAPID READING

■ Mastery Test

Read this selection as rapidly as you can without sacrificing comprehension. Then record your time in the space provided and answer the comprehension questions that follow.

DON'T LET YOUR FAMILY'S HEALTH GO UP IN SMOKE

"My dad died on me," seven-year-old Ian said. "Then I kept thinking Mom would die too." He shadowed his mother from room to room and clung to her.   1

And she clung to Ian. Her husband had died at age thirty-six of emphysema.   2
The last time she'd seen him alive in the hospital, pallid and gasping for air, he was smoking a cigarette.

He'd been a pack-a-day smoker since age fourteen and had tried many times   3
to quit. But nicotine is one of the most physically addicting substances there are—which is why Ian's father became part of the national statistics: among pack-a-day males who start smoking as young teenagers, three times as many die between ages thirty-five and forty-nine as nonsmokers. He was one of the 350,000 Americans who die every year from cigarette-related diseases.

Chilling statistics show that cigarette smoking is the largest single cause of   4
preventable death in the United States today. Tobacco contributes to an estimated 30 percent of all cancer deaths, according to a 1982 report by the U.S. Surgeon General.

Beyond these statistics, a surge of new research now makes it clear that cigarettes   5
damage far more than the smoker. All members of the smoker's family suffer from the physical and psychological effects of smoking.

"Secondhand Smoke"

One important thing smokers don't consider is the effect of "secondhand" or   6
"sidestream" smoke wafting from the tip of the cigarette between puffs. This is what is inhaled—willy-nilly—by everyone in the vicinity of the smoker. New research has revealed a sobering fact: tar, nicotine, carbon monoxide, and other harmful constituents of cigarette smoke are more highly concentrated in sidestream smoke than in the "mainstream" smoke that smokers inhale directly into their own lungs. For example, the concentration of cancer-causing nitrosamines in sidestream smoke exceeds that found in mainstream smoke by up to fifty times. Carbon monoxide concentration is $2^{1}/_{2}$ times higher in sidestream than in mainstream smoke. Indeed, since over 90 percent of cigarette smoke is composed of toxic gases, innocent bystanders get much more than their share of poison.

Let's take a look at what cigarettes can do—and are doing—to members of the   7
average family.

Preteens and Teenagers

A powerful aid in getting parents to give up smoking, and to encourage kids   8
not to start, should be found in the following national statistics:

Youngsters whose parents smoke are far more likely to take up smoking themselves. If both parents smoke, the child is about twice as likely to start as a
youngster from a "no-smoke" family.

Preteen and teenage smoking habits are major determinants of lifelong cigarette
consumption. The earlier the start, the greater the eventual risk of smoking-related
illness and death.

What of those teenagers who claim they are "nothing" smokers? ("Only three   9
cigarettes a day, Mom! That's *nothing*. Some of my friends smoke a pack a day or
more!") Can this type of limited smoking have harmful effects?

Dr. Joanne Luoto, acting director of the federal Office on Smoking and Health,   10
says: "No research has been done on the chronic effects of three-a-day smoking in
this age group. However, studies on adults who habitually smoke one to ten cigarettes
a day have clearly shown that there *is* no known 'safe' level of smoking."

"Furthermore," Dr. Luoto adds, "the addictive potential of cigarettes should not   11
be underestimated by teenagers. Any youngster who believes that he or she can
smoke 'only a few cigarettes a day' is risking the development of an addiction that
is one of the most difficult of all to break."

Mom and Dad

Perhaps the best single test of the health hazards of cigarettes was unwittingly   12
sponsored by the movies in the 1930s. Men had been smoking for centuries. But
not women. Actresses started lighting up on screen, and cigarettes emerged as a
catalyst for romance. The theme spread to print ads. Within a decade, it had become
"in" for women to smoke.

The scene now shifts from glamorous to grim. Cancer of the lungs was once   13
almost unknown among women. It takes two to three decades for lung cancer to
develop. And two to three decades after women started smoking almost as much as
men, lung cancer among women became almost as common as among men. So did
the other cigarette-related diseases and death rates. As a report by the U.S. Surgeon
General put it, "Women who smoke like men now die like men who smoke. There
can be no doubt that smoking is truly slow-moving suicide."

Women face extra dangers. Female smokers who use "the pill" have a five times   14
greater risk of heart attack than nonsmokers who use oral contraceptives. Also, the
smoking "pill" taker's risk of dying from other circulatory diseases is increased ten
to twenty times—depending on age and amount smoked.

What Can We Do?

The good news is that there has been an impressive decline in smoking among   15
all segments of our population. The bad news is that fifty-four million Americans
still smoke.

How can families protect themselves against the proven health hazards? Here   16
are two ways:

- Preteens should be warned of peer pressures to smoke that will engulf them in
  junior high, and they should be encouraged to form a no-smokers group, making
  it "cool" *not* to smoke. It's hard for teens not to smoke when their friends do.
  They need your support. But don't threaten or punish. That will only make the
  kids want to smoke more. Tell them the facts—with understanding.

- Encourage your youngsters not to start. And forget the apologetic adage: "Do
  as I say, not as I do." You can't expect your child not to start if you can't
  stop. There are stop-smoking groups in most communities; or you can ask your
  physician to recommend professional help. Whatever method you choose, get
  your whole family in on the act. You'll need their help not only to get off—but
  to stay off. That "just one" slip-up is not uncommon. But remember, if at first you
  don't succeed, quit, quit, quit again!

If you or someone you love is one of the one in three Americans who smoke,   17
remember: Stopping will give you and your loved ones the incomparable gift of a
longer, healthier life.

Check Your Understanding

1. *True or false?* _____ The harmful constituents of cigarette smoke are more
   highly concentrated in "mainstream" smoke.

2. How many people die every year from cigarette-related diseases?
   a. 100,000
   b. 150,000
   c. 200,000
   d. 350,000

3. Movies of the 1930s encouraged _____ to smoke.

4. Ninety percent of cigarette smoke is composed of
   a. tar.
   b. nicotine.
   c. toxic gases.
   d. carbon dioxide.

5. Female smokers who use "the pill" have a five times greater risk of
   a. heart attack.
   b. birth defects.
   c. circulatory disease.
   d. skin cancer.

6. If you want to stop smoking, you should do all of the following *except*
   a. ask a doctor for help.
   b. ask your family to leave you alone while you're trying to quit.
   c. join a stop-smoking group in your community.
   d. keep trying to quit even if you slip up a few times.

7. *True or false?* _____ Teenage smoking habits are a major determinant of lifelong consumption.

8. How long does it take for lung cancer to develop?
   a. five years
   b. one decade
   c. fifteen years
   d. two to three decades

9. *True or false?* _____ Cigarette smoking is the largest single cause of preventable death in the United States today.

10. Which statement best expresses the main idea of the selection?
    a. Smoking is more hazardous to women than to men.
    b. Cigarettes are harmful to every member of the family.
    c. "Sidestream" smoke is more dangerous than "mainstream" smoke.
    d. Smoking-related diseases and deaths are on the rise.

Score: Number correct (_____) × 10 = _____%

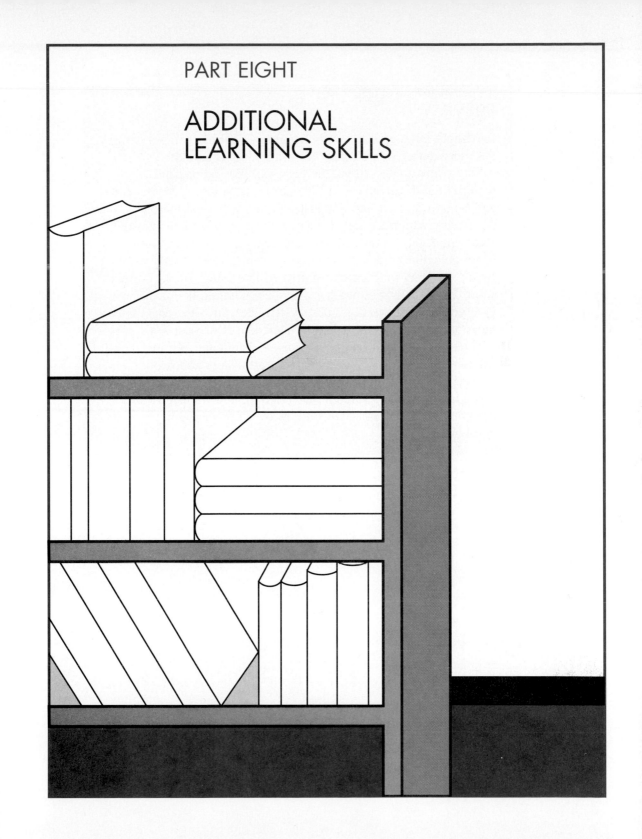

PART EIGHT

ADDITIONAL LEARNING SKILLS

PREVIEW

Part Eight takes up some extra learning skills that will help you get more out of your studies. "Reading Graphs and Tables" explains how to understand the technical illustrations and tabular material that often appear in textbooks. In "Studying Mathematics and Science" you'll find tips that will help you deal more effectively with math and science courses. A related chapter is "Reading Literature and Making Inferences," which provides some guidelines that will better equip you to read literary works. Next, "Reading for Pleasure: A List of Interesting Books" offers short descriptions of a number of widely admired books that will give you reading practice and may provide you with some of the most pleasurable and illuminating experiences of your life. "Understanding Connections between Reading and Writing" explains why writing is an important part of a textbook on reading and study skills, and also gives you an opportunity to practice your writing skills. Finally, "Writing a Research Paper" presents a series of basic steps to follow in preparing a paper involving research.

READING GRAPHS AND TABLES

INTRODUCTION

Sometimes, being a skillful reader means more than just the ability to read words. It can also mean being able to read the visual information presented in graphs and tables. As a student, you will probably encounter a number of graphs and tables in your textbooks. Such visual material can help you understand important ideas and details as you read. Knowing graphics will probably also help in your career work as well, for occupations in our computerized age increasingly rely on graphics to convey information.

Graphs and tables present information by using lines, images, or numbers as well as words. They often compare quantities or show how things change over a period of time. Reading a graph or table involves four steps:

- *Step 1: Read the title and any subtitles.* This important first step gives you a concise summary of all the information in the graph or table.

- *Step 2: Read any information at the top, at the bottom, and along the sides.* Such information may include an explanatory key to the material presented. It may also include a series of years, percentages, or figures.

- *Step 3: Ask yourself the purpose of the graph or table.* Usually, the title can be turned into a question beginning with *What, How much* or *many,* or *How.* The purpose of the graph or table is to answer that question.

- *Step 4: Read the graph or table.* As you read, keep in mind the purpose of the material.

Using these four steps, let us analyze the sample graph and table that follow.

SAMPLE GRAPH

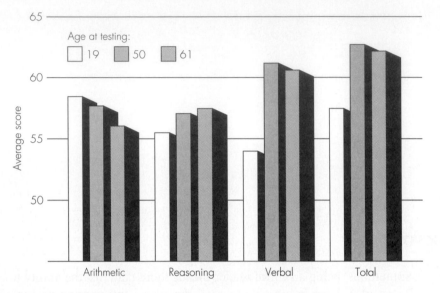

CHANGES IN SKILLS-TEST SCORES RELATED TO AGE

Step 1: The title of the graph is "Changes in Skills-Test Scores Related to Age." Thus, the information will show us how test scores change as people age.

Step 2: Near the top of the graph is a key labeled "Age at testing." Different degrees of shading on the graph represent people at age nineteen (lightest tone), age fifty (medium tone), and age sixty-one (darkest tone). Along the bottom of the graph are the words "Arithmetic," "Reasoning," "Verbal," and "Total." The graph will show test scores in these three areas in addition to total scores. Along the side of the graph is a series of numbers representing average scores, ranging from fifty to sixty-five.

Step 3: We can turn the title of the graph into the question "How are changes in skills-test scores related to age?" The purpose of the graph is to answer that question. The graph will show us how people's test scores changed as they aged.

Step 4: Read the graph and try to answer the following questions. Write your answers in the spaces provided.

1. At what age is verbal ability at its highest? _____

2. At what age are total skills scores highest? _____

3. Which age group is best at arithmetic? _____

4. Which age group has the lowest scores in reasoning ability? _____

As the medium-toned bar in the graph (which represents age fifty) is highest in the cluster above verbal ability, that age group had the best scores. And again, the age-fifty group is highest in total scores. The lightest-toned bar (which represents age nineteen) is highest in the arithmetic cluster; that group had the best scores. In reasoning ability, the age-nineteen group (lightest bar) had the lowest scores.

SAMPLE TABLE

EFFECTS ON FETUS OF DISEASE ORGANISMS

Disease	Months of risk	Most common effects	Prevention/ treatment	How transmitted
Gonorrhea*	9	Conjunctivitis of newborn; blindness; serious general infection	Testing/treatment of mother before delivery; drops of silver nitrate in eyes of all newborns	Infant infected during passage through infected vaginal canal
Herpes simplex II	9	Serious infection; can be fatal	Possibly cesarean section to avoid passage of fetus through vaginal canal	Probably during passage through infected vaginal canal; possibly crosses placenta
Rubella	1–3	Cardiac defects, cataracts, deafness	Immunization of mother before pregnancy	Crosses placenta
Toxoplasmosis*	4–5	Underdeveloped brain, blindness, etc., at birth or later in life	Pregnant women should avoid handling cat litter, eating raw meat	Crosses placenta
Syphilis	5–9	Bone, tooth deformities; progressive nervous system damage; stillbirth; brain damage later in life	Testing and treating mother before fifth month	Crosses placenta after fifth month

*May be noticeable symptoms in mother.

Follow the four steps listed on page 519; then try to answer the following questions about the sample table. Write your answers in the spaces provided.

1. What is the title of the table? _____

   _____

2. During which months does syphilis pose a threat to a fetus?

   _____

3. What are the effects of rubella on a fetus? _____

   _____

4. How is toxoplasmosis transmitted to a fetus? _____

   _____

Since the title of the table is "Effects on Fetus of Disease Organisms," the table will answer the question "What are the effects on a fetus of certain disease organisms?" By reading the information along the top and side of the table, we can answer the next three questions. Under "Months of risk," we find that syphilis is a threat during months five through nine. Under "Most common effects," we see that rubella causes cardiac defects, cataracts, and deafness. Under "How transmitted," we find that toxoplasmosis crosses the placenta.

PRACTICE IN READING GRAPHS AND TABLES

Activity 1

1. Follow the four steps listed on page 519; then try to answer the questions about the graph on the opposite page.

   a. What is the purpose of this graph? _____

      _____

   b. The goals of what group are being charted here? _____

      _____

Graph for Activity 1

LIFE GOALS OF AMERICAN FIRST-YEAR COLLEGE
STUDENTS, 1967–1990

Source: UCLA Higher Education Research Institute.

c. What are the two life goals the students were asked to rate?

_____

_____

d. In what year did over 80 percent of the students rate "developing a meaningful
philosophy of life" as very important to them? _____

_____

e. Which trend rose strongly during the years 1967–1990? _____

_____

2. Follow the four reading steps listed on page 519; then try to answer the questions about the table below.

MODEL OF THE AMERICAN CLASS STRUCTURE

Proportion of households	Class	Education	Occupation	Family income
1%	Capitalist	Prestige university	Investors, heirs, executives	Over $500,000, mostly from assets
10–15%	Upper middle	College, often with postgraduate study	Upper managers and professionals; medium business people	$75,000 or more
30–35%	Middle	At least high school; often some college or apprenticeship	Lower managers; semiprofessionals; sales, nonretail; elite craftspeople; supervisors	About $50,000
40–45%	Working	High school	Operatives; low-paid craftspeople; clerical workers; retail sales workers	About $30,000
20–25%	Poor	Some high school	Service workers; laborers; low-paid operatives and clericals	Below $20,000
1%	Underclass	Primary school	Unemployed or part-time; welfare recipients	Below $15,000

Source: Adapted from D. Gilbert and J. A. Kahl, *The American Class Structure: A New Synthesis,* 3d Ed. (Pacific Grove, CA: Dorsey Press, 1987), table 11-1, p. 332.

a. What is the purpose of this table? _____

_____

b. What proportion of households belong to the underclass?_____

_____

c. As a trend, does the education level increase, decrease, or remain the same as class rises?_____

_____

d. What occupations do members of the middle class generally hold?_____

_____

_____

e. Generally, how much more do members of the middle class make than members of the working class?_____

_____

Activity 2

1. Follow the four reading steps listed on page 519; then try to answer the questions on the following page about the graph below.

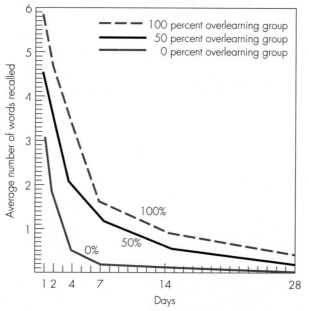

EFFECTS OF OVERLEARNING IN RETENTION OF MATERIAL

- – – 100 percent overlearning group
- —— 50 percent overlearning group
- —— 0 percent overlearning group

Average number of words recalled

Days

a. What is the purpose of the graph? _____

_____

b. How many units did the group which overlearned material by 100 percent remember at the end of the first day?
   a. 5.8
   b. 4.6
   c. 3.1
   d. 2.0

c. How many units did the group which overlearned material by 50 percent remember at the end of the second day?
   a. 5.0
   b. 3.7
   c. 1.6
   d. 1.0

d. Which group had the greatest memory loss in the week after the material

   was learned? _____

2. Follow the four reading steps listed on page 519; then try to answer the questions about the table on the opposite page.

   a. What is the purpose of the table? _____

   _____

   b. Did the number of nursing jobs increase or decrease between 1980 and

   1990? _____

   c. How many postal clerk jobs will be available in 1990? _____

   _____

   d. How many *more* cashiers' jobs will there be in 1990 than there were in 1980?

   _____

   e. How many high school teaching jobs will be eliminated between 1980

   and 1990? _____

Table for Activity 2

HELP WANTED (NUMBERS OF JOBS IN THOUSANDS)

	1980	1990	+ or −
Ten best prospects			
Secretaries	2,469	3,169	+700
Nurses' aides	1,175	1,682	+507
Janitors	2,751	3,253	+502
Salesclerks	2,880	3,359	+479
Cashiers	1,993	2,445	+452
Nurses	1,104	1,542	+438
Truck drivers	1,696	2,111	+415
Fast-food workers	806	1,206	+400
Clerks	2,395	2,772	+377
Waiters	1,711	2,072	+361
Ten worst prospects			
Postal clerks	316	310	−6
Clergy	296	287	−9
Shoe machine operators	65	54	−11
Compositors and typesetters	128	115	−13
Graduate assistants	132	108	−24
Servants	478	449	−29
College teachers	457	402	−55
High school teachers	1,237	1,064	−173
Farm laborers	1,175	940	−235
Farm operators	1,447	1,201	−246

STUDYING MATHEMATICS AND SCIENCE

For many people, mathematics and science courses are terrifying. There are several very understandable reasons for this feeling. Many of us, first of all, come to class weak in the basics we need to know to handle such courses. A college mathematics or biology instructor, for example, may expect students to know how to handle fractions, decimals, proportions, and simple algebra; but some of the students have forgotten (or have never learned) these skills. Without this kind of foundation, the work in the class starts out on a difficult level indeed.

Another reason students dread these courses is that there is no way to pass them without doing a great deal of hard work. Mathematics and science courses *demand* consistent attendance, complete notes, extensive homework, and intensive study sessions. Students looking for courses they can just "slide by" in are naturally wary of mathematics and science. But other students—ones who need chemistry or calculus, for example, to become medical technicians, nurses, or computer programmers—are willing to work hard; the problem is that they don't know how to deal with such courses. Their note-taking and study skills just don't seem adequate for mathematics and science.

Doing well in mathematics and science courses *is* possible. But you must be aware of the adjustments you should make when you switch to mathematics and science from your less technical subjects. The pointers that follow will help you gain control over these subjects.

- *In mathematics and science, knowledge is cumulative.* The learning that you do in mathematics and science courses is cumulative—each fact or formula you learn must rest on a basic structure of all you have learned before. You have to begin with the essentials and build your knowledge in a methodical, complete way. For this reason, *absences from class or weaknesses that are never corrected can be academically fatal.* You will not understand a simple algebra equation, for example, if you are not sure what a "variable" is. It is essential to stay current in such courses and to attack your weak points early. If you don't understand something, ask your instructor for help or visit the tutoring center. Every day you wait makes it more likely that you will do poorly in the course.

- *In mathematics and science, great emphasis is placed on specialized vocabulary, rules, and formulas.* Mathematics and science deal in precision. Everything has a specific name, and every problem can be solved with specific rules and formulas. In a way, this quality makes such courses easier because there is little fuzziness involved and few individual interpretations are required. If you know the vocabulary and have the rules down pat, you should do well.

  An important study technique for mathematics and science is the use of flashcards. These are three- by five-inch index cards that help you memorize and test yourself on terms and formulas. On one side of the card, write the term, rule, or formula you need to know (for instance, "photosynthesis," "Bohr's energy law," or "formula for weight density"). On the other side, write the information that you must memorize. Flashcards enable you to study the material conveniently and to discover quickly what you know and what exactly you are unsure of.

- *In mathematics and science, special emphasis is placed on homework.* In many mathematics and science classes, you will be given numerical problems to solve outside class. Often, these problems will not be checked by the instructor; their purpose is to give you practice in the kinds of material you will find on tests. Many students do a hurried job on any work that is not graded, or skip it completely. If you are not conscientious about this homework, however, you will be panicky before tests and unprepared for what is on them. If you want to pass your mathematics and science classes, you *must* take the responsibility for much of the necessary learning yourself by doing the problems and asking questions in class about problems that puzzle you.

■ *Taking clear notes in class is crucial.* In your class notes for mathematics and science, you will often be copying problems, diagrams, formulas, and definitions from the blackboard. In addition, you will be trying to follow your instructor's train of thought as he or she explains how a problem is solved or how a process works. Such classes obviously demand intense concentration. As you copy material from the board, be sure to include in your notes any information the instructor gives that can help you see the *connections between steps* or *the relationship of one fact to another.* For example, if an instructor is explaining and diagraming patterns of blood circulation in the human body, you should copy the diagram; you should also be sure you have definitions ("alveoli," "aorta") and any important connecting information ("blood moves from artery to capillaries").

As soon as possible after a mathematics or science class, you should clarify and expand your notes while the material is still fresh in your mind.

■ *Mathematics and science require patient, slow reading.* The information in mathematics and science tests is often densely packed; texts are filled with special terms that are often unfamiliar; blocks of text are interspersed with numerical formulas, problems to solve, charts, diagrams, and drawings. Such textbooks cannot be read quickly; for this reason, you have to keep up with the assigned reading. It is impossible to read and understand fifty pages—or even ten pages—the night before a test.

The good news about mathematics and science textbooks is that they are usually organized very clearly. They also have glossaries of terms and concise reviews at the ends of chapters. When you are reading mathematics and science books, proceed slowly. Do not skip over any unfamiliar terms; check the index or the glossary in the back of the book for the definition. With mathematics textbooks, spend time going over each sample problem. After you have gone over the sample, you might want to write out the problem on a piece of paper and then see if you remember how to solve it. With science textbooks, be sure to study the visual material that accompanies the written explanations. Study each chart or diagram until you understand it. Being able to visualize such material can be crucial when you are asked to reproduce it or write an essay on it during an exam.

You can succeed in mathematics and science classes if you are organized, persistent, and willing to work. When passing these courses is necessary to achieve your goals, the effort must be made.

READING LITERATURE AND MAKING INFERENCES

The comprehension skills you've learned in this book apply to everything you read. But to get the most out of literature, you also need to be aware of several important elements that shape fiction. And you need to know how to make inferences. Following, then, are a few guidelines to help you understand fiction more fully.

KEY ELEMENTS IN LITERATURE

Important elements in a work of literature are theme, plot, setting, characters, conflict, climax, narrator, and figures of speech:

- Look for the *theme,* or the overall idea, that the author is advancing. This is the very general idea that is behind the author's entire effort and unifies the work. For example, the theme in much of Katherine Anne Porter's writing is that separateness and misunderstanding are fundamental facts of the human condition.

- Make sure you understand the *plot*—the series of events that take place within the work. For instance, the plot of Philip Roth's short story "Goodbye, Columbus" is that boy meets girl, they fall in love, and then—because of different values—they fall out of love.

- Observe the *setting,* that is, the time and place of the plot. The setting of *The Adventures of Huckleberry Finn,* by Mark Twain, for instance, is the United States in the nineteenth century.

- Examine the *characters*—the people in the story. Each character will have his or her own unique qualities, behaviors, needs, and values.

- Be alert for the main *conflict* of a story. The conflict is the main struggle of the plot. It may take place within a character, between two or more characters, or between one or more characters and some force in the environment. For example, the conflict in *Moby-Dick* is between the hunter Captain Ahab and the animal he hunts—a white whale (the Moby-Dick of the title).

- Watch for the *climax,* the final main turning point of a story. The main conflict of a story is usually solved or explained in a final way at this point in the plot. For example, the climax of Shirley Jackson's story "The Lottery" comes when a woman's neighbors surround her and stone her to death.

- Be aware of the *speaker,* or *narrator,* who tells the story and the *tone* of that speaker. Both strongly influence the character of a work. The speaker is not the author but the fictional voice the author uses to narrate the story. In Mark Twain's *Huckleberry Finn,* for instance, the speaker is the title character, not the author. The tone is the style or manner of a piece. It reflects the speaker's attitude and is strongly related to the author's attitude and purpose as well.

- Note *figures of speech,* expressions in which words are used to mean something other than they usually do. These expressions are often comparisons which make a special point. Examples of figures of speech are "I wandered lonely as a cloud" (William Wordsworth), "my love is like a red, red rose" (Robert Burns), and "the slings and arrows of outrageous fortune" (William Shakespeare).

MAKING INFERENCES IN LITERATURE

To get the most out of reading literature, it is very important to make *inferences.* In other words, you must "read between the lines" and come to conclusions on the basis of the given information. While writers of factual material often directly *state* what they mean, writers of fiction often *show* what they mean. It is then up to the reader to infer the point of what the writer has said. For instance, a nonfiction author might write, "Harriet was angry at George." But the novelist might write, "Harriet's eyes narrowed when George spoke to her. She cut him off in mid-sentence with the words, 'I don't have time to argue with you.' " The author has *shown* us the anger with specific details rather than simply stating its existence abstractly. The reader must observe the details about Harriet and George and infer that she is angry.

Activity 1

Nowhere is inference more important than in poetry. Poetry, by its nature, implies much of its meaning. Implications are often made through figures of speech. For practice, read the poem below and then see if you can answer the questions that follow.

SIXTY-EIGHTH BIRTHDAY
James Russell Lowell

As life runs on, the road grows strange
With faces new, and near the end
The milestones into headstones change,
'Neath every one a friend.

Note: A *milestone* is a stone post set up to show the distance in miles on a road.

Activity

Answer each question by circling the inference most solidly based on the poem. Then read the explanations.

1. The speaker is
    a. very young.
    b. sixty-eight.
    c. an unknown age.

2. The poet compares life to a
    a. road with milestones.
    b. new face.
    c. friend.

3. The poem suggests that birthdays are
    a. strange roads.
    b. milestones on the road of life.
    c. friends.

4. The third line of the poem means that
    a. turning points go to our heads.
    b. change is good.
    c. eventually the road of life ends in death.

5. The poem implies that as we get older,
    a. we gain more friends.
    b. more and more of our friends die.
    c. our friends become strangers to us.

Here is an explanation for each of the five inferences about the poem:

1. The answer to the first question is *b*. The poem, of course, doesn't come out and say that the speaker is sixty-eight, but the title strongly implies it—what other purpose would there be for that title?

2. The answer to question 2 is *a*. The comparison of life to a road is implied in the first and third lines, which suggest that life runs on a road marked by milestones along it.

3. By describing life as a road with milestones, the speaker implies that birthdays can be considered the milestones—the distance markers. The answer to question 3 is thus *b*.

4. The third line of the poem says that life's milestones turn into headstones, which are stone markers set onto graves. This clearly implies that the road of life ends in death, so the answer to question 4 is *c*.

5. The answer to the final question is *b*. The point that more and more of our friends die is made fully in the fourth line, where the speaker says that under all the headstones are friends.

Activity 2

Following is a short story written by Langston Hughes, a poet and fiction writer who emerged as a major literary figure during the Harlem Renaissance of the 1920s. Read the story, and then circle the letters of the five inferences most solidly based on it.

EARLY AUTUMN

When Bill was very young, they had been in love. Many nights they had spent walking, talking together. Then something not very important had come between them, and they didn't speak. Impulsively, she had married a man she thought she loved. Bill went away, bitter about women.

Yesterday, walking across Washington Square, she saw him for the first time in years.

"Bill Walker," she said.

He stopped. At first he did not recognize her, to him she looked so old.

"Mary! Where did you come from?"

Unconsciously, she lifted her face as though wanting a kiss, but he held out his hand. She took it.

"I live in New York now," she said.

"Oh"—smiling politely. Then a little frown came quickly between his eyes.

"Always wondered what happened to you, Bill."

"I'm a lawyer. Nice firm, way downtown."

"Married yet?"

"Sure. Two kids."

"Oh," she said.

A great many people went past them through the park. People they didn't know. It was late afternoon. Nearly sunset. Cold.

"And your husband?" he asked her.

"We have three children. I work in the bursar's office at Columbia."

"You're looking very . . ." (he wanted to say old) ". . . well," he said.

She understood. Under the trees in Washington Square, she found herself desperately reaching back into the past. She had been older than he then in Ohio. Now she was not young at all. Bill was still young.

"We live on Central Park West," she said. "Come and see us sometime."

"Sure," he replied. "You and your husband must have dinner with my family some night. Any night. Lucille and I'd love to have you."

The leaves fell slowly from the trees in the Square. Fell without wind. Autumn dusk. She felt a little sick.

"We'd love it," she answered.

"You ought to see my kids." He grinned.

Suddenly the lights came on up the whole length of Fifth Avenue, chains of misty brilliance in the blue air.

"There's my bus," she said.

He held out his hand, "Good-by."

"When . . ." she wanted to say, but the bus was ready to pull off. The lights on the avenue blurred, twinkled, blurred. And she was afraid to open her mouth as she entered the bus. Afraid it would be impossible to utter a word.

Suddenly she shrieked very loudly, "Good-by!" But the bus door had closed.

The bus started. People came between them outside, people crossing the street, people they didn't know. Space and people. She lost sight of Bill. Then she remembered she had forgotten to give him her address—or ask him for his—or tell him that her youngest boy was named Bill, too.

1. Authors of fiction often choose settings that symbolically reflect a story. In this case, the characters' stage of life is echoed in the author's choices of
   a. city and park.
   b. season and time of day.
   c. transportation and temperature.

2. Hughes portrayed the awkwardness of the meeting by indicating a contrast between
   a. the woman's and Bill's jobs.
   b. New York City and Ohio.
   c. what the characters say and what they mean.

3. The suggestion that Bill was still young and the woman was not implies that
   a. she was actually many, many years older than he.
   b. her life had aged her more rapidly than his life had aged him.
   c. he was an exercise buff who had taken especially good care of himself.

4. The story suggests that Bill
   a. did not regret having not married the woman.
   b. plans on inviting the woman and her husband over for dinner.
   c. still wished that nothing had come between him and the woman when they were young.

5. The last few words of the story suggest that
   a. the boy was really Bill's son.
   b. the woman regretted naming her youngest son Bill.
   c. the woman had thought of Bill with so much longing that she named a son after him.

READING FOR PLEASURE: A LIST OF INTERESTING BOOKS

On the following pages are short descriptions of some books that might interest you. Some are popular books of the last few years; some are among the most widely read "classics"—books that have survived for generations because they deal with basic human experiences that all people can understand and share.

AUTOBIOGRAPHIES AND OTHER NONFICTION

Maya Angelou, *I Know Why the Caged Bird Sings*
The author writes with love, humor, and honesty about growing up black and female.

Alicia Appleman-Jurman, *Alicia: My Story*
Alicia was a Jewish girl living with her family in Poland when the Germans invaded in 1941. Her utterly compelling and heartbreaking story shows some of the best and worst of which human beings are capable.

Lauren Bacall, *Lauren Bacall by Myself*
A Hollywood star tells how she broke into movies, married tough guy Humphrey Bogart, and picked up the pieces of her life when he died of cancer.

Russell Baker, *Growing Up*
Russell Baker's mother, a giant presence in his life, insisted that he make something of himself. In his autobiography, the prize-winning journalist shows that he did, with an engrossing account of his own family and growing up.

Dee Brown, *Bury My Heart at Wounded Knee*
The harsh treatment that Native Americans have suffered at the hands of a white culture is vividly detailed in this history.

Lynn Caine, *Widow*
Few people are prepared for the loss of a loved one. Caine tells how devastating it can be to be left alone.

Truman Capote, *In Cold Blood*
A frightening story about the murder of a family that is also an investigation into what made their killers tick.

Richard P. Feynman, *Surely You're Joking, Mr. Feynman!*
The apt subtitle of this book by a Nobel prize–winning scientist is "Adventures of a Curious Character." Feynman has a boundless curiosity, enthusiasm, and love of life. In no way a "stuffy scientist," he, like his book, is utterly delightful.

Anne Frank, *The Diary of a Young Girl*
To escape the Nazi death camps, Anne Frank and her family hid for years in an attic. Her journal tells a story of love, fear, and courage.

Viktor Frankl, *Man's Search for Meaning*
How do people go on when they have been stripped of everything, including human dignity? The author describes his time in a concentration camp and what he learned there about survival.

Bob Greene, *Be True to Your School*
Bob Greene is a celebrated, popular, nationally syndicated newspaper columnist. This book, based on a diary he kept when he was a teenager, will take you back to some of the happiness, hurt, and struggle to grow up that you experienced in high school.

Dick Gregory, *Nigger*
Dick Gregory, social activist, writes about the experience of being black in a racist society.

John Howard Griffin, *Black Like Me*
A white man chemically darkens his skin and travels through the South of the 1960s to experience racial prejudice and injustice firsthand.

James Herriot, *All Creatures Great and Small*
Warm and funny stories about the experiences of an English veterinarian.

Helen Keller, *The Story of My Life*
How Miss Keller, a blind and deaf girl who lived in isolation and frustration, discovered a path to learning and knowledge.

M. E. Kerr, *Me Me Me Me Me*
A charming, easy-to-read account of a young woman's growing up. The author provides a series of warm and witty stories that will be enjoyed by people of all ages.

Herbert Kohl, *Thirty-Six Children*
An idealistic and caring young teacher describes some of the challenges he faced in trying to help his students survive and learn in the hard world of an inner-city school.

Jerry Kramer, *Distant Replay*

Whether you're a sports fan or not, you will be captivated by this portrait of stars of the Green Bay Packers football team, coached by Vince Lombardi, that won the first two Super Bowls. You learn just what happens to each of them in the twenty years after their great football victories.

Malcolm X and Alex Haley, *The Autobiography of Malcolm X*

Malcolm X, the controversial black leader who was assassinated by one of his followers, writes about the experiences that drove him to a leadership role in the Black Muslims.

Mark Mathabane, *Kaffir Boy*

A powerful description of what it's like to be black and live in a South African ghetto and experience apartheid firsthand.

Mark Owens and Delia Owens, *Cry of the Kalahari*

A husband and wife give up the comforts of academic life, sell everything they own, and go to Africa to study wildlife there and to try to save some animals from destruction. They describe their adventures with hyenas, lions, and a more dangerous species of predator—human beings.

Gilda Radner, *It's Always Something*

Before her death, the beloved comedienne from *Saturday Night Live* wrote about the trials and fortunes of her life—and described how everything changed when she learned she had ovarian cancer.

Andy Rooney, *Not That You Asked . . .*

Well-known for his commentaries on *60 Minutes,* Andy Rooney has also expressed his views in this book and several other books of short essays. Rooney has a lot of everyday things to complain about and poke fun at, and he does so in an admirable writing style that is clear, simple, and to the point.

Piri Thomas, *Down These Mean Streets*

Life in a Puerto Rican ghetto is described vividly and with understanding by one who experienced it.

James Thurber, *My Life and Hard Times*

James Thurber may be the funniest writer of all time; he writes about the absurd, the fantastic, and the eccentric with enough skill to make readers laugh out loud.

Joseph A. Wapner, *A View from the Bench*

The star of a popular TV show, *The People's Court,* Judge Wapner offers a series of real-life legal tales. At the same time, he shares insights into human nature based on his many years as a municipal and superior court judge.

FICTION

Richard Adams, *Watership Down*
A wonderfully entertaining adventure story about rabbits who act a great deal like people. The plot may sound unlikely, but it will keep you on the edge of your seat.

Willa Cather, *My Antonia*
No other American writer has written so beautifully and honestly about the experiences of the immigrants who settled the vast prairies of the Midwest.

James Dickey, *Deliverance*
A group of men go rafting down a wild Georgia river and encounter beauty, violence, and self-knowledge.

Ken Follett, *Eye of the Needle*
A thriller about a Nazi spy—"The Needle"—and the woman who is the only person who can stop him.

William Golding, *Lord of the Flies*
Can a group of children, none older than twelve, survive by themselves on a tropical island in the midst of World War III? In this modern classic, Golding shows us that the real danger is not the war outside but "the beast" within all of us.

Joseph Heller, *Catch-22*
The craziness of our culture—specifically, of war and the military—is precisely captured in this landmark novel.

Frank Herbert, *Dune*
In this science-fiction classic, Paul Atreides fights to regain his lost kingdom on a strange desert planet filled with warring factions, giant sandworms, and a magical spice.

Daniel Keyes, *Flowers for Algernon*
A scientific experiment turns a retarded man into a genius. But the results are a mixture of joy and heartbreak.

Stephen King, *The Shining*
A haunted hotel, a little boy with ESP, and a deranged father—they're all together in a horror tale of isolation and insanity.

John Knowles, *A Separate Peace*
Two schoolboys enjoy a close friendship until one grows jealous of the other's many talents—and tragedy results.

Dean Koontz, *Watchers*
An incredibly suspenseful story about two dogs that undergo lab experiments.
    One dog becomes a monster programmed to kill, and seeks to track down
    the couple that knows its secret.

Harper Lee, *To Kill a Mockingbird*
A controversial trial involving a black man accused of raping a white woman
    is the centerpiece of this story about childhood, bigotry, and justice.

Bernard Malamud, *The Natural*
An aging player makes a comeback that stuns the baseball world.

Margaret Mitchell, *Gone with the Wind*
The unforgettable characters and places in this book—Scarlett O'Hara, Rhett
    Butler, Tara—have become part of our culture.

George Orwell, *1984*
The well-known expression "Big Brother Is Watching You" comes from
    this frightening novel of a time when individuals have no control over
    their lives.

Robert Peck, *A Day No Pigs Would Die*
A boy raises a pig that is intelligent and affectionate. Will the boy follow
    orders and send the animal off to be slaughtered?

Philip Roth, *Goodbye, Columbus*
The title story in this collection is about a poor boy, a rich girl, and their ill-
    fated love affair.

J. D. Salinger, *The Catcher in the Rye*
The frustrations and turmoil of being an adolescent have perhaps never been
    captured so well as in this book. The main character, Holden Caulfield,
    is honest, funny, affectionate, obnoxious, and tormented—all at the
    same time.

J. R. R. Tolkien, *The Lord of the Rings*
Enter an amazing world of little creatures known as *Hobbits*; you, like thou-
    sands of other readers, may never want to leave.

Edith Wharton, *Ethan Frome*
An engrossing story about a love triangle involving a middle-aged farmer,
    his shrewish wife, and the pretty young cousin who comes to live with
    them.

CLASSICS

George Eliot, *Middlemarch*

A long book that is likely to be one of the peak reading experiences of your life. Eliot writes with extraordinary insight and compassion about the problems that all human beings face in seeing themselves clearly and in coping with the difficulties of their lives.

Nathaniel Hawthorne, *The Scarlet Letter*

A compelling story, set in the days of the Puritans, about a young woman, her illegitimate baby, and the scarlet label she wears as her punishment.

Herman Melville, *Moby-Dick*

Two of the most famous characters in fiction—mad Captain Ahab and Moby-Dick, the white whale—battle it out as hunter and hunted.

Mark Twain, *The Adventures of Huckleberry Finn*

A rich book filled with wit, understanding, moral insight, and very human characters—definitely *not* for children only. Many people argue that this, or *Moby-Dick,* is the greatest American novel.

UNDERSTANDING CONNECTIONS BETWEEN READING AND WRITING

Have you wondered why writing assignments are included in a book called *Reading and Study Skills?* Perhaps you felt that you were capable of becoming a good reader and skilled student without taking on the additional burden of producing written assignments. Reading and writing, however, are so closely interconnected that it is virtually impossible to be competent at one without being competent at the other. The two abilities work together in several ways:

■ *Reading and writing are interrelated language skills.* Through reading, you learn, almost subconsciously, how good writers put sentences together and organize ideas. In addition, you acquire new vocabulary words. Through writing, you begin to use what you have learned by reading. You also gain intensive practice in being logical, a skill that is essential to understanding more difficult reading material.

■ *Both reading and writing are processes.* You become a better reader, or a more skillful writer, by treating each task as a process. You preview, read, and reread. Or, you prewrite, write, and rewrite. With each step, your skills become sharper and the end product—your understanding of what you have read or the paper you have written—becomes finer.

■ *Both reading and writing are vital for communication.* Competence in reading and writing is an essential survival skill if you wish to make your voice heard and your ideas known. Shutting yourself off from either reading or writing can damage your life in two ways. First, your verbal abilities suffer because you have few language models or chances to extend your word skills. Second, your message—whatever it may be, either in your personal life or on the job—is lost because you cannot get it across to other people.

Reading and writing, then, are so closely linked that practicing one helps the other—and neglecting one damages the other. This is why writing assignments have a role in this book, and why writing should be an important priority in your life as a student.

■ Writing Assignments

Here is a list of the assignments already presented.

- Write a paper about one of the questions that follow "Your Attitude: The Heart of the Matter" (page 19).
- Write a paper about one of the questions that follow "Learning Survival Strategies" (page 35).
- Write a paper about some aspect of concentration skills (page 87).
- Write a report on a book (page 300).
- Write a summary (pages 392–394).

Following are a number of other assignments, based on chapters or reading selections in the book. Before attempting any of these assignments, remember that four important steps in good writing are:

1 Make a point of some kind.
2 Support the point.
3 Organize the support.
4 Write clear sentences.

In particular, be sure to be *specific*. Vivid, concrete details will help make your paper lively and convincing.

Note: Each paper that you write should be at least one page in length.

1. Write a paper in which you respond in detail to the study situation on page 39. Apply what you have learned in the chapter to explain all the steps that Howard should take to become an effective note-taker.

2. Write a paper in which you respond in detail to the time-control situation on page 68. Apply what you have learned in the chapter to explain all the steps that Cheryl should take to control her time effectively.

3. Write a paper in which you respond in detail to the textbook study situation on page 88. Apply what you have learned in the chapter to explain all the steps that Gary should take to study effectively through textbook previewing, marking, and note-taking.

4. Write a paper in which you respond in detail to the textbook study situation on page 192. Apply what you have learned in the chapter to explain all the steps that Steve should take to improve his memory.

5. Write a paper in which you respond in detail to the study situation on page 207. Apply what you have learned in the chapter to explain all the steps that Rita should take to improve her performance on objective exams.

6. Write a paper in which you respond in detail to the class assignment situation on page 232. Apply what you have learned in the chapter to explain all the steps that Pete should take to do a good job on his library assignments.

7. Read the lecture about what love is *not* on pages 63–64. Then write a paper in which you provide examples of some of these common kinds of mistaken love. The examples may be from your own experience, from the experience of people you know, or even from the experience of characters you have read about in books or magazines or have watched in TV shows or films.

8. Read the section on concentration skills on pages 82–85. Then write a paper based on the idea that many students—from the youngest to the oldest—find it difficult to pay attention in school. Why might this be true? What aspects of school make it hard to pay attention? (Is it the setting? The teachers? The subject matter? The pressures? The boredom?) Write a paper on the steps a teacher could take to make it easier for students to pay attention. Make your steps practical ones that a concerned teacher at a specific level (primary school, high school, college) could take.

9. Read the selection on page 390 about the importance of eating breakfast. Then write a paper in which you describe and evaluate your daily eating habits. You might begin your paper with a main-idea sentence such as, "I have fairly regular and balanced eating habits" or "A nutritionist would probably not approve of my daily eating habits." If you think you should be more energetic at certain times of the day, propose how you could achieve this through a change in diet.

10. Read "Two Factors in the Success of a Marriage" on pages 403–405. Then write a paper in which you explain the reasons why your parents' marriage (or the marriage of another couple you know) has been strong or weak. Analyze the relationship in terms of the two factors stressed in the passage: maturity and reasons for marrying. Be sure to describe or provide specific details about the couple: priorities in their lives; their behavior to each other; their approach to handling minor and major problems.

11. Read the selection about getting a job on pages 409–415. Then write a paper about the job you want. Imagine that you have heard about an opening through the want ads, a friend, the placement office, or some other source. Write a cover letter in which you apply for the job. Follow the recommendations about cover letters given in the selection. Remember to create, if necessary, a specific position at a specific company.

12. Read "Caffeine: All-American Drug" on pages 429–431. Then write a paper about how you, or someone you know, broke an unhealthy habit or overcame an addiction. First, explain why the habit was formed. For instance, did it help to calm nerves? To relieve anxiety? To escape from pressures? Then detail the process by which you or the person decided to end the habit and acted to end it.

13. Read "Nesting: Adult Children at Home" on pages 443–445. Are you, or is someone you know, a "nester"? If so, write a paper describing the pluses and minuses of nesting. Provide the specific evidence needed to support the point that nesting is a primarily positive or negative situation.

14. Read the selection on frustration on pages 467–468. Then write a paper about a major obstacle in your life. You may want to classify your problem as environmental, personal, or conflict-produced frustration. Describe the obstacle in detail so that a reader can understand just how frustrating it has been for you. Then explain what steps you have taken, or intend to take, to overcome the obstacle.

15. Read the selection on mentors on page 492. Then write a paper in which you describe a mentor you have had. State in the first sentence who the person is and the person's relationship to you (friend, mother, teacher, etc.). Then show through specific examples (the person's words and actions) why he or she has been so special for you.

16. Read the selection on page 505 on "toe-to-head relaxation," a method of helping children fall asleep. Then write a paper about a method you use to make yourself relax. Explain your process of relaxation step by step, including even the smallest details—the clothes you wear, the furniture you rest on, the things you say to yourself, and so on.

17. Read the selection on smoking on pages 513–515. Then write a paper in which you analyze several cigarette ads to determine why they help persuade people to smoke—despite common knowledge that smoking can be fatal. Pay particular attention to the ads' slogans and to the ages and implied life-styles of people portrayed in the ads.

WRITING A RESEARCH PAPER

The process of writing a research paper can be divided into six steps. We'll look at each of those steps and then consider a sample paper.

STEPS IN WRITING A RESEARCH PAPER

Step 1: Select Your Topic

Select a topic that you can readily research. First of all, go to the *Subjects section* of your library book file, as described on page 235, and see whether there are at least three books on your general topic. For example, if you initially choose over-the-counter drugs as your topic, see if you can find at least three books on this topic. Also, make sure that the books are available on the library shelves.

Next, go to the *Magazine Index* or *Readers' Guide,* as described on page 239, to see if you find five or more articles on your subject.

If both books and articles are at hand, pursue your topic. Otherwise, you may have to choose another topic. You cannot write a paper on a topic for which research materials are not readily available.

Step 2: Limit Your Topic

Read about your topic, limit it, and make the purpose of your paper clear. A research paper should develop a *limited* topic. It should be narrow and deep rather than broad and shallow. Therefore, as you read through books and articles on your general topic, look for ways to limit it.

For instance, in reading through materials on the general topic of over-the-counter drugs, you might decide to limit your topic to the reasons why such drugs are so popular. Or, after reading about adoption, you might decide to limit your paper to the problems that single people have in adopting a child. The broad subject of death could be reduced to unfair pricing practices in funeral homes; divorce might be limited to its most damaging effects on the children of divorced parents.

Do not expect to limit your topic and make your purpose clear all at once. You may have to do quite a bit of reading as you work out the limited purpose of your paper. Note that many research papers have one of two general purposes. Your purpose might be to make and defend a point of some kind. For example, your purpose in a paper might be to provide evidence that gambling should be legalized. Or, depending on your course and instructor, your purpose might simply be to present information about a particular subject. For example, you might be asked to do a paper that describes the latest scientific findings about what happens when we dream.

Step 3: Take Notes on Your Topic

Take notes as you continue to read about your topic. Take notes on whatever seems relevant to or significant for your limited topic. Write your notes on sheets of loose-leaf paper. Your notes can be in the form of *direct quotations* or *summaries in your own words,* or a *combination* of the two.

Here is a copy of notes that one student took while doing a paper on over-the-counter drugs:

Advertising to doctors by the drug industry

"The industry spends roughly $2,500 per physician on advertising every year." Most of what doctors know comes from the biased salespersons of drug companies. It is common for companies to provide doctors with information that underplays the dangers of their drugs and exaggerates their effectiveness.

Goode, 99.

Keep the following points in mind when taking notes:

- Write on one side of a sheet only, so that it will be easy to refer to your notes as you are writing your paper.
- Put only one kind of information, from one source, on any one sheet. For example, the sample above has information on only one idea from one source (a book by Erich Goode).
- Identify the source and page number under your notes.
- Put quotation marks around all material which you take word for word from any source.
- Include at the top of the sheet a heading that summarizes the content of the notes. This heading will help you organize the different kinds of information that you gather on your topic.

Be sure to document information and ideas that you take from other sources. If you do not do this, you will be stealing (the formal term is *plagiarizing*)— using someone else's work as your own work. It can usually be assumed that a good deal of the material in research writing will need to be documented.

Step 4: Plan Your Paper

Plan the paper, making clear your point and your support for the point. As you take notes, think constantly about the specific content and organization of your paper. Begin making decisions about the exact information you will present and the arrangement of that information. Prepare a basic outline of your paper that shows both its point and the areas of support for the point.

See if you can divide your support into at least three different areas.

Step 5: Keep a Record of Your Sources

Keep a written record of all your sources. On a sheet of paper, record the information below about each source:

For Books	For Magazines
Author	Author
Title	Title of article
Place of publication	Title of magazine
Publisher	Volume number (if available)
Date of publication	Pages
Call number	Date

You will need this information later, because you are expected to place at the end of your paper a list of all the sources you consulted.

Step 6: Write Your Paper

After you have finished your reading and note-taking, you should be ready to proceed with the writing of your paper. Make a final outline and use it as a guide to write the first draft of your paper. Your paper should have five basic parts:

■ A *title page,* which should give the title of the paper, your name, and the date. Center all of these on the sheet, as shown in the sample on the facing page.

■ An *opening page,* which should include an introductory paragraph that (1) attracts the reader's interest, (2) states the point of the paper, and (3) gives the plan of development that the paper will follow. The sample (page 551) shows the first page of a paper, with some explanatory labels. Note that to cite a source within your paper, you should provide in parentheses both the author's name and the relevant page number. Do not give the name of a book or article. That will appear in the list of sources at the end of the paper.

■ The *body* of the paper, which will develop all the areas of support for your point.

■ A *concluding paragraph,* which may consist of a summary, a final thought, or both. Note that your final thought might be in the form of a recommendation.

■ A *final page,* with an alphabetical list of "Works Cited," which should include all the sources you have used. See the sample (page 553).

This is the title page of a sample research paper.

The title should be centered and in capitals.

Your name should be placed two spaces under by.

Near the bottom put the course title and date; you may also include the course section number and the instructor's name.

DEPENDENCY ON
OVER-THE-COUNTER DRUGS
IN THE UNITED STATES

by

Linda Coleman

Sociology 101

November 28, 1993

Leave about three inches of blank space between the top of the first page and the title of the paper. The text of the pages that follow should begin about one inch from the top.

DEPENDENCY ON OVER-THE-COUNTER DRUGS IN THE UNITED STATES

(Three spaces)

Double spacing between lines of the text.

Walk into any supermarket, pharmacy, or discount department store in the United States, and you will find shelf after shelf devoted to drugs. Taking over-the-counter (OTC) medication is a way of life for most Americans. There's a nonprescription drug available for every ailment, from headaches to hemorrhoids. Fatigue, stress, anxiety, depression, insomnia, and overweight can be banished by little colored pills, soothing ointments, and magical liquids. Americans want to believe that "for whatever ails or bothers you, there is a chemical solution on the counter" (Hughes and Brewin 255). There are several reasons why Americans are so dependent on over-the-counter drugs. They are heavily advertised by the drug industry and readily available to consumers; also, they appeal to our desire for quick, simple solutions to our problems.

1¹/₂-inch margin at left

About one-inch margin at right

The sale of OTC medication means big business. One reason why such drugs are so popular, and sales are so high, is advertising. Advertisers send us positive messages about nonprescription drugs: they are safe, they are reliable, they are convenient, and practically everyone uses them. Faced with a heavy barrage of slick promotion, consumers stock their pockets, purses, and medicine chests with all types of drugs.

1

Page numbering starts with the first page of the text. Page 1 is numbered at the bottom. Leave about a one-inch margin at the bottom of the page.

*The heading should be in capitals and
centered. Three spaces should follow before
the first entry.*

10

WORKS CITED

Goode, Erich. Drugs in American Society. New York: McGraw-Hill, 1989.

Hughes, Richard, and Robert Brewin. The Tranquilizing of America: Pill Popping
   and the American Way of Life. New York: Harcourt Brace Jovanovich, 1979.

"Is Bayer Better?" Consumer Reports July 1982: 347–349.

Leber, Max. The Corner Drugstore. New York: Warner Books, 1983.

"Rich Profits from New Lines." Business Week January 11, 1982: 70–74.

Sanberg, Paul R. Over-the-Counter Drugs: Harmless or Hazardous? New York:
   Chelsea House Publishers, 1986.

Stuller, Jay. "Bad Medicine? (Misuse of over-the-counter and prescription
   medication)." The American Legion Magazine April 1990: 34–38.

ACKNOWLEDGMENTS

Adapted and reprinted by permission from *The American Heritage Dictionary,* paperback edition, Copyright © 1983 by Houghton Mifflin Company. Excerpts on pages 270, 272, 279, and 483.

Ronald B. Adler, adapted from *Talking Straight.* Copyright © 1977 by Holt, Rinehart, and Winston. Reprinted by permission of Holt, Rinehart, and Winston, CBS College Publishing. Selection 4 on page 332; Selection on page 346; Selection 1 on page 380; Selection 1 on pages 401–402.

Ronald B. Adler and Neil Towne, adapted from *Looking Out/Looking In,* 3d ed. Copyright © 1981 by Holt, Rinehart, and Winston. Reprinted by permission of Holt, Rinehart, and Winston, CBS College Publishing. Selection 1 on page 499.

Elliot Aronson, from *The Social Animal,* 3d ed. Copyright © 1980 by W. H. Freeman and Company. All rights reserved. Reprinted by permission. Selection 4 on page 325.

Michael S. Bassis, Richard J. Gelles, and Ann Levine, from *Sociology: An Introduction.* Selection on pages 149–186.

Selection in its entirety: Chapter 8 from M. Bassis et al., *Sociology: An Introduction,* 4th ed. © 1991. Used by permission of McGraw-Hill.

Table 8-1: From D. Gilbert and J. A. Kahl, *The American Class Structure: A New Synthesis,* 3d ed. (Belmont, CA: Dorsey Press, 1987), Table 11-1, p. 332. © 1987. Used by permission of Wadsworth Publishing Co.

Figure 8-1: From "The Biolsi Family," *The New York Times,* October 3, 1989. Copyright © 1989 by The New York Times Company. Reprinted by permission.

Table 8-2: From Davis, James Allan, and Smith, Tom W.: *General Social Surveys, 1972–1988* (machine-readable data file). Principal Investigator James A. Davis; Director and Co-Principal Investigator, Tom W. Smith. NORC ed. Chicago: National Opinion Research Center, producer, 1988; Storrs, CT: The Roper Center for Public Opinion Research, University of Connecticut, distributor. 1 data file (23,356 logical records) and 1 codebook (790 pp.)

Figure 8-3: Adapted from *Minding America's Business* by Ira C. Magaziner and Robert B. Reich. Reprinted with the permission of Prentice-Hall Law & Business.

Figure 8-4: Data from current populations surveys; G. O. Jaynes and R. M. Williams, Jr., Eds., *A Common Destiny: Blacks and American Society.* Copyright © 1989 by the National Academy of Science, National Academy Press, Washington, D.C.

Table 8-3: From L. J. D. Wacquant, "The Ghetto, the State, and the New Capitalist Economy," in *Dissent,* Fall 1989, Table 1, p. 509. © 1989. Used by permission of the Foundation for the Study of Independent Social Ideas.

Figure 8-5: Data from current populations surveys; G. U. Jaynes and R. M. Williams, Jr., Eds., *A Common Destiny: Blacks and American Society.* Copyright © 1989 by the National Academy of Science, National Academy Press, Washington, D.C.

Figure 8-6: Data adapted from J. D. Wright, "The Worthy and Unworthy Homeless." Published by permission of Transaction Publishers, from Transaction Society, vol. 25, No. 5 (July/August 1988), pp. 64–69. Copyright © 1988 by Transaction Publishers.

Figure 8-7: Reprinted with the permission of The Free Press, a Division of Macmillan, Inc., from *The American Occupational Structure* by Peter M. Blau and Otis Dudley Duncan. Copyright © 1967 by Peter M. Blau and Otis Dudley Duncan.

Table 8-5: Adapted from *World Development Report 1989* by the World Bank. Copyright © 1989 by the International Bank for Reconstruction and Development/The World Bank. Reprinted by permission of Oxford University Press, Inc.

Helen L. Bee and Sandra K. Mitchell, adapted from *The Developing Person: A Life-Span Approach.* Copyright © 1980 by Helen Bee Douglas and Sandra K. Mitchell. Selection on pages 91–92; Selection 2 on page 361; Selection 4 on page 362; Selection 4 on page 492; Selection 2 on page 493.

James F. Calhoun and Joan Ross Acocella, adapted from *Psychology of Adjustment and Human Relationships,* 3d ed. Copyright © 1990 by McGraw-Hill, Inc. Selection on page 112; Selection on page 203; Selection 1 on page 213; Selection 1 on page 320; Selection 1 on pages 328–329; Selection 4 on page 335; Selection 2 on page 372; Selection on page 495; Selection 2 on page 499.

Clarke G. Carney, Cinda Field Wells, and Don Struefert, from *Career Planning; Skills to Build Your Future.* Copyright © 1981 by Litton Educational Publishing, Inc. Reprinted by permission. Selection 3 on pages 331–332; Selection 2 on page 350; Selection 2 on page 355; Selection 3 on page 389; Selection 5 on page 492.

James C. Coleman and Constance L. Hammen, from *Contemporary Psychology and Effective Behavior.* Copyright © 1974 by Scott, Foresman and Company. Reprinted by permission. Selection on page 338.

Dennis Coon, adapted by permission from *Introduction to Psychology,* 2d ed. Copyright © 1981 by West Publishing Company. All rights reserved. Selection 1 on page 333; Selection 3 on page 378.

Dorothy E. Dusek and Daniel A. Giardano, from *Drugs: A Factual Account,* 5th ed. Copyright © 1993 by McGraw-Hill, Inc. Selection on page 116.

"Early Autumn" from *Something in Common* by Langston Hughes. Copyright 1963 by Langston Hughes. Copyright renewed 1991 by Arnold Rampersad and Ramona Bass. Reprinted by permission of Hill and Wang, a division of Farrar, Straus and Giroux, Inc. Selection on pages 534–535.

Paul R. Ehrlich, Richard W. Holm, and Irene L. Brown, adapted from *Biology and Society.* Copyright © 1976 by McGraw-Hill, Inc. Selection on page 196.

D. Stanley Eitzen, adapted from *Social Problems.* Copyright © 1980 by Allyn and Bacon, Inc. Selection 3 on page 355; Selection 3 on page 365; Selection 3 on page 373; Selection 2 on page 390; Selection 3 on page 500.

D. Stanley Eitzen and George H. Sage, from *Sociology of American Sport,* 2d ed. Copyright © 1978 by William C. Brown Company, Publishers. Reprinted by permission. Selection 4 on page 389.

Carol R. Ember and Melvin Ember, from *Cultural Anthropology,* 3d ed. Copyright © 1981 by Prentice-Hall, Inc. Reprinted by permission. Selection 3 on page 362.

FYI: Unexpected Answers to Everyday Questions, based on the award-winning ABC-TV program with Hal Linden. Copyright © 1982 by the American Broadcasting Companies, Inc. Reprinted by permission of M. Evans and Company, Inc., New York, New York 10017. Selection 1 on page 388; Selection 1 on page 390; Selection 1 on page 395; Selection 1 on page 505.

Kenneth J. Gergen and Mary M. Gergen, from *Social Psychology.* Copyright © 1981 by Harcourt Brace Jovanovich, Inc. Selection 3 on page 323; Selection 4 on page 365.

William J. Goode, from *Principles of Sociology.* Copyright © 1977 by McGraw-Hill, Inc. Reprinted by permission. Selection 3 on page 324.

Norman A. Graebner, Gilbert C. Fite, and Philip L. White, from *A History of the American People.* Copyright © 1975 by McGraw-Hill, Inc. Reprinted by permission. Selection 1 on page 371.

Linda Carol Graham, "Child Abuse: A Revolution in Treatment." Adapted with permission from *The Philadelphia Inquirer,* issue of March 16, 1980. Selection 3 on pages 433–435.

Samuel Guilino, "Helping Your Child Learn to Be a Better Reader." Reprinted from *Family Weekly.* Selection on page 393.

Richard M. Hodgett, adapted from *Introduction to Business,* 2d ed. Copyright © 1981 by Addison-Wesley Publishing Company, Inc. Selection 2 on page 329; Selection 3 on page 329; Selection 3 on page 341; Selection 4 on page 364; Selection 2 on page 365; Selection 2 on page 376; Selection 3 on page 382; Selection 2 on page 498.

Paul B. Horton and Chester L. Hunt, adapted from *Sociology,* 4th ed. Copyright © 1976 by McGraw-Hill, Inc. Reprinted by permission. Selection on page 319.

Steve Huntley, "Why So Many People Ignore Traffic Laws." Reprinted from *U.S. News and World Report,* issue of February 7, 1983. Copyright © 1983 by U.S. News and World Report, Inc. Selection 1 on pages 425–427.

Saundra Hybels and Richard L. Weaver II, from *Communicating Effectively,* 3d ed. Copyright © 1992 by McGraw-Hill, Inc. Selection on pages 120–123.

Jerome Kagan and Ernest Havemann, abridged from *Psychology: An Introduction,* 4th ed. Copyright © 1980 by Harcourt Brace Jovanovich, Inc. Reprinted by permission of the publisher. Selection 3 on pages 406–408.

John Kellmayer, "Students in Shock." Reprinted by permission. Selection 6 on pages 447–449.

Barbara Kozier and Glenora Lea Erb, adapted from *Fundamentals of Nursing.* Copyright © 1970 by Addison-Wesley Publishing Company, Inc. Selection 2 on page 381.

Jacqueline I. Kroschwitz and Melvin Winokur, from *Chemistry: A First Course.* Copyright © 1980 by McGraw-Hill, Inc. Reprinted by permission of the publisher. Selection 3 on page 321.

Mary Ann Lamanna and Agnes Reidmann, adapted from *Marriages and Families.* Copyright © 1981 by Wadsworth, Inc. Reprinted by permission. Selection 2 on pages 403–405.

Donald J. Leonard, from *Shurter's Communication in Business,* 4th ed. Copyright © 1979 by McGraw-Hill, Inc. Reprinted by permission. Selection 2 on page 363.

Marvin R. Levey, Mark Dignan, and Janet H. Shirreffs, from *Life and Health.* Copyright © 1992 by McGraw-Hill, Inc. Selection on page 102; Selection on pages 136–139.

Donald Light, Jr., and Suzanne Keller, adapted from *Sociology,* 2d ed. Copyright © 1979 by Alfred A. Knopf, Inc. Reprinted by permission. Selection 4 on page 321; Selection 4 on page 323; Selection 4 on page 330; Selection 1 on page 340; Selection 2 on page 388; Selection 3 on page 391; Selection on pages 509–510.

Stephen E. Lucas, from *The Art of Public Speaking,* 4th ed. Copyright © 1992 by McGraw-Hill, Inc. Selection on pages 124–127.

John J. Makay and Ronald C. Fetzer, from *Business Communication Skills.* Copyright © 1980 by Litton Educational Publishing, Inc. Reprinted by permission. Selection 3 on page 494.

Peggy Mann, "Don't Let Your Family's Health Go Up in Smoke." *Families* magazine, issue of May 1982. Selection on pages 513–515.

James Leslie McCary, from *Human Sexuality: A Brief Edition.* Copyright © 1973 by D. Van Nostrand Company. Reprinted by permission. Selection on page 349.

Clifford T. Morgan and Richard A. King, adapted from *Introduction to Psychology,* 5th ed. Copyright © 1975 by McGraw-Hill, Inc. Reprinted by permission. Selection on pages 467–468.

W. A. Owens, "Age and Mental Abilities." *Journal of Educational Psychology.* Copyright © 1966 by the American Psychological Association. Graph on page 528.

Diane E. Papalia and Sally Wendkos Olds, from *Human Development,* 2d ed. Copyright © 1981 by McGraw-Hill, Inc. Reprinted by permission. Selection 1 on page 331; Selection 1 on page 361.

Thomas E. Patterson, from *The American Democracy,* 2d ed. Copyright © 1993 by McGraw-Hill, Inc. Selection on page 118.

John H. Posthlewaith and Janet L. Hopson, from *The Nature of Life,* 2d ed. Copyright © 1992 by McGraw-Hill, Inc. Selection on page 105.

Virginia Nichols Quinn, from *Applying Psychology,* 2d ed. Copyright © 1990 by McGraw-Hill, Inc. Selection on page 106; Selection on pages 132–135.

David J. Rachman et al., from *Business Today,* 7th ed. Copyright © 1993 by McGraw-Hill, Inc. Selection on page 103; Selection on page 114.

Spencer A. Rathus and Jeffrey S. Nevid, from *Adjustment and Growth,* 2d ed. Copyright © 1983 by CBS College Publishing. Reprinted by permission of Holt, Rinehart, and Winston, CBS College Publishing. Selection 2 on page 322; Selection 2 on page 324; Selection 3 on page 363; Selection 2 on page 506.

Ian Robertson, adapted from *Sociology.* 2d ed. Copyright © 1981 by Worth Publishers, Inc. Reprinted by permission. Selection 2 on page 356; Selection 4 on page 391; Selection 2 on page 395; Selection 1 on page 493; Selection 3 on page 506.

Zick Rubin and Elton B. McNeil, from *The Psychology of Being Human,* 3d ed. Copyright © 1981 by Zick Rubin. Selection 3 on page 334.

Gail Saffron, "Caffeine: All-American Drug." Copyright 1990. Reprinted by permission. Selection 2 on pages 429–431.

Luella Fern Sanders, "The Smart Way to Buy a New Car." Reprinted by permission. Selection on pages 437–441.

Richard T. Schaefer and Robert P. Lamm, from *Sociology,* 4th ed. Copyright © 1992 by McGraw-Hill, Inc. Selection on page 101; Selection on 110; Selection on pages 128–131.

Charles D. Schewe and Reuben M. Smith, from *Marketing: Concepts and Applications.* Copyright © 1980 by McGraw-Hill, Inc. Reprinted by permission. Selection 1 on page 497.

Dan Steinhoff, *The World of Business.* Copyright © 1979 by McGraw-Hill, Inc. Reprinted by permission. Selection 2 on page 331.

Elbert W. Stewart, adapted from *Sociology: The Human Science,* 2d ed. Copyright © 1981 by McGraw-Hill, Inc. Reprinted by permission. Selection on page 204.

Bernard A. Weisberger, from *The Impact of Our Past.* Copyright © 1976 by McGraw-Hill, Inc. Reprinted by permission. Selection 1 on page 322; Selection 4 on page 500; Selection 4 on page 507.

INDEX

INDEX